# EP Math
# Geometry
# Workbook
# Answers

Easy Peasy

All-in-One
Homeschool

This workbook, made by permission of Easy Peasy All-in-One Homeschool, is based on the math component of Easy Peasy's curriculum. For EP's online curriculum, visit allinonehomeschool.com.

ISBN: 9798394004162

Note that the worked-out solutions do not restate the problems but rather show the subsequent steps.

**LESSON 1** ·········································

1. $\sqrt{4 \cdot 2} = \sqrt{2^2 \cdot 2} = 2\sqrt{2}$

2. $3 \cdot \sqrt{4 \cdot 3} = 3 \cdot \sqrt{2^2 \cdot 3} = 3 \cdot 2\sqrt{3} = 6\sqrt{3}$

3. $(5 + 1)\sqrt{3} = 6\sqrt{3}$

4. $2\sqrt{3} + \sqrt{3} = (2 + 1)\sqrt{3} = 3\sqrt{3}$

5. $4 \cdot 2\sqrt{2} - 4\sqrt{2} = 8\sqrt{2} - 4\sqrt{2} = 4\sqrt{2}$

6. $2\sqrt{5} - 2\sqrt{7} + 3\sqrt{7} = 2\sqrt{5} + \sqrt{7}$

7. $\sqrt{5 \cdot 10} = \sqrt{50} = 5\sqrt{2}$

8. $3 \cdot 2 \cdot \sqrt{2 \cdot 6} = 6\sqrt{12} = 6 \cdot 2\sqrt{3} = 12\sqrt{3}$

9. $\sqrt{\dfrac{18}{2}} = \sqrt{9} = 3$    10. $\dfrac{1}{2} \cdot \sqrt{28} = \dfrac{1}{2} \cdot 2\sqrt{7} = \sqrt{7}$

11. $\dfrac{1}{\sqrt{5}} \cdot \dfrac{\sqrt{5}}{\sqrt{5}} = \dfrac{\sqrt{5}}{5}$    12. $\dfrac{2}{\sqrt{2}} \cdot \dfrac{\sqrt{2}}{\sqrt{2}} = \dfrac{2\sqrt{2}}{2} = \sqrt{2}$

13. $\dfrac{6\sqrt{7}}{\sqrt{3}} \cdot \dfrac{\sqrt{3}}{\sqrt{3}} = \dfrac{6\sqrt{21}}{3} = 2\sqrt{21}$

14. $2\sqrt{2} + \sqrt{2} = 3\sqrt{2}$

15. $2\sqrt{5} - 4\sqrt{5} = -2\sqrt{5}$

16. $2 \cdot 2\sqrt{6} + 3 \cdot 3\sqrt{6} = 4\sqrt{6} + 9\sqrt{6} = 13\sqrt{6}$

17. $\sqrt{18} = 3\sqrt{2}$

18. $3\sqrt{28} = 3 \cdot 2\sqrt{7} = 6\sqrt{7}$

19. $6\sqrt{75} = 6 \cdot 5\sqrt{3} = 30\sqrt{3}$

20. $\sqrt{\dfrac{36}{3}} = \sqrt{12} = 2\sqrt{3}$    21. $\dfrac{10}{\sqrt{5}} \cdot \dfrac{\sqrt{5}}{\sqrt{5}} = \dfrac{10\sqrt{5}}{5} = 2\sqrt{5}$

22. $\dfrac{8\sqrt{3}}{\sqrt{2}} \cdot \dfrac{\sqrt{2}}{\sqrt{2}} = \dfrac{8\sqrt{6}}{2} = 4\sqrt{6}$

**LESSON 2** ·········································

1. Subtract 3 from both sides:   $4x = 8$
   Divide both sides by 4:      $x = 2$

2. Add 8 to both sides:       $3x = 21$
   Divide both sides by 3:     $x = 7$

3. Add 7 to both sides:       $-2x = 12$
   Divide both sides by –2:    $x = -6$

4. Subtract 2x from both sides:  $2x - 8 = 0$
   Add 8 to both sides:          $2x = 8$
   Divide both sides by 2:       $x = 4$

5. Simplify each side:        $3 - 3x = 9$
   Subtract 3 from both sides:  $-3x = 6$
   Divide both sides by –3:    $x = -2$

   Alternatively, you could divide both sides by 3 first and then solve $1 - x = 3$.

6. Simplify each side:        $6x + 2 = 4x$
   Subtract 4x from both sides: $2x + 2 = 0$
   Subtract 2 from both sides:  $2x = -2$
   Divide both sides by 2:      $x = -1$

7. Cross multiply:           $10x = 4 \cdot 15$
   Divide both sides by 10:    $x = 6$

   Alternatively, you could simplify 15/10 to 3/2 first and then cross multiply to get $2x = 12$.

8. Cross multiply:           $8x = 12 \cdot 6$
   Divide both sides by 8:     $x = 9$

9. Cross multiply:           $21(x + 3) = 35 \cdot 15$
   Divide both sides by 21:    $x + 3 = 25$
   Subtract 3 from both sides:  $x = 22$

10. Subtract 3x from both sides:  $-y = -3x - 8$
    Divide both sides by –1:     $y = 3x + 8$

11. Subtract x from both sides:   $-2y = -8x + 6$
    Divide both sides by –2:      $y = 4x - 3$

12. $x = 7/3$         13. $x = 2$

14. $3x = 9$          15. $3x + 9 = 0$
    $x = 3$               $3x = -9$
                          $x = -3$

16. $16x - 9 = 7$      17. $-2x + 20 = 6$
    $16x = 16$             $-2x = -14$
    $x = 1$               $x = 7$

18. $4x = 5 \cdot 20$   19. $10x = 5 \cdot 9$
    $x = 25$              $x = 9/2$

20. $6(x + 3) = 2 \cdot 15$   21. $y = -3x + 4$
    $x + 3 = 5$
    $x = 2$

22. $-6y = -3x + 12$    23. $y - x + 5 = 4x + 4$
    $y = (1/2)x - 2$        $y + 5 = 5x + 4$
                            $y = 5x - 1$

## LESSON 3

1. $\text{slope} = \dfrac{8-5}{3-0} = 1$

2. $\text{slope} = \dfrac{3-(-2)}{-1-4} = -1$

3. $y - (-2) = x - 6$
   $y + 2 = x - 6$
   $y = x - 8$

4. $y - (-3) = -5(x - 1)$
   $y + 3 = -5x + 5$
   $y = -5x + 2$

5. $m = \dfrac{3-(-3)}{1-(-2)} = 2$
   $y - 3 = 2(x - 1)$
   $y - 3 = 2x - 2$
   $y = 2x + 1$

6. It is a vertical line through the $x$-axis at 5.

7. $x$-axis: $y = 0$
   $y$-axis: $x = 0$

8. If $x = 0$, then $y = 2$.
   If $y = 0$, then $x = -2$.
   → Your line should pass through the $x$-axis at –2 and the $y$-axis at 2.

9. If $x = 0$, then $y = -1$.
   If $y = 0$, then $x = 1/2$.
   → Your line should pass through the $x$-axis at 1/2 and the $y$-axis at –1.

10. If $x = 0$, then $y = 2$.
    If $y = 0$, then $x = 3$.
    → Your line should pass through the $x$-axis at 3 and the $y$-axis at 2.

11. $m = \dfrac{-5-7}{2-(-1)} = -4$

12. $m = \dfrac{4-6}{2-3} = 2$

13. $m = \dfrac{3-3}{-2-1} = 0$

14. $y - 1 = -2(x - 3)$
    $y - 1 = -2x + 6$
    $y = -2x + 7$

15. $y - 0 = 3(x - (-2))$
    $y - 0 = 3(x + 2)$
    $y = 3x + 6$

16. $m = \dfrac{8-4}{7-3} = 1$
    $y - 4 = x - 3$
    $y = x + 1$

17. $m = \dfrac{-9-3}{-2-1} = 4$
    $y - 3 = 4(x - 1)$
    $y - 3 = 4x - 4$
    $y = 4x - 1$

18. $y = 1$ for any $x$.
    → Your line should be a horizontal line through the $y$-axis at 1.

19. If $x = 0$, then $y = 5$.
    If $y = 0$, then $x = 5$.
    → Your line should pass through the $x$-axis at 5 and the $y$-axis at 5.

20. If $x = 0$, then $y = -3$.
    If $y = 0$, then $x = 2$.
    → Your line should pass through the $x$-axis at 2 and the $y$-axis at –3.

## LESSON 4

1. Plug eq1 into eq2:  $2x + (-x + 1) = 6$
   Solve eq2 for $x$:   $x + 1 = 6$
                        $x = 5$
   Use eq1 to find $y$:  $y = -5 + 1 = -4$
   Write the solution:  $(5, -4)$

2. Solve eq2 for $y$:    $y = 3x - 7$
   Plug eq2 into eq1:   $2x + 3(3x - 7) = 1$
   Solve eq1 for $x$:   $11x - 21 = 1$
                        $x = 2$
   Use eq2 to find $y$:  $y = 3(2) - 7 = -1$
   Write the solution:  $(2, -1)$

3. Solve eq1 for $x$:    $x = y + 4$
   Plug eq1 into eq2:   $(y + 4) + 3y = -8$
   Solve eq2 for $y$:   $4y + 4 = -8$
                        $y = -3$
   Use eq1 to find $x$:  $x = -3 + 4 = 1$
   Write the solution:  $(1, -3)$

4. Add eq1 to eq2:      $6x = 12$
   Solve for $x$:       $x = 2$
   Plug $x$ into eq1:    $2 + y = 5$
   Solve for $y$:       $y = 3$
   Write the solution:  $(2, 3)$

5. Subtract eq2 from eq1 × 3:
   $$3x - 3y = -12$$
   $$-\,(3x - 2y = -7)$$
   $$\overline{\phantom{aaaaa}-y = -5}$$
   Solve for $y$:       $y = 5$
   Plug $y$ into eq1:    $x - 5 = -4$
   Solve for $x$:       $x = 1$
   Write the solution:  $(1, 5)$

6. Add eq2 to eq1 × 2:
   $$6x + 4y = 8$$
   $$+\,(7x - 4y = -8)$$
   $$\overline{\phantom{aaa}13x \phantom{aaaa}= 0}$$
   Solve for $x$:       $x = 0$
   Plug $x$ into eq1:    $3(0) + 2y = 4$
   Solve for $y$:       $y = 2$
   Write the solution:  $(0, 2)$

7. Multiply eq1 by 4:    $12x + 16y = 8$
   Multiply eq2 by 3:    $-(12x + 15y = 9)$
   Subtract the equations:  $\overline{\phantom{aaaaaaaa}y = -1}$
   Plug $y$ into eq1:    $3x + 4(-1) = 2$
   Solve for $x$:       $x = 2$
   Write the solution:  $(2, -1)$

8. Multiply eq1 by 2:    $8x - 6y = -4$
   Multiply eq2 by 3:    $+\,(9x + 6y = 21)$
   Add the equations:   $\overline{\phantom{aa}17x \phantom{aaaa}= 17}$
   Solve for $x$:       $x = 1$
   Plug $x$ into eq1:    $4(1) - 3y = -2$
   Solve for $y$:       $y = 2$
   Write the solution:  $(1, 2)$

**9.** Solution: $(1, -1)$

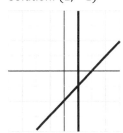

**10.** Solution: $(-2, 0)$

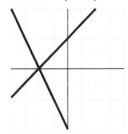

**11.** Plug eq1 into eq2.
$3x + 5(-2) = -7$
$3x - 10 = -7$
$x = 1$
Solution: $(1, -2)$

**12.** eq1 + eq2
$9x = -9$
$x = -1$
$7(-1) + y = 0$
$y = 7$
Solution: $(-1, 7)$

**13.** eq1 + eq2
$-y = 2$
$y = -2$
$x - 4(-2) = 11$
$x = 3$
Solution: $(3, -2)$

**14.** Plug eq1 into eq2.
$5x + (x + 4) = 4$
$x = 0$
$y = 0 + 4$
$y = 4$
Solution: $(0, 4)$

**15.** eq1 × 2 − eq2
$x = -1$
$3(-1) + y = 1$
$y = 4$
Solution: $(-1, 4)$

**16.** eq1 − eq2
$9y = -9$
$y = -1$
$3x + 2(-1) = 4$
$x = 2$
Solution: $(2, -1)$

**17.** Plug eq1 into eq2.
$x = 2y$
$3(2y) - 4y = 6$
$y = 3$
$x = 2(3) = 6$
Solution: $(6, 3)$

**18.** eq1 × 2 − eq2 × 3
$-11y = 22$
$y = -2$
$3x + 2(-2) = 5$
$x = 3$
Solution: $(3, -2)$

**19.** Solution: $(-1, 1)$

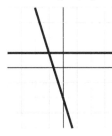

**20.** Solution: $(0, -1)$

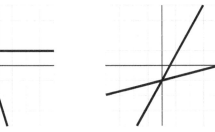

## LESSON 5

**1.** $x^2 + 3x + 2x + 6$
$= x^2 + 5x + 6$

**2.** $10x^2 - 5x - 8x + 4$
$= 10x^2 - 13x + 4$

**3.** $x^2 + 2 \cdot x \cdot 1 + 1^2$
$= x^2 + 2x + 1$

**4.** $(5x)^2 - 2 \cdot 5x \cdot 4 + 4^2$
$= 25x^2 - 40x + 16$

**5.** $x^2 + 6x + 9$
$= (x + 3)^2$

**6.** $x^2 - 4x + 4$
$= (x - 2)^2$

**7.** $(x + 3)(x - 4) = 0$
$x = -3, x = 4$

**8.** $x^2 + 4x + 4 = 6 + 4$
$(x + 2)^2 = 10$
$x + 2 = \pm\sqrt{10}$
$x = -2 \pm \sqrt{10}$

**9.** $a = 1, b = 1, c = -1$
$x = \dfrac{-1 \pm \sqrt{5}}{2}$

**10.** By factoring:
$(x - 2)(x + 3) = 0$
$x = 2, x = -3$

**11.** By comp. the square:
$x^2 - 2x = 1$
$x^2 - 2x + 1 = 1 + 1$
$(x - 1)^2 = 2$
$x - 1 = \pm\sqrt{2}$
$x = 1 \pm \sqrt{2}$

**12.** By factoring:
$(x + 2)^2 = 0$
$x + 2 = 0$
$x = -2$

**13.** $x^2 + x - 6x - 6$
$= x^2 - 5x - 6$

**14.** $x^2 - 2 \cdot x \cdot 3 + 3^2$
$= x^2 - 6x + 9$

**15.** $(2x)^2 + 2 \cdot 2x \cdot 5 + 5^2$
$= 4x^2 + 20x + 25$

**16.** $x^2 - 2x + 1$
$= (x - 1)^2$

**17.** $x^2 + 8x + 16$
$= (x + 4)^2$

**18.** $x^2 + 12x + 36$
$= (x + 6)^2$

**19.** $x^2 = 8$
$x = \pm\sqrt{8}$
$x = \pm 2\sqrt{2}$

**20.** $(x + 2)(x - 3) = 0$
$x = -2, x = 3$

**21.** $(x - 3)^2 = 0$
$x - 3 = 0$
$x = 3$

**22.** $x(x + 5) = 0$
$x = 0, x = -5$

**23.** $(x + 3)(x + 4) = 0$
$x = -3, x = -4$

**24.** $a = 5, b = -5, c = 1$
$x = \dfrac{5 \pm \sqrt{5}}{10}$

## LESSON 6

**1.** $A, B, C$

**2.** $\overline{AB}, \overline{BC}, \overline{AC}$

**3.** $\overrightarrow{AB}, \overrightarrow{BC}, \overrightarrow{AC}$
$\overrightarrow{BA}, \overrightarrow{CB}, \overrightarrow{CA}$

**4.** $\angle BAC, \angle BDE$

**5.** $\overline{AC}, \overline{BD}$

**6.** $\overline{BD}, \overline{BE}$

**7.** $\overrightarrow{AB}, \overrightarrow{BA}$

**8.** $\overleftrightarrow{NM}$

**9.** $\overline{TS}$

**10.** No other name

**11.** $\angle E, \angle FED$

**12.** $A$, $B$, and $C$ are collinear. **13.** $\overrightarrow{BA}, \overrightarrow{BC}, \overrightarrow{BD}, \overrightarrow{BE}$

$D$, $B$, and $E$ are collinear.

**14.** $\overline{AB}, \overline{BC}, \overline{BD}$ **15.** $\overrightarrow{DB}, \overrightarrow{BE}, \overrightarrow{DE}$

$\overleftrightarrow{BD}, \overleftrightarrow{EB}, \overleftrightarrow{ED}$

**16 ~ 21.** *Answers may vary. Samples are given.*

**16.**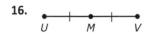

**17.**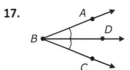

**18.**

←———→ $l$
←———→ $m$
←———→ $n$

**19.**

$d$ ↕    ↕ $e$     $f$

**20.**

$P$ — $Q$ — $R$ — $S$

**21.**

$X$ — $Y$ — $Z$

**22.** $x^2 + 6x = 1$         ⇢ $x + 3 = \pm\sqrt{10}$

$x^2 + 6x + 9 = 1 + 9$         $x = -3 \pm \sqrt{10}$

$(x + 3)^2 = 10$

## LESSON 7

**1.** a. Line $l$, points $A$ and $B$

b. Lines $m$ and $n$, point $O$

c. Plane $M$

d. Planes $M$ and $P$, line $t$

**2.** There are infinitely many points on a line.
You need two points to determine a line.

**3.** $AB + BC = AC$         ⇢ $-2x = -8$

$9 + (x + 1) = 3x + 2$         $x = 4$

$x + 10 = 3x + 2$         $AC = 3(4) + 2 = 14$

**4.** $m\angle ABD + m\angle DBC = m\angle ABC$

$(x + 5) + (7x + 15) = 180$     ⇢ $8x = 160$

$8x + 20 = 180$         $x = 20$

**5.** infinitely many lines

**6.** no; By the Parallel Postulate, there is exactly one line
passing through point $F$ parallel to line $s$. So, lines $t$
and $u$ cannot both be parallel to line $s$.

**7.** By the Perpendicular Postulate, you can draw exactly
one line through point $F$ perpendicular to line $s$.

**8.** never **9.** sometimes

**10.** always **11.** sometimes

**12.** always **13.** sometimes

**14.** always **15.** never

**16.** $AB = BC = BD = 5$

$AC = AB + BC = 5 + 5 = 10$

**17.** $m\angle ABD + m\angle DBC = m\angle ABC$

$m\angle DBC = m\angle ABC - m\angle ABD = 180° - 30° = 150°$

**18.** $AC = 2BD$

$5x + 4 = 2(x + 5)$         ⇢ $3x = 6$

$5x + 4 = 2x + 10$         $x = 2$

**19.** $m\angle ABD + m\angle DBC = m\angle ABC$

$(x + 7) + (6x - 2) = 180$     ⇢ $7x = 175$

$7x + 5 = 180$         $x = 25$

**20.** By the Parallel Postulate, you can draw exactly one line
through point $D$ parallel to line $\overleftrightarrow{AC}$.

**21.** eq1 + eq2         ⇢ $3 + y = 5$

$4x = 12$         $y = 2$

$x = 3$         Solution: $(3, 2)$

**22.** false; $\overrightarrow{PQ}$ is a ray with endpoint $P$, but $\overrightarrow{QP}$ is a ray with
endpoint $Q$.

## LESSON 8

**1.** obtuse **2.** true; $90° + 90° = 180°$

**3.** $\angle 4, \angle 5$ **4.** $\angle 3, \angle 5$

**5.** $\angle 2, \angle 3$ **6.** $\angle 3, \angle 5$; adjacent to $\angle 4$

**7.** $m\angle 1 = 90°$; $m\angle 2 = 57°$

$m\angle 3 = 90 - m\angle 2 = 90 - 57 = 33°$

$m\angle 4 = 180 - m\angle 3 = 180 - 33 = 147°$

$m\angle 5 = 180 - m\angle 4 = 180 - 147 = 33°$

**8.** $m\angle 1 = 90°$; $m\angle 3 = 35°$

$m\angle 2 = 90 - m\angle 3 = 90 - 35 = 55°$

$m\angle 4 = 180 - m\angle 3 = 180 - 35 = 145°$

$m\angle 5 = 180 - m\angle 4 = 180 - 145 = 35°$

**9.** $m\angle 3 = 180 - m\angle 4 = 180 - 150 = 30°$

$m\angle 5 = 180 - m\angle 4 = 180 - 150 = 30°$

**10.** true; $\angle 3$ and $\angle 5$ always measure $180° - m\angle 4$.

**11.** $\angle q, \angle Q, \angle PQR, \angle RQP$; acute

**12.** $\angle b, \angle B, \angle ABC, \angle CBA$; obtuse

**13.** $\angle t, \angle T, \angle STU, \angle UTS$; right

**14.** complementary **15.** none

**16.** vertical **17.** supplementary

**18.** vertical **19.** supplementary

**20.** vertical angles **21.** supplementary angles

$4x = 56$         $7x + 131 = 180$

$x = 14$         $7x = 49$

$x = 7$

22. complementary angles

$62 + (2x - 8) = 90$    $\rightarrow$    $2x = 36$

$2x + 54 = 90$        $x = 18$

23. false; Angles in a linear pair are supplementary.

24. true

25. true

26. false; Two obtuse angles add up to more than 180°, so they cannot be supplementary.

27. Complementary angles add up to 90°. So, if they are congruent, then each must measure 45°.

28. The two angles in a linear pair add up to 180°. So, if they are congruent, then each must measure 90°.

29. Vertical angles are congruent. So, if they are complementary, then each must measure 45°.

30. A right angle measures 90°, so the supplement of a right angle measures 180 – 90 = 90° as well.

31. $8\sqrt{3} - 3\sqrt{3} = 5\sqrt{3}$

32. $AB + BC = AC$    $\rightarrow$    $x = 6$

$x + 2x = 18$       $AB = x = 6$

## LESSON 9 ·······························································

1. $\angle 2$ and $\angle 6$, $\angle 3$ and $\angle 7$    2.   $\angle 2$ and $\angle 7$
$\angle 4$ and $\angle 8$

3. $\angle 4$ and $\angle 5$        4.   $\angle 4$ and $\angle 6$

5. $\angle 1$ and $\angle 3$, $\angle 2$ and $\angle 4$    6.   $\angle 1$ and $\angle 8$, $\angle 4$ and $\angle 5$
$\angle 5$ and $\angle 7$, $\angle 6$ and $\angle 8$

7. $\angle 2$ and $\angle 7$, $\angle 3$ and $\angle 6$    8.   $\angle 2$ and $\angle 3$, $\angle 6$ and $\angle 7$

9. $\angle 2 \cong \angle 3$ (vertical angles)

$\angle 2 \cong \angle 6$ (corresponding angles)

$\angle 2 \cong \angle 7$ (alternate exterior angles)

$\angle 5 \cong \angle 8$ (vertical angles)

$\angle 5 \cong \angle 1$ (corresponding angles)

$\angle 5 \cong \angle 4$ (alternate interior angles)

10. $m\angle 1 = 78°$; $m\angle 2 = 102°$; $m\angle 4 = 102°$

$m\angle 3 = m\angle 1 = 78°$ (corresponding angles)

$m\angle 5 = m\angle 2 = 102°$ (vertical angles)

$m\angle 6 = m\angle 1 = 78°$ (vertical angles)

$m\angle 7 = m\angle 2 = 102°$ (alternate interior angles)

$m\angle 8 = m\angle 1 = 78°$ (alternate exterior angles)

There are many ways to find these angle measures that are all correct. For example, you could say $m\angle 6 = m\angle 3 = 78°$ as alternate interior angles.

11. alternate exterior      12. consecutive interior

13. complementary        14. corresponding

15. vertical             16. alternate interior

17. vertical angles        corresponding angles

$a = 113$               $b = 113$

18. supplementary angles    alternate interior angles

$a + 118 = 180$         $a = 90 - b$

$a = 62$                $b = 28$

19. alternate exterior angles   supplementary angles

$3a = 93$               $3a + b = 180$

$a = 31$                $b = 87$

20. Any two adjacent angles of a parallelogram are consecutive interior angles, so they are supplementary.

21. $\angle 1$ and $\angle 2$ are supplementary and add up to 180°. $\angle 3$ and $\angle 4$ are supplementary and add up to 180°. So, the four angles add up to 360°.

22. Set $y = 0$, then $x = 3$. So, the $x$-intercept is (3, 0).

23. two pairs

24. $180° - 50° = 130°$

## LESSON 10 ·······························································

1. $\angle 1$ and $\angle 4$, $\angle 2$ and $\angle 3$    2.   $\angle 1$ and $\angle 5$, $\angle 2$ and $\angle 6$
$\angle 5$ and $\angle 8$, $\angle 6$ and $\angle 7$       $\angle 3$ and $\angle 7$, $\angle 4$ and $\angle 8$

3. $\angle 1$ and $\angle 8$, $\angle 2$ and $\angle 7$    4.   $\angle 3$ and $\angle 6$, $\angle 4$ and $\angle 5$

5. $\angle 3$ and $\angle 5$, $\angle 4$ and $\angle 6$

6. false; They are corresponding angles.

7. Lines $l$ and $m$ must be parallel because $\angle 11$ and $\angle 14$ are alternate interior angles on lines $l$ and $m$ when line $v$ is the transversal.

8. Lines $u$ and $v$ must be parallel because $\angle 6$ and $\angle 13$ are consecutive interior angles on lines $u$ and $v$ when line $m$ is the transversal.

9. $l \parallel m$ if corresponding angles are congruent.

$8y + 10 = 5y + 34$    $\rightarrow$    $y = 8$

$3y = 24$

10. yes; $(9x - 29)°$ and $(8y + 10)°$ form a linear pair, so they must add up to 180°. If $x = 15$ and $y = 8$, then $(9x - 29) + (8y + 10) = 106 + 74 = 180$. So, both pairs of lines can be parallel at the same time.

11. yes; Alternate interior angles are congruent.

12. no

13. yes; Corresponding angles are congruent.

14. corresponding angles    15. alternate exterior angles

$150 - x = 113$           $x - 84 = 116$

$x = 37$                 $x = 200$

16. The two angles must be supplementary since the angle corresponding to 118° is supplementary to $(7 - 5x)°$.

$118 + (7 - 5x) = 180$    $\rightarrow$    $x = -11$

$-5x = 55$

**17.** alternate interior     **18.** alternate exterior

**19.** corresponding     **20.** consecutive interior

**21.** $u \parallel v$ (corresponding angles)

**22.** $l \parallel m$ (alternate exterior angles)

**23.** $l \parallel m$ (consecutive interior angles)

**24.** $\angle 1 \cong \angle 4$ (vertical angles)

    $\angle 1 \cong \angle 5$ (corresponding angles)

    $\angle 1 \cong \angle 8$ (alternate exterior angles)

    $\angle 1 \cong \angle 9$ (corresponding angles)

    $\angle 1 \cong \angle 12$ (alternate exterior angles)

    $\angle 1 \cong \angle 13$ ($\angle 5 \cong \angle 13$ as corresponding angles)

    $\angle 1 \cong \angle 16$ ($\angle 5 \cong \angle 16$ as alternate exterior angles)

**25.** $l \parallel m$ because corresponding angles are congruent when lines $l$ and $m$ are cut by transversal $u$.

    $u \parallel v$ because alternate exterior angles are congruent when lines $u$ and $v$ are cut by transversal $l$.

**26.** $\overline{AF} \parallel \overline{BE}$ because $\angle AFE \cong \angle BED$ as corresponding angles when $\overline{AF}$ and $\overline{BE}$ are cut by transversal $\overline{FD}$.

    $\overline{AC} \parallel \overline{FD}$ because $\angle ABE \cong \angle BED$ as alternate interior angles when $\overline{AC}$ and $\overline{FD}$ are cut by transversal $\overline{BE}$

**27.** false; When two non-parallel lines are cut by a transversal, corresponding angles are not congruent.

## LESSON 11

**1.** acute        **2.** 180°

**3.** $\angle 2 \cong \angle 4$ as alternate interior angles.

    $\angle 3 \cong \angle 5$ as alternate interior angles.

**4.** $m\angle 2 = m\angle 4$ because $\angle 2 \cong \angle 4$.

    $m\angle 3 = m\angle 5$ because $\angle 3 \cong \angle 5$.

    So, $m\angle 1 + m\angle 2 + m\angle 3$ is equal to $m\angle 1 + m\angle 4 + m\angle 5$, which is a straight angle of 180°.

**5.** equilateral and equiangular

**6.** isosceles and obtuse

**7.** $(x - 29) + 38 + 70 = 180$    **8.** $(x + 17) + 60 + 90 = 180$
    $x + 79 = 180$                 $x + 167 = 180$
    $x = 101$                    $x = 13$

**9.** $m\angle 1 = 180 - 125 = 55°$   **10.** $m\angle 1 = 81 + 43 = 124°$
    $m\angle 2 = 55 + m\angle 1$           $m\angle 2 = 180 - m\angle 1$
        $= 55 + 55 = 110°$          $= 180 - 124 = 56°$

**11.**       **12.**

**13.** not possible

**14.** $x + 37 + 90 = 180$    **15.** $x + 46 + 100 = 180$
    $x = 53$                  $x = 34$

**16.** $5x + 30 + 120 = 180$    **17.** $x = 45 + 45 = 90$
    $5x = 30$
    $x = 6$

**18.** $4x + 6 = 68 + 74$     **19.** $x - 19 + 73 = 103$
    $4x = 136$                $x = 49$
    $x = 34$

**20.** Use the interior angle sum of $\triangle ABC$.
    $m\angle ECF = 180 - 90 - m\angle A = 180 - 90 - 62 = 28°$

**21.** Use the interior angle sum of $\triangle BCD$.
    $m\angle EBF = 180 - 90 - m\angle D = 180 - 90 - 70 = 20°$

**22.** $m\angle ABE$ and $m\angle EBF$ are complementary.
    $m\angle ABE = 90 - m\angle EBF = 90 - 20 = 70°$

**23.** $m\angle AED$ is an exterior angle of $\triangle ABE$.
    $m\angle AED = m\angle A + m\angle ABE = 62 + 70 = 132°$

**24.** $7x + 5x = 180$, so $x = 15$.

**25.** A linear pair must be adjacent, but supplementary angles do not have to be adjacent.

## LESSON 12

**1.**  $\triangle$ angle sum = 180     **2.**  $\triangle$ angle sum = 180
    $x + 38 + 70 = 180$           $x + 46 + 100 = 180$
    $x = 72$                     $x = 34$

**3.**  101° is an exterior angle.  **4.**  parallelogram, rhombus
    $x + 68 = 101$                rectangle, square
    $x = 33$                 **5.**  rhombus, square

**6.**  $98 + (4x - 26) + 90 + 90 = 360$    ⇢  $4x = 108$
    $4x + 252 = 360$                          $x = 27$

**7.**  $2x + 70 + (x + 55) + 70 = 360$    ⇢  $3x = 165$
    $3x + 195 = 360$                        $x = 55$

**8.**  $89 + (3x + 25) + 90 + 90 = 360$    ⇢  $3x = 66$
    $3x + 294 = 360$                        $x = 22$

**9.**  $(3x - 42) + 2x + 98 + 104 = 360$   ⇢  $5x = 200$
    $5x + 160 = 360$                        $x = 40$

**10.** always              **11.** sometimes

**12.** always              **13.** never

**14.** rhombus, square     **15.** rectangle, square

**16.** parallelogram, rhombus, rectangle, square, trapezoid

**17.** parallelogram, rhombus, rectangle, square

**18.** All sides are congruent.   ⇢  $2a + 8 = 5b + 4$
    $3a = 2a + 8$                $2(8) + 8 = 5b + 4$
    $a = 8$                   $b = 4$

**19.** All sides are congruent.

$5c + 2 = 3c + 8$

$c = 3$

$5c + 2 = 17 - 5d$

$5(3) + 2 = 17 - 5d$

$d = 0$

**20.** Each pair of adjacent sides is congruent.

$3s = 27;\ s = 9$

$4t = 5t - 9;\ t = 9$

**21.** Non-parallel sides are congruent.

$5x = 6 - x$

$x = 1$

**22.** The three angles in a triangle always add up to 180°, so the third angle is $180 - 25 - 60 = 95°$.

## LESSON 13

**1.** △ angle sum = 180

$x + 60 + 90 = 180$

$x = 30$

**2.** quad. angle sum = 360

$x + 92 + 80 + 86 = 360$

$x = 102$

**3.** quad. exterior angle sum = 360

$x + 96 + 90 + 85 = 360;\ x = 89$

**4.** An octagon has 8 sides, so you can draw 5 diagonals from one of the vertices. These diagonals form 6 triangles.

**5.** $2x + 102 + 78 + 90 = 180(5 - 2)$

$2x + 270 = 540;\ x = 135$

**6.** $x + 136 + 130 + 103 + 123 + 128 = 180(6 - 2)$

$x + 620 = 720;\ x = 100$

**7.** $x + 77 + 83 + 84 + 50 = 360$

$x + 294 = 360;\ x = 66$

**8.** $2x + 39 + 90 + 58 + 71 = 360$

$2x + 258 = 360;\ x = 51$

**9.** $180(5 - 2) = 540°$

**10.** $180(6 - 2) = 720°$

**11.** $180(8 - 2) = 1080°$

**12.** interior angle = $180(5 - 2)/5 = 108°$

exterior angle = $360/5 = 72°$

**13.** interior angle = $180(6 - 2)/6 = 120°$

exterior angle = $360/6 = 60°$

**14.** interior angle = $180(8 - 2)/8 = 135°$

exterior angle = $360/8 = 45°$

**15.** $x + 98 + 123 + 102 + 95 = 180(5 - 2)$

$x + 418 = 540;\ x = 122$

**16.** $6x + 65 + 82 + 75 = 180(4 - 2)$

$6x + 222 = 360;\ x = 23$

**17.** $2x + 115 + 115 + 115 + 115 = 180(6 - 2)$

$2x + 460 = 720;\ x = 130$

**18.** $5x + (5x + 10) + 80 + 80 = 360$

$10x + 170 = 360;\ x = 19$

**19.** $7x + 73 + 76 + 80 + 82 = 360$

$7x + 311 = 360;\ x = 7$

**20.** The exterior angle of $(180 - 9x)°$ is $9x°$.

$9x + 90 + 76 + 81 + 41 = 360$

$9x + 288 = 360;\ x = 8$

**21.** $180(n - 2)/n = 150$

$180(n - 2) = 150n$

$30n = 360$

$n = 12$ sides

**22.** $360/n = 72$

$360 = 72n$

$n = 5$ sides

**23.** no; If a triangle has two obtuse angles, then the sum of its interior angles will be more than 180°.

## LESSON 14

**1.** $A$, $B$, and $C$ are collinear. $E$, $B$, and $F$ are collinear.

**2.** $\overline{AB}, \overline{BC}, \overline{BE}, \overline{BF}$

**3.** $\overrightarrow{BA}, \overrightarrow{BC}, \overrightarrow{BD}, \overrightarrow{BE}, \overrightarrow{BF}$

**4.** $\overleftrightarrow{AB}, \overleftrightarrow{BC}, \overleftrightarrow{AC}$
$\overrightarrow{BA}, \overrightarrow{CB}, \overrightarrow{CA}$

**5.** $AC = 2BC$

$18 = 2(2x + 5)$

$9 = 2x + 5$

$x = 2$

**6.** $m\angle DBE + m\angle EBC = 90$

$(72 - 4y) + (9y - 2) = 90$

$5y + 70 = 90$

$y = 4$

**7.** sometimes

**8.** always

**9.** never

**10.** vertical angles

$90 - x = 58$

$x = 32$

**11.** supplementary angles

$(6x - 2) + 8x = 180$

$14x - 2 = 180$

$x = 13$

**12.** alternate exterior

**13.** consecutive interior

**14.** corresponding

**15.** alternate interior

**16.** alternate exterior angles

$5x = 120$

$x = 24$

**17.** corresponding angles

$4x = 64$

$x = 16$

**18.** $180/3 = 60°$

**19.** $180 - 60 = 120°$
Or $360/3 = 120°$

**20.** rectangle, square

**21.** yes; A square has four congruent sides.

**22.** no; A circle is made of a curve.

**23.** $180(5 - 2) = 540°$

**24.** $360/6 = 60°$

**25.** △ angle sum = 180

$x + 34 + 100 = 180$

$x = 46$

**26.** 88° is an exterior angle.

$45 + x = 88$

$x = 43$

**27.** quad. angle sum = 360

$x + 113 + 91 + 75 = 360$

$x + 279 = 360;\ x = 81$

**28.** exterior angle sum = 360

$5x + 82 + 8x + 9x + 58 = 360$

$22x + 140 = 360;\ x = 10$

**29.** $x = 3$

**30.** $y - 5 = -2(x - 1)$

**31.** $(2, 0)$

**32.** $(x - 1)(x + 3)$

## LESSON 15 ·······························

**1.** rectangle

**2.** trapezoid.

**3.** rhombus

**4.** kite

**5.** parallelogram

**6.** square

**7.** 3 lines of symmetry

**8.** 1 line of symmetry

**9.** rhombus
2 lines of symmetry

rectangle
2 lines of symmetry

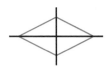 

square
4 lines of symmetry

kite
1 line of symmetry

 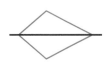

**10.** parallelogram (angle = 180°, order = 2)

rhombus (angle = 180°, order = 2)

rectangle (angle = 180°, order = 2)

square (angle = 90°, order = 4)

**11.** rhombus, rectangle, square

**12.** See the kite above.  **13.** See the square above.

**14.** See the rectangle above.

**15.** order = 5, angle = 360/5 = 72°

A regular pentagon looks exactly the same every (360/5)°, or 5 times in one full turn.

In general, the order of rotational symmetry of a regular polygon is equal to the number of sides. The angle of rotational symmetry is 360 divided by the number of sides.

**16.** order = 6
angle = 360/6 = 60°

**17.** order = 8
angle = 360/8 = 45°

**18.** Reflectional
No rotational

**19.** No reflectional
Rotational
(180°, 2)

**20.** Reflectional
Rotational
(180°, 2)

**21.** Reflectional
No rotational

**22.** Reflectional
No rotational

**23.** No reflectional
Rotational
(180°, 2)

**24.** $m\angle 1 = 90°$ (corresponding angles)

**25.** $m\angle 1 = 90°$ (corresponding angles)

$m\angle 2 = 140°$ (corresponding angles)

$m\angle 3 = 180 - m\angle 2 = 40°$ (supplementary angles)

$m\angle 4 = 180 - 90 - m\angle 3 = 50°$ (△ angle sum = 180)

**26.** true; A linear pair is 2 adjacent supplementary angles.

## LESSON 16 ·······························

**1.** $\overline{P'Q'}$

**2.** Function notation:  $T_{2,5}(x, y) = (x + 2, y + 5)$

Mapping notation:  $(x, y) \rightarrow (x + 2, y + 5)$

Vector notation:   <2, 5>

**3.** Translate each vertex 1 unit right and 1 unit up by adding 1 to each $x$-value and 1 to each $y$-value.

$A(-2, 2) \rightarrow A'(-2 + 1, 2 + 1) = A'(-1, 3)$

$B(2, 3) \rightarrow B'(2 + 1, 3 + 1) = B'(3, 4)$

**4.** Translate each vertex 2 units right and 3 units down by adding 2 to each $x$-value and −3 to each $y$-value.

$A(-2, 2) \rightarrow A'(-2 + 2, 2 - 3) = A'(0, -1)$

$B(2, 3) \rightarrow B'(2 + 2, 3 - 3) = B'(4, 0)$

**5.** Translate each vertex 5 units right by adding 5 to each $x$-value.

$A(-2, 2) \rightarrow A'(-2 + 5, 2) = A'(3, 2)$

$B(2, 3) \rightarrow B'(2 + 5, 3) = B'(7, 3)$

**6.** The $x$-value is decreased by 3. The $y$-value is increased by 7. So, the rule is $(x, y) \rightarrow (x - 3, y + 7)$.

**7.** Translate each vertex 4 units up by adding 4 to each $y$-value.

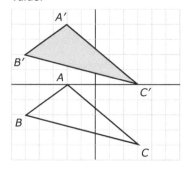

$A'(-2, 4)$
$B'(-5, 2)$
$C'(3, 0)$

**8.** Translate each vertex 5 units right and 4 units down by adding 5 to each $x$-value and –4 to each $y$-value.

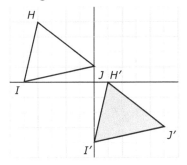

$H'(1, 0)$
$I'(0, -4)$
$J'(5, -3)$

**9.** Translate each vertex 6 units left and 3 units up by adding –6 to each $x$-value and 3 to each $y$-value.

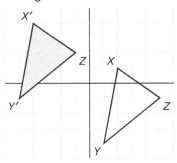

$X'(-4, 4)$
$Y'(-5, -1)$
$Z'(-1, 2)$

**10.** Add 3 to the $x$-value.

$P(-1, 6) \rightarrow P'(-1 + 3, 6) = P'(2, 6)$

**11.** Add –7 to the $x$-value and 5 to the $y$-value.

$P(-1, 6) \rightarrow P'(-1 - 7, 6 + 5) = P'(-8, 11)$

**12.** Add 8 to the $x$-value and –4 to the $y$-value.

$P(-1, 6) \rightarrow P'(-1 + 8, 6 - 4) = P'(7, 2)$

**13.** The triangle is translated 4 units right and 5 units up. So, the rule is $(x, y) \rightarrow (x + 4, y + 5)$.

**14.** The triangle is translated 4 units right and 3 units down. So, the rule is $(x, y) \rightarrow (x + 4, y - 3)$.

**15.** The triangle is translated 6 units left and 1 unit up. So, the rule is $(x, y) \rightarrow (x - 6, y + 1)$.

**16.** The $x$-value is decreased by 3. The $y$-value is increased by 5. So, the rule is <–3, 5>.

**17.** The $x$-value is increased by 8. The $y$-value is increased by 9. So, the rule is <8, 9>.

**18.** The $x$-value is increased by 3. The $y$-value is decreased by 11. So, the rule is <3, –11>.

**19.** The translation maps $(x, y)$ to $(x, y - 2)$.

$(x, y - 2)$ becomes $(0, 0)$ when $x = 0$ and $y = 2$.

So, this translation maps $(0, 2)$ to the origin.

**20.** The translation maps $(x, y)$ to $(x - 4, y)$.

$(x - 4, y)$ becomes $(0, 0)$ when $x = 4$ and $y = 0$.

So, this translation maps $(4, 0)$ to the origin.

**21.** The translation maps $(x, y)$ to $(x - 2, y + 5)$.

$(x - 2, y + 5)$ becomes $(0, 0)$ when $x = 2$ and $y = -5$.

So, this translation maps $(2, -5)$ to the origin.

**22.** false; If a triangle has two angles of 45°, then the third angle is 180 – 45 – 45 = 90°. It is a right triangle.

**23.** 2 lines of symmetry

## LESSON 17 ·······························································

**1.** $\overline{QQ'}$

**2.** Reflect each vertex over the $x$-axis.

$E$ is 1 unit above the $x$-axis, so $E'$ will be 1 unit below the $x$-axis. Similarly, $F'$ will be 2 units below the $x$-axis.

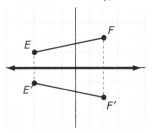

$E'(-3, -1)$
$F'(2, -2)$

**3.** Reflect each vertex over the line $y = -x$.

$C$ is on the line of reflection, so $C'$ will be the same point as $C$. $D'$ will be exactly opposite to $D$.

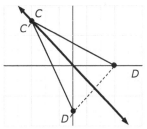

$C'(-3, 3)$
$D'(0, -3)$

**4.** Over the $x$-axis: $P(-1, 6) \rightarrow P'(-1, -6)$

Over the $y$-axis: $P(-1, 6) \rightarrow P'(1, 6)$

Over the line $y = x$: $P(-1, 6) \rightarrow P'(6, -1)$

Over the line $y = -x$: $P(-1, 6) \rightarrow P'(-6, 1)$

**6.** The sign of the $y$-value is changed. So, the line of reflection is the $x$-axis and the rule is $r_{x\text{-}axis}(x, y) = (x, -y)$.

**7.** Reflect each vertex over the line $y = 1$.

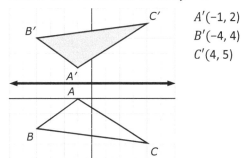

$A'(-1, 2)$
$B'(-4, 4)$
$C'(4, 5)$

**8.** Reflect each vertex over the line $x = -1$.

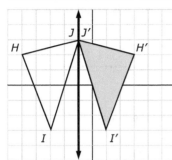

$H'(3, 2)$
$I'(1, -3)$
$J'(-1, 3)$

**9.** Reflect each vertex over the line $y = x$.

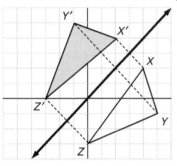

$X'(2, 4)$
$Y'(-1, 5)$
$Z'(-3, 0)$

**10.** $P(3, -5) \rightarrow P'(3, 5)$      **11.** $P(3, -5) \rightarrow P'(-3, -5)$

**12.** $P(3, -5) \rightarrow P'(-5, 3)$      **13.** $P(3, -5) \rightarrow P'(5, -3)$

**14.** $P(3, -5) \rightarrow P'(-1, -5)$      **15.** $P(3, -5) \rightarrow P'(3, 9)$

**16.** The sign of the $x$-value is changed. So, the line of reflection is the $y$-axis and the rule is $r_{y\text{-}axis}(x, y) = (-x, y)$.

**17.** The sign of the $y$-value is changed. So, the line of reflection is the $x$-axis and the rule is $r_{x\text{-}axis}(x, y) = (x, -y)$.

**18.** The $x$- and $y$-values are switched. The signs of the $x$- and $y$-values are changed. So, the line of reflection is the line $y = -x$ and the rule is $r_{y=-x}(x, y) = (-y, -x)$.

**19.** Two vertices are in Quadrant III.

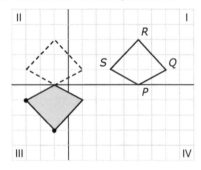

**20.** The translation rule is $(x, y) \rightarrow (x - 7, y + 5)$. So, the new coordinates of $B$ are $(-10, 6)$.

**21.** The point before the reflection is $(-1, 6)$. This means that the translation maps $(2, 5)$ to $(-1, 6)$. So, the translation rule is $(x, y) \rightarrow (x - 3, y + 1)$.

Apply these transformations to $Q$. The translation maps $Q(4, -3)$ to $Q'(1, -2)$. The reflection maps $Q'(1, -2)$ to $Q''(-2, 1)$. So, the new coordinates of $Q$ are $(-2, 1)$.

**22.** slope $= (4 - 8)/(3 - 2) = -2$

**23.** $(x + 1)^2$

**24.** no; A kite has no rotational symmetry.

## LESSON 18 ·······································································

**1.** $m\angle POP' = 90°$

**2.** $Q(4, 0) \rightarrow Q'(0, 4)$      **3.** $R(-1, 3) \rightarrow R'(1, -3)$

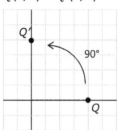 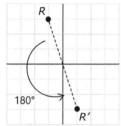

**4.** Rotate 90°:    $P(-1, 6) \rightarrow P'(-6, -1)$

Rotate 180°:   $P(-1, 6) \rightarrow P'(1, -6)$

Rotate 270°:   $P(-1, 6) \rightarrow P'(6, 1)$

**6.** The $x$- and $y$-values are switched. The sign of the original $x$-value is changed. So, the angle of rotation is 270° and the rule is $R_{0,270°}(x, y) = (y, -x)$.

**7.** Rotate each vertex 90° about the origin.

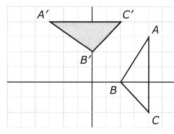

$A'(-3, 4)$
$B'(0, 2)$
$C'(2, 4)$

**8.** Rotate each vertex 180° about the origin.

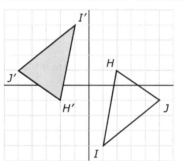

$H'(-2, -1)$
$I'(-1, 4)$
$J'(-5, 1)$

**9.** Rotate each vertex 270° about the origin.

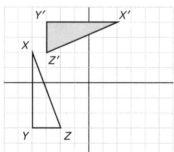

$X'(2, 4)$
$Y'(-3, 4)$
$Z'(-3, 2)$

**10.** $P(3, -5) \rightarrow P'(5, 3)$    **11.** $P(3, -5) \rightarrow P'(-3, 5)$

**12.** $P(3, -5) \rightarrow P'(-5, -3)$    **13.** $P(3, -5) \rightarrow P'(-5, -3)$

**14.** $P(3, -5) \rightarrow P'(-3, 5)$    **15.** $P(3, -5) \rightarrow P'(5, 3)$

**16.** The signs of the $x$- and $y$-values are changed. So, the angle of rotation is 180° and the rule is $R_{0,180°}(x, y) = (-x, -y)$.

**17.** The $x$- and $y$-values are switched. The sign of the original $y$-value is changed. So, the angle of rotation is 90° and the rule is $R_{0,90°}(x, y) = (-y, x)$.

**18.** The $x$- and $y$-values are switched. The sign of the original $x$-value is changed. So, the angle of rotation is 270° and the rule is $R_{0,270°}(x, y) = (y, -x)$.

**19.** The point before the rotation is (–2, –3). The point before the reflection is (–3, –2). This means that the translation maps (2, 5) to (–3, –2). So, the translation rule is $(x, y) \rightarrow (x - 5, y - 7)$.

Apply these transformations to $Q$. The translation maps $Q(9, 7)$ to $Q'(4, 0)$. The reflection maps $Q'(4, 0)$ to $Q''(0, 4)$. The rotation maps $Q''(0, 4)$ to $Q'''(0, -4)$. So, the new coordinates of $Q$ are (0, –4).

**20.** The image is in Quadrant II.

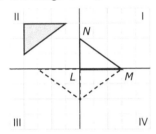

**21.** interior angle sum = $180(n - 2) = 180(4 - 2) = 360°$

**22.** The translation maps $P(3, 7)$ to $P'(0, 7)$.
The reflection maps $P'(0, 7)$ to $P''(0, -7)$.
So, the final image is (0, –7).

## LESSON 19

**1.** $P'Q' = 3PQ = 3(4) = 12$

**2.** $(x, y) \rightarrow (x/2, y/2)$
$A(-2, 0) \rightarrow A'(-1, 0)$
$B(0, 2) \rightarrow B'(0, 1)$
$C(2, 0) \rightarrow C'(1, 0)$

**3.** $(x, y) \rightarrow (3x, 3y)$
$S(2, 2) \rightarrow S'(6, 6)$
$T(1, -1) \rightarrow T'(3, -3)$
$U(2, -2) \rightarrow U'(6, -6)$

**4.** $(x, y) \rightarrow (-2x, -2y)$
$A(-2, 0) \rightarrow A'(4, 0)$
$B(0, 2) \rightarrow B'(0, -4)$
$C(2, 0) \rightarrow C'(-4, 0)$

**5.** $(x, y) \rightarrow (-x, -y)$
$S(2, 2) \rightarrow S'(-2, -2)$
$T(1, -1) \rightarrow T'(-1, 1)$
$U(2, -2) \rightarrow U'(-2, 2)$

**6.** a rotation of 180° about the origin

**7.** The $x$- and $y$-values are multiplied by 1/2. So, the scale factor is 1/2 and the rule is $D_{0,1/2}(x, y) = (x/2, y/2)$.

**8.** $P'Q' = k \times PQ$
$6 = 4k$
$k = 3/2$

$\rightarrow Q'R' = k \times QR$
$= (3/2)(8) = 12$

**9.** Dilate each vertex about the origin by scale factor 2.

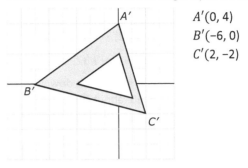

$A'(0, 4)$
$B'(-6, 0)$
$C'(2, -2)$

**10.** Dilate each vertex about the origin by scale factor –1.

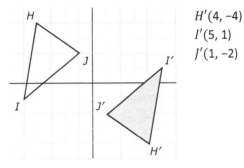

$H'(4, -4)$
$I'(5, 1)$
$J'(1, -2)$

**11.** Dilate each vertex about the origin by scale factor 1/3.

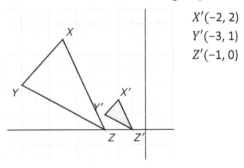

$X'(-2, 2)$
$Y'(-3, 1)$
$Z'(-1, 0)$

**12.** The $x$- and $y$-values are multiplied by 1/3. So, the scale factor is 1/3 and the rule is $D_{0,1/3}(x, y) = (x/3, y/3)$.

**13.** The $x$- and $y$-values are multiplied by 4. So, the scale factor is 4 and the rule is $D_{0,4}(x, y) = (4x, 4y)$.

**14.** The $x$- and $y$-values are multiplied by –2. So, the scale factor is –2 and the rule is $D_{0,-2}(x, y) = (-2x, -2y)$.

**15.** Find $k$.          Find $x$.          Find $y$.
$S'T' = k \cdot ST$    $\rightarrow$ $T'U' = k \cdot TU$    $\rightarrow$ $S'U' = k \cdot SU$
$6 = 2k$          $x = (3)3$          $18 = 3y$
$k = 3$          $x = 9$          $y = 6$

**16.** $S'T' = k \cdot ST$    $\rightarrow$ $T'U' = k \cdot TU$    $\rightarrow$ $S'U' = k \cdot SU$
$10 = 8k$          $25 = (5/4)x$          $y = (5/4)12$
$k = 5/4$          $x = 20$          $y = 15$

**17.** $T'U' = k \cdot TU$    $\rightarrow$ $S'T' = k \cdot ST$    $\rightarrow$ $S'U' = k \cdot SU$
$6 = 21k$          $10 = (2/7)x$          $y = (2/7)14$
$k = 2/7$          $x = 35$          $y = 4$

**18.** right angle + sum of two acute angles = 180°

sum of two acute angles = 180 – 90 = 90°

## LESSON 20

**1.** Translate by <2, 4>:  $P(3, -2) \rightarrow P'(5, 2)$

**2.** Reflect over $x = 1$:  $P(3, -2) \rightarrow P'(-1, -2)$

**3.** Rotate 90° about $O$:  $P(3, -2) \rightarrow P'(2, 3)$

**4.** a translation of 1 unit right and 4 units down
followed by a rotation of 90° about the origin

**5.** The translation maps $P(-3, 6)$ to $P'(-2, 2)$.
The rotation maps $P'(-2, 2)$ to $P''(-2, -2)$.
So, the final image is $P''(-2, -2)$.

**6.** The rotation maps $P(-3, 6)$ to $P'(3, -6)$.
The reflection maps $P'(3, -6)$ to $P''(3, 6)$.
So, the final image is $P''(3, 6)$.

**7 ~ 9.**  *Answers may vary. Samples are given.*

**7.** A reflection over the $x$-axis followed by
a translation of 1 unit down will map $\triangle HIJ$ to $\triangle RST$.

**8.** A rotation of 90° about the origin followed by
a translation of 2 units left and 2 units down
will map $\triangle HIJ$ to $\triangle XYZ$.

**9.** A translation of 4 units down followed by
a reflection over the $y$-axis will map $\triangle ABC$ to $\triangle DEF$.

**10.** a translation of 3 units right and 4 units up

**11.** a rotation of 180° about the origin

**12.** Translate by <3, –2>:  $P(1, 6) \rightarrow P'(4, 4)$
Reflect over $y = x$:   $P'(4, 4) \rightarrow P''(4, 4)$

**13.** Rotate 90° about $O$:  $P(1, 6) \rightarrow P'(-6, 1)$
Reflect over $x = 1$:   $P'(-6, 1) \rightarrow P''(8, 1)$

**14.** Translate by <–3, 3>:  $P(1, 6) \rightarrow P'(-2, 9)$
Rotate 180° about $O$:  $P'(-2, 9) \rightarrow P''(2, -9)$

**15 ~ 17.**  *Answers may vary. Samples are given.*

**15.** a translation of 2 units right and 2 units up
and then a reflection over the $y$-axis

**16.** a rotation of 180° about the origin
and then a translation of 1 unit up

**17.** a rotation of 90° about the origin
and then a translation of 2 units left and 3 units down

**18.** a translation of 2 units left and 4 units up

**19.** a translation of 10 units up; Use a simple point like (0, 0) to find the translation rule.

**20.** a rotation of 180° about the origin

**21.** $m\angle ABP = m\angle PBC$  ⌐→ $m\angle ABP = 10 + 3 = 13°$
$x + 3 = 2x - 7$        $m\angle ABC = 2 \cdot m\angle ABP$
$x = 10$            $= 26°$

## LESSON 21

**1.** Translate by <3, –5>:  $P(1, -2) \rightarrow P'(4, -7)$

**2.** Reflect over $y = 1$:  $P(1, -2) \rightarrow P'(1, 4)$

**3.** Rotate 180° about $O$:  $P(1, -2) \rightarrow P'(-1, 2)$

**4.** Reflect over $y = x$:  $P(-2, 3) \rightarrow P'(3, -2)$
Translate by <3, –2>:  $P'(3, -2) \rightarrow P''(6, -4)$

**5.** Rotate 180° about $O$:  $P(-2, 3) \rightarrow P'(2, -3)$
Reflect over the $y$-axis:  $P'(2, -3) \rightarrow P''(-2, -3)$

**6.** Translate by <–1, 4>:  $P(-2, 3) \rightarrow P'(-3, 7)$
Rotate 90° about $O$:  $P'(-3, 7) \rightarrow P''(-7, -3)$

**7 ~ 8.**  *Answers may vary. Samples are given.*

**7.** a reflection over the $y$-axis
and then a translation of 1 unit left and 3 units down

**8.** a rotation of 180° about the origin
and then a translation of 3 units left

**9.** Translate by <2, –4>:  $P(-3, 6) \rightarrow P'(-1, 2)$
Dilate about $O$ by 3:  $P'(-1, 2) \rightarrow P''(-3, 6)$

**10 ~ 12.**  *Answers may vary. Samples are given.*

**10.** A dilation about the origin by scale factor 2
followed by a reflection over the $y$-axis
will map $\triangle HIJ$ to $\triangle RST$.

**11.** A dilation about the origin by scale factor 3
followed by a translation of 6 units left and 6 units
down will map $\triangle HIJ$ to $\triangle XYZ$.

**12.** A dilation about the origin by a scale factor of 2
followed by a reflection over the $y$-axis will map $\triangle ABC$
to $\triangle DEF$.

**13.** Translate by <–5, 7>:  $P(2, -4) \rightarrow P'(-3, 3)$
Dilate about $O$ by 1/3:  $P'(-3, 3) \rightarrow P''(-1, 1)$

**14.** Dilate about $O$ by 0.5:  $P(2, -4) \rightarrow P'(1, -2)$
Reflect over the $x$-axis:  $P'(1, -2) \rightarrow P''(1, 2)$

**15.** Dilate about $O$ by 2:  $P(2, -4) \rightarrow P'(4, -8)$
Rotate 180° about $O$:  $P'(4, -8) \rightarrow P''(-4, 8)$

**16 ~ 21.**  *Answers may vary. Samples are given.*

**16.** a reflection over the $x$-axis
and then a translation of 2 units left

**17.** a dilation about the origin by scale factor 1/2
and then a reflection over the $x$-axis

**18.** a dilation about the origin by scale factor 2/3
and then a translation of 2 units right and 4 units up

**19.** a rotation of 180° about the origin
and then a translation of 1 unit up

**20.** a dilation about the origin by scale factor 1/2
and then a translation of 3 units left and 4 units up

**21.** a reflection over the $y$-axis
and then a translation of 3 units down

**22.** A) false; A reflection creates a mirror image.

B) false; A translation moves every point of the figure
the same distance in the same direction.

C) true

D) true; A rotation is a rigid transformation.

E) false; A 90° clockwise rotation is the same as a 270°
counterclockwise rotation.

F) true

G) false; A dilation with a scale factor of 3 makes a
figure three times bigger.

H) false; A composition of rigid transformations is also
a rigid transformation.

I) true

J) false; A composition of reflections over two
intersecting lines can be described as a single
rotation.

**23.** false; A ray has one endpoint.

**24.** true

**25.** true

## LESSON 22 ·····························································

**1.** 2 lines of symmetry
angle = 180°, order = 2

**2.** 1 line of symmetry
no rotational symmetry

**3.** Translate 2 units right and 5 units down.

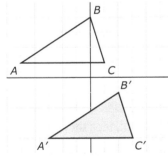

$A'(-3, -4)$
$B'(2, -1)$
$C'(-3, -4)$

**4.** Reflect over the line $x = 1$.

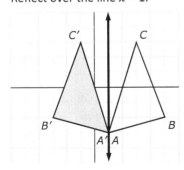

$A'(1, -3)$
$B'(-3, -2)$
$C'(-1, 3)$

**5.** Rotate 180° about the origin.

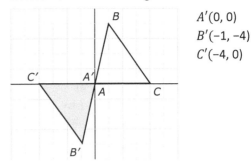

$A'(0, 0)$
$B'(-1, -4)$
$C'(-4, 0)$

**6.** Dilate about the origin by scale factor 2.

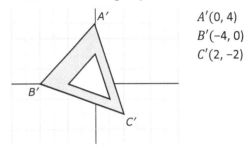

$A'(0, 4)$
$B'(-4, 0)$
$C'(2, -2)$

**7.** The $x$-value is increased by 4. The $y$-value is decreased
by 6. So, the rule is $(x, y) \rightarrow (x + 4, y - 6)$.

**8.** The sign of the $x$-value is changed. So, the line of
reflection is the $y$-axis.

**9.** The signs of the $x$- and $y$-values are changed. So, the
angle of rotation is 180°.

**10.** The $x$- and $y$-values are multiplied by 1/3. So, the scale
factor is 1/3.

**11.** Find $k$.

$S'T' = k \cdot ST$
$4 = 3k$
$k = 4/3$

Find $x$.

$T'U' = k \cdot TU$
$x = (4/3)9$
$x = 12$

Find $y$.

$S'U' = k \cdot SU$
$20 = (4/3)y$
$y = 15$

**12.** $S'T' = k \cdot ST$
$15 = 6k$
$k = 5/2$

$T'U' = k \cdot TU$
$5 = (5/2)x$
$x = 2$

$S'U' = k \cdot SU$
$y = (5/2)8$
$y = 20$

**13.** Translate by <4, −1>:    $P(-2, 1) \rightarrow P'(2, 0)$
Reflect over the $x$-axis:  $P'(2, 0) \rightarrow P''(2, 0)$

**14.** Rotate 90° about $O$:    $P(-2, 1) \rightarrow P'(-1, -2)$
Dilate about $O$ by 4:    $P'(-1, -2) \rightarrow P''(-4, -8)$

**15 ~ 18.** *Answers may vary. Samples are given.*

**15.** a reflection over the $y$-axis
and then a translation of 1 unit left and 5 units down

**16.** a rotation of 180° about the origin
and then a translation of 1 unit right and 1 unit up

**17.** a dilation about the origin by scale factor 1/2
and then a translation of 4 units left and 3 units down

**18.** a dilation about the origin by scale factor 2/3,
a reflection over the $y$-axis,
and then a translation of 2 units right and 1 unit up

**19.** a translation of 1 unit left and 2 units up; A composition of translations is a translation.

**20.** a translation of 6 units down; A composition of reflections over two parallel lines is a translation. Use a simple point like (0, 0) to find the rule.

**21** The translation maps $(x, y)$ to $(x, y - 3)$.

The reflection maps $(x, y - 3)$ to $(x, -(y - 3))$.

So, the rule is $(x, y) \rightarrow (x, -y + 3)$.

**22.** The reflection maps $(x, y)$ to $(y, x)$.

The dilation maps $(y, x)$ to $(2y, 2x)$.

So, the rule is $(x, y) \rightarrow (2y, 2x)$.

**23.** $\dfrac{3}{\sqrt{3}} \cdot \dfrac{\sqrt{3}}{\sqrt{3}} = \dfrac{3\sqrt{3}}{3} = \sqrt{3}$  **24.** rhombus, square

## LESSON 23 ·················································

**1.** $XY = 2XP = 2(5) = 10$    **2.** $x = 180 - 30 = 150$

**3.** $\triangle$ angle sum = 180    **4.** translation

$90 + 20 + y = 180$    reflection

$y = 70$    rotation

**5.** Each term is 3 more than the previous term. The next two terms are 18 and 21.

**6.** Each term has one more 5 than the previous term. The next two terms are 555555 and 5555555.

**7.** Each figure has one more square horizontally than the previous figure. The next two figures are:

**8.** The product of two negative numbers is positive.

**9.** If $\angle 1$ and $\angle 2$ form a linear pair and $\angle 2$ is acute, then $\angle 1$ is obtuse.

**10.** If $P$ bisects $\overline{XY}$ and $Q$ bisects $\overline{XP}$, then $XY = 4XQ$.

**11.** *Answers may vary. Sample(s):*

When $a = 1$, $b = 2$, and $c = 0$, $ac = bc$ but $a \neq b$.

**12.** Three collinear points cannot form a triangle.

**13.** Each term is 2 more than the previous term. The next two terms are 11 and 13.

**14.** The numerator increases by 1 and the denominator decreases by 1. The next two terms are 5/5 and 6/4.

**15.** Each figure has one more column of two dots than the previous figure. The next two figures are:

● ● ● ●    ● ● ● ● ●
● ● ● ●    ● ● ● ● ●

**16.** The square of an odd number is odd.

**17.** The sum of the interior angles of a pentagon is 540°.

**18.** The preimage and the image of a translation are congruent.

**19 ~ 21.** *Answers may vary. Samples are given.*

**19.** 21 is not a prime number.

**20.** $2x = 1$ does not have an integer solution.

**21.** 100° does not have a complementary angle.

**22.** The sum of three consecutive integers is three times the second integer.

**23.** The sum of the first $n$ positive odd integers is $n^2$.

**24.** true; A square is equilateral and equiangular.

**25.** false; Line $l$ is perpendicular to and bisects $\overline{AA'}$ and $\overline{BB'}$

## LESSON 24 ·················································

**1.** false; 2 is prime but even.

**2.** true

**3.** false; See the diagram on the right.

**4.** If an angle is a straight angle, then it measures 180°.

If an angle measures 180°, then it is a straight angle.

**5.** If two angles are right angles, then they are congruent and supplementary.

If two angles are congruent and supplementary, then they are right angles.

**6.** If a figure is a square, then it has four right angles and four congruent sides.

If a figure has four right angles and four congruent sides, then it is a square.

**7.** Angles are congruent if and only if they have the same measure.

If angles are congruent, then they have the same measure.

If angles have the same measure, then they are congruent.

**8.** Two angles are complementary if and only if their sum is 90°.

If two angles are complementary, then their sum is 90°.

If the sum of two angles is 90°, then they are complementary.

**9.** A quadrilateral is a parallelogram if and only if its opposite sides are parallel.

If a quadrilateral is a parallelogram, then its opposite sides are parallel.

If the opposite sides of a quadrilateral are parallel, then it is a parallelogram.

**10.** By the Law of Detachment, you can conclude that figure $PQRS$ has four congruent sides.

**11.** By the Law of Syllogism, you can conclude that if $\angle 1$ and $\angle 2$ are vertical angles, then $m\angle 1 = m\angle 2$.

12. If points are on the same line, they are collinear.

    If points are collinear, then they are on the same line.

13. If a triangle is equiangular, then it is equilateral.

    If a triangle is equilateral, then it is equiangular.

14. If two figures are congruent, then they have the same shape and size.

    If two figures have the same shape and size, then they are congruent.

15. Two angles are a linear pair if and only if they are adjacent and supplementary.

    If two angles are a linear pair, then they are adjacent and supplementary.

    If two angles are adjacent and supplementary, then they are a linear pair.

16. Lines are parallel if and only if they are coplanar and do not intersect.

    If lines are parallel, then they are coplanar and do not intersect.

    If lines are coplanar and do not intersect, then they are parallel.

17. A polygon is regular if and only if it is equiangular and equilateral.

    If a polygon is regular, then it is equiangular and equilateral.

    If a polygon is equiangular and equilateral, then it is regular.

18. By the Law of Syllogism, you can conclude that if $x^2 > 25$, then $x < -5$ or $x > 5$.

19. By the Law of Detachment, you can conclude that lines $l$ and $m$ intersect in exactly one point.

20. It is not possible to draw a conclusion.

21. By the Law of Detachment, you can conclude that the interior angles of figure $ABC$ add up to 180°.

22. $AB = 2AM$        $\dashrightarrow$   $x = 3$

    $5x + 3 = 2(x + 6)$     $MB = AM = 3 + 6 = 9$

    $3x = 9$

23. Translate by <-1, 3>:   $P(2, -1) \rightarrow P'(1, 2)$

    Dilate about $O$ by 3:   $P'(1, 2) \rightarrow P''(3, 6)$

## LESSON 25

1. Distributive Property
2. Transitive Property
3. Addition Property
4. Substitution Property
5. Reflexive Property
6. Subtraction Property
7. Symmetric Property
8. Substitution Property
9. Multiplication Property
10. Transitive Property
11. Reflexive Property
12. Transitive Property
13. Symmetric Property
14. Transitive Property

15. Subtraction Property
    Division Property
16. Substitution Property
    Subtraction Property
17. Symmetric Property
18. Symmetric Property
19. Addition Property
20. Transitive Property
21. Substitution Property
22. Transitive Property
23. Substitution Property
    Subtraction Property
    Division Property
24. Substitution Property
    Addition Property
    Division Property

25. Let $x$ be the smaller angle. Then the larger angle will be $2x$. Supplementary angles add up to 180°. Set up and solve the equation $x + 2x = 180$, and you get $x = 60$. So, the smaller angle measures 60°.

## LESSON 26

1. 1. Given
   2. Addition Property; Add $BC$ to both sides.
   4. Substitution Property

2.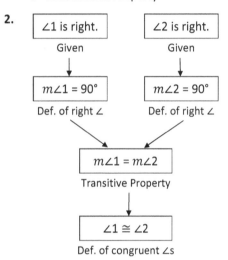

3.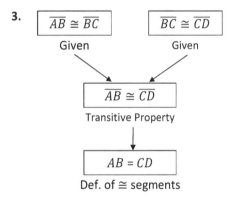

4. Because a midpoint divides a segment into two congruent segments, $\overline{AM} \cong \overline{MB}$ by the definition of midpoint.

   Congruent segments have equal lengths. So, by the definition of congruent segments, $AM = MB$.

**5.** An angle bisector divides an angle into two congruent angles, meaning that $\angle AOB \cong \angle BOC$ by the definition of angle bisector.

Congruent angles have equal measures. So, by the definition of congruent angles, $m\angle AOB = m\angle BOC$.

**6.** 1. $B$ is the midpoint of $\overline{AC}$.
   $C$ is the midpoint of $\overline{BD}$.
   2. Definition of midpoint
   4. Definition of congruent segments

**7.** 1. $\angle 1 \cong \angle 2$; $\angle 1$ is supplementary to $\angle 3$.
   2. Definition of congruent angles
   3. Definition of supplementary angles
   4. Substitution Property
   5. $\angle 2$ is supplementary to $\angle 3$.
   5. Definition of supplementary angles

**8.** 2. Definition of midpoint
   3. Definition of congruent segments
   4. Segment Addition Postulate
   5. Substitution Property

**9.** 3. Definition of right angle
   4. $m\angle A + m\angle B + m\angle C = 180°$
   5. $90 + m\angle B + m\angle C = 180°$
   6. Subtraction Property; Subtract 90 from both sides.

**10.** no; Lines $l$ and $m$ are parallel if consecutive interior angles are supplementary. Because 75 + 95 is not 180, the two lines are not parallel.

# LESSON 27 ·······································

**1.** 2. Definition of right angle
   3. Transitive Property
   4. Definition of congruent angles

**2.** Assume $x < 6$ is false. Then $x \geq 6$. Use algebra to try to make $x \geq 6$ equal to the given statement. Multiplying each side by 3 and subtracting 2 would produce $3x - 2 \geq 16$. This contradicts the given statement that $3x - 2 < 16$. Therefore, our assumption is wrong and $x < 6$ must be true.

**3.** Assume $m\angle 1 \not\leq 180°$. Then $m\angle 1 > 180°$. An angle measure cannot be negative. So if $m\angle 1 > 180°$, then $m\angle 1 + m\angle 2 > 180°$. This contradicts the given statement that $\angle 1$ and $\angle 2$ are supplementary ($m\angle 1 + m\angle 2 = 180°$). Therefore, our assumption is wrong and $m\angle 1 \leq 180°$ must be true.

**4.** Assume $n$ is odd. Then you can write $n$ as $2k + 1$ for some integer $k$. Now find $n^2 + 1$.

$$n^2 + 1 = (2k + 1)^2 + 1 = 4k^2 + 4k + 2 = 2(2k^2 + 2k + 1)$$

This means that $n^2 + 1$ is even, which contradicts the given statement. Therefore, our assumption that $n$ is odd must be false. This proves that $n$ is even.

**5.** Assume $m\angle A \neq 60°$. An equiangular triangle has three congruent angles, so the interior angle sum of $\triangle ABC = 3(m\angle A)$. If $m\angle A \neq 60°$, then $3(m\angle A)$ cannot be 180°. This contradicts the fact that the interior angle sum of a triangle is 180°. Therefore, our assumption that $m\angle A \neq 60°$ cannot be true, which proves that $m\angle A = 60°$.

**6.** B, D, A, C          **7.** A, C, D, B

**8.** D, A, C, B, E

**9.** Assume $5x - 7 = 33$. Solve the equation $5x - 7 = 33$ by adding 7 to both sides and dividing both sides by 5. Then you would get $x = 8$, which contradicts the given statement. Therefore, $5x - 7 \neq 33$ must be true.

**10.** Assume $x$ is even, and let $x = 2k$ for some integer $k$. Then $7x - 4 = 7(2k) - 4 = 14k - 4 = 2(7k - 2)$, which is even. This contradicts the given statement. Therefore, our assumption is wrong and $x$ must be odd.

**11.** Assume $\angle A$ is not obtuse. Then $m\angle A \leq 90°$. A regular hexagon has six congruent angles, so the interior angle sum of $ABCDEF = 6(m\angle A)$. If $m\angle A \leq 90$, then $6(m\angle A) \leq 540°$. This contradicts the fact that the interior angle sum of a hexagon is $180(6 - 2) = 720°$. Therefore, our assumption is wrong and $\angle A$ must be obtuse.

**12.** Assume $ABCD$ is a parallelogram. A parallelogram is a quadrilateral whose opposite sides are parallel, which means that $\overline{AB} \parallel \overline{CD}$ and $\overline{AD} \parallel \overline{BC}$ by the definition of parallelogram. This contradicts the given statement. Therefore, $ABCD$ is not a parallelogram.

**13.** $(x, y) \rightarrow (-y, x)$          **14.** Division Property

# LESSON 28 ·······································

**1.** translation, reflection, rotation

**2.** translation, reflection, rotation, dilation

**3.** translation, reflection, rotation

**4.** reflection, rotation

**5.** dilation

**6 ~ 20.** *Answers may vary. Samples are given.*

**6.** A reflection over the $x$-axis followed by a translation of 1 unit down will map $\triangle HIJ$ to $\triangle RST$. Therefore, the two triangles are congruent.

**7.** A rotation of 90° about the origin followed by a translation of 2 units left and 2 units down will map $\triangle HIJ$ to $\triangle XYZ$. Therefore, the two triangles are congruent.

**8.** A dilation about the origin by scale factor 2 followed by a reflection over the $y$-axis will map $\triangle HIJ$ to $\triangle RST$. Therefore, the two triangles are similar.

**9.** A dilation about the origin by scale factor 3 followed by a translation of 6 units left and 6 units down will map $\triangle HIJ$ to $\triangle XYZ$. Therefore, the two triangles are similar.

10. A translation to map $\overline{AC}$ to $\overline{BE}$ followed by a reflection over $\overline{BE}$ will map $\triangle ABC$ to $\triangle BDE$. Therefore, the two triangles are congruent.

11. A translation to map $\overline{ED}$ to $\overline{HG}$ followed by a reflection over $\overline{HG}$ will map $\triangle BDE$ to $\triangle FGH$. Therefore, the two triangles are congruent.

12. A reflection over the $x$-axis followed by a translation of 2 units left will map $\triangle ABC$ to $\triangle DEF$. Therefore, the two triangles are congruent.

13. A rotation of 180° about the origin followed by a translation of 1 unit up will map $\triangle ABC$ to $\triangle DEF$. Therefore, the two triangles are congruent.

14. A reflection over the $y$-axis followed by a translation of 4 units down will map $\triangle ABC$ to $\triangle DEF$. Therefore, the two triangles are congruent.

15. A dilation about the origin by scale factor 2 followed by a reflection over the $x$-axis will map $\triangle ABC$ to $\triangle DEF$. Therefore, the two triangles are similar.

16. A dilation about the origin by scale factor 2/3 followed by a translation of 2 units right and 4 units up will map $\triangle ABC$ to $\triangle DEF$. Therefore, the two triangles are similar.

17. A dilation about the origin by scale factor 1/2, a reflection over the $y$-axis, and then a translation of 2 units right and 1 unit up will map $\triangle ABC$ to $\triangle DEF$. Therefore, the two triangles are similar.

18. A translation to map $\overline{AB}$ to $\overline{DE}$ will map $\triangle ABC$ to $\triangle DEF$. Therefore, the two triangles are congruent.

19. A rotation of 180° about $C$ will map $\triangle ABC$ to $\triangle DEC$. Therefore, the two triangles are congruent.

20. A translation to map $\overline{BC}$ to $\overline{CE}$ followed by a reflection over $\overline{CE}$ will map $\triangle ABC$ to $\triangle DCE$. Therefore, the two triangles are congruent.

21. false; Counterexamples may vary. A sample is shown.

22. Lines $l$ and $m$ intersect in exactly one point.

## LESSON 29

1.  a. If ∠1 and ∠2 form a linear pair, then they are supplementary and $m\angle 1 + m\angle 2 = 180°$.

    b. If ∠3 and ∠4 are right angles, then ∠3 ≅ ∠4.

    c. If ∠5 is complementary to ∠7 and ∠6 is complementary to ∠7, then ∠5 ≅ ∠6.

    d. If ∠8 is supplementary to ∠10 and ∠9 is supplementary to ∠10, then ∠8 ≅ ∠9.

    e. If ∠11 and ∠12 are vertical angles, then ∠11 ≅ ∠12.

2.  $m\angle 3 = 90°$ and $m\angle 4 = 90°$

3.  1. ∠5 is complementary to ∠7.
       ∠6 is complementary to ∠7.
    2. Definition of complementary angles
    3. $m\angle 5 + m\angle 7 = m\angle 6 + m\angle 7$
    5. Definition of congruent angles

4.  1. ∠8 is supplementary to ∠10.
       ∠9 is supplementary to ∠10.
    3. $m\angle 8 + m\angle 10 = m\angle 9 + m\angle 10$
    4. Subtraction Property
    5. Definition of congruent angles

5.  1. ∠11 and ∠12 are vertical angles.
    3. ∠11 and ∠13 are supplementary.
       ∠12 and ∠13 are supplementary.
    4. ∠11 ≅ ∠12

6.  supplementary angles
    $7x + 131 = 180$
    $x = 7$

7.  complementary angles
    $3x + 6x = 90$
    $x = 10$

8.  vertical angles
    $4x = 56$
    $x = 14$

9 ~ 11.  See Problems 3, 4, and 5.

12. Statements (Reasons)
    1. ∠1 ≅ ∠2 (Given)
    2. ∠1 ≅ ∠3 (Vertical angles are congruent.)
    3. ∠2 ≅ ∠3 (Transitive Property)
    4. ∠2 ≅ ∠4 (Vertical angles are congruent.)
    5. ∠3 ≅ ∠4 (Transitive Property)

13. Statements (Reasons)
    1. $\overrightarrow{PE} \perp \overrightarrow{PG}, \overrightarrow{PF} \perp \overrightarrow{PH}$ (Given)
    2. ∠EPG and ∠FPH are right angles. (Definition of perpendicular)
    3. ∠1 is complementary to ∠2, ∠3 is complementary to ∠2 (Definition of complementary angles)
    4. ∠1 ≅ ∠3 (Angles complementary to the same angle are congruent. See Theorem 29.2.)

14. Statements (Reasons)
    1. ∠1 is complementary to ∠3, ∠2 is complementary to ∠4, ∠3 ≅ ∠4 (Given)
    2. $m\angle 1 + m\angle 3 = 90°$, $m\angle 2 + m\angle 4 = 90°$ (Definition of complementary angles)
    3. $m\angle 1 + m\angle 3 = m\angle 2 + m\angle 4$ (Transitive Property)
    4. $m\angle 3 = m\angle 4$ (Definition of congruent angles)
    5. $m\angle 1 + m\angle 3 = m\angle 2 + m\angle 3$ (Substitution Property)
    6. $m\angle 1 = m\angle 2$ (Subtraction Property)
    7. ∠1 ≅ ∠2 (Definition of congruent angles)

15. Statements (Reasons)
   1. ∠1 is supplementary to ∠3, ∠2 is supplementary to ∠4, ∠3 ≅ ∠4 (Given)
   2. $m\angle 1 + m\angle 3 = 180°$, $m\angle 2 + m\angle 4 = 180°$ (Definition of supplementary angles)
   3. $m\angle 1 + m\angle 3 = m\angle 2 + m\angle 4$ (Transitive Property)
   4. $m\angle 3 = m\angle 4$ (Definition of congruent angles)
   5. $m\angle 1 + m\angle 3 = m\angle 2 + m\angle 3$ (Substitution Property)
   6. $m\angle 1 = m\angle 2$ (Subtraction Property)
   7. ∠1 ≅ ∠2 (Definition of congruent angles)

16. $P(4, 5) \rightarrow P'(-5, 4)$

## LESSON 30

1. ∠1 and ∠4, ∠2 and ∠3
   ∠5 and ∠8, ∠6 and ∠7
2. ∠1 and ∠5, ∠2 and ∠6
   ∠3 and ∠7, ∠4 and ∠8
3. ∠1 and ∠8, ∠2 and ∠7
4. ∠3 and ∠6, ∠4 and ∠5
5. ∠3 and ∠5, ∠4 and ∠6
6. Post 30.1: $l \parallel m$ if and only if ∠1 ≅ ∠5.
   Thm 30.1: $l \parallel m$ if and only if ∠1 ≅ ∠8.
   Thm 30.2: $l \parallel m$ if and only if ∠4 ≅ ∠5.
   Thm 30.3: $l \parallel m$ if and only if ∠3 and ∠5 are supplementary ($m\angle 3 + m\angle 5 = 180°$).
7. 2. If lines are ∥, then corresponding angles are ≅.
   3. Vertical angles are congruent.
   4. Transitive Property
8. 2. Vertical angles are congruent.
   3. Transitive Property
   4. If corresponding angles are ≅, then lines are ∥.
9. 2. Vertical angles are congruent.
   3. If lines are ∥, then corresponding angles are ≅.
   4. Transitive Property
10. 2. Vertical angles are congruent.
    3. Transitive Property
    4. If corresponding angles are ≅, then lines are ∥.
11. 2. If lines are ∥, then corresponding angles are ≅.
    3. Definition of congruent angles
    5. Angles that form a linear pair add up to 180°.
    6. Substitution Property (Steps 3 and 5)
    7. Definition of supplementary angles
12. 2. Definition of linear pair
    3. Angles that form a linear pair are supplementary.
    4. Angles supplementary to the same angle are ≅.
    5. If corresponding angles are ≅, then lines are ∥.
13. vertical angles          corresponding angles
    a = 113                   b = 113

14. supplementary angles      alternate interior angles
    a + 118 = 180             a = 90 − b
    a = 62                    b = 28
15. alternate exterior angles    supplementary angles
    3a = 93                      3a + b = 180
    a = 31                       b = 87
16 ~ 18. See Problems 7, 10, and 11.
19. Statements (Reasons)
    1. $s \parallel t$, $u \parallel v$ (Given)
    2. ∠1 ≅ ∠5, ∠5 ≅ ∠13 (If lines are parallel, then corresponding angles are congruent.)
    3. ∠1 ≅ ∠13 (Transitive Property)
20. Statements (Reasons)
    1. $s \parallel t$, $u \parallel v$ (Given)
    2. ∠6 ≅ ∠2 (If lines are parallel, then corresponding angles are congruent.)
    3. ∠2 ≅ ∠11 (If lines are parallel, then alternate interior angles are congruent.)
    4. ∠6 ≅ ∠11 (Transitive Property)
21. Statements (Reasons)
    1. $s \parallel t$, ∠3 ≅ ∠14 (Given)
    2. ∠3 ≅ ∠7 (If lines are parallel, then corresponding angles are congruent.)
    3. ∠7 ≅ ∠14 (Transitive Property)
    4. $u \parallel v$ (If alternate exterior angles are congruent, then lines are parallel.)
22. If two angles form a linear pair, then they are adjacent and supplementary.

    If two angles are adjacent and supplementary, then then they form a linear pair.

## LESSON 31

1. yes; Corresponding angles are congruent.
2. no
3. yes; Alternate exterior angles are congruent.
4. Thm 31.1: If $s \parallel t$ and $s \perp u$, then $t \perp u$.
   Thm 31.2: If $s \perp u$ and $t \perp u$, then $s \parallel t$.
   Thm 31.3: If ∠1 ≅ ∠2, then $m \perp n$.
5. 3. If lines are ∥, then corresponding angles are ≅.
   4. Definition of congruent angles
   6. Definition of perpendicular lines
6. 2. Definition of perpendicular lines
   4. If corresponding angles are ≅, then lines are ∥.
7. $m\angle 1 + m\angle 2 = 180°$; $m\angle 1 + m\angle 1 = 180°$
   $2m\angle 1 = 180°$; $m\angle 1 = 90°$

**8.** Given: $l \parallel m,\ m \parallel n$

Prove: $l \parallel n$

Proof: Statements (Reasons)

1. $l \parallel m,\ m \parallel n$ (Given)
2. $\angle 1 \cong \angle 2,\ \angle 2 \cong \angle 3$ (If lines are parallel, then corresponding angles are congruent.)
3. $\angle 1 \cong \angle 3$ (Transitive Property)
4. $l \parallel n$ (If corresponding angles are congruent, then lines are parallel.)

**9.** $m\angle 1 = m\angle 2 = m\angle 3 = 90°$ (Def. of perpendicular lines)

**10.** $m\angle 1 = m\angle 2 = 90°$ (Theorem 31.1)

**11.** $m\angle 1 = m\angle 2 = 90°$ (Theorem 31.3)

**12 ~ 14.** See Problems 5, 6, and 7.

**15.** Statements (Reasons)

1. $a \parallel b,\ b \perp d,\ c \perp d$ (Given)
2. $b \parallel c$ (Lines that are perpendicular to the same line are parallel. See Theorem 31.2.)
3. $a \parallel c$ (Transitive Property of Parallel Lines)

**16.** Statements (Reasons)

1. $\angle 1 \cong \angle 2,\ \angle 3 \cong \angle 4$ (Given)
2. $a \parallel b$ (If alternate exterior angles are congruent, then lines are parallel.)
3. $b \parallel c$ (If alternate interior angles are congruent, then lines are parallel.)
4. $a \parallel c$ (Transitive Property of Parallel Lines)

**17.** 3 lines of symmetry

**18.** The product of three negative numbers is negative.

**19.** Assume two angles are both obtuse.

## LESSON 32

**1 ~ 3.** See Lessons 11 and 13.

**4.** $\triangle$ angle sum = 180

$3x + 4x + 124 = 180$

$x = 8$

**5.** 103 is an exterior angle.

$x - 19 + 73 = 103$

$x = 49$

**6.** exterior angle sum of any polygon = 360°

$x + 77 + 83 + 84 + 50 = 360$

$x = 66$

**7.** Thm 32.1: $m\angle 1 + m\angle 2 + m\angle 3 = 180°$

Thm 32.2: $m\angle 4 = m\angle 1 + m\angle 2$

**8.** 2. If lines are $\parallel$, then alternate interior angles are $\cong$.

3. Definition of congruent angles

5. Substitution Property

**9.** 2. Definition of linear pair

3. Angles that form a linear pair add up to 180°.

4. Angles in a triangle add up to 180°.

5. $m\angle 1 + m\angle 2 + m\angle 3 = m\angle 3 + m\angle 4$

6. $m\angle 1 + m\angle 2 = m\angle 4$

**10.** … can be divided into 3 triangles …

… the interior angle sum of each triangle is 180°, …

… 180 × 3 = 540° …

**11.** … forms 5 linear pairs …

… sum of 5 linear pairs is 180° × 5 …

… sum of 5 interior angles is 180° × 3 …

… sum of 5 exterior angles is 180° × 5 − 180° × 3 …

**12 ~ 13.** See Problems 8 and 9.

**14.** 3. Angles in a triangle add up to 180°.

4. Substitution Property

5. Subtraction Property

**15.** Statements (Reasons)

1. $\overline{AC} \perp \overline{BC},\ \overline{CD} \perp \overline{AB}$ (Given)
2. $\angle ACB$ are $\angle ADC$ right angles. (Definition of perpendicular)
3. $\triangle ABC$ and $\triangle ACD$ are right triangles. (Definition of right triangles)
4. In $\triangle ABC$, $\angle A$ and $\angle B$ are complementary. In $\triangle ACD$, $\angle A$ and $\angle ACD$ are complementary. (Acute angles in a right triangle are complementary. See Problem 14.)
5. $\angle B \cong \angle ACD$ (Angles complementary to the same angle are congruent. See Theorem 29.2.)

**16.** interior angle sum = $180(n - 2) = 180(10 - 2) = 1440°$

**17.** Distributive Property

## LESSON 33

**1.** the line itself

**2.** a parallel line

**3.** the line itself

**4.** the line itself

**5.** the line itself

**6.** a parallel line

**7.** a straight angle

**8.** … $\overrightarrow{OA}$ maps onto $\overrightarrow{OB}$ and $\overrightarrow{OC}$ maps onto $\overrightarrow{OD}$ …

… angle $\angle BOD$ formed by $\overrightarrow{OB}$ and $\overrightarrow{OD}$ …

**9.** … $m$ maps onto a line through $Q$. …

… $m$ maps onto a line parallel to $m$. …

… our translation maps $l$ onto $l$ and $m$ onto $n$, …

… angle $\angle 1$ formed by lines $l$ and $m$ …

… angle $\angle 2$ formed by lines $l$ and $n$. …

**10.** … $A$ maps onto $A$ …

… $B$ maps onto $C$ …

… our reflection maps $\overline{AB}$ onto $\overline{AC}$. …

11. $M$ maps onto itself because $M$ is on line $l$, the line of reflection.

12. $\overline{MP}$ maps onto $\overline{MQ}$ because
    - $M$ maps onto itself because $M$ is on line $l$.
    - $P$ maps onto $Q$ because they are at equal distances on opposite sides of line $l$.

13. Line $l$ maps onto itself because 180° rotations map a line onto itself if the center of rotation is on the line.

14. $\overline{MP}$ maps onto $\overline{MQ}$ because
    - Ray $\overrightarrow{MP}$ maps onto ray $\overrightarrow{MQ}$.
    - $P$ and $Q$ are equidistant from $M$.

15. Line $l$ maps onto itself because translations of a line along itself produce the same line.

16. Line $l$ maps onto a line that is parallel to itself and passes through $Q$. Translations of a line not along the line produce a parallel line.

17. 1. Translations preserve angle measures.
    2. If corresponding angles are $\cong$, then lines are ∥. You can also say that corresponding sides of the preimage and image in a translation are parallel.
    3. If lines are ∥, then alternate interior angles are $\cong$.
    4. Angle Addition Postulate, Def. of straight angle
    5. Substitution Property

18. Rotate $\overline{MP}$ and line $l$ by 180° about $M$. Then $\overline{MP}$ maps onto $\overline{MQ}$ because
    - Ray $\overrightarrow{MP}$ maps onto ray $\overrightarrow{MQ}$.
    - $P$ and $Q$ are equidistant from $M$.

    Also, line $l$ maps onto line $m$ because
    - $P$ is on line $l$ and $P$ maps onto $Q$, so line $l$ maps onto a line through $Q$.
    - 180° rotations map a line onto a parallel line if the center of rotation is not on the line, so line $l$ maps onto a line parallel to line $l$.
    - Line $m$ is the only line through $Q$ parallel to $l$.

    This means that our rotation maps $\angle 1$ formed by $\overline{MP}$ and line $l$ onto $\angle 2$ formed by $\overline{MQ}$ and line $m$. Rotations are rigid transformations, so $\angle 1 \cong \angle 2$.

19. $4\sqrt{3} = \sqrt{4 \cdot 4 \cdot 3} = \sqrt{48}$, so $x = 48$.

20. false; Two right angles are a counterexample.

## LESSON 34

1. 80; Each term is twice the previous item.

2. false; The angles must also be adjacent.

3. Two angles are complementary if and only if their sum is 90°.

   If two angles are complementary, then their sum is 90°.

   If the sum of two angles is 90°, then they are complementary.

4. If two planes are not parallel, then they intersect in a line.

5. Addition Property   6. Transitive Property

7. 1. Given
   2. Addition Property
   4. Substitution Property

8. B, D, A, C

9. A reflection over the $x$-axis followed by a translation of 2 units right will map $\triangle ABC$ to $\triangle DEF$. Therefore, the two triangles are congruent.

10. A dilation about the origin by scale factor 1/2 followed by a reflection over the $x$-axis will map $\triangle ABC$ to $\triangle DEF$. Therefore, the two triangles are similar.

11. See #5 in Lesson 29.   12. See #4 in Lesson 29.

13. See #7 in Lesson 30.   14. See #10 in Lesson 30

15. See #5 in Lesson 31.   16. See #6 in Lesson 31.

17. See #8 in Lesson 32.   18. See #9 in Lesson 32.

19. See #17 in Lesson 33.

20. exterior angle sum of any polygon = 360°

21. $(x, y) \rightarrow (-x, -y)$

## LESSON 35

1. $\triangle$ angle sum = 180°
   $74 + m\angle 1 + m\angle 1 = 180°$
   $m\angle 1 = 53°$

2. $m\angle 1 = 180 - 90 - 31 = 59°$
   $m\angle 2 = 180 - 90 - 31 = 59°$

3. $m\angle 1 = 180 - 40 - 58 = 82°$
   $m\angle 2 = m\angle 1 = 82°$ (vertical angles)
   $m\angle 3 = 58°$ (alternate interior angles)

4. Corresponding sides:
   $\overline{PQ} \cong \overline{XY}, \overline{QR} \cong \overline{YZ}, \overline{PR} \cong \overline{XZ}$
   Corresponding angles:
   $\angle P \cong \angle X, \angle Q \cong \angle Y, \angle R \cong \angle Z$
   Possible statements:
   $\triangle PQR \cong \triangle XYZ, \triangle PRQ \cong \triangle XZY, \triangle QPR \cong \triangle YXZ,$
   $\triangle QRP \cong \triangle YZX, \triangle RPQ \cong \triangle ZXY, \triangle RQP \cong \triangle ZYX$

5. If $\angle B \cong \angle E$ and $\angle C \cong \angle F$, then $\angle A \cong \angle D$.

6. $m\angle B = m\angle E = 64°$
   $m\angle C = m\angle F = 80°$
   $m\angle A = m\angle D = 180 - 64 - 80 = 36°$

7. Given: $\angle B \cong \angle E$, $\angle C \cong \angle F$
   Prove: $\angle A \cong \angle D$
   Proof: Statements (Reasons)
   1. $\angle B \cong \angle E$, $\angle C \cong \angle F$ (Given)
   2. $m\angle B = m\angle E$, $m\angle C = m\angle F$ (Def. of congruent $\angle$s)
   3. $m\angle A + m\angle B + m\angle C = 180$,
      $m\angle D + m\angle E + m\angle F = 180$ ($\triangle$ angle sum = 180)
   4. $m\angle A + m\angle B + m\angle C = m\angle D + m\angle E + m\angle F$ (Transitive Property)
   5. $m\angle A + m\angle E + m\angle F = m\angle D + m\angle E + m\angle F$ (Substitution Property, Steps 2 and 4)
   6. $m\angle A = m\angle D$ (Subtraction Property)
   7. $\angle A \cong \angle D$ (Def. of congruent $\angle$s)

8. 4. $\angle F \cong \angle H$

9. 5. If lines are ∥, then alternate interior angles are ≅.
   6. Vertical angles are congruent.
   7. Def. of congruent triangles

10. $\overline{DQ} \cong \overline{PV}$    11. $\angle R \cong \angle W$

12. $\triangle QRD \cong \triangle VWP$    13. $\triangle RQD \cong \triangle WVP$

14. $m\angle C = m\angle A = 75°$    15. $m\angle F = m\angle H = 52°$
    $90 + 75 + 3x = 180$         $71 + 52 + (8x + 1) = 180$
    $x = 5$                      $x = 7$

16. $m\angle N = m\angle U = 34°$
    $90 + 34 + (9x - 7) = 180$
    $x = 7$

17. Statements (Reasons)
    1. $\overline{AB} \cong \overline{AD}$, $\overline{BC} \cong \overline{DC}$ (Given)
    2. $\overline{AC} \cong \overline{AC}$ (Reflexive Property)
    3. $\angle BAC \cong \angle DAC$, $\angle B \cong \angle D$ (Given)
    4. $\angle BCA \cong \angle DCA$ (If two angles of two triangles are congruent, then the third angles are also congruent. See the Third Angle Theorem [35.1].)
    5. $\triangle ABC \cong \triangle ADC$ (Def. of congruent triangles)

18. Statements (Reasons)
    1. $\overline{PQ} \parallel \overline{SR}$, $\overline{QR} \parallel \overline{PS}$ (Given)
    2. $\angle QPR \cong \angle SRP$, $\angle QRP \cong \angle SPR$ (If lines are ∥, then alternate interior angles are ≅.)
    3. $\angle Q \cong \angle S$ (Third Angle Theorem [35.1])
    4. $\overline{PQ} \cong \overline{RS}$, $\overline{QR} \cong \overline{SP}$ (Given)
    5. $\overline{PR} \cong \overline{RP}$ (Reflexive Property)
    6. $\triangle PQR \cong \triangle RSP$ (Def. of congruent triangles)

19. $y = 7$    20. $(x, y) \rightarrow (y, x)$

1. 2. Reflexive Property
   4. If two angles of two triangles are congruent, then the third angles are also congruent. See the Third Angle Theorem [35.1].

2. If $\overline{AB} \cong \overline{DE}$, $\overline{BC} \cong \overline{EF}$, and $\overline{AC} \cong \overline{DF}$, then $\triangle ABC \cong \triangle DEF$.

3. 2. Reflexive Property

4. 3. Def. of bisect (or segment bisector)
   4. SSS

5. If $\overline{AB} \cong \overline{DE}$, $\angle B \cong \angle E$, and $\overline{BC} \cong \overline{EF}$, then $\triangle ABC \cong \triangle DEF$.

6. 2. Vertical angles are congruent.

7. 3. If lines are ∥, then alternate interior angles are ≅.
   4. Reflexive Property
   5. SAS

8. $\overline{PQ}$ and $\overline{QR}$    9. $\angle R$

10. $\triangle AUK \cong \triangle VSZ$ or $\triangle AUK \cong \triangle VZS$ by SSS.

11. $\triangle PEF \cong \triangle PGH$ by SAS.

12. Need $\overline{EF} \cong \overline{GD}$ to use SSS.
    Need $\angle EDF \cong \angle GFD$ to use SAS.

13. Need $\overline{BD} \cong \overline{CD}$ to use SSS.
    Need $\angle BAD \cong \angle CAD$ to use SAS.

14. Need $\overline{MT} \cong \overline{NS}$ to use SSS or SAS.
    Need $\angle MST \cong \angle NTS$ to use SAS.

15. $\triangle ADF \cong \triangle XPU$ by SAS.

16 ~ 19. See Problems 3, 4, 6, and 7.

20. Statements (Reasons)
    1. $\overline{BD} \perp \overline{CE}$ (Given)
    2. $\angle BCE$ and $\angle DCE$ are right angles. (Def. of perpendicular)
    3. $\angle BCE \cong \angle DCE$ (All right angles are congruent.)
    4. $C$ bisects $\overline{BD}$. (Given)
    5. $\overline{BC} \cong \overline{DC}$ (Def. of bisect)
    6. $\overline{CE} \cong \overline{CE}$ (Reflexive Property)
    7. $\triangle BCE \cong \triangle DCE$ (SAS, Steps 3, 5, and 6)

21. Statements (Reasons)
    1. $ABCD$ is a kite. (Given)
    2. $\overline{AB} \cong \overline{AD}$, $\overline{BC} \cong \overline{DC}$ (Def. of kite)
    3. $\overline{AC} \cong \overline{AC}$ (Reflexive Property)
    4. $\triangle ABC \cong \triangle ADC$ (SSS)

22. If an angle is a right angle, then it measures 90°.
    If an angle measures 90°, then it is a right angle.

1.  1. Given
    2. Reflexive Property
    3. SSS

2.  1. Given
    2. Vertical angles are congruent.
    3. SAS

3.  If $\angle A \cong \angle D$, $\overline{AB} \cong \overline{DE}$, and $\angle B \cong \angle E$,
    then $\triangle ABC \cong \triangle DEF$.

4.  2. Reflexive Property

5.  3. If lines are ∥, then alternate interior angles are ≅.
    4. ASA

6.  If $\angle B \cong \angle E$, $\angle C \cong \angle F$, and $\overline{AB} \cong \overline{DE}$,
    then $\triangle ABC \cong \triangle DEF$.

7.  3. Vertical angles are congruent.

8.  3. If lines are ∥, then alternate interior angles are ≅.
    4. Reflexive Property
    5. AAS

9.  $\triangle VUW \cong \triangle WXY$ by ASA.

10. Need $\overline{DE} \cong \overline{FG}$ to use SSS or SAS.
    Need $\angle EFD \cong \angle GDF$ to use SAS, ASA, or AAS.
    Need $\angle F \cong \angle G$ to use AAS.

11. Need $\overline{ZS} \cong \overline{KU}$ to use SSS.
    Need $\angle V \cong \angle A$ to use SAS.

12. $\triangle ABD \cong \triangle ACD$ by AAS.

13. $\triangle MST \cong \triangle NST$ by ASA or AAS.

14. $\triangle PEF \cong \triangle PGH$ by AAS.

15 ~ 18. See Problems 4, 5, 7, and 8.

19. Statements (Reasons)
    1. $\overline{FG} \parallel \overline{EH}$, $\overline{FE} \parallel \overline{GH}$ (Given)
    2. $\angle FEG \cong \angle HGE$, $\angle FGE \cong \angle HEG$ (If lines are ∥, then alternate interior angles are ≅.)
    3. $\overline{GE} \cong \overline{EG}$ (Reflexive Property)
    4. $\triangle EFG \cong \triangle GHE$ (ASA)

20. Statements (Reasons)
    1. $\overline{AB} \cong \overline{DE}$ (Given)
    2. $\overline{AB} \perp \overline{BE}$, $\overline{DE} \perp \overline{BE}$ (Given)
    3. $\angle ABC$ and $\angle DEC$ are right angles. (Def. of perpendicular)
    4. $\angle ABC \cong \angle DEC$ (All right angles are congruent.)
    5. $\angle ACB \cong \angle DCE$ (Vertical angles are congruent.)
    6. $\triangle ABC \cong \triangle DEC$ (AAS, Steps 1, 4, and 5)

21. B, D, C, A

1.  *Answers may vary. Sample(s):*
    If $\overline{AB} \cong \overline{DE}$, $\overline{BC} \cong \overline{EF}$, and $m\angle C = m\angle F = 90°$,
    then $\triangle ABC \cong \triangle DEF$.
    If $\overline{AB} \cong \overline{DE}$, $\overline{BC} \cong \overline{EF}$, and $\angle C$ and $\angle F$ are right angles, then $\triangle ABC \cong \triangle DEF$.
    If $\triangle ABC$ and $\triangle DEF$ are right triangles with right angles $C$ and $F$ respectively, $\overline{AB} \cong \overline{DE}$, and $\overline{BC} \cong \overline{EF}$, then $\triangle ABC \cong \triangle DEF$.

2.  3. Given
    4. Reflexive Property

3.  2. $\angle DFE$ and $\angle DFG$
    3. $\triangle DFE$ and $\triangle DFG$
    5. Reflexive Property
    6. HL

4.  2. Reflexive Property
    3. AAS

5.  2. Def. of bisect
    4. SAS
    5. CPCTC

6.  $\triangle XYZ \cong \triangle UVW$ by ASA.

7.  $\triangle STU \cong \triangle WVU$ by AAS.

8.  Need $\overline{PF} \cong \overline{PH}$ to use SSS or SAS.
    Need $\angle E \cong \angle G$ to use SAS, ASA, or AAS.
    Need $\angle F \cong \angle H$ to use AAS.

9.  $\triangle LMN \cong \triangle STU$ by SAS.

10. $\triangle PQD \cong \triangle PRD$ by HL.

11. $\triangle ABC \cong \triangle ADC$ by SSS.

12. $5a + 7 = 3a + 11$
    $a = 2$

13. $12 = a + 7$ and $3a = 5b$
    $a = 5$, $b = 3$

14. $4a + 10 = 30$ and $36 = 6a + b$
    $a = 5$, $b = 6$

15 ~ 18. See Problems 2, 3, 4, and 5.

19. Statements (Reasons)
    1. $\overline{AB} \parallel \overline{DC}$, $\overline{AC} \parallel \overline{DE}$ (Given)
    2. $\angle B \cong \angle DCE$, $\angle ACB \cong \angle E$ (If lines are ∥, then corresponding angles are ≅.)
    3. $C$ bisects $\overline{BE}$. (Given)
    4. $\overline{BC} \cong \overline{CE}$ (Def. of bisect)
    5. $\triangle ABC \cong \triangle DCE$ (ASA, Steps 2 and 4)
    6. $\overline{AC} \cong \overline{DE}$ (CPCTC)

20. Statements (Reasons)
    1. $DEFG$ is a square. (Given)
    2. $\overline{DE} \cong \overline{EF} \cong \overline{FG} \cong \overline{GD}$ (Def. of square)
    3. $\overline{DF} \cong \overline{FD}$ (Reflexive Property)
    4. $\triangle DEF \cong \triangle DGF$ (SSS)
    5. $\angle EDF \cong \angle GDF$ (CPCTC)

21. A, B, C, F

# LESSON 39 ·········································

1. 2. Reflexive Property
   3. AAS

2. 2. Def. of bisect
   4. SAS
   5. CPCTC

3. 3. Def. of congruent segments
   6. Substitution Property (Steps 4 and 5)
   7. Def. of congruent segments
   9. SAS
   10. CPCTC

4. 3. If lines are ∥, then corresponding angles are ≅.
   5. Def. of congruent segments
   6. Addition Property
   7. Segment Addition Postulate
   8. Substitution Property (Steps 6 and 7)
   9. Def. of congruent segments
   10. SAS
   11. CPCTC

5. 3. All right angles are congruent.
   5. Def. of bisect (or segment bisector)
   6. Reflexive Property
   7. SAS
   10. Reflexive Property
   11. SAS
   12. CPCTC

**6 ~ 8.** See Problems 3, 4, and 5.

9. Statements (Reasons)
   1. $\overline{EF} \perp \overline{FG}, \overline{HG} \perp \overline{FG}$ (Given)
   2. ∠EFG and ∠HGF are right ∠s. (Def. of right ∠)
   3. △EFG and △HGF are right △s. (Def. of right △)
   4. $\overline{EG} \cong \overline{HF}$ (Given)
   5. $\overline{FG} \cong \overline{GF}$ (Reflexive Property)
   6. △EFG ≅ △HGF (HL)

10. Statements (Reasons)
    1. $\overline{AB} \cong \overline{AD}, \overline{BE} \cong \overline{DE}$ (Given)
    2. $\overline{AE} \cong \overline{AE}$ (Reflexive Property)
    3. △ABE ≅ △ADE (SSS)
    4. ∠BAE ≅ ∠DAE (CPCTC)
    5. $\overline{AC} \cong \overline{AC}$ (Reflexive Property)
    6. △ABC ≅ △ADC (SAS, Steps 1, 4, and 5)

11. $c = 9$; $x^2 + 6x + 9 = (x + 3)^2$

12. a line

13. ∠1 and ∠2 are supplementary.
    $x + 3x = 180$; $x = 45$

# LESSON 40 ·········································

1. △ angle sum = 180
   $x + 46 + 100 = 180$
   $x = 34$

2. △ angle sum = 180
   $x - 13 + 56 + 90 = 180$
   $x = 47$

3. 105 is an exterior angle.
   $x + 35 = 105$
   $x = 70$

4. Thm 40.1: If $\overline{AB} \cong \overline{AC}$, then ∠B ≅ ∠C.
   Thm 40.2: If ∠E ≅ ∠F, then $\overline{DE} \cong \overline{DF}$.
   Thm 40.3: If $\overline{PQ} \cong \overline{QR} \cong \overline{PR}$, then ∠P ≅ ∠Q ≅ ∠R.
   Thm 40.4: If ∠S ≅ ∠T ≅ ∠U, then $\overline{ST} \cong \overline{TU} \cong \overline{SU}$.

5. 3. Def. of bisect
   4. Reflexive Property
   5. SAS
   6. CPCTC

6. 3. Def. of bisect
   4. Reflexive Property
   5. AAS
   6. CPCTC

7. $x + x + (x - 6) = 180$
   $x = 62$

8. $3(7x - 3) = 180$
   $x = 9$

9. $a = 24$

10. $a = b = 15$

11. $a = 43$
    $b = 180 - 2(43) = 94$

12. $a = b = 60$

13. $32 + 2a = 180$
    $a = 74$

14. $7a + 5 = 12$
    $a = 1$

15. $a = 180 - 120 = 60$
    $b = a = 60$
    $c = 180 - a - b = 60$

16. $4a + 9 = 8a - 7$
    $a = 4$

17. $4a + 2(a + 15) = 180$
    $a = 25$

18. $90 + 2a = 180$
    $a = 45$
    $36 + 2(a + b) = 180$
    $b = 27$

19. $a = 72$
    $b = 180 - a = 108$
    $b + 2c = 180$
    $c = 36$

20. $a = 180 - 62 = 118$
    $a + 2b = 180$
    $b = 31$
    $62 + 2c = 180$
    $c = 59$

21. Statements (Reasons)
    1. equilateral △ABC (Given)
    2. $\overline{AB} \cong \overline{BC}, \overline{AB} \cong \overline{AC}, \overline{BC} \cong \overline{AC}$ (Def. of equilateral triangle)
    3. ∠A ≅ ∠C, ∠B ≅ ∠C, ∠A ≅ ∠B (Base Angles Theorem [40.1])
    4. △ABC is equiangular. (Def. of equiangular triangle)

**22.** Statements (Reasons)

1. equiangular $\triangle ABC$ (Given)
2. $\angle A \cong \angle C$, $\angle B \cong \angle C$, $\angle A \cong \angle B$ (Def. of equiangular triangle)
3. $\overline{AB} \cong \overline{BC}$, $\overline{AB} \cong \overline{AC}$, $\overline{BC} \cong \overline{AC}$ (Base Angles Converse [40.2])
4. $\triangle ABC$ is equilateral. (Def. of equilateral triangle)

**23.** right, vertical, straight

**24.** $m\angle B = m\angle E = 80°$

$m\angle C = 180 - m\angle A - m\angle B = 180 - 45 - 80 = 55°$

## LESSON 41

**1.** … they lie on the line of reflection $\overline{DF}$ . …

… $B''$ maps onto $E$ …

**2.** … they lie on the line of reflection $\overline{DF}$ . …

… $E$ is the only point …

… $B'$ must map onto $E$ …

**3.** 1. Base angles of an isosceles triangle are congruent.

   **2.** $m\angle DB'F$

   $= m\angle DB'E + m\angle FB'E$

   $= m\angle DEB' + m\angle FEB'$

   $= m\angle DEF$

   Because $m\angle DB'F = m\angle DEF$, $\angle DB'F \cong \angle DEF$.

**4.** 1. Given

   2. Given

   3. If two angles of two triangles are congruent, then the third angles are also congruent. See the Third Angle Theorem [35.1].

   4. ASA

**5.** *Answer formats may vary.*

   Statements (Reasons)

   1. a. $\overline{BC} \cong \overline{EF}$ (Given)

      b. $\overline{AC} \cong \overline{XF}$ (Construction)

      c. $\angle C \cong \angle EFX$ (All right angles are congruent.)

      d. $\triangle ABC \cong \triangle XEF$ (SAS)

   2. a. $\overline{AB} \cong \overline{DE}$ (Given)

      b. $\overline{AB} \cong \overline{XE}$ (CPCTC, Step 1d)

      c. $\overline{XE} \cong \overline{DE}$ (Transitive Property)

      d. $\triangle EXD$ is isosceles. (Def. of isosceles triangle)

   3. a. $\overline{XE} \cong \overline{DE}$ (Step 2c)

      b. $\angle X \cong \angle D$ (Base Angles Theorem [40.1])

      c. $\angle EFX \cong \angle EFD$ (All right angles are congruent.)

      d. $\triangle XEF \cong \triangle DEF$ (AAS)

   4. a. $\triangle ABC \cong \triangle XEF$ (Step 1d)

      b. $\triangle XEF \cong \triangle DEF$ (Step 3d)

      c. $\triangle ABC \cong \triangle DEF$ (Transitive Property)

**6.** *Answers may vary. Sample(s):*

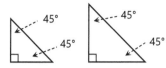

**7.** $\triangle ABC$ and $\triangle ABD$ are not congruent, even though two corresponding sides and an angle are congruent ($\overline{AB} \cong \overline{AB}$, $\overline{BC} \cong \overline{BD}$, and $\angle A \cong \angle A$). This shows that the SSA criterion is not enough to prove congruence.

**8.** rotate, translate

**9 ~ 17.** *Answers on transformations may vary.*

**9.** Translate so that $\overline{RT}$ maps to $\overline{XZ}$.

**10.** Reflect over $\overline{RT}$, then translate so that $\overline{RT}$ maps to $\overline{XZ}$.

**11.** Rotate counterclockwise so that $\overline{RT} \parallel \overline{XZ}$, then translate so that $\overline{RT}$ maps to $\overline{XZ}$.

**12.** $\triangle ABC \cong \triangle CDE$ by AAS.

Reflect over $\overline{BC}$, then translate so that $\overline{BC}$ maps to $\overline{DE}$.

**13.** $\triangle DEG \cong \triangle FEG$ by ASA.

Reflect over $\overline{EG}$.

**14.** no; AAA is not enough to prove congruence.

**15.** no; SSA is not enough to prove congruence.

**16.** $\triangle HIJ \cong \triangle HKJ$ by SAS.

Reflect over $\overline{HJ}$.

**17.** $\triangle ABC \cong \triangle DCE$ by HL.

Reflect over $\overline{BC}$, then translate so that $\overline{BC}$ maps to $\overline{CE}$.

**18.** slope $= (-2 - 4)/(1 - (-1)) = -3$

**19.** Let $x$ be the angle. Then its complement is $90 - x$.

$x = 2(90 - x)$ and $x = 60$, so the angle is 60°.

## LESSON 42

**1.** If $\angle B \cong \angle E$ and $\angle C \cong \angle F$, then $\angle A \cong \angle D$.

**2.** If $\overline{AB} \cong \overline{DE}$, $\overline{BC} \cong \overline{EF}$, and $\overline{AC} \cong \overline{DF}$, then $\triangle ABC \cong \triangle DEF$.

**3.** If $\overline{AB} \cong \overline{DE}$, $\angle B \cong \angle E$, and $\overline{BC} \cong \overline{EF}$, then $\triangle ABC \cong \triangle DEF$.

**4.** If $\angle A \cong \angle D$, $\overline{AB} \cong \overline{DE}$, and $\angle B \cong \angle E$, then $\triangle ABC \cong \triangle DEF$.

**5.** If $\angle B \cong \angle E$, $\angle C \cong \angle F$, and $\overline{AB} \cong \overline{DE}$, then $\triangle ABC \cong \triangle DEF$.

**6.** If $\overline{AB} \cong \overline{DE}$, $\overline{BC} \cong \overline{EF}$, and $m\angle C = m\angle F = 90°$, then $\triangle ABC \cong \triangle DEF$.

**7.** 2. Reflexive Property
3. SSS

**8.** 3. Def. of bisect
4. SSS

**9.** 3. Alt. interior ∠s are ≅.
4. Reflexive Property
5. SAS

**10.** 2. Reflexive Property
3. ASA

**11.** 3. Alt. interior ∠s are ≅.
4. ASA

**12.** 2. Vertical ∠s are ≅.
3. AAS

**13.** 2. Def. of right triangle
4. Reflexive Property
5. HL

**14.** 2. Def. of ⊥ lines
3. Def. of right △
5. Reflexive Property
6. HL

**15.** 2. Def. of bisect
3. Vertical ∠s are ≅.
4. SAS
5. CPCTC

**16.** 2. Reflexive Property
3. SSS
5. Reflexive Property
6. SAS
7. CPCTC

**17.** 2. Def. of congruent segments
4. Subtraction Property
6. Transitive Property (Steps 4 and 5)
8. Def. of congruent segments
9. SSS

**18.** A) false; A ray has one endpoint.
B) true
C) false; The vertices of a triangle are not collinear.
D) true; See Postulate 7.2.
E) true
F) false; Angles in a linear pair are supplementary.

**19.** A, E
B and D make $u \parallel v$.
C does not make any lines parallel.

## LESSON 43

**1.** $\overline{AB} \cong \overline{XY}, \overline{BC} \cong \overline{YZ}, \overline{AC} \cong \overline{XZ}$
$\angle A \cong \angle X, \angle B \cong \angle Y, \angle C \cong \angle Z$

**2.** $m\angle B = m\angle Y = 75°$
$m\angle C = 180 - m\angle A - m\angle B = 180 - 60 - 75 = 45°$

**3.** $\triangle DEG \cong \triangle FEG$ by ASA.

**4.** $\triangle AUK \cong \triangle VSZ$ or $\triangle AUK \cong \triangle VZS$ by SSS.

**5.** $\triangle PEF \cong \triangle PGH$ by SAS.

**6.** There is not enough information.

**7.** $\triangle HIJ \cong \triangle JKH$ by HL.

**8.** $\triangle XYD \cong \triangle XZD$ by AAS.

**9.** There is not enough information.

**10.** $\triangle ABD \cong \triangle ACD$ by SSS.

**11.** There is not enough information.

**12.** $\triangle ABC \cong \triangle DEF$ by SAS.

**13.** $\triangle STV \cong \triangle SUV$ by HL.

**14.** There is not enough information.

**15.** 2. Alt. interior ∠s are ≅.
3. Reflexive Property
4. ASA
5. CPCTC

**16.** 3. Reflexive Property
4. AAS
5. CPCTC

**17.** An equiangular triangle is equilateral.
$7a = 4a + 15 = 6b - 1$
$a = 5, b = 6$

**18.** Base angles of an isosceles triangle are congruent.
$2a + 2(a - 4) = 180$
$a = 47$

**19 ~ 20.** *Answers on transformations may vary.*

**19.** $\triangle DEG \cong \triangle FEG$ by ASA.
Reflect over $\overline{EG}$.

**20.** $\triangle LMN \cong \triangle PQR$ by HL.
Rotate by 180° about any vertex, then translate so that $\overline{NM}$ maps to $\overline{RQ}$.

**21.** A reflection over the $y$-axis followed by a translation of 1 unit left and 4 units up will map $\triangle ABC$ to $\triangle DEF$. Therefore, the two triangles are congruent.

**22.** A dilation about the origin by scale factor 1/2, a reflection over the $x$-axis, and then a translation of 3 units left and 2 units up will map $\triangle ABC$ to $\triangle DEF$. Therefore, the two triangles are similar.

## LESSON 44

**1.** $2\sqrt{3} - 3\sqrt{3} = -\sqrt{3}$

**2.** $\frac{5}{\sqrt{5}} = \frac{5}{\sqrt{5}} \cdot \frac{\sqrt{5}}{\sqrt{5}} = \frac{5\sqrt{5}}{5} = \sqrt{5}$
$\sqrt{5} + \sqrt{45} = \sqrt{5} + 3\sqrt{5} = 4\sqrt{5}$

**3.** $2x - 6 = 3x + 5$
$-x = 11$
$x = -11$

**4.** $x^2 + 2x = 6$
$x^2 + 2x + 1 = 6 + 1$
$(x + 1)^2 = 7$
$x + 1 = \pm\sqrt{7}$
$x = -1 \pm \sqrt{7}$

**5.** eq1 + eq2
$5x = 5$
$x = 1$
$2(1) + y = 7$
$y = 5$
Solution: $(1, 5)$

**6.** eq1 × 2 − eq2
$13y = 26$
$y = 2$
$2x + 5(2) = 10$
$x = 0$
Solution: $(0, 2)$

7. $y - 2 = -2(x - 3)$
$y - 2 = -2x + 6$
$y = -2x + 8$

8. $m = \dfrac{-4 - 5}{0 - 1} = 9$
$b = -4$
$y = 9x - 4$

9. $A$, $P$, and $B$ are collinear.
$C$, $P$, and $D$ are collinear.

10. true; See Postulate 7.2.

11. $AB = 2AP$
$5x + 13 = 2(x + 5)$
$3x = -3$
$x = -1$

$\rightarrow BP = AP = -1 + 5 = 4$
$AB = 2AP = 2(4) = 8$

12. supplementary angles
$(4x + 5) + 3x = 180$
$7x = 175$
$x = 25$

13. vertical angles
$3x + 2 = 101$
$3x = 99$
$x = 33$

14. vertical angles
$a = 113$
corresponding angles
$b = 113$

15. alternate exterior angles
$3a = 93$
$a = 31$
supplementary angles
$3a + b = 180$
$b = 87$

16. △ angle sum = 180
$38 + 70 + (x - 29) = 180$
$x = 101$

17. interior angle sum = $180(n - 2) = 180(5 - 2) = 540°$
$90 + 2x + 102 + 78 = 540$
$x = 135$

18. interior angle = $180(6 - 2)/6 = 120°$
exterior angle = $360/6 = 60°$

19. The angle sum of a regular polygon is equal to one interior angle multiplied by the number of angles, and the number of angles is equal to the number of sides.

Let $n$ be the number of sides. Then $180(n - 2) = 108n$. Solve for $n$ to get $n = 5$. So, the polygon has 5 sides.

20. An equilateral triangle has 3 lines of symmetry, and its angle of rotational symmetry is 360/3 = 120°.

21. $(x, y) \rightarrow (x + 3, y - 7)$

22. $B(-4, 5) \rightarrow B'(-4, -5)$

23. $C(1, -8) \rightarrow P'(8, 1)$

24. scale factor = 4

25. a rotation of 180° about the origin; A composition of reflections over two intersecting lines is a rotation.

26. a reflection over the $x$-axis
and then a translation of 2 units left

27. a dilation about the origin by scale factor 1/2
and then a reflection over the $x$-axis

28. translation

29. The intercepts are at (−1, 0) and (0, 1). These are translated to (−1, 3) and (0, 4), then reflected to (1, 3) and (0, 4). The slope-intercept equation of a line passing through (1, 3) and (0, 4) is $y = -x + 4$.

## LESSON 45

1. Each term is 4 times the previous term. The next two terms are 20 and 24.

2. Each time the arrow rotates clockwise by 90°.

3. false; 2 is prime but even.

4. If an angle is a right angle, then it measures 90°.
If an angle measures 90°, then it is a right angle.

5. If two figures are congruent, then they have the same shape and size.
If two figures have the same shape and size, then they are congruent.

6. A point is the midpoint of a segment if and only if it divides the segment into two congruent segments.

7. Lines $l$ and $m$ do not intersect.

8. Addition Property

9. Transitive Property

10. 2. Def. of right angle
3. Transitive Property
4. Def. of ≅ angles

11. 2. Def. of ≅ segments
3. Addition Property
5. Substitution Prop.
6. Def. of ≅ segments

12. Assume $x < 5$ is false. Then $x \geq 5$. Use algebra to try to make $x \geq 5$ equal to the given statement. Multiplying each side by 4 and adding 5 would produce $4x + 5 \geq 25$. This contradicts the given statement that $4x + 5 < 25$. Therefore, our assumption is wrong and $x < 5$ is true.

13. Assume $\angle B$ is obtuse. An obtuse angle is greater than 90°. By the given statement, $\angle A$ is obtuse. So if $\angle B$ is also obtuse, then $\angle A$ and $\angle B$ add up to greater than 180°. This contradicts the fact that the three angles in a triangle add up to 180°. Therefore, our assumption is wrong and $\angle B$ is not obtuse.

14. A rotation of 90° about the origin followed by a translation of 2 units left and 3 units down will map $\triangle ABC$ to $\triangle DEF$. Therefore, the two triangles are congruent.

15. A dilation about the origin by scale factor 2/3, a reflection over the $y$-axis, and then a translation of 2 units right and 1 unit up will map $\triangle ABC$ to $\triangle DEF$. Therefore, the two triangles are similar.

16. 2. Reflexive Property
3. SSS

17. 2. Def. of congruent segments
4. Segment Addition Postulate
6. Def. of congruent segments
7. Reflexive Property
8. SAS (Steps 1, 6, and 7)
9. CPCTC

**18.** An equiangular triangle is equilateral.

$15 = 7a - 6 = 2b + 7$

$a = 3, b = 4$

**19.** Base angles of an isosceles triangle are congruent.

$a = 180 - 2(33) = 114$

$b = 180 - a = 66$

$c = b = 66$

## LESSON 46

**1.** Plug eq1 into eq2.    Plug $y$ into eq1.

$2(y + 5) + y = 7$    $x = -1 + 5 = 4.$

$y = -1$    Solution: $x = 4, y = -1$

**2.** If lines are parallel, then corresponding angles are $\cong$.

**3.** $m\angle 3 = 180 - m\angle 1 - m\angle 2 = 45°$

$m\angle 4 = m\angle 2 = 55°$

$m\angle 5 = m\angle 3 = 45°$

**4.** *Answers may vary. Sample(s):*

If $\overline{PQ}$ is a midsegment of $\triangle ABC$,
then $\overline{PQ} \parallel \overline{AC}$ and $PQ = AC/2$.

If $\overline{AP} \cong \overline{PB}$ and $\overline{BQ} \cong \overline{QC}$,
then $\overline{PQ} \parallel \overline{AC}$ and $PQ = AC/2$.

If $P$ and $Q$ are midpoints of $\overline{AB}$ and $\overline{BC}$ respectively,
then $\overline{PQ} \parallel \overline{AC}$ and $PQ = AC/2$.

**5.** $5x - 8 = 2(11)$

$x = 6$

**6.** $6x = 2(4x - 3)$

$x = 3$

**7.** corresponding angles

$m\angle 1 = m\angle 2 = 51°$

$m\angle 3 = 52°$

**8.** corresponding angles

$m\angle 1 = 90°$

$m\angle 2 = m\angle 3 = 55°$

**9.** $XY = 2(4) = 8$

$YZ = 2(6) = 12$

$XZ = 2(5) = 10$

perimeter = 30

**10.** $XY = 6/2 = 3$

$YZ = 5$

$XZ = 4$

perimeter = 12

**11.** $16 = 2x$

$x = 8$

**12.** $7x + 6 = 2(5x)$

$x = 2$

**13.** Set up two equations:    $x + 6y = 8$ and $5x - 4y = 6$

Solve eq1 for $x$:    $x = 8 - 6y$

Plug $x$ into eq2:    $5(8 - 6y) - 4y = 6$

Solve eq2 for $y$:    $y = 1$

Use eq1 to find $x$:    $x = 8 - 6(1) = 2$

Write the solution:    $x = 2, y = 1$

**14.** $x = 180 - 90 - 38 = 52$

$y = x = 52$

**15.** $x = 77$

$y = z = 40$

**16.** $x = y = 75$

$z = 35$

**17.** $\overline{XU}, \overline{UZ}$

**18.** $\angle YST, \angle TUZ$ (corresponding to $\angle X$)

$\angle STU$ (alternate interior to $\angle YST$ and $\angle TUZ$)

**19.** $\triangle SYT, \triangle UTZ, \triangle TUS$

The four triangles are congruent by SSS.

**20.** perimeter of $\triangle XYZ = XY + YZ + XZ$

$= XY + 2TZ + 2ST$

$= 100 + 2(36) + 2(60) = 292$

perimeter of $\triangle STU = (1/2)(\text{perimeter of } \triangle XYZ)$

$= (1/2)(292) = 146$

**21.** *Answer formats may vary.*

Statements (Reasons)

1. a. $\overline{BQ} \cong \overline{QC}$ (Given)

b. $\overline{AB} \parallel \overline{CR}$ (Construction)

c. $\angle B \cong \angle QCR$ (Alternate interior $\angle$s are $\cong$.)

d. $\angle BQP \cong \angle CQR$ (Vertical $\angle$s are $\cong$.)

e. $\triangle BQP \cong \triangle CQR$ (ASA, Steps 1a, 1c and 1d)

2. a. $\overline{QP} \cong \overline{QR}$ (CPCTC, Step 1e)

b. $\overline{PB} \cong \overline{RC}$ (CPCTC, Step 1e)

3. a. $\overline{BP} \cong \overline{PA}$ (Given)

b. $\overline{PA} \cong \overline{RC}$ (Transitive Property, Steps 2b and 3a)

4. a. $\angle APC \cong \angle RCP$ (Alternate interior $\angle$s are $\cong$.)

b. $\overline{PC} \cong \overline{CP}$ (Reflexive Property)

c. $\triangle APC \cong \triangle RCP$ (SAS, Steps 3b, 4a, and 4b)

5. a. $\angle PCA \cong \angle CPR$ (CPCTC, Step 4c)

6. a. $\overline{PQ} \parallel \overline{AC}$ (Alternate interior $\angle$s are $\cong$.)

7. a. $\overline{PR} \cong \overline{AC}$ (CPCTC, Step 4c)

8. a. $PR = PQ + QR$ (Segment Addition Postulate)

b. $PQ = QR$ (Def. of congruent segments, Step 2a)

c. $PR = PQ + PQ$ (Substitution Property)

d. $PR = 2PQ$ (Simplify.)

e. $PR = AC$ (Def. of congruent segments, Step 7a)

f. $AC = 2PQ$ (Transitive Property)

**22.** 3. Def. of bisect (or angle bisector)

4. Reflexive Property

5. SAS

6. CPCTC

## LESSON 47

**1.** SAS    **2.** HL

**3.** *Answers may vary. Sample(s):*

Thm 47.1: $C$ is on the perpendicular bisector of $\overline{AB}$
if and only if $C$ is equidistant from $A$ and $B$.

Thm 47.1: $\overleftrightarrow{CK} \perp \overline{AB}$ and $\overleftrightarrow{CK}$ bisects $\overline{AB}$
if and only if $CA = CB$.

Thm 47.2: If $C$ is the circumcenter of $\triangle XYZ$,
then $CX = CY = CZ$.

Thm 47.2: If $\overline{CS}, \overline{CT}$, and $\overline{CU}$ are the perpendicular
bisectors of $\triangle XYZ$, then $CX = CY = CZ$.

4. $\overline{XS} \cong \overline{SY}$
   $\overline{YT} \cong \overline{TZ}$
   $\overline{CZ} \cong \overline{CX} \cong \overline{CY}$

5. $7x - 1 = 34$
   $x = 5$

6. $3x + 4 = 5x - 8$
   $x = 6$

7. $5x = x + 12$
   $x = 3$

8. $9x - 8 = 4x + 7$
   $x = 3$

9. $5x = 3x + 2$
   $x = 1$
   $CY = CX = 5(1) = 5$

10. $\triangle CSX \cong \triangle CSY$, $\triangle CTY \cong \triangle CTZ$, $\triangle CUX \cong \triangle CUZ$

    By the definition of circumcenter, $\overline{CS}$, $\overline{CT}$, and $\overline{CU}$ are perpendicular bisectors. Look at $\triangle CSX$ and $\triangle CSY$.

    $\triangle CSX \cong \triangle CSY$ by SAS because $\overline{XS} \cong \overline{YS}$ by the definition of segment bisector, $\angle CSX \cong \angle CSY$ as right angles, and $\overline{CS} \cong \overline{CS}$ by the Reflexive Property. Similarly, $\triangle CTY \cong \triangle CTZ$ and $\triangle CUX \cong \triangle CUZ$ by SAS. Alternatively, you could use Theorem 47.1 to prove the triangles congruent by SSS or HL.

11. $x - 7 = 12$
    $x = 19$

12. $7x = 5x + 8$
    $x = 4$

13. $7x - 8 = 3x + 4$
    $x = 3$

14. $2x + 5 = 15 - 8x$
    $x = 1$

15. $5x + 30 + 90 = 180$
    $x = 12$

16. $x = y = z = 7$

17. $XS = SY$
    $10 - x = 4x$
    $x = 2$
    $XY = 2XS = 2(10 - 2) = 16$

18. $CX = CY = CZ$
    $2x = x + 5$
    $x = 5$
    $CZ = CX = 2(5) = 10$

19. See Problem 10 above.

20. Statements (Reasons)
    1. $\overleftrightarrow{CK} \perp \overline{AB}$ (Given)
    2. $\angle CKA$ and $\angle CKB$ are right angles. (Def. of perpendicular)
    3. $\angle CKA \cong \angle CKB$ (All right angles are congruent.)
    4. $\overleftrightarrow{CK}$ bisects $\overline{AB}$. (Given)
    5. $\overline{AK} \cong \overline{BK}$ (Def. of bisect)
    6. $\overline{CK} \cong \overline{CK}$ (Reflexive Property)
    7. $\triangle CKA \cong \triangle CKB$ (SAS, Steps 3, 5, and 6)
    8. $\overline{CA} \cong \overline{CB}$ (CPCTC)
    9. $CA = CB$ (Def. of congruent segments)

21. Statements (Reasons)
    1. $CA = CB$ (Given)
    2. $\overline{CA} \cong \overline{CB}$ (Def. of congruent segments)
    3. Draw a line through $C$ perpendicular to $\overline{AB}$ at $K$. (Construction)
    4. $\angle CKA$ and $\angle CKB$ are right angles. (Def. of perpendicular)
    5. $\triangle CKA$ and $\triangle CKB$ are right triangles. (Def. of right triangles.)
    6. $\overline{CK} \cong \overline{CK}$ (Reflexive Property)
    7. $\triangle CKA \cong \triangle CKB$ (HL, Steps 2 and 6)
    8. $\overline{AK} \cong \overline{BK}$ (CPCTC)
    9. $\overleftrightarrow{CK}$ bisects $\overline{AB}$. (Def. of bisect)
    10. $\overleftrightarrow{CK}$ is the perpendicular bisector of $\overline{AB}$. (Def. of perpendicular bisector, Steps 3 and 9)
    11. $C$ is on $\overleftrightarrow{CK}$, the perpendicular bisector of $\overline{AB}$. (Def. of point on a line)

22. Statements (Reasons)
    1. $\overline{CS}$, $\overline{CT}$, and $\overline{CU}$ are perpendicular bisectors. (Given)
    2. $CX = CY$, $CY = CZ$, $CZ = CX$ (Any point on the perpendicular bisector of a segment is equidistant from the endpoints of the segment.)
    3. $CX = CY = CZ$ (Transitive Property)

23. number of triangles formed $= n - 2 = 7 - 2 = 5$
    interior angle sum $= 180(n - 2) = 180(7 - 2) = 900°$

## LESSON 48

1. $x = 2(15) = 30$

2. $13 = 5x - 7$
   $x = 4$

3. $4x = x + 15$
   $x = 5$

4. *Answers may vary. Sample(s):*
   Thm 48.1: $K$ is on the angle bisector of $\angle BAC$ if and only if $K$ is equidistant from $\overrightarrow{AB}$ and $\overrightarrow{AC}$.
   Thm 48.1: $\overrightarrow{AK}$ bisects $\angle BAC$ if and only if $\overline{KB} \perp \overrightarrow{AB}$, $\overline{KC} \perp \overrightarrow{AC}$, and $KB = KC$.
   Thm 48.2: If $C$ is the incenter of $\triangle XYZ$, then $CS = CT = CU$.
   Thm 48.2: If $\overline{CX}$, $\overline{CY}$, and $\overline{CZ}$ are the angle bisectors of $\triangle XYZ$, then $CS = CT = CU$.

5. $\angle CXS \cong \angle CXU$
   $\angle CYT \cong \angle CYS$
   $\overline{CU} \cong \overline{CS} \cong \overline{CT}$

6. $14 = 7 - x$
   $x = -7$

7. $x + 25 = 7x + 1$
   $x = 4$

8. $40 = 9x - 5$
   $x = 5$

**9.** $4x + 7 = 7x - 14$

$x = 7$

**10.** $8x = 5x + 9$

$x = 3$

$CT = CS = 8(3) = 24$

**11.** $\triangle CXS \cong \triangle CXU, \triangle CYS \cong \triangle CYT, \triangle CZT \cong \triangle CZU$

By the definition of incenter, $\overline{CX}$, $\overline{CY}$, and $\overline{CZ}$ are angle bisectors. Look at $\triangle CXS$ and $\triangle CXU$.

$\triangle CXS \cong \triangle CXU$ by AAS because $\angle CXS \cong \angle CXU$ by the definition of angle bisector, $\angle CSX \cong \angle CUX$ as right angles, and $\overline{CX} \cong \overline{CX}$ by the Reflexive Property. Similarly, $\triangle CYS \cong \triangle CYT$ and $\triangle CZT \cong \triangle CZU$ by AAS.

Alternatively, you could use Theorem 48.1 to prove the triangles congruent by HL.

**12.** $x = 8$

**13.** $15 = 9x - 12$

$x = 3$

**14.** $5x = 4x + 5$

$x = 5$

**15.** $5x - 17 = 19 - 4x$

$x = 4$

**16.** $5x + 1 = x + 9$

$x = 2$

**17.** $90 + 25 + x = 180$

$x = 65$

**18.** $CS = CT$

$x + 7 = 3x - 5$

$x = 6$

$CU = CS = 6 + 7 = 13$

**19.** $m\angle CZT = m\angle CZU = 20°$

$m\angle ZCT = 180 - 90 - 20$

$= 70°$

**20.** See Problem 11 above.

**21.** Statements (Reasons)

1. $\overrightarrow{AK}$ bisects $\angle BAC$. (Given)
2. $\angle BAK \cong \angle CAK$ (Def. of angle bisector)
3. $\overline{KB} \perp \overrightarrow{AB}, \overline{KC} \perp \overrightarrow{AC}$ (Given)
4. $\angle ABK$ and $\angle ACK$ are right angles. (Def. of perpendicular)
5. $\angle ABK \cong \angle ACK$ (All right angles are congruent.)
6. $\overline{AK} \cong \overline{AK}$ (Reflexive Property)
7. $\triangle ABK \cong \triangle ACK$ (AAS, Steps 2, 5, and 6)
8. $\overline{KB} \cong \overline{KC}$ (CPCTC)
9. $KB = KC$ (Def. of congruent segments)

**22.** Statements (Reasons)

1. $KB = KC$ (Given)
2. $\overline{KB} \cong \overline{KC}$ (Def. of congruent segments)
3. $\overline{KB} \perp \overrightarrow{AB}, \overline{KC} \perp \overrightarrow{AC}$ (Given)
4. $\angle ABK$ and $\angle ACK$ are right angles. (Def. of perpendicular)
5. $\triangle ABK$ and $\triangle ACK$ are right triangles. (Def. of right triangle)
6. $\overline{AK} \cong \overline{AK}$ (Reflexive Property)
7. $\triangle ABK \cong \triangle ACK$ (HL, Steps 2 and 6)
8. $\angle BAK \cong \angle CAK$ (CPCTC)
9. $\overrightarrow{AK}$ bisects $\angle BAC$. (Def. of angle bisector)

**23.** Statements (Reasons)

1. $\overline{CX}$, $\overline{CY}$, and $\overline{CZ}$ are angle bisectors. $\overline{XY} \perp \overline{CS}, \overline{YZ} \perp \overline{CT}, \overline{XZ} \perp \overline{CU}$ (Given)
2. $CS = CU, CS = CT, CT = CU$ (Any point on the bisector of an angle is equidistant from the sides of the angle.)
3. $CS = CT = CU$ (Transitive Property)

**24.** $\angle 1 \cong \angle 2$ because alternate interior angles are congruent when lines are parallel. $\angle 2 \cong \angle 3$ because vertical angles are congruent. Because the three angles are congruent, $m\angle 1 = m\angle 2 = m\angle 3 = 110°$.

## LESSON 49

**1.** $x = 14/2 = 7$

**2.** $7x - 2 = 19$

$x = 3$

**3.** $90 + 24 + x = 180$

$x = 66$

**4.** $x = 2NB = 6$

$y = 3NB = 9$

**5.** $x = (1/2)AN = 4$

$y = 3NB = 12$

**6.** $x = (2/3)AB = 12$

$y = (1/3)AB = 6$

**7.** Answers may vary. Sample(s):

If $C$ is the centroid of $\triangle XYZ$, then $XC = (2/3)XT$, $YC = (2/3)YU$, and $ZC = (2/3)ZS$.

If $\overline{XT}$, $\overline{YU}$, and $\overline{ZS}$ are the medians of $\triangle XYZ$, then $XC = (2/3)XT$, $YC = (2/3)YU$, and $ZC = (2/3)ZS$.

**8.**  a.  true; $T$ is the midpoint of $\overline{YZ}$.

b.  false; $XS = SY$ and $XU = UZ$.

c.  true

d.  true

e.  false; $CS = ZS/3 = ZC/2$

**9.** $YC = (2/3)YU$

$YU = (3/2)YC = (3/2)(16) = 24$

$CU = YU - YC = 24 - 16 = 8$

You could first find $CU$ and then $YU$:

$CU = YC/2 = 8$ and $YU = 3CU = 24$.

**10.** $ER = 3CR$

$7x + 5 = 3(4x)$

$x = 1$

$EC = 2CR = 2(4) = 8$

**11.** $AB = 2 \times AF$

**12.** $AP = (2/3) \times AD$

**13.** $PE = (1/3) \times BE$

**14.** $CF = 3 \times PF$

**15.** $ML = KM = 4$

$KL = 2KM = 8$

**16.** $JT = (2/3)JM = 10$

$TM = (1/3)JM = 5$

**17.** $TN = KT/2 = 6$

$KN = 3TN = 18$

**18.** $JT = 2TM$

$3x - 1 = 2(2x - 8)$

$x = 15$

**19.** false; A centroid is always inside a triangle because the medians are always inside the triangle.

**20 ~ 22.** *Answer formats may vary.*

**20.** Statements (Reasons)

1. $\overline{PQ} \cong \overline{PR}$, $\overline{PK}$ is a median. (Given)
3. $K$ is a midpoint. (Def. of median)
4. $\overline{QK} \cong \overline{RK}$ (Def. of midpoint)
5. $\overline{PK} \cong \overline{PK}$ (Reflexive Property)
6. $\triangle PQK \cong \triangle PRK$ (SSS)
7. $\angle QPK \cong \angle RPK$ (CPCTC)
8. $\overline{PK}$ is an angle bisector. (Def. of angle bisector)

**21.** Statements (Reasons)

1. $\overline{PQ} \cong \overline{PR}$, $\overline{PK}$ is an angle bisector. (Given)
2. $\angle QPK \cong \angle RPK$ (Def. of angle bisector)
3. $\overline{PK} \cong \overline{PK}$ (Reflexive Property)
4. $\triangle PQK \cong \triangle PRK$ (SAS)
5. $\overline{QK} \cong \overline{RK}$ (CPCTC)
6. $K$ is a midpoint. (Def. of midpoint)
7. $\overline{PK}$ is a median. (Def. of median)

**22.** Statements (Reasons)

1. a. $\overline{XE}$ and $\overline{ZD}$ are medians. (Given)
   b. $D$ and $E$ are midpoints. (Def. of medians)
   c. $\overline{DE}$ is a midsegment of $\triangle XYZ$. (Def. of midsegment)
   d. $\overline{DE} \parallel \overline{XZ}$ (Triangle Midsegment Theorem [46.1])
   e. $G$ and $F$ are midpoints. (Construction)
   f. $\overline{GF}$ is a midsegment of $\triangle CXZ$. (Def. of midsegment)
   g. $\overline{GF} \parallel \overline{XZ}$ (Triangle Midsegment Theorem [46.1])
   h. $\overline{DE} \parallel \overline{GF} \parallel \overline{XZ}$ (Transitive Property, Steps 1d and 1g)

2. a. $DE = XY/2$, $GF = XY/2$ (Triangle Midsegment Theorem [46.1])
   b. $DE = GF$ (Transitive Property)
   c. $\overline{DE} \cong \overline{GF}$ (Def. of congruent segments)

3. a. $\angle CDE \cong \angle CFG$, $\angle CED \cong \angle CGF$ (If lines parallel, then alternate interior $\angle$s are $\cong$.)
   b. $\triangle CDE \cong \triangle CFG$ (ASA, Steps 2c and 3a)

4. a. $\overline{CE} \cong \overline{CG}$ (CPCTC, Step 3b)
   b. $\overline{CG} \cong \overline{GX}$ (Def. of midpoint, Step 1e)
   c. $\overline{CE} \cong \overline{CG} \cong \overline{GX}$ (Transitive Property)
   d. $CE = CG = GX$ (Def. of congruent segments)

5. a. $CX = CG + GX$ (Segment Addition Postulate)
   b. $CX = CE + CE$ (Substitution Property)
   c. $CX = 2CE$ (Simplify.)

*(The proof continues on the next column.)*

**22.** 6. a. $\overline{CD} \cong \overline{CF}$ (CPCTC, Step 3b)
   b. $\overline{CF} \cong \overline{FZ}$ (Def. of midpoint, Step 1e)
   c. $\overline{CD} \cong \overline{CF} \cong \overline{FZ}$ (Transitive Property)
   d. $CD = CF = FZ$ (Def. of congruent segments)
   e. $CZ = CF + FZ$ (Segment Addition Postulate)
   f. $CZ = CD + CD$ (Substitution Property)
   g. $CZ = 2CD$ (Simplify)

**23.** parallel, perpendicular

# LESSON 50

**1.** right triangle
$x + 60 + 90 = 180$
$x = 30$

**2.** acute triangle
$x + 38 + 70 = 180$
$x = 72$

**3.** obtuse triangle
$x + 30 + 30 = 180$
$x = 120$

**4.** perpendicular bisector

**5.** angle bisector

**6.** median

**7.** $\overline{EQ}$

**8.** outside

**9.** In $\triangle MKN$, $m\angle N = 180 - m\angle MKN - m\angle KMN$
$= 180 - 90 - 55 = 35°$
In $\triangle LMN$, $m\angle L = 180 - m\angle LMN - m\angle N$
$= 180 - 90 - 35 = 55°$

**10.** $\overline{LM}, \overline{MN}, \overline{MK}$

**11.** The orthocenter is $M$.

**12.** false; An altitude can be inside the triangle, outside of the triangle, or one side of the triangle.

**13.** true; The altitudes of an acute triangle are always inside the triangle.

**14.** $\overline{AE}, \overline{BD}$

**15.** $\overline{AB}, \overline{BC}, \overline{BF}$

**16.** The centroid is $G$.

**17.** The orthocenter is $B$.

**18.** In $\triangle XYP$, $m\angle QXP = 180 - m\angle P - m\angle Y$
$= 180 - 90 - 32 = 58°$
$m\angle QXZ = m\angle QXP - m\angle ZXP = 58 - 29 = 29°$
In $\triangle QZX$, $m\angle QZX = 180 - m\angle ZQX - m\angle QXZ$
$= 180 - 90 - 29 = 61°$

**19.** $\triangle XYZ$ is an obtuse triangle, so the orthocenter is outside of the triangle.

**20.** $\triangle XYZ$ is not isosceles because the base angles $\angle QXZ$ and $\angle Y$ are not congruent.

**21 ~ 24.** *Answer formats may vary.*

21. Statements (Reasons)
    1. $\overline{PQ} \cong \overline{PR}$, $\overline{PK}$ is a median. (Given)
    3. $K$ is a midpoint. (Def. of median)
    4. $\overline{QK} \cong \overline{RK}$ (Def. of midpoint)
    5. $\overline{PK} \cong \overline{PK}$ (Reflexive Property)
    6. $\triangle PQK \cong \triangle PRK$ (SSS)
    7. $\angle PKQ \cong \angle PKR$ (CPCTC)
    8. $\angle PKQ$ & $\angle PKR$ are a linear pair. (Def. of linear pair)
    8. $\overline{PK} \perp \overline{QR}$ (Two lines intersecting to form a linear pair of congruent angles are perpendicular. See Theorem 31.3.)
    9. $\overline{PK}$ is an altitude. (Def. of altitude)

22. Statements (Reasons)
    1. $\overline{PQ} \cong \overline{PR}$, $\overline{PK}$ is an altitude. (Given)
    2. $\overline{PK} \perp \overline{QR}$ (Def. of altitude)
    3. $\angle PKQ$ and $\angle PKR$ are right angles. (Def. of perpendicular)
    4. $\triangle PQK$ and $\triangle PRK$ are right triangles. (Def. of right triangle)
    5. $\overline{PK} \cong \overline{PK}$ (Reflexive Property)
    6. $\triangle PQK \cong \triangle PRK$ (HL, Steps 1 and 5)
    7. $\overline{QK} \cong \overline{RK}$ (CPCTC)
    8. $K$ is a midpoint. (Def. of midpoint)
    9. $\overline{PK}$ is a median. (Def. of median)

23. Statements (Reasons)
    1. $\overline{PE}$ is an altitude of isosceles $\triangle PQF$. (Given)
    2. $\overline{PE}$ is a median of $\triangle PQF$. (An altitude of an isosceles triangle is also a median. See Problem 22.)
    3. $E$ is the midpoint of $\overline{QF}$. (Def. of median)
    4. $\overline{QE} \cong \overline{EF}$ (Def. of midpoint)
    5. $QE = EF$ (Def. of congruent segments)
    6. $QF = QE + EF = 2QE$ (Segment Addition Postulate, Substitution Property)
    7. $\overline{PF}$ is a median of $\triangle PQR$. (Given)
    8. $F$ is the midpoint of $\overline{QR}$. (Def. of median)
    9. $\overline{QF} \cong \overline{FR}$ (Def. of midpoint)
    10. $QF = FR$ (Def. of congruent segments)
    11. $QR = QF + FR = 2QF = 2(2QE) = 4QE$ (Segment Addition Postulate, Substitution Property)

24. Statements (Reasons)
    1. $\triangle PQF$ is isosceles with $\overline{PQ} \cong \overline{PF}$. (Given)
    2. $\angle Q \cong \angle PFE$ (Base Angles Theorem [40.1])
    3. $m\angle Q = m\angle PFE$ (Def. of congruent angles)
    4. $\triangle FPR$ is isosceles with $\overline{FP} \cong \overline{FR}$. (Given)
    5. $\angle R \cong \angle FPR$ (Base Angles Theorem [40.1])
    6. $m\angle R = m\angle FPR$ (Def. of congruent angles)
    7. $m\angle PFE = m\angle R + m\angle FPR$ (Triangle Exterior Angle Theorem [32.2])
    8. $m\angle Q = m\angle R + m\angle R = 2m\angle R$ (Substitution Property, Steps 3, 6 and 7)

25. altitude, median, perpendicular bisector, angle bisector

26. exterior angle sum of any polygon = 360°
    one exterior angle = $360/n = 360/12 = 30°$

27. $P(3, -2) \rightarrow P'(2, 2) \rightarrow P''(-2, 2)$

28. Base angles of an isosceles triangle are congruent.
    $6x = 7x - 5$
    $x = 5$
    base angle = $6(5) = 30°$
    vertex angle = $180 - 2(30) = 120°$

# LESSON 51

1. angle bisector
2. perpendicular bisector
3. altitude
4. median
5. altitude
6. median
7. perpendicular bisector
8. angle bisector
9. altitude
10. altitude, median, perpendicular bisector, angle bisector
11. See Lessons 47 through 50.
12. orthocenter
13. circumcenter
14. incenter
15. centroid
16. orthocenter
17. circumcenter
18. $5x = 7x - 8$
    $x = 4$
19. $56 + (x + 18) + 90 = 180$
    $x = 16$
    Note that $x + 18 \neq 36$.
20. $56 + 2(x + 7) + 90 = 180$
    $x = 10$
21. perpendicular bisectors
22. angle bisectors
23. medians
24. altitudes
25. vertices
26. sides
27. on

**28.** *Answer formats may vary.*

A midsegment is parallel to the third side (Theorem 46.1). $\overline{DE}$ is a midsegment of $\triangle ABC$, so $\overline{DE} \parallel \overline{AC}$.

A line perpendicular to one of two parallel lines is also perpendicular to the other (Theorem 31.1). $\overline{DE} \parallel \overline{AC}$ and $\overline{AC} \perp \overline{BC}$, so $\overline{DE} \perp \overline{BC}$.

For the same reason, $\overline{DF} \parallel \overline{BC}$ and thus $\overline{DF} \perp \overline{AC}$.

**29.** median (midpoint $F$ of $\overline{AC}$),

altitude ($\overline{DF} \perp \overline{AC}$),

perpendicular bisector (both altitude and median),

angle bisector ($\triangle ADF \cong \triangle CDF$ by SAS)

Notice that $\triangle ADF \cong \triangle CDF$ by SAS because $\overline{AF} \cong \overline{CF}$ by the definition of midpoint, $\angle DFA \cong \angle DFC$ as right angles, and $\overline{DF} \cong \overline{DF}$ by the Reflexive Property.

**30.** Because $\overline{DE} \perp \overline{BC}$ and $E$ bisects $\overline{BC}$, $\overline{DE}$ is the perpendicular bisector of $\overline{BC}$. Similarly, $\overline{DF}$ is the perpendicular bisector of $\overline{AC}$.

Because $D$ is where perpendicular bisectors of $\triangle ABC$ intersect, it is the circumcenter of $\triangle ABC$ by definition.

The circumcenter of a right triangle is the midpoint of the hypotenuse.

**31.** false; Translations, reflections, and rotations are rigid transformations, so they produce congruent figures.

**32.** The two angles in a linear pair add up to 180°. So, if they are congruent, then each must measure 90°.

# LESSON 52

**1.** Thm 52.1: If $AB > BC$, then $m\angle C > m\angle A$.

Thm 52.2: If $m\angle C > m\angle A$, then $AB > BC$.

Thm 52.3: $AB + BC > AC$,

$\qquad AB + AC > BC$,

$\qquad BC + AC > AB$

**2.** $EF < DE < DF$, so $m\angle D < m\angle F < m\angle E$.

**3.** $QR < PR < PQ$, so $m\angle P < m\angle Q < m\angle R$.

**4.** $m\angle D = 180 - 98 - 39 = 43°$

$m\angle F < m\angle D < m\angle E$, so $DE < EF < DF$.

**5.** $m\angle R = 180 - 41 - 71 = 68°$

$m\angle P < m\angle R < m\angle Q$, so $QR < PQ < PR$.

**6.** yes; The following inequalities are all true.

$\qquad 5 + 7 > 10 \qquad 5 + 10 > 7 \qquad 7 + 10 > 5$

**7.** Let $x$ be the third side.

$\qquad x + 4 > 5 \qquad\quad x + 5 > 4 \qquad\quad 4 + 5 > x$

$\qquad\quad x > 1 \qquad\qquad x > -1 \qquad\qquad x < 9$

Solve the inequalities to get $1 < x < 9$. So, the third side must be longer than 1 and shorter than 9.

**8.** $m\angle Q = 180 - 90 - 43 = 47°$

$m\angle P < m\angle Q < m\angle R$, so $QR < PR < PQ$.

**9.** $m\angle Z = 180 - 94 - 45 = 41°$

$m\angle Z < m\angle X < m\angle Y$, so $XY < YZ < XZ$.

**10.** $BC < AB < AC$, so $m\angle A < m\angle C < m\angle B$.

**11.** yes; $4 + 6 > 9$, $4 + 9 > 6$, and $6 + 9 > 4$ are all true.

**12.** no; $2 + 7 > 9$ is false.

**13.** yes; $5 + 5 > 5$ is true.

**14.** $x + 3 > 5$ gives $x > 2$.

$x + 5 > 3$ gives $x > -2$

$3 + 5 > x$ gives $x < 8$.

So, the third side must be longer than 2 and shorter than 8.

**15.** $x + 4 > 9$ gives $x > 5$.

$x + 9 > 4$ gives $x > -5$

$4 + 9 > x$ gives $x < 13$.

So, the third side must be longer than 5 and shorter than 13.

**16.** $x + 7 > 8$ gives $x > 1$.

$x + 8 > 7$ gives $x > -1$

$7 + 8 > x$ gives $x < 15$.

So, the third side must be longer than 1 and shorter than 15.

**17 ~ 19.** *Answer formats may vary.*

**17.** Statements (Reasons)

1. a. $m\angle B = m\angle 1 + m\angle 3$ (Angle Addition Postulate)

   b. $m\angle B > m\angle 1$ (Def. of greater than)

   Note that, if $a = b + c$ and $c > 0$, then $a > b$ by the definition of greater than.

2. a. $m\angle 2 = m\angle A + m\angle 3$ (Triangle Exterior Angle Theorem [32.2])

   b. $m\angle 2 > m\angle A$ (Def. of greater than)

3. a. $BC = DC$ (Construction)

   b. $m\angle 1 = m\angle 2$ (Base Angles Theorem [40.1].)

4. a. $m\angle B > m\angle 2$ (Substitution, Steps 1b and 3b)

   b. $m\angle B > m\angle A$ (Transitive Prop., Steps 2b and 4a)

**18.** 1. $m\angle B < m\angle A$ (Triangle Side-Angle Theorem [52.1])

2. $m\angle B = m\angle A$ (Base Angles Theorem [40.1])

3. Both cases contradict the given statement. So, our assumption is false and $AC > BC$ must be true.

**19.** Statements (Reasons)

1. a. $m\angle ACD = m\angle 2 + m\angle 3$ (Angle Addition Post.)

   b. $m\angle ACD > m\angle 2$ (Def. of greater than)

2. a. $BC = BD$ (Construction)

   b. $m\angle 1 = m\angle 2$ (Base Angles Theorem [40.1])

   c. $m\angle ACD > m\angle 1$ (Substitution, Steps 1b and 2b)

3. a. $AD > AC$ (Apply Theorem 52.1 to $\triangle ADC$.)

4. a. $AD = AB + BD$ (Segment Addition Postulate)

   b. $AD = AB + BC$ (Substitution, Steps 2a and 4a)

   c. $AB + BC > AC$ (Substitution, Steps 3a and 4b)

**20.** The midsegment between any two sides of a triangle is parallel to and half the length of the third side. See the Triangle Midsegment Theorem [46.1].

**21.** A centroid divides a median in the ratio 2:1.
$AP = (2/3)AD = (2/3)(12) = 8$
$PD = (1/3)AD = (1/3)(12) = 4$

## LESSON 53

**1.** Add 7 to all sides: $\quad 8 < 4x < 16$
Divide all sides by 4: $\quad 2 < x < 4$

**2.** $x + 5 > 9$ gives $x > 4$. $\quad$ —> So, the third side must be longer than 4 and shorter than 14.
$x + 9 > 5$ gives $x > -4$
$5 + 9 > x$ gives $x < 14$.

**3.** Thm 53.1: If $\overline{AB} \cong \overline{DE}$, $\overline{BC} \cong \overline{EF}$, and $m\angle B > m\angle E$, then $AC > DF$.
Thm 53.2: If $\overline{AB} \cong \overline{DE}$, $\overline{BC} \cong \overline{EF}$, and $AC > DF$, then $m\angle B > m\angle E$.

**4.** $85° > 82°$, so $x > y$. $\qquad$ **5.** $57° > 54°$, so $x > y$.

**6.** $30 < 31$, so $m\angle 1 < m\angle 2$. $\quad$ **7.** $40 > 38$, so $m\angle 1 > m\angle 2$.

**8.** $54 - 6x > 45$ because $45° > 36°$.
$54 - 6x > 0$ because side lengths must be positive.
Solve each inequality to get $x < 3/2$ and $x < 9$.
Combine the two inequalities to get $x < 3/2$.

**9.** $4x - 1 < 39$ because $30 < 33$.
$4x - 1 > 0$ because angles must be positive.
Solve each inequality to get $x < 10$ and $x > 1/4$.
Combine the two inequalities to get $1/4 < x < 10$.

**10.** $90° > 80°$, so $x > y$. $\qquad$ **11.** $180 - 93 = 87°$
$87° < 93°$, so $x < y$.

**12.** $68° = 68°$, so $x = y$. $\qquad$ **13.** $25 > 24$, so $m\angle 1 > m\angle 2$.

**14.** $44 < 44$, so $m\angle 1 = m\angle 2$. $\quad$ **15.** $16 < 18$, so $m\angle 1 < m\angle 2$.

**16.** $25 - 5x > 15$ and $25 - 5x > 0$
$x < 2$ and $x < 5$
$x < 2$

**17.** $6x - 1 > 2x$ and $6x - 1 > 0$ and $2x > 0$
$x > 1/4$ and $x > 1/6$ and $x > 0$
$x > 1/4$

**18.** $4x + 2 > 54$ and $4x + 2 > 0$
$x > 13$ and $x > -1/2$
$x > 13$

**19 ~ 20.** *Answer formats may vary.*

**19.** 1. Base angles of an isosceles triangle are congruent. $\triangle ABD$ is isosceles, so $m\angle 3 = m\angle 1 + m\angle 2$.
  2. Angles must be positive. $m\angle 3 = m\angle 1 + m\angle 2$ and $m\angle 1 > 0$, so $m\angle 3 > m\angle 2$ by the definition of greater than.
   Note that, if $a = b + c$ and $c > 0$, then $a > b$ by the definition of greater than.
  3. $m\angle 3 + m\angle 4 > m\angle 3$ by the definition of greater than. Because $m\angle 3 > m\angle 2$, $m\angle 3 + m\angle 4 > m\angle 2$ by the Transitive Property.
  4. The larger angle has the longer opposite side. In $\triangle ADF$, $m\angle 3 + m\angle 4 > m\angle 2$ and thus $AC > DF$.

**20.** 1. By the Hinge Theorem [53.1], $AC < DF$.
  2. $\triangle ABC \cong \triangle DEF$ by SAS, so $AC = DF$.
  3. Both cases contradict the given statement. So, our assumption is false and $m\angle B > m\angle E$ must be true.

**21.** reflection

**22.** false; Counterexamples may vary. Any $a$, $b$, and $c$ where $a \neq b$ and $c = 0$ can be a counterexample.

## LESSON 54

**1.** 2. Def. of centroid
  5. A midsegment is half the length of the third side. See Theorem 46.1.

**2.** 2. Def. of midsegment
  3. A midsegment is parallel to the third side. See Theorem 46.1.
  4. A line perpendicular to one of two parallel lines is also perpendicular to the other. See Theorem 31.1.
  6. Def. of circumcenter

**3.** 2. Alternate interior $\angle$s on parallel lines are $\cong$.
  3. Reflexive Property
  4. AAS
  6. The sum of two sides of a triangle is greater than the third side. See Theorem 53.3.

**4.** 2. Def. of bisect
  3. Triangle Exterior Angle Theorem [32.2]
  4. Substitution Property
  6. The larger angle has the longer opposite side. See Theorem 52.2.

**5.** 2. Def. of bisect
  3. Reflexive Property
  4. SAS
  5. CPCTC
  6. Def. of midpoint
  7. Def. of median

**6.** 2. A midsegment is half the length of the third side. See Theorem 46.1.

    4. Substitution Property

    6. Substitution Property

**7.** Statements (Reasons)

    1. $m\angle C = 90°$ (Given)

    2. $m\angle A + m\angle B + m\angle C = 180°$ (Angles in a triangle add up to 180°. See the Triangle Sum Theorem [32.1].)

    3. $m\angle A + m\angle B = 180 - m\angle C$ (Subtraction Property)

    4. $m\angle A + m\angle B = 180 - 90$ (Substitution Property)

    5. $m\angle A + m\angle B = 90$ (Simplify.)

    6. $m\angle A < 90$, $m\angle B < 90$ (Def. of less than)

    7. $m\angle A < m\angle C$, $m\angle B < m\angle C$ (Substitution Property)

    8. $BC < AB$, $AC < AB$ (The larger angle has the longer opposite side. See Theorem 52.2.)

**8.** Statements (Reasons)

    1. $\angle 3$ is an exterior angle. (Given)

    2. $m\angle 3 = m\angle 1 + m\angle 2$ (Triangle Exterior Angle Theorem [32.2])

    3. $m\angle 3 > m\angle 1$, $m\angle 3 > m\angle 2$ (Def. of greater than)

**9.** a translation of 10 units down; A composition of reflections over two parallel lines is a translation. Use a simple point like (0, 0) to find the rule.

**10.** Lines $t$ and $u$ are perpendicular. See Theorem 31.1.

**11.** Let $x$ be the vertex angle and $2x$ be the base angle.

$x + 2x + 2x = 180$; $x = 36$

The triangle has angles 36°, 72°, and 72°.

## LESSON 55

**1.** median

**2.** altitude

**3.** perpendicular bisector

**4.** angle bisector

**5.** midsegment

**6.** altitude, median, perpendicular bisector, angle bisector

**7.** $5x - 8 = 2(16)$

    $x = 8$

**8.** consecutive interior $\angle$s

    $140 + (7x + 5) = 180$

    $x = 5$

**9.** $9x - 8 = 4x + 7$

    $x = 3$

**10.** $90 + 62 + 2(7x) = 180$

    $x = 2$

**11.** $5x - 8 = 3x$

    $x = 4$

**12.** $58 + (x + 15) + 90 = 180$

    $x = 17$

**13.** $\overline{TZ}$, $\overline{SU}$

**14.** $\angle XSU$, $\angle UTZ$ (corresponding to $\angle Y$)

    $\angle TUS$ (alternate interior to $\angle XSU$ and $\angle UTZ$)

**15.** $\triangle SXU$, $\triangle TUZ$, $\triangle UTS$ (congruent by SSS)

**16.** perimeter of $\triangle STU = (1/2)$(perimeter of $\triangle XYZ$)

    $= (1/2)(18 + 22 + 24) = 32$

**17.** circumcenter

**18.** $YT = YZ/2 = 24/2 = 12$

    $YC = XC = 18$

**19.** *Answer formats may vary.*

Any point on the perpendicular bisector of a segment is equidistant from the endpoints of the segment (Theorem 47.1).

Because $\overline{CS}$ is a perpendicular bisector, $CX = CY$.
Because $\overline{CT}$ is a perpendicular bisector, $CY = CZ$.
By the Transitive Property, $CX = CY = CZ$.
So, $C$ is equidistant from $X$, $Y$, and $Z$.

You could say that $CX = CY$ and $CY = CZ$ because $\triangle CSX \cong \triangle CSY$ and $\triangle CTY \cong \triangle CTZ$ by SAS.

**20.** centroid

**21.** $CT = XC/2 = 10/2 = 5$

    $XT = 3CT = 3(5) = 15$

**22.** *Answer formats may vary.*

Statements (Reasons)

    1. $\overline{YX} \cong \overline{YZ}$, $\overline{YU}$ is a median. (Given)

    3. $U$ is a midpoint. (Def. of median)

    4. $\overline{XU} \cong \overline{ZU}$ (Def. of midpoint)

    5. $\overline{YU} \cong \overline{YU}$ (Reflexive Property)

    6. $\triangle YXU \cong \triangle YZU$ (SSS)

    7. $\angle XYU \cong \angle ZYU$ (CPCTC)

    8. $\overline{YU}$ is an angle bisector. (Def. of angle bisector)

**23.** no; $8 + 8 > 16$ is false.

**24.** $x + 7 > 3$ gives $x > -4$.

    $x + 3 > 7$ gives $x > 4$

    $7 + 3 > x$ gives $x < 10$.

    → So, the third side must be longer than 4 and shorter than 10.

**25.** $m\angle B = 180 - 70 - 45 = 65°$

    $m\angle C < m\angle B < m\angle A$, so $AB < AC < BC$.

**26.** $57° > 54°$, so $x > y$.

**27.** 3. Def. of perpendicular

    4. Def. of right triangle

    5. Reflexive Property

    6. HL

    7. CPCTC

    8. Def. of midpoint

    9. Def. of median

**28.** acute; The third angle is $180 - 46 - 50 = 84°$.

**29.** If a point is the incenter of a triangle, then it is equidistant from the sides of the triangle.

1. Solve eq1 for $x$:　　$x = y + 2$
   Plug eq1 into eq2:　$2(y + 2) = 3y + 4$
   Solve eq2 for $y$:　　$2y + 4 = 3y + 4$
   　　　　　　　　　　$y = 0$
   Use eq1 to find $x$:　$x = 0 + 2 = 2$
   Write the solution:　$x = 2, y = 0$

2. false; They are supplementary.

3. Thm 56.1: If $ABCD$ is a parallelogram,
   　　　　then $\overline{AB} \cong \overline{CD}$ and $\overline{BC} \cong \overline{DA}$.

   Thm 56.2: If $ABCD$ is a parallelogram,
   　　　　then $m\angle A + m\angle B = 180°$,
   　　　　　　$m\angle B + m\angle C = 180°$,
   　　　　　　$m\angle C + m\angle D = 180°$, and
   　　　　　　$m\angle D + m\angle A = 180°$.

   Thm 56.3: If $ABCD$ is a parallelogram,
   　　　　then $\angle A \cong \angle C$ and $\angle B \cong \angle D$.

   Thm 56.4: If $ABCD$ is a parallelogram,
   　　　　then $\overline{AP} \cong \overline{CP}$ and $\overline{BP} \cong \overline{DP}$.

4. $x = 21$
   $y = 15$

5. $x + 7 = 10$
   $3y - 5 = 10$
   $x = 3, y = 5$

6. $x = 115°$
   $y = z = 180 - 115 = 65°$

7. $x = 99°$
   $y = z = 180 - 99 = 81°$

8. Write the equations:　$EM = GM$ and $FM = HM$
   　　　　　　　　　　$x + y = 15$ and $3x = 2y + 5$
   Solve eq1 for $x$:　　$x = 15 - y$
   Plug eq1 into eq2:　$3(15 - y) = 2y + 5$
   Solve eq2 for $y$:　　$y = 8$
   Use eq1 to find $x$:　$x = 15 - 8 = 7$
   Find $EG$ and $FH$:　$EG = 2GM = 2(15) = 30$
   　　　　　　　　　　$FH = 2FM = 2(3)(7) = 42$

9. $a = 8$
   $b = 5$
   $c = 180 - 70 = 110$
   $d = 70$
   $e = c = 110$

10. $5a - 9 = 6$
    $a = 3$
    $b = 180 - 67 = 113$
    $c = 67$
    $d = b = 113$

11. $9 - 4a = 3a - 5$
    $3b = 72$
    $a = 2, b = 24$

12. $m\angle PQR + m\angle QRS = 180$ ⇢ $m\angle PQR = m\angle RSP$
    $115 + (3x + 14) = 180$ ┆ $115 = 8y - 13$
    $x = 17$ ┄┘ $y = 16$

13. $PR = 2PK$ ⇢ $QS = 2QK$
    $x + 7 = 2(x + 1)$ ┆ $y + 5 = 2(7 - y)$
    $x = 5$ ┄┘ $y = 3$

14. Write the equations:　$PK = RK$ and $QK = SK$
    　　　　　　　　　　$2x - 6 = 6y$ and $x + 9 = 5y + 8$
    Solve eq2 for $x$:　　$x = 5y - 1$
    Plug eq2 into eq1:　$2(5y - 1) - 6 = 6y$
    Solve eq1 for $y$:　　$y = 2$
    Use eq2 to find $x$:　$x = 5(2) - 1 = 9$
    Write the solution:　$x = 9, y = 2$

15. 3. Alternate interior $\angle$s on parallel lines are $\cong$.
    4. Reflexive Property
    5. ASA

16. 2. Def. of parallelogram
    3. Alternate interior $\angle$s on parallel lines are $\cong$.
    4. Opposite sides of a parallelogram are congruent.
    5. ASA
    6. CPCTC

17. Statements (Reasons)
    1. $\square ABCD$ (Given)
    2. $\overline{BA} \parallel \overline{CD}, \overline{BC} \parallel \overline{AD}$ (Def. of parallelogram)
    3. $\angle A$ and $\angle B$ are supplementary; $\angle B$ and $\angle C$ are supplementary. (Consecutive interior angles on parallel lines are supplementary.)
    4. $m\angle A + m\angle B = 180°, m\angle B + m\angle C = 180°$ (Def. of supplementary angles)

18. Statements (Reasons)
    1. $\square ABCD$ (Given)
    2. $\overline{BA} \parallel \overline{CD}, \overline{BC} \parallel \overline{AD}$ (Def. of parallelogram)
    3. $\angle A$ and $\angle B$ are supplementary; $\angle B$ and $\angle C$ are supplementary; $\angle C$ and $\angle D$ are supplementary. (Consecutive interior angles on parallel lines are supplementary.)
    4. $\angle A \cong \angle C, \angle B \cong \angle D$ (Angles supplementary to the same angle are congruent. See Theorem 29.3.)

19. Statements (Reasons)
    1. $\square LMNR, \square LPQR$ (Given)
    2. $\overline{MN} \cong \overline{LR}, \overline{LR} \cong \overline{PQ}$ (Opposite sides of a parallelogram are congruent.)
    3. $\overline{MN} \cong \overline{PQ}$ (Transitive Property)

20. Statements (Reasons)
    1. $\square EFGH, \square EPQR$ (Given)
    2. $\angle E \cong \angle G, \angle E \cong \angle Q$ (Opposite angles of a parallelogram are congruent.)
    3. $\angle G \cong \angle Q$ (Transitive Property)

21. $(y - 3) = 2(x - (-1))$

22. true

## LESSON 57 ·······················

1. Opposite sides are congruent, so $x = 16$ and $y = 12$.

2. Opposite angles are congruent, so $x = 62$.
   Consecutive angles are supplementary, so $y = z = 118$.

3. Diagonals bisect each other, so $x = 4$ and $y = 6$.

4. Thm 57.1: If $\overline{AB} \cong \overline{CD}$ and $\overline{BC} \cong \overline{DA}$,
   then $ABCD$ is a parallelogram.

   Thm 57.2: If $\angle A \cong \angle C$ and $\angle B \cong \angle D$,
   then $ABCD$ is a parallelogram.

   Thm 57.3: If $\overline{AP} \cong \overline{CP}$ and $\overline{BP} \cong \overline{DP}$,
   then $ABCD$ is a parallelogram.

   Thm 57.4: If $\overline{AD} \parallel \overline{BC}$ and $\overline{AD} \cong \overline{BC}$,
   then $ABCD$ is a parallelogram.

5. yes; Angles in a quadrilateral add up to 360°, so the
   fourth angle is $360 - 83 - 83 - 97 = 97°$. Opposite
   angles are congruent, so it is a parallelogram.

6. no; The diagonals must bisect each other.

7. Opposite sides must be congruent.
   $2x + 9 = 5x - 3$       $x + y = 13$
   $x = 4$                $y = 9$

8. A pair of sides must be parallel and congruent.
   $2x = x + 7$         $4y = 64$
   $x = 7$             $y = 16$

9. yes; Opposite sides are congruent.

10. no; There is not enough information.

11. yes; Opposite angles are congruent.

12. yes; One pair of sides is parallel and congruent.

13. yes; The diagonals bisect each other.

14. no; There is not enough information.

15. $(x + 15) + 2x = 180$  ·⟶ $x + 15 = 2y$
    $x = 55$                 --┘ $y = 35$

16. $4x = 8$           ·⟶ $10 - x = 5y - 2$
    $x = 2$         --┘ $y = 2$

17. $5x = x + 16$    ·⟶ $7y = 49$
    $x = 4$           --┘ $y = 7$

18. 2. Reflexive Property
    3. SSS
    4. CPCTC
    5. If alternate interior angles are congruent, then lines
       are parallel.

19. 2. Angles in a quadrilateral add up to 360°.
    4. Division Property
    5. Def. of supplementary angles
    6. If consecutive interior angles are supplementary,
       then lines are parallel.

20. Statements (Reasons)
    1. $\overline{AP} \cong \overline{CP}$, $\overline{BP} \cong \overline{DP}$ (Given)
    2. $\angle APB \cong \angle CPD$, $\angle BPC \cong \angle DPA$ (Vertical $\angle$s $\cong$.)
    3. $\triangle APB \cong \triangle CPD$, $\triangle BPC \cong \triangle DPA$ (SAS)
    4. $\overline{AB} \cong \overline{CD}$, $\overline{BC} \cong \overline{DA}$ (CPCTC)
    5. $ABCD$ is a parallelogram. (A quadrilateral is a
       parallelogram if opposite sides are congruent.)

21. Statements (Reasons)
    1. $\overline{AD} \parallel \overline{BC}$, $\overline{AD} \cong \overline{BC}$ (Given)
    2. $\angle BCA \cong \angle DAC$ (If lines are parallel, then alternate
       interior $\angle$s are $\cong$.)
    3. $\overline{AC} \cong \overline{AC}$ (Reflexive Property)
    4. $\triangle ABC \cong \triangle CDA$ (SAS)
    5. $\angle BAC \cong \angle DCA$ (CPCTC)
    6. $\overline{BA} \parallel \overline{CD}$ (If alternate interior $\angle$s are $\cong$, then lines
       are parallel.)
    7. $ABCD$ is a parallelogram. (Def. of parallelogram)

22. false; Counterexamples may vary. A triangle with
    angles 120°, 30°, and 30° is a counterexample.

23. If a triangle is isosceles, then it is an acute triangle.
    If a triangle is an acute triangle, then it is isosceles.

## LESSON 58 ·······················

1. Opposite sides are congruent, so $a = 8$ and $b = 5$.
   Consecutive angles are supplementary, so $c = e = 110$.
   Opposite angles are congruent, so $d = 70$.

2. Diagonals bisect each other, so $x = 8$ and $y = 9$.

3. Opposite sides are congruent, so $5x = x + 16$ and $x = 4$.
   Opposite sides are parallel, so $7y = 49$ and $y = 7$.

4. Thm 58.1: $\square ABCD$ is a rhombus if and only if
   $\overline{AC} \perp \overline{BD}$.

   Thm 58.2: $\square ABCD$ is a rhombus if and only if
   $\overline{AC}$ bisects $\angle BAD$ and $\angle BCD$, and
   $\overline{BD}$ bisects $\angle ABC$ and $\angle ADC$.

   Thm 58.3: $\square EFGH$ is a rectangle if and only if
   $\overline{EG} \cong \overline{FH}$.

5. true; A rhombus is a parallelogram. The diagonals of a
   parallelogram bisect each other.

6. A square is a parallelogram, a rhombus, and a square.
   Its diagonals are congruent and perpendicular. They
   bisect each other and opposite angles.

7. Diagonals bisect opposite angles, so $m\angle 1 = 59°$.
   Alt. interior $\angle$s are congruent, so $m\angle 2 = 59°$.
   Alt. interior $\angle$s are congruent, so $m\angle 3 = m\angle 1 = 59°$.
   A triangle has 180°, so $m\angle 4 = 180 - m\angle 3 - 59 = 62°$.
   Opposite angles are congruent, so $m\angle 5 = m\angle 4 = 62°$.

   You could say $m\angle 1 = m\angle 2 = m\angle 3 = 59°$ as base angles
   of congruent isosceles triangles.

8. Diagonals are perpendicular, so $m\angle1 = 90°$.
   Diagonals bisect opposite angles, so $m\angle2 = 31°$.
   Alt. interior $\angle$s are congruent, so $m\angle3 = m\angle2 = 31°$.
   A triangle has 180°, so $m\angle4 = 180 - 90 - m\angle2 = 59c$.
   Diagonals bisect opposite angles, so $m\angle5 = m\angle4 = 59°$.

9. $FH = EG$          $\rightarrow$  $x = 5$
   $4x + 10 = 6x$  ---⌐  $FH = EG = 6(5) = 30$

10. a. $\overline{BC}, \overline{CD}, \overline{DA}$ (All sides are congruent.)
    b. $\angle BPC, \angle CPD, \angle DPA$ (Diagonals are perpendicular.)
    c. $\angle ADP, \angle CBP, \angle CDP$ ($\triangle ABD$ and $\triangle CBD$ are congruent isosceles triangles, so their base angles are congruent.)

11. a. $\overline{EG}$ (Diagonals are congruent.)
    b. $\overline{EQ}, \overline{GQ}, \overline{HQ}$ (Diagonals are congruent and bisect each other because a rectangle is a parallelogram.)
    c. $\triangle EFG, \triangle GHE, \triangle HGF$ (Opposite sides are congruent and diagonals are congruent, so the triangles are congruent by SSS.)

12. Diagonals bisect opposite angles, so $m\angle1 = 62°$.
    Alt. interior $\angle$s are congruent, so $m\angle2 = 62°$.
    Alt. interior $\angle$s are congruent, so $m\angle3 = m\angle1 = 62°$.
    A triangle has 180°, so $m\angle4 = 180 - m\angle3 - 62 = 56°$.
    Opposite angles are congruent, so $m\angle5 = m\angle4 = 56°$.

13. Diagonals bisect opposite angles, so $m\angle1 = 60°$.
    Diagonals are perpendicular, so $m\angle2 = 90°$.
    Alt. interior $\angle$s are congruent, so $m\angle3 = 60°$.
    Diagonals bisect opposite angles, so $m\angle4 = m\angle3 = 60°$.
    A triangle has 180°, so $m\angle5 = 180 - 90 - m\angle3 = 30°$.

14. Opposite angles are congruent, so $m\angle1 = 112°$.
    Base $\angle$s of an isosceles triangle are $\cong$, so $m\angle2 = m\angle3$.
    A triangle has 180°, so $112 + m\angle2 + m\angle3 = 180$ and $m\angle2 = m\angle3 = 34°$.
    Diagonals bisect opposite angles, so $m\angle4 = m\angle3 = 34°$.

15. rhombus, square

16. rectangle, square

17. parallelogram, rhombus, rectangle, square

18. $CE = DF$          $\rightarrow$  $x = 4$
    $5x - 6 = 30 - 4x$  ---⌐  $CE = DF = 5(4) - 6 = 14$

19. $PQ = RS$          $\rightarrow$  $x = 3$
    $x + 4 = 5x - 8$  ---⌐  perimeter $= 4PQ = 4(7) = 28$

20. Statements (Reasons)
    1. $ABCD$ is a rhombus. (Given)
    2. $ABCD$ is a parallelogram, $\overline{AB} \cong \overline{BC} \cong \overline{CD} \cong \overline{DA}$ (Def. of rhombus)
    3. $\overline{BP} \cong \overline{DP}$ (Diagonals of a ▱ bisect each other. )
    4. $\overline{AP} \cong \overline{AP}$ (Reflexive Property)
    5. $\triangle APB \cong \triangle APD$ (SSS)
    6. $\angle APB \cong \angle APD$ (CPCTC)
    7. $\angle APB$ & $\angle APD$ are a linear pair. (Def. of linear pair)
    8. $\overline{AC} \perp \overline{BD}$ (Two lines intersecting to form a linear pair of congruent angles are perpendicular. See Theorem 31.3.)

21. Statements (Reasons)
    1. $ABCD$ is a parallelogram, $\overline{AC} \perp \overline{BD}$ (Given)
    2. $\angle APB$ and $\angle APD$ are right angles. (Def. of $\perp$)
    3. $\angle APB \cong \angle APD$ (All right angles are congruent.)
    4. $\overline{BP} \cong \overline{DP}$ (Diagonals of a ▱ bisect each other. )
    5. $\overline{AP} \cong \overline{AP}$ (Reflexive Property)
    6. $\triangle APB \cong \triangle APD$ (SAS)
    7. $\overline{AB} \cong \overline{AD}$ (CPCTC)
    8. $\overline{AB} \cong \overline{CD}, \overline{AD} \cong \overline{BC}$ (Opposite sides of a ▱ are congruent.)
    9. $\overline{AB} \cong \overline{BC} \cong \overline{CD} \cong \overline{DA}$ (Transitive Property)
    10. $ABCD$ is a rhombus. (Def. of rhombus)

22. Statements (Reasons)
    1. $ABCD$ is a rhombus. (Given)
    2. $\overline{AB} \cong \overline{BC} \cong \overline{CD} \cong \overline{DA}$ (Def. of rhombus)
    3. $\overline{AC} \cong \overline{AC}$ (Reflexive Property)
    4. $\triangle ABC \cong \triangle ADC$ (SSS)
    5. $\angle BAC \cong \angle DAC, \angle BCA \cong \angle DCA$ (CPCTC)
    6. $\overline{AC}$ bisects $\angle BAD$ and $\angle BCD$. (Def. of bisect)
    7. Similarly, $\overline{BD}$ bisects $\angle ABC$ and $\angle ADC$.

23. Statements (Reasons)
    1. $ABCD$ is a ▱, $\overline{AC}$ bisects $\angle BAD$ & $\angle BCD$. (Given)
    2. $\angle BAC \cong \angle DAC, \angle BCA \cong \angle DCA$ (Def. of bisect)
    3. $\overline{AC} \cong \overline{AC}$ (Reflexive Property)
    4. $\triangle ABC \cong \triangle ADC$ (ASA)
    5. $\overline{AB} \cong \overline{AD}, \overline{BC} \cong \overline{DC}$ (CPCTC)
    6. $\overline{AB} \cong \overline{CD}, \overline{AD} \cong \overline{BC}$ (Opposite sides of a ▱ are congruent.)
    7. $\overline{AB} \cong \overline{BC} \cong \overline{CD} \cong \overline{DA}$ (Transitive Property)
    8. $ABCD$ is a rhombus. (Def. of rhombus)

**24.** Statements (Reasons)

1. $EFGH$ is a rectangle. (Given)
2. $\angle EFG$ and $\angle FEH$ are right angles. (Def. of rectangle)
3. $\angle EFG \cong \angle FEH$ (All right angles are congruent.)
4. $\overline{FG} \cong \overline{EH}$ (Opposite sides of a $\square$ are congruent.)
5. $\overline{EF} \cong \overline{FE}$ (Reflexive Property)
6. $\triangle EFG \cong \triangle FEH$ (SAS)
7. $\overline{EG} \cong \overline{FH}$ (CPCTC)

**25.** Statements (Reasons)

1. $EFGH$ is a parallelogram, $\overline{EG} \cong \overline{FH}$ (Given)
2. $\overline{FG} \cong \overline{EH}$ (Opposite sides of a $\square$ are congruent.)
3. $\overline{EF} \cong \overline{FE}$ (Reflexive Property)
4. $\triangle EFG \cong \triangle FEH$ (SSS)
5. $\angle EFG \cong \angle FEH$ (CPCTC)
6. $\angle EFG \cong \angle GHE$, $\angle FEH \cong \angle HGF$ (Opposite angles of a $\square$ are congruent.)
7. $\angle EFG \cong \angle GHE \cong \angle FEH \cong \angle HGF$ (Transitive Property)
8. $EFGH$ is a rectangle. (Def. of rectangle)

**26.** B maps $P$ to $(-1, 2)$.
A, C, and D map $P$ to $(-2, 1)$.

# LESSON 59

**1.** Thm 59.1: If $\overline{MN}$ is the midsegment of trapezoid $ABCD$, then $\overline{MN} \parallel \overline{AB} \parallel \overline{DC}$ and $MN = (AB + DC)/2$.

Thm 59.2: Trapezoid $EFGH$ is isosceles if and only if $\angle E \cong \angle H$ and $\angle F \cong \angle G$.

Thm 59.3: Trapezoid $EFGH$ is isosceles if and only if $\overline{EG} \cong \overline{FG}$.

Thm 59.4: I If $KLMN$ is a kite and $\overline{KL} \cong \overline{KN}$, then $\angle L \cong \angle N$.

Thm 59.5: I If $KLMN$ is a kite and $\overline{KL} \cong \overline{KN}$, then $\overline{KM}$ bisects $\angle K$ and $\angle M$.

Thm 59.6: If $KLMN$ is a kite, then $\overline{KM} \perp \overline{LN}$.

**2.** $MN = (PQ + RS)/2$     $x = 3$
$x + 4 = (2x - 1 + 3x)/2$     $PQ = 2(3) - 1 = 5$
$2(x + 4) = 2x - 1 + 3x$     $RS = 3(3) = 9$

**3.** $m\angle P = m\angle Q = 110°$
$m\angle R = m\angle S = 180 - 110 = 70°$

**4.** Non-vertex angles are congruent, so $m\angle 1 = 106°$.
Vertex angles are bisected by a diagonal, so $m\angle 2 = 30°$.
A triangle has 180°, so $m\angle 3 = 180 - 106 - m\angle 2 = 44°$.
A triangle has 180°, so $m\angle 4 = 180 - 30 - m\angle 1 = 44°$.

You could say that $m\angle 4 = m\angle 3 = 44°$ because vertex angles are bisected by a diagonal.

**5.** Diagonals are perpendicular, so $m\angle 1 = 90°$.
A triangle has 180°, so $m\angle 2 = 180 - 62 - m\angle 1 = 28°$.
Vertex angles are bisected by a diagonal, so $m\angle 3 = 42°$.
A triangle has 180°, so $m\angle 4 = 180 - 90 - m\angle 3 = 48°$.
Vertex angles are bisected by a diagonal, so $m\angle 5 = m\angle 2 = 28°$.
A triangle has 180°, so $m\angle 6 = 180 - 90 - m\angle 5 = 62°$.

**6.** $x = (14 + 18)/2$    $\rightarrow$ $y = 80$
$x = 16$    $z = 180 - y = 100$

**7.** $24 = (x + 28)/2$    $\rightarrow$ $y = 83$
$x = 20$    $z = 180 - 83 = 97$

**8.** $12 = (7x + 2 + 5x - 2)/2$   $\rightarrow$ $y = 180 - 110 = 70$
$x = 2$    $z = 110$

**9.** Non-vertex angles are congruent, so $m\angle 1 = m\angle 2$.
A quadrilateral has 360°, so $m\angle 1 + m\angle 2 + 91 + 63 = m\angle 1 + m\angle 1 + 91 + 63 = 360$ and $m\angle 1 = m\angle 2 = 103°$.

**10.** Non-vertex angles are congruent, so $m\angle 1 = 113°$.
Vertex angles are bisected by a diagonal, so $m\angle 2 = 27°$.
A triangle has 180°, so $m\angle 3 = 180 - 113 - m\angle 2 = 40°$.
A triangle has 180°, so $m\angle 4 = 180 - 27 - m\angle 1 = 40°$.

**11.** Diagonals are perpendicular, so $m\angle 1 = 90°$.
A triangle has 180°, so $m\angle 2 = 180 - 40 - m\angle 1 = 50°$.
A triangle has 180°, so $m\angle 3 = 180 - 90 - 26 = 64°$.
Vertex angles are bisected by a diagonal, so $m\angle 4 = m\angle 2 = 50°$ and $m\angle 5 = m\angle 3 = 64°$.
A triangle has 180°, so $m\angle 6 = 180 - 90 - m\angle 4 = 40°$.

**12.** Statements (Reasons)

1. trapezoid $ABCD$, $\overline{BA} \cong \overline{CD}$ (Given)
2. $\overline{BC} \parallel \overline{AD}$ (Def. of trapezoid)
3. Draw $\overline{CK}$ such that $\overline{BA} \parallel \overline{CK}$. (Construction)
4. $ABCK$ is a parallelogram. (Def. of parallelogram)
5. $\overline{BA} \cong \overline{CK}$ (Opposite sides of a $\square$ are congruent.)
6. $\overline{CK} \cong \overline{CD}$ (Transitive Property, Steps 1 and 5)
7. $\angle CKD \cong \angle D$ (Base Angles Theorem [40.1].)
8. $\angle A \cong \angle CKD$ (Corresponding $\angle$s on $\parallel$ lines are $\cong$.)
9. $\angle A \cong \angle D$ (Transitive Property)
10. $\angle B$ and $\angle A$ are supplementary; $\angle C$ and $\angle D$ are supplementary. (Consecutive interior $\angle$s on $\parallel$ lines are supplementary.)
11. $\angle B \cong \angle C$ (Angles supplementary to congruent angles are congruent. See Theorem 29.3.)

13. Statements (Reasons)
    1. trapezoid $ABCD$, $\angle A \cong \angle D$ (Given)
    2. $\overline{BC} \parallel \overline{AD}$ (Def. of trapezoid)
    3. Draw $\overline{CK}$ such that $\overline{BA} \parallel \overline{CK}$. (Construction)
    4. $\angle A \cong \angle CKD$ (Corresponding $\angle$s on $\parallel$ lines are $\cong$.)
    5. $\angle CKD \cong \angle D$ (Transitive Property, Steps 1 and 4)
    6. $\overline{CK} \cong \overline{CD}$ (Base Angles Converse [40.2])
    7. $ABCK$ is a parallelogram. (Def. of parallelogram)
    8. $\overline{BA} \cong \overline{CK}$ (Opposite sides of a ▱ are congruent.)
    9. $\overline{BA} \cong \overline{CD}$ (Transitive Property, Steps 6 and 8)

14. Statements (Reasons)
    1. trapezoid $ABCD$, $\overline{BA} \cong \overline{CD}$ (Given)
    2. $\angle BAD \cong \angle CDA$ (Base angles of an isosceles trapezoid are congruent. See Theorem 59.2.)
    3. $\overline{AD} \cong \overline{AD}$ (Reflexive Property)
    4. $\triangle BAD \cong \triangle CDA$ (SAS)
    5. $\overline{BD} \cong \overline{CA}$ (CPCTC)

15. Statements (Reasons)
    1. trapezoid $ABCD$, $\overline{BD} \cong \overline{CA}$ (Given)
    2. $\overline{BC} \parallel \overline{AD}$ (Def. of trapezoid)
    3. Draw $\overline{CK}$ such that $\overline{CK} \parallel \overline{BD}$ and $K$ is on $\overleftrightarrow{AD}$. (Construction)
    4. $BCKD$ is a parallelogram. (Def. of parallelogram)
    5. $\overline{BD} \cong \overline{CK}$ (Opposite sides of a ▱ are congruent.)
    6. $\overline{CA} \cong \overline{CK}$ (Transitive Property, Steps 1 and 5)
    7. $\angle CAD \cong \angle K$ (Base Angles Theorem [40.1].)
    8. $\angle K \cong \angle BDA$ (Corresponding $\angle$s on $\parallel$ lines are $\cong$.)
    9. $\angle BDA \cong \angle CAD$ (Transitive Property, Steps 7 and 8)
    10. $\overline{AD} \cong \overline{AD}$ (Reflexive Property)
    11. $\triangle BDA \cong \triangle CAD$ (SAS, Steps 1, 9, and 10)
    12. $\overline{BA} \cong \overline{CD}$ (CPCTC)

16. $m\angle Z = 180 - 55 - 60 = 65°$
    $m\angle X < m\angle Y < m\angle Z$, so $YZ < XZ < XY$.

## LESSON 60 ···········································

1. A, B, D, F

2. 2. Opposite sides of a parallelogram are congruent.
   4. Opposite sides of a parallelogram are congruent.
   5. Transitive Property

3. 2. Def. of isosceles trapezoid
   3. Base angles of an isosceles trapezoid are congruent.
   4. Reflexive Property
   5. SAS

4. 2. If alternate interior $\angle$s are $\cong$, then lines are parallel.
   4. If alternate interior $\angle$s are $\cong$, then lines are parallel.
   5. Def. of parallelogram

5. 2. CPCTC
   4. CPCTC
   5. A quadrilateral is a parallelogram if opposite angles are congruent.

6. square          7. rhombus

8. rhombus          9. rectangle

10. 2. Opposite angles of a parallelogram are congruent.
    4. Opposite angles of a parallelogram are congruent.
    5. Transitive Property

11. 2. A midsegment is parallel to the third side.
    4. A midsegment is parallel to the third side.
    5. Def. of parallelogram

12. *Answer formats may vary.*
    Statements (Reasons)
    1. a. trapezoid $PQRS$ with midsegment $\overline{MN}$ (Given)
       b. $M$ and $N$ are midpoints. (Def. of midsegment)
       c. $\overline{QN} \cong \overline{NR}$ (Def. of midpoint)
       d. $\overline{PQ} \parallel \overline{ST}$ (Def. of trapezoid)
       e. $\angle PQN \cong \angle TRN$, $\angle QPN \cong \angle RTN$ (Alternate interior $\angle$s on parallel lines are congruent.)
       f. $\triangle PQN \cong \triangle TRN$ (AAS)
    2. a. $\overline{PN} \cong \overline{NT}$ (CPCTC, Step 1f)
       b. $N$ is the midpoint of $\overline{PT}$. (Def. of midpoint)
       c. $\overline{MN}$ is a midsegment of $\triangle PST$. (Def. of midsegment)
    3. a. $\overline{MN} \parallel \overline{ST}$ (A midsegment is parallel to the third side. See Theorem 46.1.)
       b. $\overline{MN} \parallel \overline{SR} \parallel \overline{PQ}$ (Transitive Property, Steps 1d and 3a)
    4. a. $\overline{PQ} \cong \overline{RT}$ (CPCTC, Step 1f)
       b. $QP = RT$ (Def. of congruent segments)
       c. $MN = ST/2$ (A midsegment is half the length of the third side. See Theorem 46.1.)
       d. $ST = SR + RT$ (Segment Addition Postulate)
       e. $ST = SR + PQ$ (Substitution, Steps 4b & 4d)
       f. $MN = (SR + PQ)/2$ (Substitution)

13. Statements (Reasons)
    1. kite $KLMN$ (Given)
    2. $\overline{KL} \cong \overline{KN}, \overline{ML} \cong \overline{MN}$ (Def. of kite)
    3. $\overline{KM} \cong \overline{KM}$ (Reflexive Property)
    4. $\triangle KLM \cong \triangle KNM$ (SSS)
    5. $\angle L \cong \angle N, \angle LKM \cong \angle NKM, \angle LMK \cong \angle NMK$ (CPCTC)

14. Statements (Reasons)
    1. kite $KLMN$ (Given)
    2. $\overline{KL} \cong \overline{KN}, \overline{ML} \cong \overline{MN}$ (Def. of kite)
    3. $\overline{KM} \cong \overline{KM}$ (Reflexive Property)
    4. $\triangle KLM \cong \triangle KNM$ (SSS)
    5. $\angle LKP \cong \angle NKP$ (CPCTC)
    6. $\overline{KP} \cong \overline{KP}$ (Reflexive Property)
    7. $\triangle LKP \cong \triangle NKP$ (SAS, Steps 2, 5, and 6)
    8. $\overline{LP} \cong \overline{NP}, \angle LPK \cong \angle NPK$ (CPCTC)
    9. $\angle LPK$ & $\angle NPK$ are a linear pair. (Def. of linear pair)
    10. $\overline{KM} \perp \overline{LN}$ (Two lines intersecting to form a linear pair of congruent angles are perpendicular. See Theorem 31.3.)

15. SAS                    16. $\overline{AB} \cong \overline{AC}$

## LESSON 61

1. Opposite sides are congruent, so $a = 16$ and $b = 10$.
   Consecutive angles are supplementary, so $c = e = 110$.
   Opposite angles are congruent, so $d = 70$.

2. Opposite sides are congruent, so $13 = 4a - 3$ and $a = 4$.
   Consecutive angles are supplementary, $b = 108$.

3. Diagonals bisect each other, so $a = 8$ and $b = 9$.

4. Opposite sides are congruent, so $3a = a + 6$ and $a = 3$.
   Opposite sides are parallel, so $b = 49$.

5. yes; Opposite sides are parallel.

6. yes; Opposite angles are congruent. The fourth angle is $360 - 80 - 80 - 100 = 100$.

7. yes; Opposite sides are congruent.

8. no; There is not enough information.

9. no; There is not enough information.

10. yes; Diagonals bisect each other.

11. Diagonals bisect opposite angles, so $m\angle 1 = 62°$.
    Alt. interior $\angle$s are congruent, so $m\angle 2 = 62°$.
    Alt. interior $\angle$s are congruent, so $m\angle 3 = m\angle 1 = 62°$.
    A triangle has 180°, so $m\angle 4 = 180 - m\angle 3 - 62 = 56°$.
    Opposite angles are congruent, so $m\angle 5 = m\angle 4 = 56°$.

12. Opposite angles are congruent, so $m\angle 1 = 118°$.
    Base $\angle$s of an isosceles triangle are $\cong$, so $m\angle 2 = m\angle 3$.
    A triangle has 180°, so $118 + m\angle 2 + m\angle 3 = 180$ and $m\angle 2 = m\angle 3 = 31°$.
    Diagonals bisect opposite angles, so $m\angle 4 = m\angle 3 = 31°$.

13. Diagonals bisect opposite angles, so $m\angle 1 = 60°$.
    Diagonals are perpendicular, so $m\angle 2 = 90°$.
    Alt. interior $\angle$s are congruent, so $m\angle 3 = 60°$.
    Diagonals bisect opposite angles, so $m\angle 4 = m\angle 3 = 60°$.
    A triangle has 180°, so $m\angle 5 = 180 - 90 - m\angle 3 = 30°$.

14. Diagonals are perpendicular, so $m\angle 1 = 90°$.
    A triangle has 180°, so $m\angle 2 = 180 - 57 - m\angle 1 = 33°$.
    Diagonals bisect opposite angles, so $m\angle 3 = 57°$.
    Alt. interior $\angle$s are congruent, so $m\angle 4 = m\angle 2 = 33°$.
    Alt. interior $\angle$s are congruent, so $m\angle 5 = 57°$.

15. The midsegment is half the sum of the bases, so $x = (7 + 9)/2 = 8$.
    Base angles are congruent, so $y = 80$.
    $y$ and $z$ are supplementary, so $z = 180 - y = 100$.

16. The midsegment is half the sum of the bases, so $12 = (14 + x)/2$ and $x = 10$.
    97° and $y$ are supplementary, so $y = 180 - 97 = 83$.
    Base angles are congruent, so $z = y = 83$.

17. Vertex angles are bisected by a diagonal, so $m\angle 1 = 33°$ and $m\angle 2 = 47°$.
    A triangle has 180°, so $m\angle 3 = 180 - 33 - 47 = 100°$.
    Non-vertex angles are congruent, so $m\angle 4 = m\angle 3 = 100°$.

18. Base angles of an isosceles triangle are congruent, so $m\angle 1 = 31°$ and $m\angle 2 = 45°$.
    A triangle has 180°, so $m\angle 3 = 180 - 31 - m\angle 1 = 118°$.
    A triangle has 180°, so $m\angle 4 = 180 - 45 - m\angle 2 = 90°$.

19. parallelogram              20. rhombus

21. isosceles trapezoid        22. rhombus

23. 2. Def. of parallelogram
    3. Alternate interior $\angle$s on parallel lines are $\cong$.
    4. Opposite sides of a parallelogram are congruent.
    5. ASA
    6. CPCTC

24. the line itself

25. $\triangle ABC$ is an isosceles triangle with $\overline{AB} \cong \overline{AC}$.

26. perimeter of $\triangle DEF = (1/2)$(perimeter of $\triangle ABC$)

## LESSON 62

1. Cross multiply: $8x = 5(12)$
   Divide both sides by 8: $x = 15/2$

2. Corresponding sides: $\overline{AB} \cong \overline{DE}, \overline{BC} \cong \overline{EF}, \overline{AC} \cong \overline{DF}$
   Corresponding angles: $\angle A \cong \angle D, \angle B \cong \angle E, \angle C \cong \angle F$

3. yes; Angles are congruent, and $18/6 = 24/8 = 27/9$.

4. no; Angles are congruent, but $6/20 \neq 12/36$

5. Corresponding angles: $\angle L \cong \angle S, \angle M \cong \angle T, \angle N \cong \angle U$
   Corresponding sides: $LM/ST = MN/TU = LN/SU$

6. Set up. $\rightarrow$ Cross multiply. $\rightarrow$ Solve.

   $\dfrac{9}{15} = \dfrac{a}{20}$ $\rightarrow$ $15a = 9(20)$ $\rightarrow$ $a = 12$

   $\dfrac{9}{15} = \dfrac{15}{b}$ $\rightarrow$ $9b = 15(15)$ $\rightarrow$ $b = 25$

7. $\dfrac{a}{16} = \dfrac{5}{20}$ $\rightarrow$ $20a = 16(5)$ $\rightarrow$ $a = 4$

   $\dfrac{2}{b} = \dfrac{5}{20}$ $\rightarrow$ $5b = 2(20)$ $\rightarrow$ $b = 8$

8. no; Angles are congruent, but $9/18 = 6/12 \neq 7/15$

9. yes; Angles are congruent, and $10/25 = 16/40 = 2/5$.

10. $\dfrac{50}{10} = \dfrac{a}{8}$ $\rightarrow$ $10a = 50(8)$ $\rightarrow$ $a = 40$

    $\dfrac{50}{10} = \dfrac{30}{b}$ $\rightarrow$ $50b = 10(30)$ $\rightarrow$ $b = 6$

11. $\dfrac{18}{12} = \dfrac{24}{a}$ $\rightarrow$ $18a = 12(24)$ $\rightarrow$ $a = 16$

    $\dfrac{18}{12} = \dfrac{27}{b}$ $\rightarrow$ $18b = 12(27)$ $\rightarrow$ $b = 18$

12. $\dfrac{4}{16} = \dfrac{a}{20}$ $\rightarrow$ $16a = 4(20)$ $\rightarrow$ $a = 5$

    $\dfrac{4}{16} = \dfrac{2}{b}$ $\rightarrow$ $4b = 16(2)$ $\rightarrow$ $b = 8$

13. $\dfrac{24}{40} = \dfrac{a}{60}$ $\rightarrow$ $40a = 24(60)$ $\rightarrow$ $a = 36$

    $\dfrac{24}{40} = \dfrac{30}{b}$ $\rightarrow$ $24b = 40(30)$ $\rightarrow$ $b = 50$

14. Let $x$ be the width of rectangle $Q$.
    $$\frac{\text{width of } P}{\text{width of } Q} = \frac{\text{length of } P}{\text{length of } Q}$$

    $\dfrac{9}{x} \quad \dfrac{15}{20}$ $\rightarrow$ $15x = 9(20)$ $\rightarrow$ $x = 12$

    Rectangle $Q$ is 12 inches wide and 20 inches long. So, the perimeter is $12 + 12 + 20 + 20 = 64$ inches.

15. Let $x$ and $y$ be the other two sides of $\triangle XYZ$. The length of the smallest side of $\triangle LMN$ is 16 cm.

    $\dfrac{16}{24} = \dfrac{20}{x}$ $\rightarrow$ $16x = 24(20)$ $\rightarrow$ $x = 30$

    $\dfrac{16}{24} = \dfrac{24}{y}$ $\rightarrow$ $16y = 24(24)$ $\rightarrow$ $y = 36$

    $\triangle XYZ$ has side lengths 24cm, 30 cm, and 36. So, the perimeter is $24 + 30 + 36 = 90$ cm.

16. A) true      B) false      C) false      D) true
    E) false      F) false      G) false      H) true

    *Counterexamples may vary. Sample(s):*
    B) a right triangle with legs 1 cm and 2 cm
       a right triangle with legs 2 cm and 3 cm

    C) a rectangle with width 1 cm and length 2 cm
       a rectangle with width 2 cm and length 3 cm

    E) a parallelogram that is a rectangle
       a parallelogram that is not a rectangle

    F) an equilateral triangle
       an isosceles triangle with angles 50°, 65° and 65°

    G) a rhombus that is a square
       a rhombus that is not a square

17. $m\angle C = 75°$
    $90 + 75 + 3x = 180$
    $x = 5$

18. $m\angle F = 52°$
    $71 + 52 + (8x + 1) = 180$
    $x = 7$

## LESSON 63

1. 2. Alternate interior $\angle$s on parallel lines are $\cong$.
   3. Reflexive Property
   4. ASA

2. If $\angle A \cong \angle D$ and $\angle B \cong \angle E$, then $\triangle ABC \sim \triangle DEF$.

3. $\angle A \cong \angle C$ because their measures are equal.
   $\angle ABE \cong \angle CBD$ because all right angles are congruent.
   So, $\triangle ABE \sim \triangle CBD$ by AA.

4. $m\angle DFE = 180 - 136 = 44°$
   $\angle DEF \cong \angle H$ because their measures are equal.
   $\angle D \cong \angle D$ by the Reflexive Property.
   So, $\triangle DEF \sim \triangle DGH$ by AA.

5.  $m\angle R = 180 - 90 - 37 = 53°$

    $\angle R \cong \angle U$ because their measures are equal.

    $\angle Q \cong \angle T$ because all right angles are congruent.

    So, $\triangle PQR \sim \triangle STU$ by AA.

6.  $\dfrac{AB}{CB} = \dfrac{BE}{BD}$

    $\dfrac{70}{42} = \dfrac{60}{DB}$

    $70DB = 42(60)$

    $DB = 36$

7.  $\dfrac{DE}{DG} = \dfrac{DE}{DE + EG} = \dfrac{EF}{GH}$

    $\dfrac{30}{30 + 45} = \dfrac{40}{GH}$

    $30GH = 40(30 + 45)$

    $GH = 100$

8.  2. Corresponding ∠s on parallel lines are ≅.
    3. Reflexive Property

9.  2. All right angles are congruent.
    4. AA

10. $\angle A \cong \angle C$ because $m\angle C = 180 - 90 - 55 = 35°$.

    $\angle ABE \cong \angle CBD$ because all right angles are congruent.

    So, $\triangle ABE \sim \triangle CBD$ by AA.

11. $\angle G \cong \angle G$ by the Reflexive Property.

    $\angle E \cong \angle HFG$ because $m\angle HFG = 180 - 130 = 50°$.

    So, $\triangle DEG \sim \triangle HFG$ by AA.

12. $m\angle T = 180 - 88 - 52 = 40°$

    $m\angle E = 180 - 88 - 38 = 54°$

    So, the triangles are not similar.

13. $\angle P \cong \angle P$ by the Reflexive Property.

    $\angle R \cong \angle PTQ$ because $m\angle PTQ = 180 - 142 = 38°$.

    So, $\triangle PRS \sim \triangle PTQ$ by AA.

14. $\angle B \cong \angle B$ by the Reflexive Property.

    $\angle BAC \cong \angle D$ because $m\angle BAC = 180 - 37 - 93 = 50°$.

    So, $\triangle BAC \sim \triangle BDA$ by AA.

15. In $\triangle IJH$, $m\angle IHJ = 180 - 43 - 92 = 45°$

    In $\triangle IHK$, $m\angle IHK = 180 - 43 - 43 = 94°$

    So, the triangles are not similar.

16. Statements (Reasons)
    1. midsegment $\overline{DE}$ (Given)
    2. $\overline{DE} \parallel \overline{BC}$ (Triangle Midsegment Theorem [46.1])
    3. $\angle ADE \cong \angle B$ (Corresponding ∠s on ∥ lines are ≅.)
    4. $\angle A \cong \angle A$ (Reflexive Property)
    5. $\triangle ADE \sim \triangle ABE$ (AA)

17. Statements (Reasons)
    1. trapezoid $WXYZ$ with bases $\overline{WX}$ and $\overline{ZY}$ (Given)
    2. $\overline{WX} \parallel \overline{ZY}$ (Def. of trapezoid)
    3. $\angle PWX \cong \angle PYZ$, $\angle PXW \cong \angle PZY$ (Alternate interior ∠s on ∥ lines are ≅.)
    4. $\triangle PWX \sim \triangle PYZ$ (AA)

18. A midsegment is half the length of the third side.

    $BC = 2DE = 2(15) = 30$

    $E$ is the midpoint of $\overline{AC}$.

    $EC = AE = 20$

    $AC = 2AE = 2(20) = 40$

19. $\dfrac{WX}{YZ} = \dfrac{PX}{PZ}$

    $\dfrac{25}{40} = \dfrac{15}{PZ}$

    $\rightarrow$  $25PZ = 40(15)$

    $PZ = 24$

    $XZ = PX + PZ$

    $= 15 + 24 = 39$

20. eq1 + eq2

    $6x = 12$

    $x = 2$

    $\rightarrow$  Use eq1 to find $y$.

    $2 + y = 5$

    $y = 3$

21. interior angle sum = $180(n - 2) = 180(12 - 2) = 1800°$

    exterior angle sum of any polygon = $360°$

## LESSON 64

1.  $15x = 6(20)$

    $x = 8$

2.  $10(x + 9) = 7(15)$

    $x = 3/2$

3.  2. Opposite sides of a parallelogram are congruent.
    3. Reflexive Property
    4. SSS

4.  2. A midsegment is parallel to the third side.
    3. Corresponding ∠s on parallel lines are ≅.
    4. Reflexive Property
    5. AA

5.  If $\dfrac{AB}{DE} = \dfrac{BC}{EF} = \dfrac{AC}{DF}$, then $\triangle ABC \sim \triangle DEF$.

6.  $DC/DB = 8/(8 + 8) = 8/16 = 1/2$

    $DE/DA = 9/(9 + 9) = 9/18 = 1/2$

    $CE/BA = 7/14 = 1/2$

    So, $\triangle DCE \sim \triangle DBA$ by SSS.

7.  $DE/XY = 18/12 = 3/2$

    $EF/YZ = 10/8 = 5/4$

    $DF/XZ = 15/10 = 3/2$

    So, the triangles are not similar.

8.  $FG/PQ = 18/12 = 3/2$

    $GH/QR = 15/10 = 3/2$

    $FH/PR = 21/14 = 3/2$

    So, $\triangle FGH \sim \triangle PQR$ by SSS.

9.  Set up.  $\rightarrow$  Cross multiply.  $\rightarrow$  Solve.

    $\dfrac{27}{18} = \dfrac{21}{a}$  $\rightarrow$  $27a = 18(21)$  $\rightarrow$  $a = 14$

    $\dfrac{27}{9} = \dfrac{18}{b}$  $\rightarrow$  $27b = 9(18)$  $\rightarrow$  $b = 6$

10. $AB/DE = 9/30 = 3/10$
    $BC/EF = 12/40 = 3/10$
    $AC/DF = 20/50 = 2/5$
    So, the triangles are not similar.

11. $\angle P \cong \angle P$ by the Reflexive Property.
    $\angle PQT \cong \angle S$ because $m\angle PQT = 180 - 143 = 37°$.
    So, $\triangle PQT \sim \triangle PSR$ by AA.

12. $CD/CE = 16/(16 + 12) = 16/28 = 4/7$
    $CG/CF = 18/(18 + 14) = 18/32 = 9/16$
    $DG/EF = 20/35 = 4/7$
    So, the triangles are not similar.

13. $\angle B \cong \angle B$ by the Reflexive Property.
    $\angle BAC \cong \angle D$ because $m\angle BAC = 180 - 37 - 93 = 50°$.
    So, $\triangle BAC \sim \triangle BDA$ by AA.

14. $m\angle S = 180 - 87 - 52 = 41°$
    $m\angle X = 180 - 87 - 40 = 53°$
    So, the triangles are not similar.

15. $OP/RS = 28/21 = 4/3$
    $PQ/SQ = 24/18 = 4/3$
    $OQ/RQ = 16/12 = 4/3$
    So, $\triangle OPQ \sim \triangle RSQ$ by SSS.

16. $\dfrac{15}{10} = \dfrac{18}{2a}$ $\rightarrow$ $15(2a) = 10(18)$ $\rightarrow$ $a = 6$

    $\dfrac{15}{10} = \dfrac{12}{b + 6}$ $\rightarrow$ $15(b + 6) = 10(12)$ $\rightarrow$ $b = 2$

17. $\dfrac{6}{18} = \dfrac{14}{14 + a}$ $\rightarrow$ $6(14 + a) = 18(14)$ $\rightarrow$ $a = 28$

    $\dfrac{6}{18} = \dfrac{12}{12 + b}$ $\rightarrow$ $6(12 + b) = 18(12)$ $\rightarrow$ $b = 24$

18. The left angle in the smaller triangle must be 51°.
    $51 + 39 + (4a + 6) = 180$
    $a = 21$

19. *Answer formats may vary.*
    Statements (Reasons)
    1. right $\triangle ABC$ with altitude $\overline{BD}$ (Given)
    2. $\angle A \cong \angle A$ (Reflexive Property)
    3. $\angle ABC \cong \angle ADB$ (All right angles are congruent.)
    4. $\triangle ABC \sim \triangle ADB$ (AA)
    5. $\angle C \cong \angle C$ (Reflexive Property)
    5. $\angle ABC \cong \angle BDC$ (All right angles are congruent.)
    6. $\triangle ABC \sim \triangle BDC$ (AA)
    7. $\triangle ABC \sim \triangle ADB \sim \triangle BDC$ (Transitive Property)

20. $\dfrac{AD}{BD} = \dfrac{BD}{CD}$ $\rightarrow$ $\dfrac{AD}{12} = \dfrac{12}{6}$ $\rightarrow$ $\begin{array}{l} 6AD = 12(12) \\ AD = 24 \end{array}$

21. centroid

22. A centroid divides a median in the ratio 2:1.
    $BP = (2/3)BE = (2/3)(15) = 10$
    $PE = (1/3)BE = (1/3)(15) = 5$

23. A midsegment is half the length of the third side.
    $DE = BC/2 = 5$

## LESSON 65

1. $18(x + 3) = 21(42)$
   $x = 46$

2. $6(x + 3) = 7(x + 4)$
   $x = -10$

3. 2. All right angles are congruent.
   3. Reflexive Property
   4. AA

4. $\angle P \cong \angle S$ because their measures are equal.
   $\angle OQP \cong \angle RQS$ because vertical angles are congruent.
   So, $\triangle OQP \sim \triangle RQS$ by AA.

5. $PQ/PS = 14/(14 + 7) = 14/21 = 2/3$
   $PR/PT = 16/(16 + 8) = 16/24 = 2/3$
   $QR/ST = 10/15 = 2/3$
   So, $\triangle PQR \sim \triangle PST$ by SSS.

6. If $\angle B \cong \angle E$ and $\dfrac{AB}{DE} = \dfrac{BC}{EF}$, then $\triangle ABC \sim \triangle DEF$.

7. $\angle S \cong \angle S$ by the Reflexive Property.
   $ST/SU = 36/(36 + 27) = 36/63 = 4/7$
   $SW/SV = 32/(32 + 24) = 32/56 = 4/7$
   So, $\triangle STW \sim \triangle SUV$ by SAS.

8. no; There is not enough information.

9. $\angle Y \cong \angle T$ because $m\angle Y = 180 - 53 - 40 = 87°$.
   $XY/ST = 20/8 = 5/2$
   $YZ/TU = 25/10 = 5/2$
   So, $\triangle XYZ \sim \triangle STU$ by SAS.

10. $m\angle ECD = 180 - 90 - 52 = 38°$
    $m\angle ACB = 180 - 104 - m\angle ECD = 38°$
    $\angle ACB \cong \angle ECD$ because their measures are equal.
    $\angle B \cong \angle D$ because all right angles are congruent.
    So, $\triangle ABC \sim \triangle EDC$ by AA.

11. $PO/PM = 14/(14 + 7) = 14/21 = 2/3$
    $PN/PL = 16/(16 + 8) = 16/24 = 2/3$
    $\angle P \cong \angle P$ by the Reflexive Property.
    So, $\triangle PON \sim \triangle PML$ by SAS.

12. $m\angle E = 180 - 121 = 59°$
    $m\angle D = 180 - 44 - m\angle E = 77°$
    $m\angle G = 180 - 44 - 76 = 60°$
    So, the triangles are not similar.

13. $\angle B \cong \angle B$ by the Reflexive Property.

$BC/BD = 18/(18 + 12) = 18/30 = 3/5$

$BF/BE = 21/(21 + 14) = 21/35 = 3/5$

So, $\triangle BCF \sim \triangle BDE$ by SAS.

14. $\angle KCL \cong \angle OCN$ because vertical angles are congruent.

$KC/OC = 48/56 = 6/7$

$LC/NL = 40/50 = 4/5$

So, the triangles are not similar.

15. $DE/XY = 9/6 = 3/2$

$EF/YZ = 12/8 = 3/2$

$DF/XZ = 15/10 = 3/2$

So, $\triangle DEF \sim \triangle XYZ$ by SSS.

16. The bottom left angle must be 38°.

$78 + 38 + (5a + 9) = 180$

$a = 11$

17. $\dfrac{16}{(16 + 8)} = \dfrac{10}{a}$ → $16a = 10(16 + 8)$ → $a = 15$

$\dfrac{16}{(16 + 8)} = \dfrac{b}{b + 7}$ → $16(b + 7) = b(16 + 8)$ → $b = 14$

18. $\dfrac{12}{18} = \dfrac{a}{a + 15}$ → $18a = 12(a + 15)$ → $a = 30$

$\dfrac{12}{18} = \dfrac{24}{24 + b}$ → $12(24 + b) = 18(24)$ → $b = 12$

19. $\triangle LMN \sim \triangle PQR$ by AA because $\angle L \cong \angle P$ and $\angle N \cong \angle R$ as corresponding angles.

$\triangle LMN \sim \triangle PXN$ by AA because $\angle L \cong \angle P$ as corresponding angles and $\angle N \cong \angle N$ by the Reflexive Property.

$\triangle PXN \sim \triangle PQR$ by AA because $\angle P \cong \angle P$ by the Reflexive Property and $\angle N \cong \angle R$ as corresponding angles.

Therefore, the three triangles are similar to each other.

20. Corresponding angles are congruent.

$m\angle M = 180 - m\angle L - m\angle XNP$

$\qquad = 180 - m\angle L - m\angle R$

$\qquad = 180 - 47 - 63 = 70°$

$m\angle Q = m\angle M = 70°$

21. Corresponding sides are proportional.

$\dfrac{LM}{PQ} = \dfrac{LN}{PR} = \dfrac{LP + PN}{PN + NR}$

$\dfrac{20}{25} = \dfrac{8 + PN}{PN + 12}$ → $20(PN + 12) = 25(8 + PN)$

$PN = 8$

22. An equiangular triangle is equilateral.

$7a = 4a + 15 = 6b - 1$

$a = 5, b = 6$

23. Base angles of an isosceles triangle are congruent.

$2a + 2(a - 4) = 180$

$a = 47$

24. $\triangle DEG \cong \triangle FEG$ by ASA.

Reflect over $\overline{EG}$.

25. $\triangle LMN \cong \triangle PQR$ by HL.

Rotate by 180° about any vertex, then translate so that $\overline{LM}$ maps to $\overline{PQ}$.

You could perform two reflections over $\overline{LM}$ and $\overline{MN}$ instead of a rotation of 180°.

## LESSON 66

1. Translate so that $\overline{RT}$ maps to $\overline{XZ}$.

2. Reflect over $\overline{RT}$, then translate so that $\overline{RT}$ maps to $\overline{XZ}$.

3. Rotate counterclockwise so that $\overline{RT} \parallel \overline{XZ}$, then translate so that $\overline{RT}$ maps to $\overline{XZ}$.

**4 ~ 6.** *Answer formats may vary.*

4. Statements (Reasons)

    1. a. $\triangle ABC \sim \triangle AB'C'$ (Dilations produce similar figures.)

    2. a. $\angle B \cong \angle B'$ (Corresponding angles of similar triangles are congruent.)

       b. $\angle B \cong \angle E$ (Given)

       c. $\angle B' \cong \angle E$ (Transitive Property)

    3. a. $k = DE/AB$ (Construction)

       b. $AB' = k \cdot AB$ (Def. of scale factor)

       c. $AB' = (DE/AB)AB$ (Substitution)

       d. $AB' = DE$ (Simplify.)

       e. $\overline{AB'} \cong \overline{DE}$ (Def. of congruent segments)

    4. a. $\angle A \cong \angle D$ (Given)

       b. $\angle B' \cong \angle E$ (Proved in Step 2.)

       c. $\overline{AB'} \cong \overline{DE}$ (Proved in Step 3.)

       b. $\triangle AB'C' \cong \triangle DEF$ (ASA)

5. Statements (Reasons)

    1. a. $\overline{PQ} \parallel \overline{EF}$ (Construction)

       b. $\angle DPQ \cong \angle E$ (Corresponding $\angle$s are $\cong$.)

       c. $\angle D \cong \angle D$ (Reflexive Property)

       d. $\triangle DPQ \sim \triangle DEF$ (AA)

    2. a. $\dfrac{DP}{DE} = \dfrac{DQ}{DF}$ (Corresponding sides of similar triangles are proportional.)

    *(The proof continues on the next page.)*

**5.** 3. a. $DP = AB$ (Construction)

    b. $\dfrac{AB}{DE} = \dfrac{DQ}{DF}$ (Substitution, Steps 2a and 3a)

    c. $\dfrac{AB}{DE} = \dfrac{AC}{DF}$ (Given)

    d. $\dfrac{DQ}{DF} = \dfrac{AC}{DF}$ (Transitive Property)

    e. $DQ = AC$ (Multiplication Property)

  4. a. $\angle A \cong \angle D$ (Given)

    b. $\overline{DP} \cong \overline{AB}, \overline{DQ} \cong \overline{AC}$ (Def. of congruent segments, Steps 3a and 3e)

    c. $\triangle ABC \cong \triangle DPQ$ (SAS)

  5. a. $\triangle ABC \sim \triangle DEF$ (Steps 4c and 1d means that you can map $\triangle ABC$ to $\triangle DPQ$ and then to $\triangle DEF$ using a sequence of rigid transformations and a dilation.)

**6.** Statements (Reasons)

1. $\triangle DPQ \sim \triangle DEF$ (AA, See Step 1 in Problem 5.)

2. $\dfrac{DP}{DE} = \dfrac{DQ}{DF} = \dfrac{PQ}{EF}$ (Corresponding sides of similar triangles are proportional.)

3. $DP = AB$ (Construction)
   $DQ = AC$ (See Step 3 in Problem 5.)

4. $PQ = BC$ (Apply the same reasoning as above.)

5. $\triangle ABC \cong \triangle DPQ$ (SSS)

6. $\triangle ABC \sim \triangle DEF$ (Steps 1 and 5)

**7.** The answer is d.

**8 ~ 13.** *Answers on transformations may vary.*

**8.** $\angle A \cong \angle A$ by the Reflexive Property.
$\angle D \cong \angle BEA$ because $m\angle BEA = 180 - 122 = 58°$.
So, $\triangle ABE \sim \triangle ACD$ by AA.

Dilate about $A$ using scale factor 3.

**9.** $\angle D \cong \angle D$ by the Reflexive Property.
$DE/DF = 12/(12 + 9) = 12/21 = 4/7$
$DH/DG = 8/(8 + 6) = 8/14 = 4/7$
So, $\triangle DEH \sim \triangle DFG$ by SAS.

Dilate about $D$ using scale factor 7/4.

**10.** $\angle P \cong \angle R$ because $m\angle P = 180 - 90 - 55 = 35°$.
$\angle PQT \cong \angle RQS$ because all right angles are congruent.
So, $\triangle PQT \sim \triangle RQS$ by AA.

Dilate about $Q$ using scale factor 7/5, then reflect over $\overline{TQ}$. You could perform the reflection first and then the dilation.

**11.** $PO/PM = 28/(28 + 14) = 28/42 = 2/3$
$PN/PL = 32/(32 + 16) = 32/48 = 2/3$
$ON/ML = 20/30 = 2/3$
$\angle P \cong \angle P$ by the Reflexive Property.
So, $\triangle PON \sim \triangle PML$ by SSS or SAS.

Dilate about $P$ using scale factor 3/2.

**12.** $m\angle ACB = 180 - 90 - 51 = 39°$
$m\angle ECD = 180 - 102 - m\angle ACB = 39°$
$\angle ACB \cong \angle ECD$ because their measures are equal.
$\angle B \cong \angle D$ because all right angles are congruent.
So, $\triangle ABC \sim \triangle EDC$ by AA.

Reflect over a line that is perpendicular to $\overline{BD}$ and passes through $C$, then dilate about $C$ using scale factor $35/25 = 7/5$.

**13.** $RQ/TU = 20/5 = 4$
$QP/UV = 16/4 = 4$
$\angle Q \cong \angle U$ because all right angles are congruent.
So, $\triangle RQP \sim \triangle TUV$ by SAS.

Rotate 90° clockwise, dilate about any vertex using scale factor 4, then translate so that $\overline{TU}$ maps to $\overline{RQ}$.

**14.** $\dfrac{AB}{AC} = \dfrac{AE}{AD}$ $\rightarrow$   $21AE = 7(24)$
$\dfrac{7}{21} = \dfrac{AE}{24}$    $AE = 8$
$DE = AD - AE = 24 - 8 = 16$

**15.** $\dfrac{AB}{ED} = \dfrac{BC}{DC}$ $\rightarrow$   $35(3x - 1) = 25(4x)$
$\dfrac{3x - 1}{4x} = \dfrac{25}{35}$    $x = 7$
$AB = 3(7) - 1 = 20$
$ED = 4(7) = 28$

**16.** $m\angle PON = m\angle M = 67°$
$m\angle PNO = 180 - m\angle P - m\angle PON$
        $= 180 - 32 - 67 = 81°$

**17.** $(x, y) \rightarrow (x + 9, y + 2)$     **18.** scale factor = 1/2

## LESSON 67

**1.** $\sqrt{4 \cdot 4 \cdot 2} = 4\sqrt{2}$

**2.** Take the square root of each side.
$x = \pm\sqrt{150} = \pm\sqrt{5 \cdot 5 \cdot 6} = \pm 5\sqrt{6}$

**3.** $x^2 = 5 \cdot 15$
$x = \pm\sqrt{5 \cdot 15} = \pm\sqrt{5 \cdot 5 \cdot 3} = \pm 5\sqrt{3}$

**4.** $\triangle ABC \sim \triangle ACD \sim \triangle CBD$

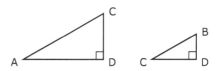

5. $\triangle EFG \sim \triangle EGH \sim \triangle GFH$

6. $\triangle KLM \sim \triangle LNM \sim \triangle KNL$

7. $\triangle PSR \sim \triangle PQS \sim \triangle SQR$

8. $\dfrac{\text{hypotenuse of largest } \triangle}{\text{hypotenuse of middle } \triangle} = \dfrac{\text{shorter leg of largest } \triangle}{\text{shorter leg of middle } \triangle}$

$\dfrac{10}{8} = \dfrac{6}{x}$  →  $10x = 8(6)$  →  $x = 24/5$

9. $\dfrac{\text{shorter leg of smallest } \triangle}{\text{shorter leg of middle } \triangle} = \dfrac{\text{longer leg of smallest } \triangle}{\text{longer leg of middle } \triangle}$

$\dfrac{7}{x} = \dfrac{x}{14}$  →  $x^2 = 7(14)$  →  $x = 7\sqrt{2}$

10. $\dfrac{\text{hypotenuse of largest } \triangle}{\text{hypotenuse of smallest } \triangle} = \dfrac{\text{shorter leg of largest } \triangle}{\text{shorter leg of smallest } \triangle}$

$\dfrac{15 + 5}{x} = \dfrac{x}{5}$  →  $x^2 = 5(15 + 5)$  →  $x = 10$

11.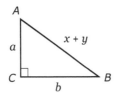

   a. $\triangle CDB \sim \triangle ADC$:  $\dfrac{h}{x} = \dfrac{y}{h} = \dfrac{b}{a}$

   b. $\triangle CDB \sim \triangle ACB$:  $\dfrac{h}{a} = \dfrac{y}{b} = \dfrac{b}{x + y}$

   c. $\triangle ADC \sim \triangle ACB$:  $\dfrac{x}{a} = \dfrac{h}{b} = \dfrac{a}{x + y}$

12. $\triangle DEF \sim \triangle EGF \sim \triangle DGE$

13. $\triangle PSR \sim \triangle PQS \sim \triangle SQR$

14. $\triangle WXZ \sim \triangle WYX \sim \triangle XYZ$

15. $\dfrac{\text{longer leg of middle } \triangle}{\text{longer leg of smallest } \triangle} = \dfrac{\text{shorter leg of middle } \triangle}{\text{shorter leg of smallest } \triangle}$

$\dfrac{14}{x} = \dfrac{x}{8}$  →  $x^2 = 14(8)$  →  $x = 4\sqrt{7}$

16. $\dfrac{\text{longer leg of middle } \triangle}{\text{longer leg of smallest } \triangle} = \dfrac{\text{shorter leg of middle } \triangle}{\text{shorter leg of smallest } \triangle}$

$\dfrac{6}{x} = \dfrac{x}{3}$  →  $x^2 = 6(3)$  →  $x = 3\sqrt{2}$

17. $\dfrac{\text{hypotenuse of largest } \triangle}{\text{hypotenuse of smallest } \triangle} = \dfrac{\text{shorter leg of largest } \triangle}{\text{shorter leg of smallest } \triangle}$

$\dfrac{x + 6}{12} = \dfrac{12}{6}$  →  $6(x + 6) = 12(12)$  →  $x = 18$

18. $\dfrac{\text{longer leg of middle } \triangle}{\text{longer leg of smallest } \triangle} = \dfrac{\text{shorter leg of middle } \triangle}{\text{shorter leg of smallest } \triangle}$

$\dfrac{x}{5\sqrt{3}} = \dfrac{5\sqrt{3}}{5}$  →  $5x = (5\sqrt{3})(5\sqrt{3})$  →  $x = 15$

19. $\dfrac{\text{hypotenuse of largest } \triangle}{\text{hypotenuse of middle } \triangle} = \dfrac{\text{longer leg of largest } \triangle}{\text{longer leg of middle } \triangle}$

$\dfrac{20}{16} = \dfrac{16}{x}$  →  $20x = 16(16)$  →  $x = 64/5$

20. $\dfrac{\text{longer leg of middle } \triangle}{\text{longer leg of smallest } \triangle} = \dfrac{\text{shorter leg of middle } \triangle}{\text{shorter leg of smallest } \triangle}$

$\dfrac{4x}{10} = \dfrac{10}{x}$  →  $4x^2 = 10(10)$  →  $x = 5$

21. $\triangle ABC \sim \triangle ACD$ by AA because they both have a right angle and share $\angle A$.

   $\triangle ABC \sim \triangle CBD$ by AA because they both have a right angle and share $\angle B$.

   Because $\triangle ABC \sim \triangle ACD$ and $\triangle ABC \sim \triangle CBD$, their corresponding angles are all congruent. Therefore, the three triangles are similar to each other.

22. The altitudes of a right triangle intersect at the vertex of the right angle.

23. orthocenter

## LESSON 68 ··························································

1. $\triangle PQR \sim \triangle PRS \sim \triangle RQS$

2. $\dfrac{\text{longer leg of middle } \triangle}{\text{longer leg of smallest } \triangle} = \dfrac{\text{shorter leg of middle } \triangle}{\text{shorter leg of smallest } \triangle}$

$\dfrac{8}{x} = \dfrac{x}{4}$  →  $x^2 = 8(4)$  →  $x = 4\sqrt{2}$

$\dfrac{\text{hypotenuse of smallest } \triangle}{\text{hypotenuse of largest } \triangle} = \dfrac{\text{shorter leg of smallerst } \triangle}{\text{shorter leg of largest } \triangle}$

$\dfrac{y}{8 + 4} = \dfrac{4}{y}$  →  $y^2 = 4(8 + 4)$  →  $y = 4\sqrt{3}$

3. $\sqrt{4(8)} = \sqrt{4 \cdot 4 \cdot 2} = 4\sqrt{2}$

4. $CD^2 = AD \cdot BD$
   $AC^2 = AD \cdot AB$
   $BC^2 = BD \cdot BA$

5. $YK^2 = XK \cdot ZK$
   $XY^2 = XK \cdot XZ$
   $ZY^2 = ZK \cdot ZX$

6. $GE^2 = DE \cdot FE$
   $DG^2 = DE \cdot DF$
   $FG^2 = FE \cdot FD$

7. $h^2 = xy$
   $a^2 = x(x + y)$
   $b^2 = y(x + y)$

**8.** $x^2 = 6(12)$ and $y^2 = 6(6 + 12)$

$x = 6\sqrt{2}$ $y = 6\sqrt{3}$

**9.** $x^2 = 9(4)$ and $y^2 = 9(9 + 4)$

$x = 6$ $y = 3\sqrt{13}$

**10.** $(4\sqrt{3})^2 = 4x$ and $y^2 = 4(4 + x) = 4(4 + 12)$

$x = 12$ $y = 8$

**11.** $\sqrt{5(10)} = \sqrt{5 \cdot 5 \cdot 2} = 5\sqrt{2}$

**12.** $\sqrt{8(18)} = \sqrt{2 \cdot 2 \cdot 2 \cdot 3 \cdot 3 \cdot 2} = 12$

**13.** $\sqrt{9(25)} = \sqrt{3 \cdot 3 \cdot 5 \cdot 5} = 15$

**14.** $x^2 = 5(10)$ and $y^2 = 5(5 + 10)$

$x = 5\sqrt{2}$ $y = 5\sqrt{3}$

**15.** $(2\sqrt{15})^2 = 10x$ and $y^2 = x(10 - x) = 6(4)$

$x = 6$ $y = 2\sqrt{6}$

**16.** $x^2 = 7(21)$ and $y^2 = 7(7 + 21)$

$x = 7\sqrt{3}$ $y = 14$

**17.** $4^2 = x(2x)$ and $y^2 = 2x(2x + x)$

$x^2 = 8$ $y^2 = 6x^2 = 6(8)$

$x = 2\sqrt{2}$ $y = 4\sqrt{3}$

**18.** $15^2 = 9(x + 15)$ and $y^2 = 9(9 + x + 15) = 9(34)$

$x = 10$ $y = 3\sqrt{34}$

**19.** $20^2 = x(4x)$ and $y^2 = x(x + 4x)$

$x^2 = 100$ $y^2 = 5x^2 = 5(100)$

$x = 10$ $y = 10\sqrt{5}$

**20 ~ 21.** By Theorem 67.1, these three triangles are similar.

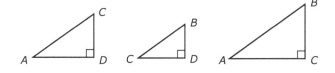

**20.** Statements (Reasons)

1. right $\triangle ABC$, hypotenuse $\overline{AB}$, altitude $\overline{CD}$ (Given)
2. $\triangle ACD \sim \triangle CBD$ (Theorem 67.1)
3. $\dfrac{AD}{CD} = \dfrac{CD}{BD}$ (Corresponding sides of similar triangles are proportional.)
4. $CD^2 = AD \cdot BD$ (Cross multiply.)

**21.** Similarly,

$\triangle ACD \sim \triangle ABC$, so $\dfrac{AD}{AC} = \dfrac{AC}{AB}$ and $AC^2 = AD \cdot AB$.

$\triangle CBD \sim \triangle ABC$, so $\dfrac{BD}{BC} = \dfrac{BC}{BA}$ and $BC^2 = BD \cdot BA$.

**22.** vertex

**23.** complementary

**24.** vertices

**25.** congruent, bisectors of each other

## LESSON 69

**1.** Corresponding sides must be proportional.

$\dfrac{10}{15} = \dfrac{14}{14 + QS}$ → $10(14 + QS) = 15(14)$

$QS = 7$

$\dfrac{10}{15} = \dfrac{16}{16 + RT}$ → $10(16 + RT) = 15(16)$

$RT = 8$

**2.** true; $\angle PQR \cong \angle S$ because corresponding angles of similar triangles are congruent. $\angle PQR$ and $\angle S$ are corresponding angles on $\overline{QR}$ and $\overline{ST}$ cut by $\overline{PS}$. Two lines cut by a transversal are parallel if corresponding angles are congruent. Therefore, $\overline{QR}$ is parallel to $\overline{ST}$.

**3.** a. $\dfrac{AP}{PB} = \dfrac{AQ}{QC}$   b. $\dfrac{DE}{EF} = \dfrac{LM}{MN}$

**4.** a. $\dfrac{a}{b} = \dfrac{d}{e}$   b. $\dfrac{b}{c} = \dfrac{e}{f}$

c. $\dfrac{e}{d} = \dfrac{b}{a}$   d. $\dfrac{a}{b + c} = \dfrac{d}{e + f}$

**5.** $\dfrac{10}{12} = \dfrac{x}{18}$

$12x = 10(18)$

$x = 15$

**6.** $\dfrac{16}{24} = \dfrac{20}{x}$

$16x = 24(20)$

$x = 30$

**7.** $\dfrac{5}{x} = \dfrac{6}{4}$

$6x = 5(4)$

$x = 10/3$

**8.** $\dfrac{x}{5} = \dfrac{4}{x}$

$x^2 = 4(5)$

$x = 2\sqrt{5}$

**9.** $\dfrac{16}{12} = \dfrac{20}{x}$

$16x = 12(20)$

$x = 15$

**10.** $\dfrac{x}{7} = \dfrac{24}{8}$

$8x = 7(24)$

$x = 21$

**11.** $\dfrac{20}{12} = \dfrac{15}{3x}$

$3x(20) = 12(15)$

$x = 3$

**12.** $\dfrac{18}{x + 5} = \dfrac{15}{x}$

$18x = 15(x + 5)$

$x = 25$

**13.** $\dfrac{4}{x + 2} = \dfrac{6}{2x + 1}$

$4(2x + 1) = 6(x + 2)$

$x = 4$

**14.** $\dfrac{5x}{14} = \dfrac{4x + 2}{12}$

$5x(12) = 14(4x + 2)$

$x = 7$

**15.** $\dfrac{4}{3} = \dfrac{5}{x}$

$4x = 3(5)$

$x = 15/4$

**16.** $\dfrac{x}{8} = \dfrac{5}{x}$

$x^2 = 8(5)$

$x = 2\sqrt{10}$

**17.** $\dfrac{8}{6x} = \dfrac{5x}{15}$

$(6x)(5x) = 8(15)$

$x^2 = 4$

$x = 2$

**18.** $\dfrac{a}{b} + 1 = \dfrac{c}{d} + 1$

$\dfrac{a}{b} + \dfrac{b}{b} = \dfrac{c}{d} + \dfrac{d}{d}$

$\dfrac{a+b}{b} = \dfrac{c+d}{d}$

**19.** $\dfrac{a}{b} + \dfrac{b}{b} = \dfrac{c}{d} + \dfrac{d}{d}$

$\dfrac{a}{b} + 1 = \dfrac{c}{d} + 1$

$\dfrac{a}{b} = \dfrac{c}{d}$

**20.** Statements (Reasons)

1. $\dfrac{PB}{AP} = \dfrac{QC}{AQ}$ (Given)

2. $\dfrac{PB + AP}{AP} = \dfrac{QC + AQ}{AQ}$ (Property of proportions)

3. $AB = AP + PB$,
   $AC = AQ + QC$ (Segment Addition Postulate)

4. $\dfrac{AB}{AP} = \dfrac{AC}{AQ}$ (Substitution Property)

5. $\angle A \cong \angle A$ (Reflexive Property)

6. $\triangle APQ \sim \triangle ABC$ (SAS, Steps 4 and 5)

7. $\angle APQ \cong \angle B$ (Corresponding angles of similar triangles are congruent.)

8. $\overline{PQ} \parallel \overline{BC}$ (If corresponding angles are congruent, then lines are parallel.)

**21.** Statements (Reasons)

1. $\overline{PQ} \parallel \overline{BC}$ (Given)

2. $\angle APQ \cong \angle B$ (Corresponding $\angle$s on $\parallel$ lines are $\cong$.)

3. $\angle A \cong \angle A$ (Reflexive Property)

4. $\triangle APQ \sim \triangle ABC$ (AA)

5. $\dfrac{AB}{AP} = \dfrac{AC}{AQ}$ (Corresponding sides of similar triangles are proportional.)

6. $AB = AP + PB$,
   $AC = AQ + QC$ (Segment Addition Postulate)

7. $\dfrac{PB + AP}{AP} = \dfrac{QC + AQ}{AQ}$ (Substitution Property)

8. $\dfrac{PB}{AP} = \dfrac{QC}{AQ}$ (Property of proportions)

**22.** Given: $\overleftrightarrow{DL} \parallel \overleftrightarrow{EM} \parallel \overleftrightarrow{FN}$

Prove: $\dfrac{DE}{EF} = \dfrac{LM}{MN}$

Proof:

1. $\overleftrightarrow{DL} \parallel \overleftrightarrow{EM} \parallel \overleftrightarrow{FN}$ (Given)

2. Draw $\overline{DPN}$. (Construction)

3. $\dfrac{DE}{EF} = \dfrac{DP}{PN}$ in $\triangle DFN$ (Theorem 69.1)

4. $\dfrac{DP}{PN} = \dfrac{LM}{MN}$ in $\triangle DLN$ (Theorem 69.1)

5. $\dfrac{DE}{EF} = \dfrac{LM}{MN}$ (Transitive Property)

**23.** A) true; Translations produce congruent figures.

B) false; Dilations produce similar figures.

C) true; Dilations produce similar figures.

D) true; Translations and dilations preserve angles.

E) true; $YZ = 3QR$ and $QR = BC$, so $YZ = 3BC$.

F) false; Translations and dilations preserve angles.

## LESSON 70

**1.** $x^2 = 8$

$x = \pm 2\sqrt{2}$

**2.** $(3x - 2)(x + 1) = 0$

$x = 2/3, x = -1$

**3.** $\dfrac{8}{12} = \dfrac{x}{6}$

$12x = 8(6)$

$x = 4$

**4.** $\dfrac{3x}{8} = \dfrac{15}{2x}$

$(3x)(2x) = 8(15)$

$x^2 = 20$

$x = 2\sqrt{5}$

**5.** $\dfrac{AD}{BD} = \dfrac{AC}{BC}$ or $\dfrac{AC}{AD} = \dfrac{BC}{BD}$

**6.** a, b, and d are correct.

**7.** $\dfrac{5}{7} = \dfrac{7}{x}$

$5x = 7(7)$

$x = 49/5$

**8.** $\dfrac{10}{x} = \dfrac{15}{12}$

$15x = 10(12)$

$x = 8$

**9.** $\dfrac{x}{27 - x} = \dfrac{24}{12}$

$12x = 24(27 - x)$

$x = 18$

**10.** $\dfrac{x}{7} = \dfrac{15}{10}$

$10x = 7(15)$

$x = 21/2$

**11.** $\dfrac{4}{x} = \dfrac{15}{18}$

$15x = 4(18)$

$x = 24/5$

**12.** $\dfrac{x}{20 - x} = \dfrac{18}{12}$

$12x = 18(20 - x)$

$x = 12$

**13.** $\dfrac{14}{12} = \dfrac{20}{10x}$

$14(10x) = 12(20)$

$x = 12/7$

**14.** $\dfrac{x+1}{x+5} = \dfrac{26}{39}$

$39(x + 1) = 26(x + 5)$

$x = 7$

**15.** $\dfrac{25}{4x} = \dfrac{7x}{28}$

$(4x)(7x) = 25(28)$

$x^2 = 25$

$x = 5$

**16.** $\dfrac{3x}{5x} = \dfrac{4x}{6x+1}$

$(5x)(4x) = (3x)(6x + 1)$

$2x^2 - 3x = 0$

$x(2x - 3) = 0$

$x = 3/2$

**17.** $\dfrac{20}{3x} = \dfrac{3x+3}{9}$

$(3x)(3x + 3) = 20(9)$

$x^2 + x - 20 = 0$

$(x + 5)(x - 4) = 0$

$x = 4$

**18.** $\dfrac{x-1}{8} = \dfrac{6}{x+1}$

$(x - 1)(x + 1) = 8(6)$

$x^2 = 49$

$x = 7$

**19.** $\dfrac{AP}{PX} = \dfrac{AQ}{QY} = \dfrac{AR}{RZ}$

**20.** $\dfrac{AP}{AX} = \dfrac{PQ}{XY} = \dfrac{PR}{XZ} = \dfrac{AR}{AZ}$

**21.** $\dfrac{XY}{YZ} = \dfrac{AX}{AZ}$

**22.** $\dfrac{AP}{PQ} = \dfrac{AR}{RQ}$

**23.** *Answer formats may vary.*

Statements (Reasons)

1. $\overline{DC} \parallel \overline{BP}$ (Construction)

   $\angle 1 \cong \angle 3$ (Corresponding ∠s on ∥ lines are ≅.)

2. $\angle 2 \cong \angle 4$ (Alternate interior ∠s on ∥ lines are ≅.)

3. $\angle 1 \cong \angle 2$ (Given)

   $\angle 3 \cong \angle 4$ (Transitive Property)

4. $\overline{BC} \cong \overline{PC}$ (Base Angles Converse [40.2])

   $BC = PC$ (Def. of congruent segments)

5. $\dfrac{AD}{DB} = \dfrac{AC}{PC}$ (Triangle Side Splitter Theorem [69.1])

6. $\dfrac{AD}{DB} = \dfrac{AC}{BC}$ (Substitution Property, Steps 4 and 5)

**24.** Addition Property

Division Property

**25.** Substitution Property

Subtraction Property

Division Property

## LESSON 71

**1.** 2. Corresponding ∠s on parallel lines are ≅.

3. Reflexive Property

**2.** 2. All right angles are congruent.

3. Reflexive Property

4. AA

**3.** 2. A midsegment is parallel to the third side.

3. Corresponding ∠s on parallel lines are ≅.

4. Reflexive Property

5. AA

**4.** 3. Alternate interior ∠s on parallel lines are ≅.

4 Vertical angles are congruent.

5. AA

6. CSSTP

**5.** 2. Vertical angles are congruent.

3. AA

**6.** 2. Base Angles Theorem [40.1]

3. Transitive Property

4. Reflexive Property

5. AA

6. CASTC

**7.** 2. Def. of perpendicular

3. All right angles are congruent.

5. AA

**8.** 2. Vertical angles are congruent.

3. AA

4. CSSTP

**9.** Statements (Reasons)

1. $AB = 3AD$, $AC = 3AE$ (Given)

2. $\dfrac{AB}{AD} = \dfrac{3AD}{AD} = 3$, $\dfrac{AC}{AE} = \dfrac{3AE}{AE} = 3$ (Division property)

3. $\dfrac{AB}{AD} = \dfrac{AC}{AE}$ (Transitive Property)

4. $\angle A \cong \angle A$ (Reflexive Property)

5. $\triangle ABC \sim \triangle ADE$ (SAS)

**10.** Statements (Reasons)

1. $\angle B \cong \angle PCA$ (Given)

2. $\angle P \cong \angle P$ (Reflexive Property)

3. $\triangle PBC \sim \triangle PCA$ (AA)

4. $\dfrac{PB}{PC} = \dfrac{PC}{PA}$ (CSSTP, Corresponding sides of similar triangles are proportional.)

5. $PC^2 = PA \cdot PB$ (Cross multiply.)

**11.** Opposite angles are congruent, so $m\angle 1 = 118°$.

Base ∠s of an isosceles triangle are ≅, so $m\angle 2 = m\angle 3$.

A triangle has 180°, so $118 + m\angle 2 + m\angle 3 = 180$ and $m\angle 2 = m\angle 3 = 31°$.

Diagonals bisect opposite angles, so $m\angle 4 = m\angle 3 = 31°$.

**12.** Vertex angles are bisected by a diagonal, so $m\angle 1 = 28°$ and $m\angle 2 = 42°$.

A triangle has 180°, so $m\angle 3 = 180 - 28 - 42 = 110°$.

Non-vertex angles are ≅, so $m\angle 4 = m\angle 3 = 110°$.

# LESSON 72 ·······························

1. Use the Leg Rule [68.2].
$10^2 = 5(5 + x)$
$x = 15$

2. $\dfrac{21}{15} = \dfrac{x}{10}$
$15x = 21(10)$
$x = 14$

3. $\dfrac{24}{x} = \dfrac{30}{20}$
$30x = 24(20)$
$x = 16$

4. $\dfrac{12}{20} = \dfrac{x}{15}$
$20x = 12(15)$
$x = 9$ ft

5. $\dfrac{6}{30} = \dfrac{1.6}{x}$
$6x = 30(1.6)$
$x = 8$ m

6. $\dfrac{520}{x} = \dfrac{560}{350}$
$560x = 520(350)$
$x = 325$ ft

7. $\dfrac{560}{560 + 350} = \dfrac{152}{y}$
$560y = 152(560 + 350)$
$y = 247$ ft

8. $\dfrac{48}{32} = \dfrac{36}{x}$
$48x = 32(36)$
$x = 24$ inches

9. $\dfrac{1.6}{x} = \dfrac{2}{12}$
$2x = 1.6(12)$
$x = 9.6$ m

10. $\dfrac{10}{10 + 10} = \dfrac{5.2}{x}$
$10x = (5.2)(10 + 10)$
$x = 10.4$ ft

11. $\dfrac{3}{32} = \dfrac{1.5}{x}$
$3x = 32(1.5)$
$x = 16$ m

12. $\dfrac{3}{9} = \dfrac{12 - x}{12}$
$9(12 - x) = 3(12)$
$x = 8$ ft

13. $AB$, $AD$, $BC$

14. Use the Altitude Rule.
$QS^2 = PS \cdot RS$
$QS^2 = 80(240)$
$QS = 80\sqrt{3}$
   $\approx 138.6$ yd

15. Use the Leg Rule.
$QP^2 = PS \cdot PR$
$QP^2 = 80(80 + 240)$
$QP = 160$
distance $= QP + PS$
   $= 240$ yd

16. no; 5 + 8 > 15 is false. The sum of two sides of a triangle must be greater than the third side.

17. The larger angle has the longer opposite side.
$m\angle C = 180 - 55 - 63 = 62°$
$m\angle A < m\angle C < m\angle B$, so $BC < AB < AC$.

18. Consecutive angles of a parallelogram are supplementary, so $x + 3x = 180$ and $x = 45$.

Opposite angles of a parallelogram are congruent, so the parallelogram has angles 45°, 135°, 45°, and 135°.

# LESSON 73 ·······························

1. $x^2 = 5(20)$
$x = 10$

2. $x(x + 8) = 8(x + 1)$
$x^2 = 8$
$x = \pm 2\sqrt{2}$

3. Corresponding angles are congruent.
$90 + 56 + (5x + 4) = 180$; $x = 6$

4. Corresponding sides are proportional.
$\dfrac{18}{12} = \dfrac{24}{a}$ → $18a = 12(24)$ → $a = 16$
$\dfrac{18}{12} = \dfrac{27}{b}$ → $18b = 12(27)$ → $b = 18$

5. $m\angle A = 180 - 90 - 54 = 36°$
$m\angle D = 180 - 90 - 35 = 55°$
So, the triangles are not similar.

6. $\angle K \cong \angle K$ by the Reflexive Property.
$\angle KLO \cong \angle M$ because $m\angle KLO = 180 - 130 = 50°$.
So, $\triangle KLO \sim \triangle KMN$ by AA.

7. $NO/NP = 14/(14 + 7) = 14/21 = 2/3$
$NM/NL = 15/(15 + 9) = 15/24 = 5/8$
$OM/PL = 10/15 = 2/3$
So, the triangles are not similar.

8. $RS/XY = 12/18 = 2/3$
$ST/YZ = 10/15 = 2/3$
$RT/XZ = 8/12 = 2/3$
So, $\triangle RST \sim \triangle XYZ$ by SSS.

9. $\angle KML \cong \angle OMN$ as vertical angles.
$KM/OM = 24/30 = 4/5$
$LM/NM = 20/25 = 4/5$
So, $\triangle KML \sim \triangle OMN$ by SAS.

10. $\angle Y \cong \angle T$ because $m\angle Y = 180 - 40 - 53 = 87°$.
$XY/ST = 30/10 = 3/1$
$YZ/TU = 24/8 = 3/1$
So, $\triangle XYZ \sim \triangle STU$ by SAS.

11. $\angle B \cong \angle B$ by the Reflexive Property.
$BC/BD = 18/(18 + 12) = 18/30 = 3/5$
$BF/BE = 21/(21 + 14) = 21/35 = 3/5$
So, $\triangle BCF \sim \triangle BDE$ by SAS.

Dilate about $B$ using scale factor 5/3.

12. $m\angle ACB = 180 - 90 - 51 = 39°$
$m\angle ECD = 180 - 102 - m\angle ACB = 39°$
$\angle ACB \cong \angle ECD$ because their measures are equal.
$\angle B \cong \angle D$ because all right angles are congruent.
So, $\triangle ABC \sim \triangle EDC$ by AA.

Reflect over a line that is perpendicular to $\overline{BD}$ and passes through $C$, then dilate about $C$ by 7/5.

**13.** $x^2 = 6(3)$ and $y^2 = 3(3 + 6)$

  $x = 3\sqrt{2}$    $y = 3\sqrt{3}$

**14.** $8^2 = x(4x)$ and $y^2 = x(x + 4x)$

  $x^2 = 16$    $y^2 = 5x^2 = 5(16)$

  $x = 4$    $y = 4\sqrt{5}$

**15.** $\dfrac{8}{6} = \dfrac{10}{x}$

  $8x = 6(10)$

  $x = 15/2$

**16.** $\dfrac{x - 2}{x + 2} = \dfrac{26}{39}$

  $39(x - 2) = 26(x + 2)$

  $x = 10$

**17.** $\dfrac{4}{10} = \dfrac{5}{x}$

  $4x = 5(10)$

  $x = 25/2$

**18.** $\dfrac{8}{6x} = \dfrac{5x}{15}$

  $(6x)(5x) = 8(15)$

  $x^2 = 4$

  $x = 2$

**19.** 3.  Alternate interior ∠s on parallel lines are ≅.

  4   Vertical angles are congruent.

  5.  AA

  6.  CSSTP (Corresponding sides of similar triangles are proportional.)

**20.** $\dfrac{18}{24} = \dfrac{12}{x}$

  $18x = 24(12)$

  $x = 16$ ft

**21.** $\dfrac{6}{30} = \dfrac{1.6}{x}$

  $6x = 30(1.6)$

  $x = 8$ m

**22.** The midsegment of a trapezoid is half the sum of the bases. An isosceles trapezoid has congruent legs.

  The bases of this trapezoid are 8 and 10, so the length of the midsegment is (8 + 10)/2 = 9.

## LESSON 74

**1.**  $\sqrt{20} = \sqrt{4 \cdot 5} = 2\sqrt{5}$

**2**  Subtract 5 from both sides:  $(x + 3)^2 = 20$

  Take the square root:  $x + 3 = \pm\sqrt{20}$

  Simplify the square root:  $x + 3 = \pm 2\sqrt{5}$

  Subtract 3 from both sides:  $x = -3 \pm 2\sqrt{5}$

**3.**  $a^2 = 10(10 + 5)$ and $b^2 = 5(5 + 10)$

  $a = 5\sqrt{6}$    $b = 5\sqrt{3}$

**4.**  $c^2 = a^2 + b^2$ or $AB^2 = AC^2 + BC^2$

**5.**  $x^2 = 4^2 + 8^2$

  $x^2 = 80$

  $x = 4\sqrt{5}$

**6.**  $9^2 = 7^2 + (x + 1)^2$

  $(x + 1)^2 = 32$

  $x + 1 = 4\sqrt{2}$

  $x = -1 + 4\sqrt{2}$

**7.**  $b^2 = xc$

  $a^2 + b^2 = yc + xc = c(y + x) = c^2$

**8.**  no; $8^2 \ne 4^2 + 5^2$

**9.**  yes; $10^2 = 6^2 + 8^2$

**10.**  yes; $26^2 = 10^2 + 24^2$

**11.**  $x^2 = 5^2 + 5^2$

  $x^2 = 50$

  $x = 5\sqrt{2}$

**12.**  $11^2 = 9^2 + x^2$

  $x^2 = 40$

  $x = 2\sqrt{10}$

**13.**  $x^2 = 12^2 + 9^2$

  $x^2 = 225$

  $x = 15$

  You could use a multiple of the 3-4-5 triple.

**14.**  $20^2 = 16^2 + x^2$

  $x^2 = 144$

  $x = 12$

  You could use a multiple of the 3-4-5 triple.

**15.**  $10^2 = 5^2 + (x - 5)^2$

  $(x - 5)^2 = 75$

  $x - 5 = 5\sqrt{3}$

  $x = 5 + 5\sqrt{3}$

**16.**  $(2x)^2 = x^2 + (4\sqrt{3})^2$

  $4x^2 = x^2 + 48$

  $x^2 = 16$

  $x = 4$

**17.**  $13^2 = 5^2 + x^2$

  $x^2 = 144$

  $x = 12$ ft

  You could use the 5-12-13 triple.

**18.**  $x^2 = 8^2 + 15^2$

  $x^2 = 289$

  $x = 17$ km

  You could use the 8-15-17 triple.

**19.** a.  area $= (a + b)^2 = a^2 + 2ab + b^2$

  b.  area = 4 right triangles + small square

  $= 4 \times \dfrac{1}{2} ab + c^2 = 2ab + c^2$

  c.  $a^2 + 2ab + b^2 = 2ab + c^2$ (Set the two areas equal.)

  $a^2 + b^2 = c^2$ (Subtract $2ab$ from both sides.)

**20.** a.  The bases of a trapezoid are the parallel sides, so the bases of this trapezoid are $a$ and $b$.

  The height of a trapezoid is the perpendicular distance between the bases, so the height of this trapezoid is $b + a$.

  area $= \dfrac{1}{2}(a + b)(b + a) = \dfrac{1}{2}(a + b)^2$

  b.  area = three right triangles

  $= \dfrac{1}{2} ab + \dfrac{1}{2} ab + \dfrac{1}{2} c^2 = ab + \dfrac{1}{2} c^2$

  c.  $\dfrac{1}{2}(a + b)^2 = ab + \dfrac{1}{2} c^2$ (Set the two areas equal.)

  $(a + b)^2 = 2ab + c^2$ (Multiply both sides by 2.)

  $a^2 + 2ab + b^2 = 2ab + c^2$ (Expand the left side.)

  $a^2 + b^2 = c^2$ (Subtract $2ab$ from both sides.)

**21.**  $\overrightarrow{BA}, \overrightarrow{BC}, \overrightarrow{BD}$

**22.**  $AB + BC = AC$

  $(x + 4) + x = 12$

  $x = 4$

**23.**  Let $x = m\angle ABD$.

  $m\angle DBC = 5x$

  $x + 5x = 180$

  $x = 30$

  $m\angle ABD = 30°$

# LESSON 75

1. $m\angle 1 > m\angle 2$

2. $m\angle 1 < m\angle 3$

3. $x^2 = 10^2 + 15^2$
   $x^2 = 325$
   $x = 5\sqrt{13}$

4. $(5\sqrt{2})^2 = 5^2 + x^2$
   $x^2 = 25$
   $x = 5$

5. $12^2 = 6^2 + x^2$
   $x^2 = 108$
   $x = 6\sqrt{3}$

6. Thm 75.1: If $c^2 = a^2 + b^2$, then $\triangle ABC$ is a right $\triangle$.
   Thm 75.2: If $c^2 < a^2 + b^2$, then $\triangle ABC$ is acute.
   Thm 75.3: If $c^2 > a^2 + b^2$, then $\triangle ABC$ is obtuse.

7. yes; $41^2 = 9^2 + 40^2$

8. obtuse; $(5\sqrt{3})^2 > 4^2 + 7^2$

9. no; $12^2 \neq 9^2 + 8^2$

10. yes; $(6\sqrt{2})^2 = 6^2 + 6^2$

11. no; $(5\sqrt{6})^2 \neq 5^2 + 11^2$

12. acute; $8^2 < 4^2 + 7^2$

13. obtuse; $6^2 > 5^2 + (\sqrt{10})^2$

14. right; $25^2 = 7^2 + 24^2$

15. $12^2 = 9^2 + x^2$
    $x^2 = 63$
    $x = 3\sqrt{7}$
    The two right triangles are congruent by HL. Each right triangle has hypotenuse 12 and legs $x$ and 9.

16. $x^2 = 2^2 + 2^2$       $y^2 = x^2 + 2^2$
    $x^2 = 8$               $y^2 = (2\sqrt{2})^2 + 2^2$
    $x = 2\sqrt{2}$         $y^2 = 12$
                            $y = 2\sqrt{3}$

17. $x^2 = 6^2 + 8^2$       $x^2 = 4^2 + y^2$
    $x^2 = 100$             $10^2 = 4^2 + y^2$
    $x = 10$                $y^2 = 84$
                            $y = 2\sqrt{21}$

18. *Answer formats may vary.*
    Statements (Reasons)
    1. Draw a right $\triangle XYZ$ with $a$, $b$, and $z$. (Construction)
       $z^2 = a^2 + b^2$ (Pythagorean Theorem [74.1])
    2. $c^2 = a^2 + b^2$ (Given)
       $z^2 = c^2$ (Transitive Property)
    3. $z = c$ (Take the square root.)
    4. $\triangle ABC \cong \triangle XYZ$ (SSS)

19. Statements (Reasons)
    1. Draw a right $\triangle XYZ$ as in Problem 18. (Construction)
    2. $z^2 = a^2 + b^2$ (Pythagorean Theorem [74.1])
    3. $c^2 < a^2 + b^2$ (Given)
    4. $c^2 < z^2$ (Substitution Property)
    5. $c < z$ (Take the square root.)
    6. $m\angle C < m\angle Z$ (Converse of Hinge Theorem [53.2])
    7. $m\angle C < 90°$ (Substitution Property)
    8. $\triangle ABC$ is acute. (Def. of acute triangle)

20. Statements (Reasons)
    1. Draw a right $\triangle XYZ$ as in Problem 18. (Construction)
    2. $z^2 = a^2 + b^2$ (Pythagorean Theorem [74.1])
    3. $c^2 > a^2 + b^2$ (Given)
    4. $c^2 > z^2$ (Substitution Property)
    5. $c > z$ (Take the square root.)
    6. $m\angle C > m\angle Z$ (Converse of Hinge Theorem [53.2])
    7. $m\angle C > 90°$ (Substitution Property)
    8. $\triangle ABC$ is obtuse. (Def. of obtuse triangle)

21. $P(3, -2) \rightarrow P'(0, 0) \rightarrow P''(0, 0)$

22. a translation of 4 units left and 4 units down; A composition of translations is a translation.

23. similar; A dilation is a similarity transformation.

# LESSON 76

1. $\dfrac{1}{\sqrt{2}} \cdot \dfrac{\sqrt{2}}{\sqrt{2}} = \dfrac{\sqrt{2}}{2}$

2. $\dfrac{6}{\sqrt{3}} \cdot \dfrac{\sqrt{3}}{\sqrt{3}} = \dfrac{6\sqrt{3}}{3} = 2\sqrt{3}$

3. $x^2 = 1^2 + 1^2$
   $x^2 = 2$
   $x = \sqrt{2}$

4. $2^2 = 1^2 + x^2$
   $x^2 = 3$
   $x = \sqrt{3}$

5. a. hypotenuse = $\sqrt{2} \times$ leg
   b. hypotenuse = 2 × shorter leg
      longer leg = $\sqrt{3}$ × shorter leg

6. $a = 9$
   $b = 9\sqrt{2}$

7. $3 = a\sqrt{3}$
   $a = \dfrac{3}{\sqrt{3}} = \sqrt{3}$
   $b = 2a = 2\sqrt{3}$

8. $a = 2(8) = 16$
   $b = 8\sqrt{3}$
   $c = b/2 = 4\sqrt{3}$
   $d = c\sqrt{3} = 12$

9. $a = 10$
   $b = 10\sqrt{2}$
   $c = b/2 = 5\sqrt{2}$
   $d = c\sqrt{3} = 5\sqrt{6}$

10. $3\sqrt{2} = a\sqrt{2}$
    $a = b = 3$

11. $a = 10/2 = 5$
    $b = a\sqrt{3} = 5\sqrt{3}$

12. $a = 7\sqrt{3}$
    $b = 2(7) = 14$

13. $a = 5$
    $b = 5\sqrt{2}$

14. $6 = a\sqrt{3}$
    $a = \dfrac{6}{\sqrt{3}} = 2\sqrt{3}$
    $b = 2a = 4\sqrt{3}$

15. $9 = a\sqrt{3}$
    $a = \dfrac{9}{\sqrt{3}} = 3\sqrt{3}$
    $b = 2a = 6\sqrt{3}$

16. $a = 3\sqrt{2}$
    $b = a = 3\sqrt{2}$
    $c = a\sqrt{2} = 6$

17. $a = 4/2 = 2$
    $b = a\sqrt{3} = 2\sqrt{3}$
    $c = b = 2\sqrt{3}$
    $d = c\sqrt{2} = 2\sqrt{6}$

**18.** $a = \sqrt{6}$

$b = a\sqrt{2} = \sqrt{12} = 2\sqrt{3}$

$c = \sqrt{6}\sqrt{3} = \sqrt{18} = 3\sqrt{2}$

$d = 2\sqrt{6}$

**19.** Statements (Reasons)

1. $\triangle ABC$ is a 45°-45°-90° triangle. (Given)
2. $\overline{AB} \cong \overline{BC}$ (Base Angles Converse [40.2])
3. $AB = BC$ (Def. of congruent segments)
4. $AC^2 = AB^2 + BC^2$ (Pythagorean Theorem [74.1])
5. $AC^2 = AB^2 + AB^2$ (Substitution Property)
6. $AC^2 = 2AB^2$ (Simplify.)
7. $AC = AB\sqrt{2}$ (Take the square root.)

**20.** Statements (Reasons)

1. $\triangle ABC$ is a 30°-60°-90° triangle. (Given)
2. Construct $\triangle ABD$ such that $BC = BD$. (Construction)

First, prove that $\triangle ABC \cong \triangle ABD$.

3. $\overline{BC} \cong \overline{BD}$ (Def. of congruent segments)
4. $\overline{AB} \cong \overline{AB}$ (Reflexive Property)
5. $\angle ABC \cong \angle ABD$ (All right angles are congruent.)
6. $\triangle ABC \cong \triangle ABD$ (SAS)

Second, prove that $\triangle ACD$ is equilateral.

7. $\angle C \cong \angle D, \angle CAB \cong \angle DAB$ (CPCTC)
8. $m\angle C = m\angle D, m\angle CAB = m\angle DAB$ (Def. of congruent angles)
9. $m\angle C = 60°, m\angle CAB = 30°$ (Given)
10. $m\angle C = m\angle D = 60°, \ m\angle CAB = m\angle DAB = 30°$ (Transitive Property)
11. $m\angle CAD = m\angle CAB + m\angle DAB = 30 + 30 = 60°$ (Angle Addition Postulate)
12. $\triangle ACD$ is equiangular. (Def. of equiangular triangle)
13. $\triangle ACD$ is equilateral. (All equiangular triangles are equilateral. See Theorem 40.4.)

Third, prove that $AC = 2BC$.

14. $AC = CD$ (Def. of equilateral triangle)
15. $CD = BC + BD$ (Segment Addition Postulate)
16. $CD = BC + BC = 2BC$ (Substitution, Steps 2 and 15)
17. $AC = 2BC$ (Transitive Property, Steps 14 and 16)

Lastly, prove that $AB = BC\sqrt{3}$.

18. $AC^2 = AB^2 + BC^2$ (Pythagorean Theorem [74.1])
19. $AB^2 = AC^2 - BC^2$ (Subtraction Property)
20. $AB^2 = (2BC)^2 - BC^2$ (Substitution, Steps 17 and 19)
21. $AB^2 = 4BC^2 - BC^2 = 3BC^2$ (Simplify.)
22. $AB = BC\sqrt{3}$ (Take the square root.)

**21.** longer leg = $\sqrt{3}$ (shorter leg) = $6\sqrt{3}$

hypotenuse = 2 (shorter leg) = 12

perimeter = $6 + 6\sqrt{3} + 12 = 18 + 6\sqrt{3}$ cm

**22.** An isosceles right triangle is a 45-45-90 triangle.

hypotenuse = $\sqrt{2}$ (leg) = $5\sqrt{2}$

perimeter = $5 + 5 + 5\sqrt{2} = 10 + 5\sqrt{2}$ in

**23.** A diagonal divides a square into two congruent 45-45-90 triangles. In each 45-45-90 triangle, the legs are the sides of the square, and the hypotenuse is the diagonal of the square.

leg of right triangle = side length = 36/4 = 9

hypotenuse of right triangle = $\sqrt{2}$ (leg) = $9\sqrt{2}$

diagonal = hypotenuse of right triangle = $9\sqrt{2}$ in

**24.** An altitude divides an equilateral triangle into two congruent 30-60-90 triangles. In each 30-60-90 triangle, the longer leg is the altitude of the equilateral triangle, and the shorter leg is half the side length of the equilateral triangle.

shorter leg of right triangle = half the side length = 4

longer leg of right triangle = $\sqrt{3}$ (shorter leg) = $4\sqrt{3}$

altitude = longer leg of right triangle = $4\sqrt{3}$ cm

**25.** In an isosceles triangle, the median to the base is also an altitude and an angle bisector. In an isosceles triangle with base angle 30°, the median to the base divides the triangle into two congruent 30-60-90 triangles. In each 30-60-90 triangle, the shorter leg is the median of the isosceles triangle, and the longer leg is half the base of the isosceles triangle.

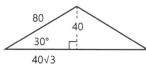

shorter leg of right triangle = median = 40

longer leg of right triangle = $\sqrt{3}$ (shorter leg) = $40\sqrt{3}$

hypotenuse of right triangle = 2 (shorter leg) = 80

perimeter = 2 (hypotenuse) + 2 (longer leg)

$= 160 + 80\sqrt{3}$ mm

**26.** SSS, SAS, HL

**27.** altitude $(\overline{AD} \perp \overline{BC})$

median $(\overline{BD} \cong \overline{CD})$

perpendicular bisector $(\overline{AD} \perp \overline{BC}$ and $\overline{BD} \cong \overline{CD})$

angle bisector $(\triangle ABD \cong \triangle ACD$ and $\angle BAD \cong \angle CAD)$

## LESSON 77

1. $x^2 = 4^2 + 8^2$
   $x^2 = 80$
   $x = 4\sqrt{5}$

2. $x = 7\sqrt{3}$

3. $x = 5\sqrt{2}$

4. $\sin D = \dfrac{8}{17}$    $\cos D = \dfrac{15}{17}$    $\tan D = \dfrac{8}{15}$

   $\sin E = \dfrac{15}{17}$    $\cos E = \dfrac{8}{17}$    $\tan E = \dfrac{15}{8}$

5. $\sin D = \dfrac{5}{13}$    $\cos D = \dfrac{12}{13}$    $\tan D = \dfrac{5}{12}$

   $\sin E = \dfrac{12}{13}$    $\cos E = \dfrac{5}{13}$    $\tan E = \dfrac{12}{5}$

6. $\sin D = \cos D = \dfrac{4}{4\sqrt{2}} = \dfrac{1}{\sqrt{2}} = \dfrac{\sqrt{2}}{2}$    $\tan D = \dfrac{4}{4} = 1$

   $\sin E = \cos E = \dfrac{4}{4\sqrt{2}} = \dfrac{1}{\sqrt{2}} = \dfrac{\sqrt{2}}{2}$    $\tan E = \dfrac{4}{4} = 1$

7. $\sin 15° = 0.25881... ≈ 0.2588$
   $\cos 60° = 0.5$
   $\tan 75° = 3.73205... ≈ 3.7321$

8. $\sin 30° = \dfrac{x}{2x} = \dfrac{1}{2}$

   $\cos 30° = \dfrac{x\sqrt{3}}{2x} = \dfrac{\sqrt{3}}{2}$

   $\tan 30° = \dfrac{x}{x\sqrt{3}} = \dfrac{1}{\sqrt{3}} = \dfrac{\sqrt{3}}{3}$

9. $12^2 = 8^2 + x^2$
   $x^2 = 80$
   $x = 4\sqrt{5}$

10. $x^2 = 7^2 + 14^2$
    $x^2 = 245$
    $x = 7\sqrt{5}$

11. $15^2 = 5^2 + x^2$
    $x^2 = 200$
    $x = 10\sqrt{2}$

12. $\sin A = \dfrac{x}{12} = \dfrac{4\sqrt{5}}{12} = \dfrac{\sqrt{5}}{3}$

    $\cos A = \dfrac{8}{12} = \dfrac{2}{3}$

    $\tan A = \dfrac{x}{8} = \dfrac{4\sqrt{5}}{8} = \dfrac{\sqrt{5}}{2}$

13. $\sin R = \dfrac{14}{x} = \dfrac{14}{7\sqrt{5}} = \dfrac{2}{\sqrt{5}} = \dfrac{2\sqrt{5}}{5}$

    $\cos R = \dfrac{7}{x} = \dfrac{7}{7\sqrt{5}} = \dfrac{1}{\sqrt{5}} = \dfrac{\sqrt{5}}{5}$

    $\tan R = \dfrac{14}{7} = 2$

14. $\sin Y = \dfrac{x}{15} = \dfrac{10\sqrt{2}}{15} = \dfrac{2\sqrt{2}}{3}$

    $\cos Y = \dfrac{5}{15} = \dfrac{1}{3}$

    $\tan Y = \dfrac{x}{5} = \dfrac{10\sqrt{2}}{5} = 2\sqrt{2}$

15. $\sin 10° ≈ 0.1736$

16. $\cos 20° ≈ 0.9397$

17. $\tan 57° ≈ 1.5399$

18. $\sin 60° = \dfrac{x\sqrt{3}}{2x} = \dfrac{\sqrt{3}}{2}$

19. $\cos 60° = \dfrac{x}{2x} = \dfrac{1}{2}$

20. $\tan 45° = \dfrac{x}{x} = 1$

21. interior angle sum $= 180(n - 2) = 180(8 - 2) = 1080°$

22. Let $x$ be the base angle.
    $2x + 50 = 180$; $x = 65$
    So, each base angle measures 65°.

## LESSON 78

1. Multiply both sides by $x$:    $0.2x = 4$
   Multiply both sides by 10:    $2x = 40$
   Divide both sides by 2:    $x = 20$

2. acute, complementary

3. $x = 12$; (5, 12, 13) is a Pythagorean triple.

4. $\sin D = \cos E = \dfrac{5}{13}$

5. $\cos 22° = 0.92718... ≈ 0.9272$

6. $\sin 30° = \cos(90° - 30°) = \cos 60°$
   $\cos 30° = \sin(90° - 30°) = \sin 60°$

7. The tangent of an acute angle is the reciprocal of the tangent of its complement. In other words, the tangents of complementary angles multiply to 1.

8. $\sin 36° = \dfrac{a}{10}$    and    $\cos 36° = \dfrac{b}{10}$

   $a = 10 \sin 36°$        $b = 10 \cos 36°$

   $a ≈ 5.9$            $b ≈ 8.1$

**9.** $\tan 61° = \dfrac{14}{a}$ and $\sin 61° = \dfrac{14}{b}$

$a\tan 61° = 14$ $\qquad b\sin 61° = 14$

$a = \dfrac{14}{\tan 61°}$ $\qquad b = \dfrac{14}{\sin 61°}$

$a \approx 7.8$ $\qquad b \approx 16$

**10.** $\tan 53° = \dfrac{a}{7}$ and $\cos 53° = \dfrac{7}{b}$

$a = 7\tan 53°$ $\qquad b\cos 53° = 7$

$a \approx 9.3$ $\qquad b = \dfrac{7}{\cos 53°}$

$\qquad\qquad\qquad\qquad b \approx 11.6$

**11.** $x = 4$; (3, 4, 5) is a Pythagorean triple.

$\sin\theta = \dfrac{4}{5}$ $\qquad \cos\theta = \dfrac{3}{5}$ $\qquad \tan\theta = \dfrac{4}{3}$

**12.** $x = 13$; (5, 12, 13) is a Pythagorean triple.

$\sin\theta = \dfrac{12}{13}$ $\qquad \cos\theta = \dfrac{5}{13}$ $\qquad \tan\theta = \dfrac{12}{5}$

**13.** $x = \sqrt{3}$; Use the side ratios of a 30-60-90 triangle

$\sin\theta = \dfrac{1}{2}$ $\qquad \cos\theta = \dfrac{\sqrt{3}}{2}$ $\qquad \tan\theta = \dfrac{1}{\sqrt{3}} = \dfrac{\sqrt{3}}{3}$

**14.** $\sin 34° = \dfrac{a}{8}$ and $\cos 34° = \dfrac{b}{8}$

$a = 8\sin 34°$ $\qquad b = 8\cos 34°$

$a \approx 4.5$ $\qquad b \approx 6.6$

**15.** $\tan 26° = \dfrac{a}{11}$ and $\cos 26° = \dfrac{11}{b}$

$a = 11\tan 26°$ $\qquad b\cos 26° = 11$

$a \approx 5.4$ $\qquad b = \dfrac{11}{\cos 26°}$

$\qquad\qquad\qquad\qquad b \approx 12.2$

**16.** $\tan 37° = \dfrac{9}{a}$ and $\sin 37° = \dfrac{9}{b}$

$a\tan 37° = 9$ $\qquad b\sin 37° = 9$

$a = \dfrac{9}{\tan 37°}$ $\qquad b = \dfrac{9}{\sin 37°}$

$a \approx 11.9$ $\qquad b \approx 15$

**17.** $\cos 53° = \dfrac{a}{17}$ and $\sin 53° = \dfrac{b}{17}$

$a = 17\cos 53°$ $\qquad b = 17\sin 53°$

$a \approx 10.2$ $\qquad b \approx 13.6$

**18.** $\sin 65° = \dfrac{6}{a}$ and $\tan 65° = \dfrac{6}{b}$

$a\sin 65° = 6$ $\qquad b\tan 65° = 6$

$a = \dfrac{6}{\sin 65°}$ $\qquad b = \dfrac{6}{\tan 65°}$

$a \approx 6.6$ $\qquad b \approx 2.8$

**19.** $\tan 29° = \dfrac{a}{14}$ and $\cos 29° = \dfrac{14}{b}$

$a = 14\tan 29°$ $\qquad b\cos 29° = 14$

$a \approx 7.8$ $\qquad b = \dfrac{14}{\cos 29°}$

$\qquad\qquad\qquad\qquad b \approx 16$

**20.** $\sin 35° = \cos(90° - 35°) = \cos 55°$

$\cos 35° = \sin(90° - 35°) = \sin 55°$

**21.** $a°$ and $b°$ are complementary, so $\cos b° = \sin a° = 3/5$.

**22.** $c°$ and $d°$ are complementary, so $\tan c° = 2$.

**23.** $\sin 50° = \dfrac{a}{8}$ and $\sin 40° = \dfrac{a}{b} = \dfrac{6.1}{b}$

$a = 8\sin 50°$ $\qquad b\sin 40° = 6.1$

$a \approx 6.1$ $\qquad b = \dfrac{6.1}{\sin 40°}$

$\qquad\qquad\qquad\qquad b \approx 9.5$

**24.** $\tan 68° = \dfrac{a}{5}$ and $\tan 74° = \dfrac{a}{b} = \dfrac{12.4}{b}$

$a = 5\tan 68°$ $\qquad b\tan 74° = 12.4$

$a \approx 12.4$ $\qquad b = \dfrac{12.4}{\tan 74°}$

$\qquad\qquad\qquad\qquad b \approx 3.6$

**25.** $\sin 26° = \dfrac{3}{a}$ and $\sin 39° = \dfrac{a}{b} = \dfrac{6.8}{b}$

$a\sin 26° = 3$ $\qquad b\sin 39° = 6.8$

$a = \dfrac{3}{\sin 26°}$ $\qquad b = \dfrac{6.8}{\sin 39°}$

$a \approx 6.8$ $\qquad b \approx 10.8$

**26.** A) Opposite sides are congruent.

E) Diagonals bisect each other.

F) One pair of sides is parallel and congruent.

| | $x$ | $\sin \theta$ | $\cos \theta$ | $\tan \theta$ |
|---|---|---|---|---|
| **1.** | 3 | $\dfrac{4}{5}$ | $\dfrac{3}{5}$ | $\dfrac{4}{3}$ |
| **2.** | $\sqrt{5}$ | $\dfrac{2}{\sqrt{5}} = \dfrac{2\sqrt{5}}{5}$ | $\dfrac{1}{\sqrt{5}} = \dfrac{\sqrt{5}}{5}$ | 2 |
| **3.** | $\sqrt{2}$ | $\dfrac{1}{\sqrt{2}} = \dfrac{\sqrt{2}}{2}$ | $\dfrac{1}{\sqrt{2}} = \dfrac{\sqrt{2}}{2}$ | 1 |

**4.** $\sin 40° = \dfrac{x}{15}$

$x = 15 \sin 40°$

$x \approx 9.6$

**5.** $\cos 53° = \dfrac{7}{x}$

$x \cos 53° = 7$

$x = \dfrac{7}{\cos 53°}$

$x \approx 11.6$

**6.** $\tan 28° = \dfrac{x}{4}$

$x = 4 \tan 28°$

$x \approx 2.1$

**7.** $\sin^{-1} (2/5) \approx 23.6°$

**8.** $\cos^{-1} (4/9) \approx 63.6°$

**9.** $\sin \theta = \dfrac{10}{17}$

$\theta = \sin^{-1} (10/17)$

$\theta \approx 36°$

**10.** $\cos \theta = \dfrac{9}{15} = \dfrac{3}{5}$

$\theta = \cos^{-1} (3/5)$

$\theta \approx 53.1°$

**11.** $\tan \theta = \dfrac{4}{8} = \dfrac{1}{2}$

$\theta = \tan^{-1} (1/2)$

$\theta \approx 26.6°$

**12.** $\sin^{-1} (0.25) \approx 14.5°$

**13.** $\cos^{-1} (1/5) \approx 78.5°$

**14.** $\tan^{-1} (3/8) \approx 20.6°$

**15.** $\sin \theta = \dfrac{5}{15} = \dfrac{1}{3}$

$\theta = \sin^{-1} (1/3)$

$\theta \approx 19.5°$

**16.** $\tan \theta = \dfrac{5}{8}$

$\theta = \tan^{-1} (5/8)$

$\theta \approx 32°$

**17.** $\cos \theta = \dfrac{9}{17}$

$\theta = \cos^{-1} (9/17)$

$\theta \approx 58°$

**18.** $\tan \theta = \dfrac{14}{7} = 2$

$\theta = \tan^{-1} (2)$

$\theta \approx 63.4°$

**19.** $\sin \theta = \dfrac{18}{22} = \dfrac{9}{11}$

$\theta = \sin^{-1} (9/11)$

$\theta \approx 54.9°$

**20.** $\cos \theta = \dfrac{5}{13}$

$\theta = \cos^{-1} (5/13)$

$\theta \approx 67.4°$

**21.** $\sin 50° = \dfrac{x}{6}$ and $\sin \theta = \dfrac{x}{7.3} = \dfrac{4.6}{7.3}$

$x = 6 \sin 50°$ $\qquad \theta = \sin^{-1} (4.6/7.3)$

$x \approx 4.6$ $\qquad \theta \approx 39.1°$

**22.** $\tan 67° = \dfrac{x}{4}$ and $\tan \theta = \dfrac{x}{3} = \dfrac{9.4}{3}$

$x = 4 \tan 67°$ $\qquad \theta = \tan^{-1} (9.4/3)$

$x \approx 9.4$ $\qquad \theta \approx 72.3°$

**23.** $\tan 25° = \dfrac{x}{8}$ and $\tan \theta = \dfrac{8}{11 + x} = \dfrac{8}{14.7}$

$x = 8 \tan 25°$ $\qquad \theta = \tan^{-1} (8/14.7)$

$x \approx 3.7$ $\qquad \theta \approx 28.6°$

**24.** A) true; Bases are parallel.

B) true; Legs are congruent.

C) false; Diagonals are congruent, but not necessarily perpendicular.

D) true; Each pair of base angles is congruent.

E) false; $MN = (PQ + SR)/2$

# LESSON 80 ·········································

**1.** cosine

$\cos 35° = \dfrac{a}{8}$

$a = 8 \cos 35°$

$a \approx 6.6$

**2.** sine

$\sin 35° = \dfrac{b}{8}$

$b = 8 \sin 35°$

$b \approx 4.6$

**3.** $z^2 = 6^2 - 4^2$

$z^2 = 20$

$z = 2\sqrt{5} \approx 4.5$

**4.** sine

$x = \sin^{-1} (4/6)$

$x \approx 41.8°$

**5.** complementary

$y = 90 - x \approx 48.2°$

**6.** Find $AB$: $AB^2 = 5^2 + 9^2 = 106$

$AB = \sqrt{106} \approx 10.3$

Find $m\angle B$: $\tan B = 5/9$

$m\angle B = \tan^{-1} (5/9) \approx 29.1°$

Find $m\angle A$: $m\angle A \approx 90 - 29.1 = 60.9°$

You could use the Triangle Sum Theorem [32.1] to find $m\angle A \approx 180 - 90 - 29.1 = 60.9°$.

**7.** Find $AC$: $AC^2 = 11^2 - 8^2 = 57$

$AC = \sqrt{57} \approx 7.5$

Find $m\angle B$: $\cos B = 8/11$

$m\angle B = \cos^{-1} (8/11) \approx 43.3°$

Find $m\angle A$: $m\angle A \approx 90 - 43.3 = 46.7°$

8.  Find $AB$:   $\cos 57° = 7 / AB$

$AB = 7 / \cos 57° \approx 12.9$

Find $BC$:   $\tan 57° = BC / 7$

$BC = 7 \tan 57° \approx 10.8$

Find $m\angle B$:   $m\angle B = 90 - 57 = 33°$

**9 ~ 10.**  *Answers may vary slightly due to rounding.*

9.  a.  $BD = 10 \sin 54° \approx 8.1$

$AD = 10 \cos 54° \approx 5.9$

$m\angle ABD = 90 - 54 = 36°$

b.  $BD \approx 8.1$ (Found in Problem 9a.)

$m\angle C \approx \tan^{-1}(8.1/10) \approx 39°$

$m\angle CBD \approx 90 - 39 = 51°$

$BC = 10 / \sin 51° \approx 12.9$

c.  $BC \approx 12.9$ (Found in Problem 9b.)

$AC = AD + DC \approx 5.9 + 10 = 15.9$

$m\angle C \approx 39°$ (Found in Problem 9b.)

$m\angle ABC = m\angle ABD + m\angle CBD \approx 36 + 51 = 87°$

10.  a.  $AC = \sqrt{14^2 + 4^2} = \sqrt{212} \approx 14.6$

$m\angle CAD = \tan^{-1}(4/14) \approx 15.9°$

$m\angle ACD \approx 90 - 15.9 = 74.1°$

b.  $BD = \sqrt{16^2 - 14^2} = \sqrt{60} \approx 7.7$

$m\angle BAD = \cos^{-1}(14/16) \approx 29°$

$m\angle B \approx 90 - 29 = 61°$

c.  $BC = BD - CD \approx 7.7 - 4 = 3.7$

$AC \approx 14.6$ (Found in Problem 10a.)

$m\angle B \approx 61°$ (Found in Problem 10b.)

$m\angle BCA \approx 180 - m\angle ACD = 180 - 74.1 = 105.9°$

$m\angle BAC = m\angle BAD - m\angle CAD \approx 29 - 15.9 = 13.1°$

11.  $x^2 = 12^2 + 9^2$

$x^2 = 225$

$x = 15$

12.  $\tan 59° = x/13$

$x = 13 \tan 59°$

$x \approx 21.6$

13.  $\cos x° = 15/16$

$x = \cos^{-1}(15/16)$

$x = 20.4°$

14.  $AB = \sqrt{7^2 + 10^2} = \sqrt{149} \approx 12.2$

$m\angle A = \tan^{-1}(10/7) \approx 55°$

$m\angle B \approx 90 - 55 = 35°$

15.  $BC = \sqrt{9^2 - 5^2} = \sqrt{56} \approx 7.5$

$m\angle A = \cos^{-1}(5/9) \approx 56.3°$

$m\angle B \approx 90 - 56.3 = 33.7°$

16.  $AB = \sqrt{8^2 + 14^2} = \sqrt{260} \approx 16.1$

$m\angle A = \tan^{-1}(14/8) \approx 60.3°$

$m\angle B \approx 90 - 60.3 = 29.7°$

17.  $BC = 7 \sin 35° \approx 4$

$AC = 7 \cos 35° \approx 5.7$

$m\angle B = 90 - 35 = 55°$

18.  $AC = 14 \tan 24° \approx 6.2$

$AB = 14 / \cos 24° \approx 15.3$

$m\angle A = 90 - 24 = 66°$

19.  $AB = 9.8 / \sin 74° \approx 10.2$

$BC = 9.8 / \tan 74° \approx 2.8$

$m\angle A = 90 - 74 = 16°$

**20 ~ 21.**  *Answers may vary slightly due to rounding.*

20.  a.  $AB = 13 / \sin 55° \approx 15.9$

$BD = 13 / \tan 55° \approx 9.1$

$m\angle A = 90 - 55 = 35°$

b.  $BD \approx 9.1$ (Found in Problem 20a.)

$m\angle CBD = \cos^{-1}(9.1/11) \approx 34.2°$

$m\angle C \approx 90 - 34.2 = 55.8°$

$DC = 11 \cos 55.8° \approx 6.2$

c.  $AB \approx 15.9$ (Found in Problem 20a.)

$AC = AD + DC \approx 13 + 6.2 = 19.2$

$m\angle A = 35°$ (Found in Problem 20a.)

$m\angle C \approx 55.8°$ (Found in Problem 20b.)

$m\angle ABC \approx 180 - 35 - 55.8 = 89.2°$

21.  a.  $AD = 7 \tan 50° \approx 8.3$

$AC = 7 / \cos 50° \approx 10.9$

$m\angle DAC = 90 - 50 = 40°$

b.  $\triangle ABD$ is a 30-60-90 triangle.

$AD \approx 8.3$ (Found in Problem 21a.)

$BD = AD\sqrt{3} = (8.3)(\sqrt{3}) \approx 14.4$

$AB = 2AD \approx 2(8.3) = 16.6$

$m\angle DAB = 90 - 30 = 60°$

c.  $AC \approx 10.9$ (Found in Problem 2a.)

$AB \approx 16.6$ (Found in Problem 2b.)

$BC = BD - CD \approx 14.4 - 7 = 7.4$

$m\angle ACB = 180 - 50 = 130°$

$m\angle BAC = 180 - 130 - 30 = 20°$

22.  Use a 30-60-90 triangle.

$a = 5\sqrt{3}$

$b = 2(5) = 10$

23.  B is similar by AA.

D is similar by SSS.

E is similar by SAS.

# LESSON 81

1. Opposite sides are congruent and parallel.
   Opposite angles are congruent.
   Consecutive angles are supplementary.

2. 50°, 130°, 50°, 130°

3. $h = 7 \sin 51° \approx 5.4$

4. area $= (11h)/2 \approx (11)(5.4)/2 = 29.7$ square units

5. $\sin 53° = \sin 127° = 0.79863...$

6. $\sin 150° = \sin 30° = \dfrac{1}{2}$

   $\sin 135° = \sin 45° = \dfrac{1}{\sqrt{2}} = \dfrac{\sqrt{2}}{2}$

   $\sin 120° = \sin 60° = \dfrac{\sqrt{3}}{2}$

7. area $= \dfrac{1}{2}(10)(10) \sin 85° \approx 49.8$

8. area $= \dfrac{1}{2}(15)(19) \sin 40° \approx 91.6$

9. area $= \dfrac{1}{2}(17)(19) \sin 106° \approx 155.2$

10. included angle $= 180 - 27 - 44 = 109°$

    area $= \dfrac{1}{2}(12)(18) \sin 109° \approx 102.1$

11. included angle $= 180 - 68 = 112$
    area $= (12)(16) \sin 112° \approx 178$

12. included angle $= 108°$
    area $= (15)(26) \sin 108° \approx 370.9$

13. area $= \dfrac{1}{2}(13)(13) \sin 39° \approx 53.2$

14. area $= \dfrac{1}{2}(16)(22) \sin 78° \approx 172.2$

15. included angle $= 180 - 35 - 40 = 105°$

    area $= \dfrac{1}{2}(25)(22) \sin 105° \approx 265.6$

16. area $= (13)(14) \sin 115° \approx 164.9$

17. included angle $= 103°$
    area $= (23)(19) \sin 103° \approx 425.8$

18. included angle $= 180 - 99 = 81°$
    area $= (16)(12) \sin 81° \approx 189.6$

19. height $= 6 \sin 60° \approx 5.2$

    area $= \dfrac{1}{2}(6)(6) \sin 60° \approx 15.6$

20. side length $= 16/4 = 4$
    area $= (4)(4) \sin 40° \approx 10.3$

21. Opposite sides of a parallelogram are congruent, so the parallelogram has side lengths of 10 and 5.
    area $= (10)(5) \sin 110° \approx 47$

22. See the kite on the right.
    perimeter $= 2(5) + 2(7) = 24$
    area = 2 congruent triangles
    $= 2(1/2)(5)(7) \sin 106°$
    $\approx 33.6$

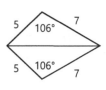

23. $\dfrac{6}{30} = \dfrac{1.6}{x}$

    $6x = 30(1.6)$

    $x = 8$ m

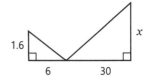

# LESSON 82

1. $\theta$ and 31° are alternate exterior angles, so $\theta = 31°$.

2. $x = 9 \tan \theta = 9 \tan 31° \approx 5.4$

3 ~ 14.  *Diagrams are not drawn to scale.*

3. $x = 1.6$
   $y = 20 \tan 35° \approx 14$
   $h = x + y \approx 15.6$
   The tree is about 15.6 m tall.

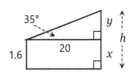

4. $x = 150 \tan 22° \approx 60.6$
   $y = 150 \tan 38° \approx 117.2$
   $h = x + y \approx 177.8$
   The taller building is about 177.8 ft tall.

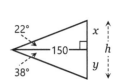

5. $x = 60 / \tan 18° \approx 184.7$
   $y = 60 / \tan 10° \approx 340.3$
   $d = y - x \approx 155.6$
   The distance between the two ships is about 155.6 m.

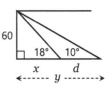

6. $x = 15 \sin 54° \approx 12.1$
   The top of the ladder reaches about 12.1 ft high.

7. $x = 80 / \sin 65° \approx 88.3$
   The length of the string is about 88.3 m.

8. $\theta = 34°$
   $x = 90 / \tan 34° \approx 133.4$
   The ship is about 133.4 ft away from the lighthouse.

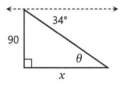

**9.** $\theta = 15°$

$x = 56 / \tan 15° \approx 209$

The boat is about 209 ft away from the lighthouse.

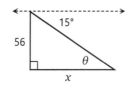

**10.** $x = 75$

$y = 150 \tan 38° \approx 117.2$

$h = x + y \approx 192.2$

The taller building is about 192.2 ft tall.

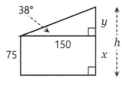

**11.** $x = 90$

$y = 120 - z = 30$

$z = y / \tan 20° \approx 82.4$

The two buildings are about 82.4 m apart.

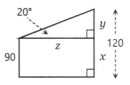

**12.** $x = 25 / \tan 48° \approx 22.5$

$y = 25 / \tan 26° \approx 51.3$

$d = y - x \approx 28.8$

The distance between the two cars is about 28.8 m.

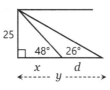

**13.** max $h = 80 \sin 65° \approx 72.5$

min $h = 80 \sin 40° \approx 51.4$

The maximum height is about 72.5 ft and the minimum height is about 51.4 ft.

**14.** $d = (100 \text{ ft/s})(5 \text{ sec}) = 500 \text{ ft}$

$h = d \sin 22° \approx 187.3$

The plane is about 187.3 ft above the ground.

**15.** $\dfrac{4}{x} = \dfrac{5}{20}$  →  $5x = 4(20)$  →  $x = 16$ ft

## LESSON 83

**1.** $\dfrac{1}{\sqrt{5}} \cdot \dfrac{\sqrt{5}}{\sqrt{5}} = \dfrac{\sqrt{5}}{5}$

**2.** $\dfrac{6}{\sqrt{2}} \cdot \dfrac{\sqrt{2}}{\sqrt{2}} = \dfrac{6\sqrt{2}}{2} = 3\sqrt{2}$

**3.** $x^2 = 5^2 + 10^2$

$x^2 = 125$

$x = 5\sqrt{5}$

**4.** $7^2 = 6^2 + x^2$

$x^2 = 13$

$x = \sqrt{13}$

**5.** yes; $29^2 = 20^2 + 21^2$

**6.** obtuse; $10^2 > 8^2 + 3^2$

**7.** $a = b = 4$

**8.** $a = 3\sqrt{3}$

$a = 2(3) = 6$

**9.** $\sin \theta = \dfrac{5}{13}$    $\cos \theta = \dfrac{12}{13}$    $\tan \theta = \dfrac{5}{12}$

**10.** $\sin \theta = \dfrac{15}{17}$    $\cos \theta = \dfrac{8}{17}$    $\tan \theta = \dfrac{15}{8}$

**11.** $\sin 35° = \dfrac{x}{7}$

$x = 7 \sin 35°$

$x \approx 4$

**12.** $\cos 52° = \dfrac{x}{12}$

$x = 12 \cos 52°$

$x \approx 7.4$

**13.** $\cos 21° = \dfrac{7}{x}$

$x \cos 21° = 7$

$x = \dfrac{7}{\cos 21°}$

$x \approx 7.5$

**14.** $\tan 59° = \dfrac{10}{x}$

$x \tan 59° = 10$

$x = \dfrac{10}{\tan 59°}$

$x \approx 6$

**15.** $\tan \theta = \dfrac{4}{11}$

$\theta = \tan^{-1}(4/11)$

$\theta \approx 20°$

**16.** $\sin \theta = \dfrac{17}{19}$

$\theta = \sin^{-1}(17/19)$

$\theta \approx 63.5°$

**17.** $\tan \theta = \dfrac{5.3}{4}$

$\theta = \tan^{-1}(5.3/4)$

$\theta \approx 53°$

**18.** $\cos \theta = \dfrac{16}{18}$

$\theta = \cos^{-1}(16/18)$

$\theta \approx 27.3°$

**19.** $BC = \sqrt{21^2 - 17^2} = \sqrt{152} \approx 12.3$

$m\angle A = \cos^{-1}(17/21) \approx 36°$

$m\angle B \approx 90 - 36 = 54°$

**20.** $AB = 9 / \cos 56° \approx 16.1$

$BC = 9 \tan 56° \approx 13.3$

$m\angle B = 90 - 56 = 34°$

**21.** area $= (1/2)(10)(15) \sin 70° \approx 70.5$

**22.** area $= (10)(18) \sin 100° \approx 177.3$

**23 ~ 24.** *Diagrams are not drawn to scale.*

**23.** $x = 13 \sin 75° \approx 12.6$

The top of the ladder reaches about 12.6 ft high.

**24.** $x = 100 \tan 20° \approx 36.4$

$y = 100 \tan 24° \approx 44.5$

$h = x + y \approx 80.9$

The taller building is about 80.9 m tall.

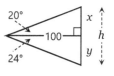

**25.** 2. Alternate interior ∠s on parallel lines are ≅.

3. Reflexive Property

4. SAS

5. CPCTC

6. If alternate interior ∠s are ≅, then lines are parallel.

7. Def. of parallelogram

## LESSON 84

1.

2. sometimes

3. 1 line; See the Parallel Postulate [7.8].

4. Use the Segment Addition Postulate [7.6].
   $DE + EF = DF$
   $x + 2x = 18; x = 6$
   $DE = x = 6$

5. 100° and $(x + 35)$ ° are congruent as vertical angles.
   $x + 35 = 100; x = 65$

6. $x$ and 118° are supplementary.
   $x = 180 - 118 = 62$

   $x$ and $y$ are congruent as alternate interior angles.
   $y = x = 62$

7. interior angle sum of a triangle = 180
   $3x + 2x + 105 = 180; x = 15$

8. interior angle sum of a pentagon = $180(5 - 2) = 540°$
   $x + 95 + 102 + 123 + 98 = 540; x = 122$

9. 4 lines of symmetry
   angle of rotational symmetry = 90°

10. The translation maps $P(2, -6)$ to $P'(-1, 0)$.
    The reflection maps $P'(-1, 0)$ to $P''(0, -1)$.
    So, the final image is $(0, -1)$.

**11 ~ 12.** *Answers may vary. Samples are given.*

11. a reflection over the $x$-axis followed by a translation of 6 units left and 1 unit up

12. a reflection over the $y$-axis followed by a dilation about the origin by scale factor 2

13. Each time the numerator doubles. The next two terms are 1/32 and 1/64.

14. Each figure has one more square horizontally than the previous figure. The next two figures are:

15. Assume $x < 4$ is false. Then $x \geq 4$. Use algebra to try to make $x \geq 4$ equal to the given statement. Multiplying each side by 2 and adding 7 would produce $2x + 7 \geq 15$. This contradicts the given statement that $2x + 7 < 15$. Therefore, our assumption is wrong and $x < 4$ is true.

16. Assume $\angle 1$ and $\angle 2$ are both obtuse. An obtuse angle is greater than 90°. So if $\angle 1$ and $\angle 2$ are both obtuse, then they add up to greater than 180°. This contradicts the given statement that $\angle 1$ and $\angle 2$ are supplementary angles which add up to 180°. Therefore, $\angle 1$ and $\angle 2$ cannot be both obtuse.

17. 2. If lines are ∥, then alternate interior angles are ≅.
    3. Def. of congruent angles
    5. Substitution Property

18. $\triangle ABC \cong \triangle ADC$ by SSS.

19. $\triangle DEG \cong \triangle FEG$ by ASA.

20. $\triangle HIJ \cong \triangle JKH$ by HL.

21. $\triangle PEF \cong \triangle PGH$ by SAS.

22. Congruent triangles have congruent angles.
    $m\angle HEG = m\angle FGE = 28°$

    Angles in a triangle add up to 180°.
    $28 + 4x + 104 = 180; x = 12$

23. Base angles of an isosceles triangle are congruent.
    $m\angle U = m\angle T = 5x°$

    Angles in a triangle add up to 180°.
    $10x + 5x + 5x = 180; x = 9$

24. $y = -x$

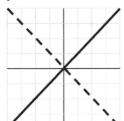

25. $(2, 0)$

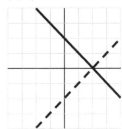

## LESSON 85

1. A midsegment is half the length of the third side.
   $3x - 8 = 2(14); x = 12$

2. A midsegment is parallel to the third side.
   Corresponding angles on parallel lines congruent.
   $5x + 1 = 56; x = 11$

3. Any point on the perpendicular bisector of a segment is equidistant from the endpoints of the segment.
   $9x - 8 = 4x + 7; x = 3$

4. An angle bisector divides an angle into two congruent angles. Angles in a triangle add up to 180°.
   $90 + 56 + 2(x - 9) = 180; x = 26$

5. A median divides the side to which it is drawn into two congruent segments.
   $7x - 8 = 3x; x = 2$

6. An altitude forms right angles with the side to which it is drawn. Angles in a triangle add up to 180°.
   $90 + 56 + (x + 18) = 180; x = 16$

7. perpendicular bisector

8. A circumcenter is equidistant from the vertices of its triangle.

   $YC = ZC = XC = 10$

9. median

10. A centroid divides a median in the ratio 2:1.

    $PE = PB/2 = 12/2 = 6$

    $BE = 3PE = 3(6) = 18$

11. no; 4 + 6 > 10 is false. The sum of two sides of a triangle must be greater than the third side.

12. The sum of two sides of a triangle must be greater than the third side. Let $x$ be the third side.

    | | | |
    |---|---|---|
    | $x + 3 > 5$ | $x + 5 > 3$ | $3 + 5 > x$ |
    | $x > 2$ | $x > -2$ | $x < 8$ |

    Combine the inequalities to get 2 < $x$ < 8. So, the third side must be longer than 2 and shorter than 8.

13. The longer side has the larger opposite angle.

    $\angle C$ is bigger than $\angle A$ because $AB > BC$.

14. Statements (Reasons)

    1. midsegments $\overline{PQ}, \overline{QR}, \overline{PR}$ (Given)

    2. $PQ = \frac{1}{2}AB, QR = \frac{1}{2}BC, PR = \frac{1}{2}AC$

       (A midsegment is half the length of the third side. See Theorem 46.1.)

    3. perimeter of $\triangle PQR = PQ + QR + PR$, perimeter of $\triangle ABC = AB + BC + AC$ (Def. of perimeter)

    4. perimeter of $\triangle PQR = \frac{1}{2}AB + \frac{1}{2}BC + \frac{1}{2}AC$

       (Substitution Property)

    5. perimeter of $\triangle PQR = \frac{1}{2}(AB + BC + AC)$

       (Distributive Property)

    6. perimeter of $\triangle PQR = \frac{1}{2}$ perimeter of $\triangle ABC$

       (Substitution Property)

15. parallelogram, rhombus, rectangle, square

16. rectangle, square

17. rhombus, square, kite

18. Opposite angles are congruent.

    $m\angle A = m\angle C = 70°$

    Consecutive angles are supplementary.

    $m\angle B = m\angle D = 180 - 70 = 110°$

19. Opposite sides are congruent.

    $AB = CD; 3x = 2x + 18; x = 18$

    Diagonals bisect each other.

    $AC = 2AE; 7y + 30 = 2(5y); y = 10$

20. $\triangle EPF \cong \triangle EPH \cong \triangle GPF \cong \triangle GPH$

    All sides are congruent. Diagonals bisect each other and are perpendicular. So, the four right triangles are congruent by SSS, SAS, or HL.

21. Diagonals bisect opposite angles.

    $m\angle F = 2(m\angle EFP) = 2(56) = 112°$

    Opposite angles are congruent.

    $m\angle H = m\angle F = 112°$

    Consecutive angles are supplementary.

    $m\angle E = m\angle G = 180 - 112 = 68°$

22. $\triangle PQR \cong \triangle QPS \cong \triangle SRQ \cong \triangle RSP$

    All angles are right angles. Opposite sides are congruent. Diagonals are congruent. So, the four right triangles are congruent by SSS, SAS, or HL.

23. Diagonals are congruent.

    $PR = QS; x + 5 = 3x - 7; x = 6$

    $PR = 6 + 5 = 11$

24. Base angles are congruent.

    $m\angle Z = m\angle Y = 68°$

    Non-base angles are supplementary.

    $m\angle W = m\angle X = 180 - 68 = 112°$

25. The midsegment is parallel to the bases. Corresponding angles on parallel lines congruent.

    $m\angle WMN = m\angle Z = 68°$

    $m\angle XNM = m\angle Y = 68°$

26. The midsegment is half the sum of the bases.

    $MN = (WX + ZY)/2 = (15 + 27)/2 = 21$

27. Angles in a triangle add up to 180°. See $\triangle STV$.

    $m\angle S = 180 - m\angle STP - m\angle SVP = 180 - 45 - 30 = 105°$

    Non-vertex angles are congruent.

    $m\angle U = m\angle S = 105°$

28. Vertex angles are bisected by a diagonal.

    $m\angle UTP = m\angle STP = 45°$

    $m\angle UVP = m\angle SVP = 30°$

29. Statements (Reasons)

    1. $\square ABCD$ (Given)

    2. $\overline{BA} \parallel \overline{CD}, \overline{BC} \parallel \overline{AD}$ (Def. of parallelogram)

    3. $\angle BAC \cong \angle DCA, \angle BCA \cong \angle DAC$ (Alternate interior $\angle$s on parallel lines are $\cong$.)

    4. $\overline{AC} \cong \overline{CA}$ (Reflexive Property)

    5. $\triangle ABC \cong \triangle CDA$ (ASA)

    6. $\overline{AB} \cong \overline{CD}, \overline{BC} \cong \overline{DA}$ (CPCTC)

## LESSON 86

1. $\angle G \cong \angle G$ by the Reflexive Property.
   $\angle E \cong \angle HFG$ because $m\angle HFG = 180 - 130 = 50°$.
   So, $\triangle DEG \sim \triangle HFG$ by AA.

2. $\angle B \cong \angle B$ by the Reflexive Property.
   $\angle BAC \cong \angle D$ because $m\angle BAC = 180 - 37 - 93 = 50°$.
   So, $\triangle BAC \sim \triangle BDA$ by AA.

3. $\angle KML \cong \angle OMN$ as vertical angles.
   $KM/OM = 55/75 = 11/15$
   $LM/NM = 50/70 = 5/7$
   So, the triangles are not similar.

4. $PQ/XY = 12/20 = 3/5$
   $QR/YZ = 9/15 = 3/5$
   $PR/XZ = 15/25 = 3/5$
   So, $\triangle PQR \sim \triangle XYZ$ by SSS.

5. Use the Leg Rule.
   $6^2 = 3(3 + x)$
   $x = 9$

6. Use the Altitude Rule.
   $8^2 = x(4x)$
   $x^2 = 16$
   $x = 4$

7. Use Theorem 70.1.
   $\dfrac{4}{x} = \dfrac{15}{18}$
   $15x = 4(18)$
   $x = 24/5$

8. Use Theorem 69.2.
   $\dfrac{8}{6x} = \dfrac{5x}{15}$
   $(6x)(5x) = 8(15)$
   $x^2 = 4$
   $x = 2$

9. Statements (Reasons)
   1. midsegment $\overline{BC}$ (Given)
   2. $\overline{BC} \parallel \overline{DE}$ (A midsegment is parallel to the 3rd side.)
   3. $\angle ABC \cong \angle D$ (Corresponding $\angle$s on $\parallel$ lines are $\cong$.)
   4. $\angle A \cong \angle A$ (Reflexive Property)
   5. $\triangle ABC \sim \triangle ADE$ (AA)
   6. $\dfrac{AB}{AD} = \dfrac{AC}{AE}$ (Corresponding sides of similar triangles are proportional.)

10. $\dfrac{20}{135} = \dfrac{24}{x} \quad \rightarrow \quad 20x = 135(24) \quad \rightarrow \quad x = 162$ m

11. $AD/AB = AE/AC = 1/3$
    $\angle A \cong \angle A$ by the Reflexive Property.
    So, $\triangle ADE \sim \triangle ABC$ by SAS.

    Corresponding sides are proportional.
    $DE/BC = 1/3$; $BC = 3DE = 3(15) = 45$ ft
    So, the pond is 45 feet wide.

12. $x^2 = 3^2 + 6^2$
    $x^2 = 45$
    $x = 3\sqrt{5}$

13. $11^2 = 9^2 + x^2$
    $x^2 = 40$
    $x = 2\sqrt{10}$

14. right; $10^2 = 8^2 + 6^2$

15. obtuse; $(5\sqrt{6})^2 > 5^2 + 11^2$

16. $a = 7\sqrt{3}$
    $b = 2(7) = 14$

17. $a = 5$
    $b = 5\sqrt{2}$

18. $\sin 30° = \dfrac{1}{2}$ $\qquad \cos 30° = \dfrac{\sqrt{3}}{2}$ $\qquad \tan 30° = \dfrac{1}{\sqrt{3}} = \dfrac{\sqrt{3}}{3}$

19. $a°$ and $b°$ are complementary. The cosine of an acute angle is equal to the sine of its complement.
    $\cos b° = \sin a° = 2/5$

20. $AC = \sqrt{14^2 - 12^2} = \sqrt{52} \approx 7.2$
    $m\angle A = \sin^{-1}(12/14) \approx 59°$
    $m\angle B \approx 90 - 59 = 31°$

21. $BC = 8 \sin 62° \approx 7.1$
    $AC = 8 \cos 62° \approx 3.8$
    $m\angle B = 90 - 62 = 28°$

22. area $= (1/2)(19)(15) \sin 40° \approx 91.6$

23. included angle $= 180 - 68 = 112°$
    area $= (12)(16) \sin 112° \approx 178$

24 ~ 25. *Diagrams are not drawn to scale.*

24. $x = 1.7$
    $y = 30 \tan 34° \approx 20.2$
    $h = x + y \approx 21.9$
    The tree is about 21.9 m tall.

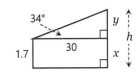

25. $\theta = 15°$
    $x = 56 / \tan 15° \approx 209$
    The boat is about 209 ft away from the lighthouse.

## LESSON 89

1. A) false; A line has no endpoints.
   B) false; Any three points are coplanar.
   C) true
   D) false; Only acute angles have complements.
   E) false; All equilateral triangles are isosceles.
   G) true

2. $(5x - 4)°$ and the angle to the right of $64°$ are corresponding angles and must be congruent.
   $5x - 4 = 180 - 64; x = 24$

3. D

4. interior angle sum $= 180(n - 2) = 180(5 - 2) = 540°$
   one interior angle $= 540/5 = 108°$

5. A) false; Dilations produce similar figures.
   B) true; Dilations produce similar figures.
   C) false; $DE = 2AB$
   D) true; Reflections and dilations preserve angles.

**6.** An angle bisector creates two congruent angles.

$m\angle ABP = m\angle PBC$

$3x + 7 = 5x - 9$; $x = 8$

$m\angle ABC = 2m\angle ABP = 2(3x + 7) = 2(31) = 62°$

**7.** The translation maps $P(3, -4)$ to $P'(2, 1)$.

The reflection maps $P'(2, 1)$ to $P''(1, 2)$.

So, the final image is (1, 2).

**8.**  A) parallelogram; Opposite angles are congruent.

B) parallelogram; Diagonals bisect each other.

C) parallelogram; Opposite sides are congruent.

D) not a parallelogram

**9.**  2.  Segment Addition Postulate

4.  Subtraction Property

**10.** D

**11.** Corresponding sides must be proportional.

$\dfrac{24}{18} = \dfrac{16}{x}$  →  $24x = 18(16)$  →  $x = 12$

$\dfrac{24}{18} = \dfrac{28}{y}$  →  $24y = 18(28)$  →  $y = 21$

**12.** The sum of two sides of a triangle must be greater than the third side. Let $x$ be the third side.

$x + 5 > 9$      $x + 9 > 5$      $5 + 9 > x$

$x > 4$        $x > -4$      $x < 14$

Combine the three inequalities to get $4 < x < 14$.

**13.** A midsegment is half the length of the third side, so the perimeter of $\triangle PQR$ is half the perimeter of $\triangle ABC$.

**14.** B, C, D

**15.** Corresponding angles are congruent.

$m\angle G = m\angle E = 75°$

Angles in a triangle add up to 180°.

$m\angle 1 = 180 - m\angle G - m\angle H = 180 - 75 - 55 = 50°$

**16.** C, B, D, A

**17.** Base angles of an isosceles triangle are congruent.

$2x = 5x - 45$; $x = 15$

base angle = 2(15) = 30°

Angles in a triangle add up to 180°.

vertex angle = 180 − 2(30) = 120°

**18.** Non-vertex angles are congruent.

$m\angle 1 = 113°$

Angles in a triangle add up to 180°.

$m\angle 2 = 180 - 27 - 113 = 40°$

**19.** C; $\cos 38° = x/13$, not $13/x$.

**20.** The altitudes are $\overline{BA}$, $\overline{BC}$ and $\overline{BF}$.

The orthocenter is $B$.

$\overline{AE}$ and $\overline{BD}$ are medians. $G$ is the centroid.

**21.**  2.  Def. of bisect (or def. of segment bisector)

3.  Vertical angles are congruent.

4.  SAS

**22.** B is similar by SSS.

C is similar by AA.

**23.** $T$ is the centroid and divides $\overline{AD}$ in the ratio 2:1.

$AD = 3TD = 3(6) = 18$

$AT = 2TD = 2(6) = 12$

**24.** Use the Altitude Rule [68.1].

$x^2 = 14(8) = 112$

$x = 4\sqrt{7}$

**25.** Use a 45-45-90 triangle.     Use a 30-60-90 triangle.

$a = 3$                  $c = 3\sqrt{3}$

$b = 3\sqrt{2}$            $d = 2(3) = 6$

**26.**  A) true; Bases are parallel.

B) true; Legs are congruent.

C) false; Diagonals are not necessarily perpendicular.

D) true; Diagonals are congruent.

**27.** Angles in a triangle add up to 180°.

$90 + 2x + (3x - 10) = 180$; $x = 20$

$m\angle B = 2(20) = 40°$

$m\angle C = 3(20) - 10 = 50°$

A) false; $AC < AB$ because $m\angle B < m\angle C$.

B) false; $AB + AC > BC$ by Theorem 52.3.

C) false; $\angle B$ is smallest, so $\overline{AC}$ is shortest.

D) true; $\angle A$ is largest, so $\overline{BC}$ is longest.

E) true

**28.** Consecutive angles of a parallelogram are supplementary, so $x + 5x = 180$ and $x = 30$.

Opposite angles of a parallelogram are congruent, so the parallelogram has angles 30°, 150°, 30°, and 150°.

**29.** $\dfrac{1.6}{x} = \dfrac{2.4}{12}$  →  $2.4x = 1.6(12)$  →  $x = 8$

The tree is 8 meters tall.

**30.** $\theta = 35°$

$x = 80 / \tan 35° \approx 114.3$

The ship is about 114.3 ft away from the lighthouse.

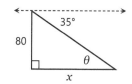

# LESSON 90

1. B, D, F

   A is false because the rays have different endpoints. C is false because two points determine a line. E is false because the supplement of an acute angle is obtuse.

2. B, C

3. A; The first step is to add 4 to both sides.

4. Use the Segment Addition Postulate [7.6].

   $AP + PB = AB$

   $2x + (3x - 2) = 18; x = 4$

   $AP = 2(4) = 8$

   $PB = 3(4) - 2 = 10$

5. Angles in a triangle add up to 180°.

   $x + 2x + 3x = 180$

   $x = 30$

   The triangle has angles measuring 30°, 60°, and 90°, so it is a right triangle.

6. Angles in a triangle add up to 180°.

   $m\angle BCA = 180 - 90 - 58 = 32°$

   If lines are parallel, then alternate interior angles are congruent.

   $m\angle 1 = m\angle BCA = 32°$

7. B

8. 3. All right angles are congruent.

   4. If corresponding angles are congruent, then lines are parallel.

9. A; A maps the point to (1, −1). B, C, and D map the point to (−1, −1).

10. Assume that $n$ is odd.

11. interior angle sum of a hexagon = 180(6 − 2) = 720°

12. A; 2 + 4 > 8 is false. The sum of two sides of a triangle must be greater than the third side.

13. D; The included angles must be congruent.

14. Use the Leg Rule [68.2].

    $12^2 = 6(6 + x)$

    $x = 18$

15. C; tan 60° = $\sqrt{3}$

16. Corresponding sides must be proportional.

    $\dfrac{16}{16 + 8} = \dfrac{x}{x + 7}$  →  $16(x + 7) = 24x$  →  $x = 14$

    $\dfrac{16}{16 + 8} = \dfrac{10}{y}$  →  $16y = 24(10)$  →  $y = 15$

17. A diagonal divides a rhombus into two congruent isosceles triangles with congruent base angles.

    $m\angle 1 = 62°$

    Angles in a triangle add up to 180°.

    $m\angle 2 = 180 - 62 - 62 = 56°$

18. In a parallelogram, opposite angles are congruent, and consecutive angles are supplementary.

    Let $4x$ and $5x$ be the two angles.

    $4x + 5x = 180; x = 20$

    The angles are 80°, 100°, 80°, and 100°.

19. D; The quadrilateral is a parallelogram because opposite sides are congruent. A rhombus is a parallelogram with perpendicular diagonals.

20. A centroid divides a median in the ratio 2:1.

    $AP = 2PD$

    $3x - 4 = 2x; x = 4$

    $AD = AP + PD = 8 + 4 = 12$

21. B, C, D, E

22. B

23. 3. If lines are parallel, then alternate interior angles are congruent.

    4. Reflexive Property

    5. ASA

24. A midsegment is half the length of the third side.

    perimeter of $\triangle STU = ST + TU + SU$

    $= XZ/2 + XY/2 + YZ/2$

    $= 15 + 13 + 12 = 40$

25. The midsegment is half the sum of the bases.

    $MN = (PQ + SR)/2$

    $7 = (5 + SR)/2$

    $SR = 9$

26. Angles in a triangle add up to 180°.

    $m\angle Z = 180 - 55 - 65 = 60°$

    The larger angle has the longer opposite side.

    $YZ < XY < XZ$ because $m\angle X < m\angle Z < m\angle Y$.

27. C

28. The triangle is obtuse because $11^2 > 7^2 + 8^2$.

29. sin 50° = x/20

    $x = 20 \sin 50° \approx 15.3$

    The top of the ladder reaches about 15.3 ft high.

30. $\dfrac{5}{h} = \dfrac{8}{24}$  →  $8h = 5(24)$  →  $x = 15$

    The tree is 15 ft tall.

**1.** Thm 91.1: Line $l$ is tangent to $\odot O$ at point $T$ if and only if $l \perp \overline{OT}$.

Thm 91.2: If $\overline{CA}$ and $\overline{CB}$ are tangent segments, then $\overline{CA} \cong \overline{CB}$.

**2.** $(x + 8)^2 = x^2 + 12^2$
$16x = 80$
$x = 5$

**3.** $14^2 = x^2 + 7^2$
$x^2 = 147$
$x = 7\sqrt{3}$

**4.** $x + 5 = 3x - 7$
$x = 6$

**5.** $9 - 3x = x - 1$
$x = 5/2$

**6.** $AD = AF = 11$
$BE = BD = 6$
$CE = CF = 12$
$\rightarrow$ perimeter
$= AB + BC + AC$
$= 17 + 18 + 23 = 58$

**7.** $AE = AH = 9$
$BE = 16 - AE = 7$
$BF = BE = 7$
$CF = CG = 10$
$DG = DH = 5$
$\rightarrow$ perimeter
$= AB + BC + CD + AD$
$= 16 + 17 + 15 + 14$
$= 62$

**8.** $(2x)^2 = x^2 + 9^2$
$x^2 = 27$
$x = 3\sqrt{3}$

**9.** $16^2 = x^2 + x^2$
$x^2 = 128$
$x = 8\sqrt{2}$

**10.** $63 + (5x + 2) + 90 = 180$
$x = 5$

**11.** $4 = 8 - x$
$x = 4$

**12.** $3x + 1 = 7x - 4$
$x = 5/4$

**13.** $x(x + 3) = 8x$
$x^2 - 5x = 0$
$x(x - 5) = 0$
$x = 5$

**14.** $BE = BD = 15$
$CE = CF = 9$
$AF = AD = 10$
$\rightarrow$ perimeter
$= AB + BC + AC$
$= 25 + 24 + 19 = 68$

**15.** $AE = AH = 6$
$BF = BE = 12$
$DG = DH = 14.6$
$CG = 20.8 - DG = 6.2$
$CF = CG = 6.2$
$\rightarrow$ perimeter
$= AB + BC + CD + AD$
$= 18 + 18.2 + 20.8 + 20.6$
$= 77.6$

**16.** $AH = AE = 14$
$DH = 18.4 - AH = 4.4$
$DG = DH = 4.4$
$CF = CG = 7.6$
$BF = 12.6 - CF = 5$
$BE = BF = 5$
$\rightarrow$ perimeter
$= AB + BC + CD + AD$
$= 19 + 12.6 + 12 + 18.4$
$= 62$

**17.** Assume that $l$ is not perpendicular to $\overline{OT}$. Then there must be a point $K$ on $l$ such that $l \perp \overline{OK}$.

By the definition of tangent, tangent line $l$ intersects circle $O$ at only $T$. This means that $K$ is outside of circle $O$ and thus $\overline{OK}$ is longer than radius $\overline{OT}$ ($OT < OK$).

But look at $\triangle OTK$. Because $l \perp \overline{OK}$, it is a right triangle with hypotenuse $\overline{OT}$. The hypotenuse is the longest side of a right triangle, meaning that $OT > OK$.

$OT < OK$ and $OT > OK$ cannot be both true. Our assumption leads to a contradiction and must be false. Therefore, $l$ must be perpendicular to $\overline{OT}$.

**18.** Assume that $l$ is not tangent to circle $O$. Then $l$ must intersect circle $O$ at another point $K$ besides $T$.

Both $T$ and $K$ are on circle $O$, so $OT = OK$ as radii.

But look at $\triangle OTK$. Because $l \perp \overline{OT}$, it is a right triangle with hypotenuse $\overline{OK}$. The hypotenuse is the longest side of a right triangle, meaning that $OT < OK$.

$OT = OK$ and $OT < OK$ cannot be both true. Our assumption leads to a contradiction and must be false. Therefore, $l$ must be tangent to circle $O$.

**19.** Statements (Reasons)
1. $\overline{CA}$ and $\overline{CB}$ are tangents to circle $P$. (Given)
2. Draw $\overline{AP}$, $\overline{BP}$, and $\overline{CP}$. (Construction)
3. $\overline{PA} \perp \overline{AC}$, $\overline{PB} \perp \overline{BC}$ (Tangent and radius are perpendicular. See Theorem 91.1.)
4. $\angle CAP$ and $\angle CBP$ are right angles. (Def. of perpendicular)
5. $\triangle CAP$ and $\triangle CBP$ are right triangles. (Def. of right triangle)
6. $\overline{AP} \cong \overline{BP}$ (All radii of a circle are congruent.)
7. $\overline{CP} \cong \overline{CP}$ (Reflexive Property)
8. $\triangle CAP \sim \triangle CBP$ (HL)
9. $\overline{CA} \cong \overline{CB}$ (CPCTC)

**20.** $\dfrac{8}{6} = \dfrac{x}{7.5}$ $\rightarrow$ $6x = 8(7.5)$ $\rightarrow$ $x = 10$

**21.** $\dfrac{x}{x + 4} = \dfrac{26}{39}$ $\rightarrow$ $39x = 26(x + 4)$ $\rightarrow$ $x = 8$

**22.** $\dfrac{8}{x} = \dfrac{x}{12}$ $\rightarrow$ $x^2 = 8(12)$ $\rightarrow$ $x = 4\sqrt{6}$

## LESSON 92

1. Tangent and radius are perpendicular, so $\triangle QAB$ is a right triangle with hypotenuse $\overline{QB}$.

   (5, 12, 13) is a Pythagorean triple, so $QA = 5$.

2. Tangent segments to a circle from a point are $\cong$.
   $DE = DF$
   $5x + 6 = 8x$; $x = 2$
   $DE = DF = 8(2) = 16$

3. $\overline{BC}$ is a minor arc, and $\overline{BAC}$ is a major arc.
   $m\overset{\frown}{ABC} = 180°$
   $m\overset{\frown}{AB} = m\angle AOB = 50°$
   $m\overset{\frown}{BC} = 180 - m\overset{\frown}{AB} = 180 - 50 = 130°$
   $m\overset{\frown}{BCA} = 360 - m\overset{\frown}{AB} = 360 - 50 = 310°$

4. $\overset{\frown}{DE} \cong \overset{\frown}{FG}$ if and only if $\angle DPE \cong \angle FPG$.

5. $m\overset{\frown}{YZ} = 180 - m\overset{\frown}{ZW} = 180 - 70 = 110°$

6. $m\overset{\frown}{XZ} = m\overset{\frown}{XW} + m\overset{\frown}{WZ} = 40 + 70 = 110°$

7. $m\overset{\frown}{XYZ} = m\overset{\frown}{XY} + m\overset{\frown}{YZ} = 140 + 110 = 250°$

8. $m\overset{\frown}{XZY} = 360 - m\overset{\frown}{XY} = 360 - 140 = 220°$

9. $50 + (6x + 8) + (3x - 1) + (9x - 3) = 360$
   $18x + 54 = 360$
   $x = 17$

10. minor arc; $m\overset{\frown}{DE} = m\angle DME = 60°$

11. minor arc; $m\overset{\frown}{CE} = m\angle CME = 90°$

12. minor arc; $m\overset{\frown}{CD} = m\overset{\frown}{CE} - m\overset{\frown}{DE} = 90 - 60 = 30°$

13. semicircle; $m\overset{\frown}{AED} = 180°$

14. minor arc; $m\overset{\frown}{AE} = m\overset{\frown}{AED} - m\overset{\frown}{DE} = 180 - 60 = 120°$

15. major arc; $m\overset{\frown}{ABE} = 360 - m\overset{\frown}{AE} = 360 - 120 = 240°$

16. yes; $\angle AMP \cong \angle DME$ as vertical angles.

17. $x + 148 = 360$
    $x = 212$

18. $x + 87 = 180$
    $x = 93$

19. $130 + 10x = 360$
    $x = 23$

20. $(7x - 4) + (5x - 8) = 180$
    $x = 16$

21. $5x = 125$
    $x = 25$

22. $90 + 116 + x + x = 360$
    $x = 77$

23. $x + 3x + 2x + 60 = 360$
    $x = 50$

24. $90 + 10x + (15x - 2) + 9x = 360$
    $x = 8$

25. $3x + 3x + (9x + 10) + (7x - 2) = 360$
    $x = 16$

26. Statements (Reasons)
    1. $\overset{\frown}{DE} \cong \overset{\frown}{FG}$ (Given)
    2. $m\overset{\frown}{DE} = m\overset{\frown}{FG}$ (Def. of congruent arcs)
    3. $m\overset{\frown}{DE} = m\angle DPE$, $m\overset{\frown}{FG} = m\angle FPG$ (Def. of arc measure)
    4. $m\angle DPE = m\angle FPG$ (Substitution Property)
    5. $\angle DPE \cong \angle FPG$ (Def. of congruent angles)

27. Statements (Reasons)
    1. $\angle DPE \cong \angle FPG$ (Given)
    2. $m\angle DPE = m\angle FPG$ (Def. of congruent angles)
    3. $m\angle DPE = m\overset{\frown}{DE}$, $m\angle FPG = m\overset{\frown}{FG}$ (Def. of arc measure)
    4. $m\overset{\frown}{DE} = m\overset{\frown}{FG}$ (Substitution Property)
    5. $\overset{\frown}{DE} \cong \overset{\frown}{FG}$ (Def. of congruent arcs)

28. Complementary angles add up to 90°. So, if they are congruent, then each must measure 45°.

29. $\sin 30° = \dfrac{1}{2}$   $\cos 30° = \dfrac{\sqrt{3}}{2}$   $\tan 30° = \dfrac{1}{\sqrt{3}} = \dfrac{\sqrt{3}}{3}$

## LESSON 93

1. $x = 7\sqrt{2}$

2. $x = 10/2 = 5$

3. shorter leg = 5
   $x = 2(5) = 10$

4. $(2x)^2 = x^2 + 9^2$
   $x^2 = 27$
   $x = 3\sqrt{3}$

5. $x + 5 = 3x - 7$
   $x = 6$

6. $(7x - 4) + (5x - 8) = 180$
   $x = 16$

7. Thm 93.1: $\overset{\frown}{AB} \cong \overset{\frown}{CD}$ if and only if $\overline{AB} \cong \overline{CD}$.
   Thm 93.2: $\overline{PG} \perp \overline{EF}$ if and only if $\overline{HE} \cong \overline{HF}$ and $\overset{\frown}{GE} \cong \overset{\frown}{GF}$.

8. $2x + 116 = 360$
   $x = 122$

9. $4x - 3 = 13$
   $x = 4$

10. $x + 50 = 180$
    $x = 130$

11. $3x + 5 = 8$
    $x = 1$

12. The longer leg of the right $\triangle$ is 18/2 = 9.
    $x^2 = 5^2 + 9^2$
    $x^2 = 106$
    $x = \sqrt{106}$

13. Let $b$ be the longer leg of the right $\triangle$. Then $x = 2b$.
    $6^2 = 4^2 + b^2$
    $b^2 = 20$
    $b = 2\sqrt{5}$
    $x = 2b = 4\sqrt{5}$

14. $x = 123$

15. $2x + 74 = 360$
    $x = 143$

16. $4x = 14 - 3x$
    $x = 2$

17. $x + 68 = 180$
    $x = 112$

**18.** $115 + (3x + 5) = 180$
$x = 20$

**19.** $8x - 11 = 3x + 4$
$x = 3$

**20** base of right $\triangle$ = 10
$x^2 = 5^2 + 10^2$
$x^2 = 125$
$x = 5\sqrt{5}$

**21.** $b$ = base of right $\triangle$
$4^2 = 2^2 + b^2$
$b^2 = 12$
$b = 2\sqrt{3}$
$x = 2b = 4\sqrt{3}$

**22.** Use a 30-60-90 triangle.
$x = 8/2 = 4$
$x + y$ = radius = 8
$y = 8 - x = 4$

**23.** Statements (Reasons)
1. $\overset{\frown}{AB} \cong \overset{\frown}{CD}$ (Given)
2. $\angle AOB \cong \angle COD$ (Congruent arcs have congruent central angles. See Theorem 92.1)
3. $\overline{OA} \cong \overline{OB} \cong \overline{OC} \cong \overline{OD}$ (All radii of a circle are $\cong$.)
4. $\triangle AOB \cong \triangle COD$ (SAS)
5. $\overline{AB} \cong \overline{CD}$ (CPCTC)

**24.** Statements (Reasons)
1. $\overline{AB} \cong \overline{CD}$ (Given)
2. $\overline{OA} \cong \overline{OB} \cong \overline{OC} \cong \overline{OD}$ (All radii of a circle are $\cong$.)
3. $\triangle AOB \cong \triangle COD$ (SSS)
4. $\angle AOB \cong \angle COD$ (CPCTC)
5. $\overset{\frown}{AB} \cong \overset{\frown}{CD}$ (Congruent central angles have congruent arcs. See Theorem 92.1)

**25.** Statements (Reasons)
1. $\overline{PG} \perp \overline{EF}$ (Given)
2. $\angle PHE$ are $\angle PHF$ right $\angle$s. (Def. of perpendicular)
3. $\triangle PHE$ and $\triangle PHF$ are right $\triangle$s. (Def. of right $\triangle$)
4. $\overline{PE} \cong \overline{PF}$ (All radii of a circle are $\cong$.)
5. $\overline{PH} \cong \overline{PH}$ (Reflexive Property)
6. $\triangle PHE \cong \triangle PHF$ (HL)
7. $\overline{HE} \cong \overline{HF}$ (CPCTC)
8. $\angle GPE \cong \angle GPF$ (CPCTC)
9. $\overset{\frown}{GE} \cong \overset{\frown}{GF}$ (Congruent central angles have congruent arcs. See Theorem 92.1)

**26.** Statements (Reasons)
1. $\overline{HE} \cong \overline{HF}$ (Given)
2. $\overline{PE} \cong \overline{PF}$ (All radii of a circle are $\cong$.)
3. $\overline{PH} \cong \overline{PH}$ (Reflexive Property)
4. $\triangle PHE \cong \triangle PHF$ (SSS)
5. $\angle PHE \cong \angle PHF$ (CPCTC)
6. $\angle PHE$ & $\angle PHF$ are a linear pair. (Def. of linear pair)
7. $\overline{PG} \perp \overline{EF}$ (Two lines intersecting to form a linear pair of congruent angles are perpendicular. See Theorem 31.3.)

**27.** Add eq1 to eq2. $\quad\rightarrow\;$ Use eq1 to find $y$.
$3x = 6 \qquad\qquad\qquad 2 - y = 3$
$x = 2 \qquad\qquad\qquad\; y = -1$
$\qquad\qquad\qquad\quad$ Solution: $x = 2$, $y = -1$

**28.** 4 pairs

**29.** $\tan b° = 1$; The legs must be congruent.

## LESSON 94

**1.** $(x + 4)^2 = x^2 + 8^2$
$x = 6$

**2.** $x + 3 = 9 - 2x$
$x = 2$

**3.** $115 + x = 180$
$x = 65$

**4.** $x + 2(122) = 360$
$x = 116$

**5.** $8 = 3x + 2$
$x = 2$

**6.** $b$ = base of right $\triangle$
$6^2 = 3^2 + b^2$
$b = 3\sqrt{3}$
$x = 2b = 6\sqrt{3}$

**7.** See Problem 7 in Lesson 93.

**8.** $\overline{ST} \cong \overline{UV}$ if and only if $OK = OL$.

**9.** $x + 2(97) = 360$
$x = 166$

**10.** $2(9x) + 62 + 100 = 360$
$x = 11$

**11.** $7x = 2x + 5$
$x = 1$

**12.** $14 = 3x + 5$
$x = 3$

**13.** $2x + 152 = 360$
$x = 104$

**14.** $x = 6$
$y = 180 - 64 = 116$

**15.** $x = 9$
$2y + 160 = 360$
$y = 100$

**16.** $110 + 2(98) + x = 360$
$x = 54$

**17.** $13 = 4x - 7$
$x = 5$

**18.** $5x - 3 = 7$
$x = 2$

**19.** Use the Pythagorean Theorem or a 45-45-90 triangle. You can use a 45-45-90 triangle because the legs of the right triangle are congruent.

legs of right $\triangle$ = 14/2 = 7
$x$ = hypotenuse = $\sqrt{2}$ × leg = $7\sqrt{2}$

**20.** Use the Pythagorean Theorem or a 3-4-5 triangle. A 3-4-5 triangle is a right triangle with sides 3, 4, and 5. Remember that (3, 4, 5) is a Pythagorean triple.

longer leg of right $\triangle$ = 8/2 = 4
$x$ = shorter leg = 6/2 = 3
$y$ = hypotenuse = 5

**21.** Use the Pythagorean Theorem or a 30-60-90 triangle. You can use a 30-60-90 triangle because the hypotenuse is twice the shorter leg.

shorter leg of right $\triangle$ = radius − 2 = 4 − 2 = 2
$x$ = longer leg = $\sqrt{3}$ × shorter leg = $2\sqrt{3}$

**21.** $m\angle APX = m\widehat{AZ} = 39°$

$m\angle PAX = 90 - m\angle APX = 90 - 39 = 51°$

$AX = \sqrt{10^2 - 8^2} = \sqrt{36} = 6$

You could use a multiple of a 3-4-5- triangle to find $AX$.

**23.** *Answer formats may vary.*

Statements (Reasons)

1. $PX = PY$ (Given)
2. $\overline{AB} \cong \overline{CD}$ (Chords equidistant from the center are congruent. See Theorem 94.1.)
3. $\widehat{AB} \cong \widehat{CD}$ (Congruent chords have congruent arcs. See Theorem 93.1)

**24.** $m\widehat{AB} = 2(m\widehat{AZ}) = 2(39) = 78°$ (Theorem 93.2)

$m\widehat{CD} = m\widehat{AB} = 78°$ (Proved in Problem 23.)

$m\widehat{BD} = 360 - 2(78) - 82 = 122°$

**25.** Statements (Reasons)

1. $\overline{OK} \perp \overline{ST}, \overline{OL} \perp \overline{UV}, \overline{ST} \cong \overline{UV}$ (Given)
2. $\overline{KS} \cong \overline{KT}, \overline{LU} \cong \overline{LV}$ (A radius perpendicular to a chord bisects the chord. See Theorem 93.2.)
3. $\overline{KT} \cong \overline{LV}$ (Halves of congruent segments are congruent. You could prove this statement in more detailed steps as shown below.)
   a. $ST = UV$ (Def. of congruent segments, Step 1)
   b. $ST = 2KT, UV = 2LV$ (Def. of bisect)
   c. $2KT = 2LV$ (Substitution Property)
   d. $KT = LV$ (Division Property)
   e. $\overline{KT} \cong \overline{LV}$ (Def. of congruent segments)
4. Draw $\overline{OT}$ and $\overline{OV}$. (Construction)
5. $\overline{OT} \cong \overline{OV}$ (All radii of a circle are congruent.)
6. $\triangle OKT \cong \triangle OLV$ (HL, Steps 3 and 5)
7. $\overline{OK} \cong \overline{OL}$ (CPCTC)

**26.** Statements (Reasons)

1. $\overline{OK} \perp \overline{ST}, \overline{OL} \perp \overline{UV}, \overline{OK} \cong \overline{OL}$ (Given)
2. Draw $\overline{OT}$ and $\overline{OV}$. (Construction)
3. $\overline{OT} \cong \overline{OV}$ (All radii of a circle are congruent.)
4. $\triangle OKT \cong \triangle OLV$ (HL, Steps 1 and 3)
5. $\overline{KT} \cong \overline{LV}$ (CPCTC)
6. $\overline{KS} \cong \overline{KT}, \overline{LU} \cong \overline{LV}$ (A radius perpendicular to a chord bisects the chord. See Theorem 93.2.)
7. $\overline{ST} \cong \overline{UV}$ (Multiples of congruent segments are congruent. You could prove this statement in more detailed steps as shown below.)
   a. $KT = LV$ (Def. of congruent segments, Step 5)
   b. $2KT = 2LV$ (Multiplication Property)
   b. $ST = 2KT, UV = 2LV$ (Def. of bisect)
   c. $ST = UV$ (Substitution Property)
   d. $\overline{ST} \cong \overline{UV}$ (Def. of congruent segments)

**27.** Statements (Reasons)

1. $\widehat{DE} \cong \widehat{DF}$ (Given)
2. $\overline{DE} \cong \overline{DF}$ (Congruent arcs have congruent chords. See Theorem 93.1.)
3. $\overline{PE} \cong \overline{PF}$ (All radii of a circle are congruent.)
4. $\overline{DP} \cong \overline{DP}$ (Reflexive Property)
5. $\triangle DPE \cong \triangle DPF$ (SSS)

In Step 2, you could say $\angle DPE \cong \angle DPF$ because congruent arcs have congruent central angles (Theorem 92.1). Then $\triangle DPE \cong \triangle DPF$ by SAS.

**28.** Statements (Reasons)

1. $\overline{AD} \cong \overline{DC}$ (Given)
2. $\overline{OB}$ bisects $\overline{AC}$. (Def. of bisect)
3. $\widehat{AB} \cong \widehat{BC}$ (A radius perpendicular to a chord bisects the arc of that chord. See Theorem 93.2.)
4. $\overline{AB} \cong \overline{BC}$ (Congruent arcs have congruent chords. See Theorem 93.1.)

**29.** Let $x$ and $2x$ be the two angles. Consecutive angles of a parallelogram are supplementary.

$x + 2x = 180; x = 60$

The angles are 60°, 120°, 60°, and 120°.

**30.** obtuse; $8^2 > 3^2 + 6^2$

## LESSON 95

**1.** $x + 63 + 90 = 180$
$x = 27$

**2.** $x + 87 = 180$
$x = 93$

**3.** $90 + 9x + 10x + 118 = 360$
$x = 8$

**4.** $2x + 116 = 360$
$x = 122$

**5.** $x = 6$
$y = 180 - 64 = 116$

**6.** Use a 3-4-5 triangle.
base of right $\triangle = 4$
$x = 3$

**7.** Thm 95.1: $m\angle ABC = m\widehat{AC}/2$ (or $m\widehat{AC} = 2m\angle ABC$)
Thm 95.2: $\angle DGE \cong \angle DFE$

**8.** $a = 136/2 = 68$

**9.** $a = 180 - 94 = 86$
$b = a/2 = 86/2 = 43$

**10.** $a = 64/2 = 32$
$b = a = 32$

**11.** $a = 2(57) = 114$
$b = 57$

**12.** $a = 2(46) = 92$

**13.** $a = 360 - 90 - 134 = 136$
$b = a/2 = 136/2 = 68$

**14.** $a = 180 - 96 = 84$
$b = a/2 = 84/2 = 42$

**15.** $a = 116$
$b = 360 - 2(116) = 128$
$c = b/2 = 128/2 = 64$

**16.** $a = 150/2 = 75$
$b = a = 75$

**17.** $a = 90$
$b = 2(90) = 180$

**18.** $a = 46/2 = 23$
$b = 90/2 = 45$

**19.** $a = 130/2 = 65$
$b = 2(35) = 70$

20. $a = 72/2 = 36$

    $b = 72$

    $c = b/2 = 72/2 = 36$

21. Statements (Reasons)

    1. inscribed $\angle ABC$, diameter $\overline{BC}$ (Given)
    2. $\overline{OA} \cong \overline{OB}$ (All radii of a circle are congruent.)
    3. $\angle A \cong \angle B$ (Base Angles Theorem [40.1])
    4. $m\angle A = m\angle B$ (Def. of congruent angles)
    5. $m\angle AOC = m\angle A + m\angle B$ (Triangle Exterior Angle Theorem [32.2])
    6. $m\angle AOC = m\angle B + m\angle B$ (Substitution)
    7. $m\angle AOC = 2m\angle B$ (Simplify.)
    8. $m\widehat{AC} = m\angle AOC$ (Def. of arc measure)
    9. $m\widehat{AC} = 2m\angle B$ (Transitive Property)

22. Statements (Reasons)

    1. inscribed $\angle ABC$, diameter $\overline{DB}$ (Given)
    2. $m\widehat{AC} = m\widehat{AD} + m\widehat{DC}$ (Arc Addition Postulate)
    3. $m\widehat{AD} = 2m\angle ABD$, $m\widehat{DC} = 2m\angle DBC$ (Proved in Problem 21.)
    4. $m\widehat{AC} = 2m\angle ABD + 2m\angle DBC$ (Substitution)
    5. $m\widehat{AC} = 2(m\angle ABD + m\angle DBC)$ (Distributive Prop.)
    5. $m\angle ABD + m\angle DBC = m\angle B$ (Angle Addition Post.)
    6. $m\widehat{AC} = 2m\angle B$ (Substitution)

23. Statements (Reasons)

    1. inscribed $\angle ABC$, diameter $\overline{DB}$ (Given)
    2. $m\widehat{AC} = m\widehat{AD} - m\widehat{CD}$ (Arc Addition Postulate)
    3. $m\widehat{AD} = 2m\angle ABD$, $m\widehat{CD} = 2m\angle CBD$ (Proved in Problem 21.)
    4. $m\widehat{AC} = 2m\angle ABD - 2m\angle CBD$ (Substitution)
    5. $m\widehat{AC} = 2(m\angle ABD - m\angle CBD)$ (Distributive Prop.)
    5. $m\angle ABD - m\angle CBD = m\angle B$ (Angle Addition Post.)
    6. $m\widehat{AC} = 2m\angle B$ (Substitution)

24. Statements (Reasons)

    1. inscribed $\angle DGE$ and $\angle DFE$ (Given)
    2. $m\angle G = m\widehat{DE}/2$, $m\angle F = m\widehat{DE}/2$ (Theorem 95.1)
    3. $m\angle G = m\angle F$ (Transitive Property)
    4. $\angle G \cong \angle F$ (Def. of congruent angles)

25. Statements (Reasons)

    1. inscribed $\angle DPE$ and $\angle FQG$, $\widehat{DE} \cong \widehat{FG}$ (Given)
    2. $m\widehat{DE} = m\widehat{FG}$ (Def. of congruent arcs)
    3. $m\widehat{DE} = 2m\angle P$, $m\widehat{FG} = 2m\angle Q$ (Theorem 95.1)
    4. $2m\angle P = 2m\angle Q$ (Transitive Property)
    5. $m\angle P = m\angle Q$ (Division Property)
    6. $\angle P \cong \angle Q$ (Def. of congruent angles)

26. B; 5 + 5 > 10 is false. The sum of two sides of a triangle must be greater than the third side.

## LESSON 96

1. Angles in a triangle add up to 180°.

   $38 + 70 + (x - 29) = 180$; $x = 101$

2. Angles in a quadrilateral add up to 360°.

   $6x + 92 + 80 + 86 = 360$; $x = 17$

3. Angles in a quadrilateral add up to 360°.

   $2x + 70 + (x + 55) + 70 = 360$; $x = 55$

4. $x + 112 = 180$

   $x = 68$

5. $2(3x) + 62 + 100 = 360$

   $x = 33$

6. height of right $\triangle$ = 7

   hypotenuse = 22/2 = 11

   $11^2 = 7^2 + x^2$

   $x = \sqrt{72} = 6\sqrt{2}$

7. $x = 110/2 = 55$

8. $x = (180 - 106)/2 = 37$

9. $x = 60$ (equilateral $\triangle$)

10. Thm 96.1: $m\angle B = 90°$ if and only if $\overline{AC}$ is a diameter.

    Thm 96.2: If $EFGH$ is inscribed in a circle, then $m\angle E + m\angle G = m\angle F + m\angle H = 180°$.

11. $a = 90$

    $b = 2(44) = 88$

12. $a = 90$

    $b = 180/2 = 90$

13. $a = 180 - 89 = 91$

    $b = 180 - 84 = 96$

14. $a = (74 + 112)/2 = 93$

    $b = 180 - a = 87$

    $c = 180 - 77 = 103$

15. $m\angle 1 = 90°$

    $m\angle 2 = 180 - m\angle 1 - 37$

    $\quad = 53°$

16. $m\angle 1 = 98/2 = 49°$

    $m\angle 2 = 180 - 90 - m\angle 1$

    $\quad = 41°$

17. $m\angle 1 = 60°$

    $m\angle 2 = 60/2 = 30°$

    $m\angle 3 = 180 - 90 - m\angle 2$

    $\quad = 60°$

18. $m\angle 1 = 180 - 58 = 122°$

    $m\angle 2 = 180 - 72 = 108°$

19. $m\angle 1 = (98 + 94)/2 = 96°$

    $m\angle 2 = (68 + 94)/2 = 81°$

    $m\angle 3 = 180 - m\angle 1 = 84°$

20. $m\angle 1 = 180 - 90 = 90$

    $m\angle 2 = (118 + 100)/2$

    $\quad = 109°$

    $m\angle 3 = 180 - m\angle 2 = 71°$

21. $\widehat{ADC}$ is the intercepted arc of $\angle B$. An intercepted arc measures twice its inscribed angle, so $m\widehat{ADC} = 2m\angle B = 2(90) = 180°$.

    By definition, a semicircle is an arc whose measure is 180° and whose endpoints are the endpoints of a diameter. So, $\widehat{ADC}$ is a semicircle and $\overline{AC}$ is a diameter.

22. A diameter divides a circle into two semicircles, so $\widehat{ADC}$ is a semicircle and $m\widehat{ADC} = 180°$. $\angle B$ is an inscribed angle of $\widehat{ADC}$. An inscribed angle measures half its intercepted arc, so $m\angle B = m\widehat{ADC}/2 = 180/2 = 90°$.

**23.** 2. An intercepted arc measures twice its inscribed angle. See Theorem 95.1.

    4. Substitution Property

    5. Division Property

**24.** Let $x$ be the number.    ➔ Solve by factoring.

$x^2 - x = 2$             $(x - 2)(x + 1) = 0$

$x^2 - x - 2 = 0$      $x = 2, x = -1$

**25.** perimeter of $\triangle DEF$ = (1/2)(perimeter of $\triangle ABC$)

                  = (1/2)(18) = 9

## LESSON 97

**1.** $a = 7$
$b = 180 - 65 = 115$

**2.** base of right $\triangle$ = 10
$a^2 = 5^2 + 10^2$
$a = \sqrt{125} = 5\sqrt{5}$

**3.** $a = 180 - 94 = 86$
$b = a/2 = 86/2 = 43$

**4.** $a = 57$
$b = 2(57) = 114$

**5.** $a = 90$
$b = 180 - 90 - 37 = 53$

**6.** $a = 180 - 89 = 91$
$b = 180 - 84 = 96$

**7.** Thm 97.1: $m\angle 1 = m\widehat{AB}/2$
Thm 97.2: $m\angle 1 = (m\widehat{DE} + m\widehat{FG})/2$

**8.** $a = 156/2 = 78$
$b = 360 - 156 = 204$

**9.** $a = 2(96) = 192$
$b = 360 - a = 168$

**10.** $a = (35 + 65)/2 = 50$
$b = 180 - a = 130$

**11.** $a = 108$
$(b + 128)/2 = 108$
$b = 88$

**12.** $m\angle 1 = 154/2 = 77°$
$m\angle 2 = 180 - m\angle 1$
      $= 103°$

**13.** $m\angle 1 = 218/2 = 109°$
$m\angle 2 = 180 - m\angle 1$
      $= 71°$

**14.** $m\angle 1 = 122/2 = 61°$
$m\angle 2 = 122/2 = 61°$
$\angle 2$ is an inscribed angle.

**15.** $m\angle 1 = (54 + 70)/2 = 62°$
$m\angle 2 = 180 - m\angle 1$
      $= 118°$

**16.** $m\angle 1 = (86 + 118)/2$
      $= 102°$
$m\angle 2 = 180 - m\angle 1$
      $= 78°$

**17.** $m\angle 1 = (90 + 134)/2$
      $= 112°$
$m\angle 2 = m\angle 1 = 112°$

**18.** $\cong$ chords have $\cong$ arcs.
$a = 152$

Use Theorem 97.1.
$b = 152/2 = 76$
$c = a/2 = 76$

**19.** A semicircle has 180°.
$a = 180 - 93 = 87$

Use Theorem 97.2.
$b = (a + 129)/2 = 108$

**20.** A circle has 360°.   ➔ Use Theorem 97.2.
$a + 2a + 3a + 4a = 360$     $b = (2a + 4a)/2$
$a = 36$                    $= (72 + 144)/2 = 108$

**21.** Statements (Reasons)

1. tangent $\overleftrightarrow{BP}$, diameter $\overline{AB}$ (Given)

2. $m\angle ABP = 90°$ (Tangent and radius are perpendicular. See Theorem 91.1)

3. $\widehat{ACB}$ is a semicircle and $m\widehat{ACB} = 180°$. (Def. of semicircle)

4. $m\widehat{ACB}/2 = 90°$ (Division Property)

5. $m\angle ABP = m\widehat{ACB}/2$ (Transitive Property)

**22.** Statements (Reasons)

1. tangent $\overleftrightarrow{BP}$, acute $\angle ABP$ (Given)

2. Draw diameter $\overline{BC}$. (Construction)

3. $m\angle CBP = m\widehat{CAB}/2$ (Proved in Problem 21.)

4. $m\angle CBA = m\widehat{CA}/2$ (Inscribed Angle Theorem [95.1])

5. $m\angle ABP = m\angle CBP - m\angle CBA$ (Angle Addition Post.)

6. $m\angle ABP = m\widehat{CAB}/2 - m\widehat{CA}/2$ (Substitution Prop.)

7. $m\angle ABP = (m\widehat{CAB} - m\widehat{CA})/2$ (Distributive Prop.)

8. $m\widehat{CAB} - m\widehat{CA} = m\widehat{AB}$ (Arc Addition Post.)

9. $m\angle ABP = m\widehat{AB}/2$ (Substitution Prop.)

**23.** Statements (Reasons)

1. tangent $\overleftrightarrow{BP}$, acute $\angle ABP$ (Given)

2. Draw diameter $\overline{BC}$. (Construction)

3. $m\angle CBP = m\widehat{CDB}/2$ (Proved in Problem 21.)

4. $m\angle ABC = m\widehat{AC}/2$ (Inscribed Angle Theorem [95.1])

5. $m\angle ABP = m\angle ABC + m\angle CBP$ (Angle Addition Post.)

6. $m\angle ABP = m\widehat{AC}/2 + m\widehat{CDB}/2$ (Substitution Prop.)

7. $m\angle ABP = (m\widehat{AC} + m\widehat{CDB})/2$ (Distributive Prop.)

8. $m\widehat{AC} + m\widehat{CDB} = m\widehat{ACB}$ (Arc Addition Post.)

9. $m\angle ABP = m\widehat{ACB}/2$ (Substitution Prop.)

**24.** Statements (Reasons)

1. chords $\overline{DF}$ and $\overline{EG}$ (Given)

2. Draw $\overline{DG}$. (Construction)

3. $m\angle G = m\widehat{DE}/2$, $m\angle D = m\widehat{FG}/2$ (Inscribed Angle Theorem [95.1])

4. $m\angle 1 = m\angle G + m\angle D$ (Triangle Exterior Angle Theorem [32.2])

5. $m\angle 1 = m\widehat{DE}/2 + m\widehat{FG}/2$ (Substitution Property)

6. $m\angle 1 = (m\widehat{DE} + m\widehat{FG})/2$ (Distributive Property)

**25.** interior angle sum = $180(n - 2) = 180(6 - 2) = 720°$
one interior angle = 720/6 = 120°

**26.** angle of rotational symmetry = 360/6 = 60°

# LESSON 98

1. Use Theorem 32.2.
   $m\angle 1 + 74 = 142$
   $m\angle 1 = 142 - 74 = 68°$

2. Use Theorem 95.1.
   $m\angle 1 = 92/2 = 46°$

3. Use Theorem 97.1.
   $m\angle 1 = 214/2 = 107°$

4. $m\angle 1 = m\widehat{CD}/2 = 130/2 = 65°$ (Theorem 95.1)
   $m\angle 2 = m\widehat{AB}/2 = 64/2 = 32°$ (Theorem 95.1)
   $m\angle 3 = m\angle 1 - m\angle 2 = 65 - 32 = 33°$ (Theorem 32.2)

5. $m\angle 1 = m\widehat{CB}/2 = 172/2 = 86°$ (Theorem 97.1)
   $m\angle 2 = m\widehat{AB}/2 = 98/2 = 49°$ (Theorem 95.1)
   $m\angle 3 = m\angle 1 - m\angle 2 = 86 - 49 = 37°$ (Theorem 32.2)

6. $m\angle 1 = m\widehat{ACB}/2 = 224/2 = 112°$ (Theorem 97.1)
   $m\angle 2 = m\widehat{AB}/2 = (360 - 224)/2 = 68°$ (Theorem 97.1)
   $m\angle 3 = m\angle 1 - m\angle 2 = 112 - 68 = 44°$ (Theorem 32.2)

7. a. $m\angle 1 = (m\widehat{CD} - m\widehat{AB})/2$
   b. $m\angle 1 = (m\widehat{CB} - m\widehat{AB})/2$
   c. $m\angle 1 = (m\widehat{ACB} - m\widehat{AB})/2$

8. $x = (153 - 37)/2 = 58$

9. $x = (162 - 66)/2 = 48$

10. $a = 360 - 196 - 74 = 90$
    $b = (196 - a)/2 = 53$

11. $a = 360 - 117 = 243$
    $b = (a - 117)/2 = 63$

12. $a = (129 - 63)/2 = 33$

13. $a = (147 - 79)/2 = 34$

14. $a = 360 - 230 = 130$
    $b = (230 - a)/2 = 50$

15. $a = 180 - 65 - 84 = 31$
    $b = (65 - a)/2 = 17$

16. $a = 360 - 110 = 250$
    $b = (a - 110)/2 = 70$

17. $(136 - a)/2 = 36$
    $136 - a = 2(36)$
    $a = 64$

18. $(a - (360 - a))/2 = 45$
    $a - (360 - a) = 2(45)$
    $a = 225$

19. $(8a - 46)/2 = 2a + 1$
    $8a - 46 = 2(2a + 1)$
    $a = 12$

20. $(6a - 50)/2 = 35 - a$
    $6a - 50 = 2(35 - a)$
    $a = 15$

21. Statements (Reasons)
    1. two secants (Given)
    2. $m\angle 3 = m\angle 1 + m\angle 2$ (Triangle Exterior Angle Theorem [32.2])
    3. $m\angle 1 = m\angle 3 - m\angle 2$ (Subtraction Property)
    4. $m\angle 3 = m\widehat{CD}/2, m\angle 2 = m\widehat{AB}/2$ (Inscribed Angle Theorem [95.1])
    5. $m\angle 1 = m\widehat{CD}/2 - m\widehat{AB}/2$ (Substitution Property)
    6. $m\angle 1 = (m\widehat{CD} - m\widehat{AB})/2$ (Distributive Property)

22. Statements (Reasons)
    1. a secant, a tangent (Given)
    2. $m\angle 3 = m\angle 1 + m\angle 2$ (Triangle Exterior Angle Theorem [32.2])
    3. $m\angle 1 = m\angle 3 - m\angle 2$ (Subtraction Property)
    4. $m\angle 3 = m\widehat{CB}/2$ (Chord-Tangent Angle Theorem [97.1])
    5. $m\angle 2 = m\widehat{AB}/2$ (Inscribed Angle Theorem [95.1])
    6. $m\angle 1 = m\widehat{CB}/2 - m\widehat{AB}/2$ (Substitution Property)
    7. $m\angle 1 = (m\widehat{CB} - m\widehat{AB})/2$ (Distributive Property)

23. Statements (Reasons)
    1. two tangents (Given)
    2. $m\angle 3 = m\angle 1 + m\angle 2$ (Triangle Exterior Angle Theorem [32.2])
    3. $m\angle 1 = m\angle 3 - m\angle 2$ (Subtraction Property)
    4. $m\angle 3 = m\widehat{ACB}/2, m\angle 2 = m\widehat{AB}/2$ (Chord-Tangent Angle Theorem [97.1])
    5. $m\angle 1 = m\widehat{ACB}/2 - m\widehat{AB}/2$ (Substitution Property)
    6. $m\angle 1 = (m\widehat{ACB} - m\widehat{AB})/2$ (Distributive Property)

24. $\angle DAC \cong \angle BCA$

25. yes; Opposite sides are congruent.

# LESSON 99

1. Take the square root of each side.
   $x = \pm\sqrt{8} = \pm 2\sqrt{2}$

2. Solve by factoring or use the quadratic formula.
   $x^2 + 2x - 15 = 0$ $\rightarrow$ $x = 3, x = -5$
   $(x - 3)(x + 5) = 0$

3. Use the quadratic formula.
   $5x = x^2 - x - 6$ $\rightarrow$ $x = \dfrac{6 \pm \sqrt{60}}{2} = 3 \pm \sqrt{15}$
   $x^2 - 6x - 6 = 0$

4. $a = (54 + 70)/2 = 62$
   $b = 180 - a = 118$

5. $a = 360 - 196 - 74 = 90$
   $b = (196 - a)/2 = 53$

6. a. $PA \cdot PB = PC \cdot PD$
   b. $PA \cdot PB = PC \cdot PD$
   c. $PA \cdot PB = PC^2$

7. $9x = 6(12)$
   $x = 8$

8. $6x = 5(x + 2)$
   $x = 10$

9. $8(8 + 15) = 10(10 + x)$
   $x = 42/5$

10. $9^2 = x(x + 8)$
    $x^2 + 8x - 81 = 0$
    $x = -4 + \sqrt{97}$

11. $x(x + 5) = 6(6 + x + 1)$
    $x^2 - x - 42 = 0$
    $(x - 7)(x + 6) = 0$
    $x = 7$

12. $8x = 6(10)$
    $x = 15/2$

**13.** $x^2 = 5(5 + 8)$
$x^2 = 65$
$x = \sqrt{65}$

**14.** $x(x + 6) = 9(9 + 4)$
$x^2 + 6x - 117 = 0$
$x = -3 + 3\sqrt{14}$

**15.** $x(x + 4) = 5(12)$
$x^2 + 4x - 60 = 0$
$(x - 6)(x + 10) = 0$
$x = 6$

**16.** $x(x + 6) = 7(7 + 9)$
$x^2 + 6x - 112 = 0$
$(x - 8)(x + 14) = 0$
$x = 8$

**17.** $x^2 = 15(15 + 10 + 7)$
$x^2 = 480$
$x = 4\sqrt{30}$

$\dashrightarrow$ $14y = 10(7)$
$y = 5$

**18.** Statements (Reasons)
1. two chords (Given)
2. $\angle A \cong \angle D, \angle C \cong \angle B$ (Inscribed angles of the same arc are congruent. See Theorem 95.2.)
3. $\triangle PAC \sim \triangle PDB$ (AA)
4. $\dfrac{PA}{PD} = \dfrac{PC}{PB}$ (Corresponding sides of similar triangles are proportional.)
5. $PA \cdot PB = PC \cdot PD$ (Cross multiply.)

**19.** Statements (Reasons)
1. two secants (Given)
2. $\angle P \cong \angle P$ (Reflexive Property)
3. $\angle B \cong \angle D$ (Inscribed angles of the same arc are congruent. See Theorem 95.2.)
4. $\triangle PBC \sim \triangle PDA$ (AA)
5. $\dfrac{PB}{PD} = \dfrac{PC}{PA}$ (Corresponding sides of similar triangles are proportional.)
6. $PA \cdot PB = PC \cdot PD$ (Cross multiply.)

**20.** Statements (Reasons)
1. a tangent, a secant (Given)
2. $\angle P \cong \angle P$ (Reflexive Property)
3. $m\angle ACP = m\overarc{AC}/2$ (A chord-tangent angle measures half its intercepted arc. See Theorem 97.1.)
3. $m\angle ABC = m\overarc{AC}/2$ (Inscribed Angle Theorem [95.1])
5. $m\angle ACP = m\angle ABC$ (Transitive Property)
6. $\angle ACP \cong \angle ABC$ (Def. of congruent angles)
4. $\triangle PAC \sim \triangle PCB$ (AA)
5. $\dfrac{PA}{PC} = \dfrac{PC}{PB}$ (Corresponding sides of similar triangles are proportional.)
6. $PA \cdot PB = PC^2$ (Cross multiply.)

**21.** Figures can have congruent angles but different side lengths.

**22.** $\dfrac{5}{h} = \dfrac{6.2}{18.6}$ $\rightarrow$ $6.2h = 5(18.6)$ $\rightarrow$ $x = 15$ ft

**1.** $x = y/2$

**2.** $x = y/2$

**3.** $x = (y + z)/2$
$ab = cd$

**4.** $x = (y - z)/2$
$a(a + b) = c(c + d)$

**5.** $x = (y - z)/2$
$a(a + b) = c^2$

**6.** $x = (y - z)/2$
$a = b$

**7.** $m\overarc{AB} = 180 - m\overarc{AD} = 180 - 114 = 66°$
$m\overarc{CD} = 180 - m\overarc{BC} = 180 - 90 = 90°$

$m\angle 1 = m\overarc{AD} = 114°$ (central angle)
$m\angle 2 = m\overarc{AD}/2 = 57°$ (inscribed angle)
$m\angle 3 = m\overarc{AD}/2 = 57°$ (inscribed angle)
$m\angle 4 = m\overarc{BC}/2 = 45°$ (inscribed angle)
$m\angle 5 = m\overarc{BC}/2 = 45°$ (inscribed angle)
$m\angle 6 = 90°$ (tangent-radius angle)
$m\angle 7 = m\overarc{CD}/2 = 45°$ (chord-tangent angle)
$m\angle 8 = (m\overarc{AD} + m\overarc{BC})/2 = 102°$ (chord-chord angle)

You could use the Triangle Exterior Angle Theorem [32.2] to find $m\angle 8 = m\angle 2 + m\angle 5 = m\angle 3 + m\angle 4 = 102°$.

**8.** $a = 128/2 = 64$

**9.** $a = 130/2 = 65$
$b = 2(35) = 70$

**10.** $a = 98/2 = 49$
$b = 180 - 90 - a = 41$

**11.** $a = 2(138) = 276$
$b = 360 - a = 84$

**12.** $(a + 90)/2 = 73$
$a + 90 = 2(73)$
$a = 56$

$\dashrightarrow$ $a + b + 90 + 136 = 360$
$b = 78$

**13.** $a = 180 - 67 - 86 = 27$
$b = (67 - a)/2 = 20$

**14.** $a^2 = 16(9) = 144$
$a = 12$

**15.** $a(a + 12) = 8(8 + 10)$
$a^2 + 12a - 144 = 0$
$a = -6 + 6\sqrt{5}$

**16.** $a^2 = 9(9 + 10)$
$a = \sqrt{171} = 3\sqrt{19}$
$9(9 + 10) = 10(10 + b)$
$b = 71/10$

**17.** Congruent chords have congruent arcs. Let $m\overarc{AD} = m\overarc{BC} = x$. A circle has 360°, so $112 + 56 + 2x = 360°$. Solve the equation to get $x = m\overarc{AD} = m\overarc{BC} = 96°$.

$m\angle 1 = m\overarc{AB}/2 = 56°$ (inscribed angle)
$m\angle 2 = m\overarc{CD}/2 = 28°$ (inscribed angle)
$m\angle 3 = m\overarc{CD}/2 = 28°$ (inscribed angle)
$m\angle 4 = m\overarc{AD}/2 = 48°$ (inscribed angle)
$m\angle 5 = m\overarc{BC}/2 = 48°$ (inscribed angle)
$m\angle 6 = (m\overarc{AB} + m\overarc{CD})/2 = 84°$ (chord-chord angle)
$m\angle 7 = 180 - m\angle 6 = 96°$ (supplementary angles)
$m\angle 8 = (m\overarc{AB} - m\overarc{CD})/2 = 28°$ (secant-secant angle)

**18.** $m\overset{\frown}{BC} = 180 - m\overset{\frown}{AB} = 180 - 70 = 110°$

$m\overset{\frown}{AE} = 180 - m\overset{\frown}{CD} - m\overset{\frown}{DE} = 180 - 70 - 38 = 72°$

$m\angle 1 = m\overset{\frown}{AB}/2 = 35°$ (inscribed angle)

$m\angle 2 = m\overset{\frown}{BC}/2 = 55°$ (inscribed angle)

$m\angle 3 = (m\overset{\frown}{CD} + m\overset{\frown}{DE})/2 = 54°$ (inscribed angle)

$m\angle 4 = m\overset{\frown}{AE} + m\overset{\frown}{DE} = 110°$ (central angle)

$m\angle 5 = m\overset{\frown}{BC}/2 = 55°$ (chord-tangent angle)

$m\angle 6 = (m\overset{\frown}{BEC} - m\overset{\frown}{BC})/2 = 70°$ (tangent-tangent angle)

$m\angle 7 = 90°$ (tangent-radius angle)

$m\angle 8 = (m\overset{\frown}{AB} - m\overset{\frown}{DE})/2 = 16°$ (secant-secant angle)

**19.** Let $x$ be the angle. Then its supplement is $180 - x$.

$x = 4(180 - x)$; $x = 144$

The angle is 144°.

**20.** $x = 5$

$y = 60 \tan 20° \approx 21.8$

$h = x + y \approx 26.8$

The tree is about 26.8 ft tall.

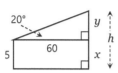

# LESSON 101

**1.** $(x, y) \rightarrow (x + 3, y - 7)$

**2.** $(x, y) \rightarrow (3x, 3y)$

**3.** 1/5 or 0.2

**4.** $b(a/b) = a$
dilation

**5.** 2. $\overline{AB} \cong \overline{AC}$
4. Reflexive Property
5. SSS

**6.** 1. diameter $\overline{AB}$, tangent $\overline{BC}$
2. Tangent and radius are perpendicular.
4. An angle inscribed in a semicircle is a right angle.
5. All right angles are congruent.
6. Reflexive Property
7. AA

**7.** A translation of 8 units left and 2 units down followed by a dilation about the origin by scale factor 3/2 will map ⊙R onto ⊙S. Therefore, the two circles are similar.

**8.** A translation of 6 units right and 1 unit down followed by a dilation about (3, −1) by scale factor 1/2 will map ⊙R onto ⊙S. Therefore, the two circles are similar.

**9.** 2. Def. of perpendicular
3. Def. of right triangle
5. Congruent arcs have congruent chords. See Theorem 93.1.
6. Congruent chords are equidistant from the center. See Theorem 94.1.
7. Reflexive Property
8. HL

**10.** Statements (Reasons)
1. diameter $\overline{AC}$, diameter $\overline{BD}$ (Given)
2. $\angle APB \cong \angle CPD$ (Vertical angles are congruent.)
3. $\overset{\frown}{AB} \cong \overset{\frown}{CD}$ (Congruent central angles have congruent arcs. See Theorem 92.1.)

**11.** Statements (Reasons)
1. tangent $\overline{AB}$, tangent $\overline{AC}$ (Given)
2. $\overline{AB} \cong \overline{AC}$ (Tangent segments to a circle from a point are congruent. See Theorem 91.2.)
3. $\overline{OB} \cong \overline{OC}$ (All radii of a circle are congruent.)
4. $\overline{OA} \cong \overline{OA}$ (Reflexive Property)
5. $\triangle OAB \sim \triangle OAC$ (SSS)
6. $\angle OAB \cong \angle OAC$ (CPCTC)

**12.** Statements (Reasons)
1. $\overset{\frown}{PQ} \cong \overset{\frown}{SR}$ (Given)
2. $\overline{PQ} \cong \overline{SR}$ (Congruent arcs have congruent chords. See Theorem 93.1.)
3. $\angle P \cong \angle S$, $\angle Q \cong \angle R$ (Inscribed angles of the same arc are congruent. See Theorem 95.2.)
4. $\triangle PQT \cong \triangle SRT$ (ASA)

**13.** Statements (Reasons)
1. $\overline{AB} \parallel \overline{CD}$ (Given)
2. Draw $\overline{BC}$. (Construction)
3. $\angle ABC \cong \angle BCD$ (Alternate interior ∠s are ≅.)
4. $m\angle ABC = m\angle BCD$ (Def. of congruent angles)
5. $m\angle ABC = m\overset{\frown}{AC}/2$, $m\angle BCD = m\overset{\frown}{BD}/2$ (An inscribed angle measures half its intercepted arc. See Theorem 95.1.)
6. $m\overset{\frown}{AC}/2 = m\overset{\frown}{BD}/2$ (Substitution Property)
7. $m\overset{\frown}{AC} = m\overset{\frown}{BD}$ (Multiplication Property)
8. $\overset{\frown}{AC} \cong \overset{\frown}{BD}$ (Def. of congruent arcs)

**14.** Vertical angles are congruent. So, if they are complementary, then each must measure 45°.

**15.** false; Only acute angles have complements. Any non-acute angle can be a counterexample.

**16.** $P$ is the centroid and divides $\overline{BE}$ in the ratio 2:1.
$BP = (2/3)BE = (2/3)15 = 10$

**17.** rhombus, square, kite

**18.** An altitude divides an equilateral triangle into two congruent 30-60-90 triangles. Use the side ratios of a 30-60-90 triangle to find the side length of the equilateral triangle.

altitude = longer leg of right triangle = $4\sqrt{3}$
side length = hypotenuse of right triangle = 8
perimeter = 3(side length) = 3(8) = 24 inches

## LESSON 102

1. $(3 + 3)^2 = x^2 + 3^2$
   $x^2 = 27$
   $x = 3\sqrt{3}$

2. $3x + 5 = 7x - 3$
   $x = 2$

3. a. semicircle; $m\overset{\frown}{STU} = 180°$
   b. minor arc; $m\overset{\frown}{TU} = 180 - m\overset{\frown}{ST} = 180 - 65 = 115°$
   c. major arc; $m\overset{\frown}{STV} = 360 - m\overset{\frown}{SV} = 360 - 135 = 225°$

4. a. minor arc; $m\overset{\frown}{AB} = 180 - m\overset{\frown}{BC} = 180 - 70 = 110°$
   b. minor arc; $m\overset{\frown}{AE} = 180 - m\overset{\frown}{CD} - m\overset{\frown}{DE}$
      $= 180 - 56 - 90 = 34°$
   c. major arc; $m\overset{\frown}{BCE} = m\overset{\frown}{BC} + m\overset{\frown}{CD} + m\overset{\frown}{DE}$
      $= 70 + 56 + 90 = 216°$

5. $2x + 124 = 360$
   $x = 118$

6. $3x - 8 = 7$
   $x = 5$

7. hypotenuse = 8
   longer leg = 12/2 = 6
   $8^2 = x^2 + 6^2$
   $x = \sqrt{28} = 2\sqrt{7}$

8. $5x + 1 = 16$
   $x = 3$

9. $a = 98/2 = 49$

10. $a = 32$
    $b = 2(32) = 64$

11. $a = 90$
    $b = 2(58) = 116$

12. $a = 180 - 88 = 92$
    $b = 180 - 96 = 84$

13. $a = 162/2 = 81$
    $b = 360 - 162 = 198$

14. $a = (73 + 81)/2 = 77$
    $b = 180 - a = 103$

15. $a = (130 - 44)/2 = 43$

16. $a = 360 - 118 = 242$
    $b = (a - 118)/2 = 62$

17. $9x = 6(12)$
    $x = 8$

18. $x(x + 8) = 4(4 + 9)$
    $x^2 + 8x - 52 = 0$
    $x = -4 + 2\sqrt{17}$

19. 2. An inscribed angle measures half its intercepted arc. See Theorem 95.1.
    4. A chord-tangent angle measures half its intercepted arc. See Theorem 97.1.
    5. Transitive Property

20. $(x, y) \to (x + 3, y + 3)$; A composition of translations is a translation.

21. $\cos x° = 12/13$; The triangle is a 5-12-13 triangle.

22. $x = 80 \tan 15° \approx 21.4$
    $y = 80 \tan 21° \approx 30.7$
    $h = x + y \approx 52.1$
    The taller building is about 52.1 m tall.

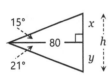

## LESSON 103

1. $a^2 = 5^2 + 10^2$
   $a^2 = 125$
   $a = 5\sqrt{5}$

2. $a = 7\sqrt{3}$
   $b = 2(7) = 14$

3. $a = 3$
   $b = 3\sqrt{2}$

4. parallelogram, rhombus, rectangle, square

5. parallelogram, rhombus, rectangle, square

6. rhombus, square, kite

7. rectangle, square

8. $A = bh = (3 + 2)(8) = 40$

9. $A = bh = 12(11) = 132$

10. Use the Pythagorean Theorem to find $h = 10$.
    $A = bh = 12(10) = 120$ units$^2$

11. Use a 30-60-90 triangle to find $h = 4\sqrt{3}$.
    Opposite sides of a rectangle are congruent, so $a = 8$.
    $A = \frac{1}{2} h(b_1 + b_2) = \frac{1}{2} (4\sqrt{3})(8 + 12) = 40\sqrt{3}$ units$^2$

12. Diagonals are perpendicular.
    Use a multiple of a 3-4-5 triangle to find $b = 9$.
    Use a 5-12-13 triangle to find $c = 5$.
    $A = \frac{1}{2} d_1 d_2 = \frac{1}{2} (12 + 12)(9 + 5) = 168$ units$^2$

13. Opposite sides are congruent.
    $A = bh = 13(14) = 182$ units$^2$

14. $A = \frac{1}{2} bh = \frac{1}{2} (5 + 11)(8) = 64$ units$^2$

15. $A = \frac{1}{2} d_1 d_2 = \frac{1}{2} (4 + 6)(3 + 3) = 30$ units$^2$

16. Diagonals bisect each other, so $a = 4$ and $b = 6$.
    $A = \frac{1}{2} d_1 d_2 = \frac{1}{2} (4 + 4)(6 + 6) = 48$ units$^2$

17. Opposite angles are congruent, so $a = 60$.
    Use a 30-60-90 triangle to find $h = 3\sqrt{3}$.
    $A = bh = 7(3\sqrt{3}) = 21\sqrt{3}$ units$^2$

18. Use a 5-12-13 triangle to find $a = c = 5$.
    Opposite sides of a rectangle are congruent, so $b = 15$.
    $A = \frac{1}{2} h(b_1 + b_2) = \frac{1}{2} (12)(15 + 5 + 15 + 5) = 240$ units$^2$

19. $a°$ and $b°$ are complementary. The cosine of an acute angle is equal to the sine of its complement.
    $\cos b° = \sin a° = 4/5$

20. A right triangle is inscribed in a circle if and only if the hypotenuse is a diameter of the circle.
    Our triangle is a 30-60-90 triangle with hypotenuse 8 cm. This means that the legs are 4 cm and $4\sqrt{3}$ cm.
    So, the perimeter is $12 + 4\sqrt{3}$ cm.

## LESSON 104

*Note that all areas are in square units.*

**1.** Use a 30-60-90 triangle to find $x = 4\sqrt{3}$.

$A = \frac{1}{2}bh = \frac{1}{2}(4\sqrt{3})(4) = 8\sqrt{3}$

**2.** Use a 45-45-90 triangle to find $x = 6$.

$A = \frac{1}{2}bh = \frac{1}{2}(6)(6) = 18$

**3.** Use a 30-60-90 triangle to find $x = 5\sqrt{3}$.

$A = \frac{1}{2}bh = \frac{1}{2}(10)(5\sqrt{3}) = 25\sqrt{3}$

**4.** $\overline{CP}$ and $\overline{CQ}$ are radii, $\angle PCQ$ is a central angle, and $\overline{CT}$ is an apothem.

**5.** $m\angle PCQ = 360/6 = 60°$
$m\angle PCT = (m\angle PCQ)/2 = 60/2 = 30°$
$m\angle CPT = 90 - m\angle PCT = 90 - 30 = 60°$

**6.** $A = \frac{1}{2}sa \cdot n = \frac{1}{2}(11.6)(8)(5) = 232$

**7.** $A = \frac{1}{2}sa \cdot n = \frac{1}{2}(3.3)(4)(8) = 52.8$

**8.** Use a 30-60-90 triangle to find $a = 3\sqrt{3}$.

$A = \frac{1}{2}sa \cdot n = \frac{1}{2}(6)(3\sqrt{3})(6) = 54\sqrt{3}$

**9.** $\overline{DE}$ and $\overline{DF}$ are radii, $\angle EDF$ is a central angle, and $\overline{DK}$ is an apothem.

**10.** $m\angle EDF = 360/8 = 45°$
$m\angle EDK = (m\angle EDF)/2 = 45/2 = 22.5°$
$m\angle DEK = 90 - m\angle EDK = 90 - 22.5 = 67.5°$

**11.** $A = \frac{1}{2}sa \cdot n = \frac{1}{2}(5)(6)(8) = 120$

**12.** $\overline{OA}$ and $\overline{OB}$ are radii, $\angle AOB$ is a central angle, and $\overline{OP}$ is an apothem.

**13.** $m\angle AOB = 360/6 = 60°$
$m\angle AOP = (m\angle AOB)/2 = 60/2 = 30°$
$m\angle OAP = 90 - m\angle AOP = 90 - 30 = 60°$

**14.** Use a 30-60-90 triangle to find missing measures. If $AB = 16$, then $AP = 8$ and $OP = 8\sqrt{3}$.

$A = \frac{1}{2}sa \cdot n = \frac{1}{2}(16)(8\sqrt{3})(6) = 384\sqrt{3}$

**15.** If $OP = 2\sqrt{3}$, then $AP = 2$ and $AB = 4$.

$A = \frac{1}{2}sa \cdot n = \frac{1}{2}(4)(2\sqrt{3})(6) = 24\sqrt{3}$

**16.** If $OA = 12$, then $AP = 6$, $AB = 12$, and $OP = 6\sqrt{3}$.

$A = \frac{1}{2}sa \cdot n = \frac{1}{2}(12)(6\sqrt{3})(6) = 216\sqrt{3}$

**17.** Use a 30-60-90 triangle to find $a = 4$ and $x = 4\sqrt{3}$.

$A = \frac{1}{2}sa \cdot n = \frac{1}{2}(2x)(a)(3) = \frac{1}{2}(8\sqrt{3})(4)(3) = 48\sqrt{3}$

**18.** Use a 45-45-90 triangle to find $a = 5$ and $x = 5$.

$A = \frac{1}{2}sa \cdot n = \frac{1}{2}(2x)(a)(4) = \frac{1}{2}(10)(5)(4) = 100$

You could use the area formula for a rectangle.
$A = bh = (2a)(2x) = (10)(10) = 100$

**19.** Use a 30-60-90 triangle to find $x = 2$ and $a = 2\sqrt{3}$.

$A = \frac{1}{2}sa \cdot n = \frac{1}{2}(2x)(a)(6) = \frac{1}{2}(4)(2\sqrt{3})(6) = 24\sqrt{3}$

**20.** Each pair of base angles is congruent, and non-base angles are supplementary. So, the other three angles are 40°, 140°, and 140°.

**21.** $PT \cdot QT = RT \cdot ST$
$8x = 4(x + 3)$
$x = 3$

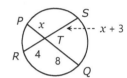

## LESSON 105

**1.** $10x = 4(15)$
$x = 6$

**2.** $14x = 6(35)$
$x = 15$

**3.** $\frac{6}{15} = \frac{10}{x}$
$6x = 10(15)$
$x = 25$

**4.** $\frac{26}{13} = \frac{10}{x}$
$26x = 13(10)$
$x = 5$

**5.**
a. The side ratio is 2:1.
b. The perimeter ratio will be 2:1.
c. The perimeter of $\triangle PQR$ is $26 + 10 + 24 = 60$.
The perimeter of $\triangle XYZ$ is $13 + 5 + 12 = 30$.
The perimeter ratio is 60:30 = 2:1.
d. The area ratio will be 4:1.
e. The area of $\triangle PQR$ is $(24)(10)/2 = 120$.
The area of $\triangle XYZ$ is $(12)(5)/2 = 30$.
The area ratio is 120:30 = 4:1.

**6.** $3^2 / 4^2 = 9/16$

**7.** $\sqrt{4} / \sqrt{25} = 2/5$

**8.** area ratio = 9/1
side ratio = 3/1
$\frac{3}{1} = \frac{15}{x}$
$3x = 15$
$x = 5$
The hypotenuse is 5 in.

**9.** perimeter ratio = 2/5
side ratio = 2/5
$\frac{2}{5} = \frac{4}{x}$
$2x = 5(4)$
$x = 10$
The longest side is 10 ft.

10. $\dfrac{50}{10} = \dfrac{a}{8}$  →  $10a = 50(8)$  →  $a = 40$

$\dfrac{50}{10} = \dfrac{30}{b}$  →  $50b = 10(30)$  →  $b = 6$

11. $\dfrac{18}{12} = \dfrac{24}{a}$  →  $18a = 12(24)$  →  $a = 16$

$\dfrac{18}{12} = \dfrac{27}{b}$  →  $18b = 12(27)$  →  $b = 18$

12. $\dfrac{4}{16} = \dfrac{a}{20}$  →  $16a = 4(20)$  →  $a = 5$

$\dfrac{4}{16} = \dfrac{2}{b}$  →  $4b = 16(2)$  →  $b = 8$

13. $\dfrac{24}{40} = \dfrac{a}{60}$  →  $40a = 24(60)$  →  $a = 36$

$\dfrac{24}{40} = \dfrac{30}{b}$  →  $24b = 40(30)$  →  $b = 50$

14. perimeter ratio = 4/3
side ratio = 4/3
$\dfrac{4}{3} = \dfrac{x}{9} = \dfrac{20}{y}$
$3x = 4(9)$, $4y = 3(20)$
$x = 12$, $y = 15$

15. area ratio = 1/4
side ratio = 1/2
$\dfrac{1}{2} = \dfrac{x}{10} = \dfrac{4}{y}$
$2x = 10$, $y = 2(4)$
$x = 5$, $y = 8$

16. $3^2 / 7^2 = 9/49$

17. $\sqrt{16} / \sqrt{25} = 4/5$

18. side ratio = 6/8 = 3/4
area ratio = 9/16

19. perimeter ratio = 2/3
area ratio = 4/9
$\dfrac{4}{9} = \dfrac{40}{x}$
$4x = 9(40)$
$x = 90$
The area is 90 cm².

20. area ratio = 25/36
perimeter ratio = 5/6
$\dfrac{5}{6} = \dfrac{20\sqrt{2}}{x}$
$5x = 6(20\sqrt{2})$
$x = 24\sqrt{2}$
The perimeter is $24\sqrt{2}$ in.

21. SSS

22. HL

## LESSON 106

1. $C = 2\pi r$
$= 2\pi(3) = 6\pi$
$\approx 6(22/7) \approx 18.9$

2. $4\pi = 2\pi r$
$4 = 2r$
$r = 2$

3. $s = \dfrac{\theta}{360} \cdot 2\pi r$
$= \dfrac{150}{360} \cdot 2\pi(6) = 5\pi$

4. $10.5\pi = \dfrac{210}{360} \cdot 2\pi r$
$r = 10.5 \cdot \dfrac{360}{210} \cdot \dfrac{1}{2} = 9$

5. $14\pi = \dfrac{\theta}{360} \cdot 2\pi(18)$
$\theta = 14(360) \cdot \dfrac{1}{2(18)} = 140°$

6. $C = 2\pi(8) = 16\pi \approx 16(22/7) \approx 50.3$

7. $C = 2\pi(2) = 4\pi \approx 4(22/7) \approx 12.6$

8. $C = \pi d = 14\pi \approx 14(22/7) \approx 44$

9. $s = \dfrac{140}{360} \cdot 2\pi(9) = 7\pi$

10. $s = \dfrac{90}{360} \cdot 2\pi(4) = 2\pi$

11. $s = \dfrac{180}{360} \cdot 2\pi(5) = 5\pi$

12. $10\pi = 2\pi r$
$10 = 2r$
$r = 5$

13. $26\pi = \pi d$
$d = 26$

14. $4\pi = \dfrac{80}{360} \cdot 2\pi r$
$r = 4 \cdot \dfrac{360}{80} \cdot \dfrac{1}{2} = 9$

15. $16\pi = \dfrac{240}{360} \cdot 2\pi r$
$r = 16 \cdot \dfrac{360}{240} \cdot \dfrac{1}{2} = 12$

16. $3\pi = \dfrac{\theta}{360} \cdot 2\pi(6)$
$\theta = 3(360) \cdot \dfrac{1}{2(6)} = 90°$

17 ~ 18. *Answers may vary slightly due to rounding.*

17. circumference of wheel = $\pi d \approx (22/7)(80) \approx 251$ cm
distance = 5,000 × circumference of wheel
$\approx 5,000 \times 251 = 1,255,000$ cm = 12.55 km
The car will travel about 13 km.

18. circumference of wheel = $\pi d \approx (22/7)(75) \approx 236$ cm
revolutions = distance / circumference
$\approx 200,000$ cm / 236 cm $\approx 847$
The wheel will make about 847 revolutions.

19. $BD < CD$ because 32° < 35°.

20. $x + 6 < 3x - 4$ and $x + 6 > 0$ and $3x - 4 > 0$
$x > 5$ and $x > -6$ and $x > 4/3$
Combine the inequalities to get $x > 5$.

## LESSON 107

1. a. Base angles are congruent, so $m\angle A = m\angle B$.
$m\angle AOB + m\angle A + m\angle B = 180°$
$120 + 2(m\angle A) = 180$
$m\angle A = 30°$
$m\angle AOP = 90 - m\angle A = 60°$

b. $\triangle OAP$ is a 30-60-90 triangle.
$OP = OA/2 = 3$
$AP = OP\sqrt{3} = 3\sqrt{3}$

1. c. $AB = 2AB = 6\sqrt{3}$

   $A = \dfrac{1}{2}bh = \dfrac{1}{2}(AB)(OP) = \dfrac{1}{2}(6\sqrt{3})(3) = 9\sqrt{3}$

2. $A = \pi r^2$

   $= \pi(3)^2 = 9\pi$

   $\approx 9(22/7) \approx 28.3$

3. $4\pi = \pi r^2$

   $4 = r^2$

   $r = 2$

4. $A = \dfrac{80}{360} \cdot \pi(9)^2 = 18\pi$

5. $A = \dfrac{210}{360} \cdot \pi(12)^2 = 84\pi$

6. sector area $= \dfrac{90}{360} \cdot \pi(2)^2 = \pi$

   triangle area $= \dfrac{1}{2}(2)(2) = 2$

   segment area $= \pi - 2$

7. sector area $= \dfrac{120}{360} \cdot \pi(12)^2 = 48\pi$

   triangle area $= \dfrac{1}{2}(12\sqrt{3})(6) = 36\sqrt{3}$

   segment area $= 48\pi - 36\sqrt{3}$

8. An isosceles triangle with vertex angle 60° is an equilateral triangle.

   Our triangle is an equilateral triangle with side length 6. Use a 30-60-90 triangle to find that the height of the triangle is $3\sqrt{3}$.

   sector area $= \dfrac{60}{360} \cdot \pi(6)^2 = 6\pi$

   triangle area $= \dfrac{1}{2}(6)(3\sqrt{3}) = 9\sqrt{3}$

   segment area $= 6\pi - 9\sqrt{3}$

   **Circumference**     **Area**

9. $C = 2\pi(9) = 18\pi$   $A = \pi(9)^2 = 81\pi$

10. $C = 2\pi(5) = 10\pi$   $A = \pi(5)^2 = 25\pi$

11. $C = 2\pi(3) = 6\pi$   $A = \pi(3)^2 = 9\pi$

    **Arc length**     **Sector area**

12. $s = \dfrac{150}{360} \cdot 2\pi(12) = 10\pi$   $A = \dfrac{150}{360} \cdot \pi(12)^2 = 60\pi$

13. $s = \dfrac{100}{360} \cdot 2\pi(9) = 5\pi$   $A = \dfrac{100}{360} \cdot \pi(9)^2 = (45/2)\pi$

14. $s = \dfrac{40}{360} \cdot 2\pi(6) = (4/3)\pi$   $A = \dfrac{40}{360} \cdot \pi(6)^2 = 4\pi$

15. $49\pi = \pi r^2$

    $49 = r^2$

    $r = 7$

16. $18\pi = \pi r^2$

    $18 = r^2$

    $r = \sqrt{18} = 3\sqrt{2}$

17. $9\pi = \dfrac{90}{360} \cdot \pi r^2$

    $r^2 = 9 \cdot \dfrac{360}{90} = 36$

    $r = 6$

18. $54\pi = \dfrac{\theta}{360} \cdot \pi(18)^2$

    $\theta = 54(360) \cdot \dfrac{1}{18(18)}$

    $\theta = 60°$

19. sector area $= \dfrac{120}{360} \cdot \pi(18)^2 = 108\pi$

    triangle area $= \dfrac{1}{2}(18\sqrt{3})(9) = 81\sqrt{3}$

    segment area $= 108\pi - 81\sqrt{3}$

20. sector area $= \dfrac{90}{360} \cdot \pi(8)^2 = 16\pi$

    triangle area $= \dfrac{1}{2}(8)(8) = 32$

    segment area $= 16\pi - 32$

21. sector area $= \dfrac{60}{360} \cdot \pi(4)^2 = (8/3)\pi$

    triangle area $= \dfrac{1}{2}(4)(2\sqrt{3}) = 4\sqrt{3}$

    segment area $= (8/3)\pi - 4\sqrt{3}$

22. Tangent and radius are perpendicular, so $\triangle QAB$ is a right triangle with hypotenuse $\overline{QB}$. Use a 5-12-13 triangle or the Pythagorean Theorem to find $QA = 5$.

## LESSON 108

**Arc length**     **Sector area**

1. $s = \dfrac{80}{360} \cdot 2\pi(9) = 4\pi$   $A = \dfrac{80}{360} \cdot \pi(9)^2 = 18\pi$

2. $s = \dfrac{210}{360} \cdot 2\pi(6) = 7\pi$   $A = \dfrac{210}{360} \cdot \pi(6)^2 = 21\pi$

3. $s = \dfrac{30}{360} \cdot 2\pi(18) = 3\pi$   $A = \dfrac{30}{360} \cdot \pi(18)^2 = 27\pi$

4. $\dfrac{120}{360} = \dfrac{x}{2\pi}$

   $360x = 120(2\pi)$

   $x = (2/3)\pi$ radians

5. $\dfrac{x}{360} = \dfrac{7\pi/4}{2\pi}$

   $2\pi x = 360(7\pi/4)$

   $x = 315°$

6. $s = \dfrac{3\pi}{4}(12) = 9\pi$

7. $A = \dfrac{1}{2} \cdot \dfrac{2\pi}{3}(6)^2 = 12\pi$

8. $A = \dfrac{1}{2} \cdot \dfrac{7\pi}{6}(12)^2 = 84\pi$

9. $A = \dfrac{1}{2} \cdot \dfrac{3\pi}{4}(8)^2 = 24\pi$

10. $\dfrac{80}{360} = \dfrac{x}{2\pi}$

    $360x = 80(2\pi)$

    $x = (4/9)\pi$ radians

11. $\dfrac{210}{360} = \dfrac{x}{2\pi}$

    $360x = 210(2\pi)$

    $x = (7/6)\pi$ radians

**12.** $\dfrac{x}{360} = \dfrac{\pi/5}{2\pi}$

$2\pi x = 360(\pi/5)$

$x = 36°$

**13.** $\dfrac{x}{360} = \dfrac{5\pi/9}{2\pi}$

$2\pi x = 360(5\pi/9)$

$x = 100°$

**Arc length**　　　　**Sector area**

**14.** $s = \dfrac{5\pi}{9}(18) = 10\pi$　　$A = \dfrac{1}{2} \cdot \dfrac{5\pi}{9}(18)^2 = 90\pi$

**15.** $s = \dfrac{4\pi}{3}(15) = 20\pi$　　$A = \dfrac{1}{2} \cdot \dfrac{4\pi}{3}(15)^2 = 150\pi$

**16.** $s = \dfrac{\pi}{6}(6) = \pi$　　　$A = \dfrac{1}{2} \cdot \dfrac{\pi}{6}(6)^2 = 3\pi$

**17.** $\dfrac{\text{sector area}}{\text{circle area}} = \dfrac{\text{arc length}}{\text{circumference}}$

$\dfrac{x}{81\pi} = \dfrac{6\pi}{18\pi} = \dfrac{1}{3} \quad \rightarrow \quad 3x = 81\pi \quad \rightarrow \quad x = 27\pi$

**18.** $\dfrac{\text{arc length}}{\text{circumference}} = \dfrac{\text{sector area}}{\text{circle area}}$

$\dfrac{x}{14\pi} = \dfrac{21\pi}{49\pi} = \dfrac{3}{7} \quad \rightarrow \quad 7x = 3(14)\pi \quad \rightarrow \quad x = 6\pi$

**19.** base of right $\triangle = 6/2 = 3$

radius = hypotenuse of
　　a 45-45-90 triangle
　　with legs 3
　　$= 3\sqrt{2}$

## LESSON 109 ·······································

**1.** $11^2 = a^2 + 5^2$

$a^2 = 96$

$a = 4\sqrt{6}$

**2.** $a = 5$

$b = 5\sqrt{2}$

**3.** $a = 7\sqrt{3}$

$b = 2(7) = 14$

**4.** $A = bh = 7(5) = 35$

**5.** $A = \dfrac{1}{2}bh = \dfrac{1}{2}(5 + 11)(8) = 64$

**6.** $A = \dfrac{1}{2}h(b_1 + b_2) = \dfrac{1}{2}(10)(10 + 6 + 12) = 140$

**7.** $A = \pi r^2 = \pi(3)^2 = 9\pi$

**8.** $A = \dfrac{1}{2}\pi r^2 = \dfrac{1}{2}\pi(6)^2 = 18\pi$

**9.** $A = \dfrac{1}{4}\pi r^2 = \dfrac{1}{4}\pi(8)^2 = 16\pi$

**10.** Use a 3-4-5 triangle to find $h = 4$.

area = square + triangle

$= 6(6) + \dfrac{1}{2}(6)(4) = 36 + 12 = 48$

**11.** area = 2 semicircles + rectangle

= 1 full circle + rectangle

$= \pi(7)^2 + 10(14) = 49\pi + 140$

**12.** Use a 45-45-90 triangle to find $r = 8$.

area = semicircle − triangle

$= \dfrac{1}{2}\pi(8)^2 - \dfrac{1}{2}(16)(8) = 32\pi - 64$

**13.** Use a 45-45-90 triangle to find $x = 8$.

Use a 30-60-90 triangle to find $y = 8\sqrt{3}$.

area $= \dfrac{1}{2}(x + y)(8) = \dfrac{1}{2}(8 + 8\sqrt{3})(8) = 32 + 32\sqrt{3}$

**14.** Use the Pythagorean Theorem to find $x = 6$.

area = large rectangle − triangle

$= 12(6) - \dfrac{1}{2}(3)(6) = 72 - 9 = 63$

**15.** area = quarter circle + rectangle

$= \dfrac{1}{4}\pi(6)^2 + 4(6) = 9\pi + 24$

**16.** area = 2 quarter circles + 2 squares

= 1 semicircle + 2 squares

$= \dfrac{1}{2}\pi(10)^2 + 2(10)(10) = 50\pi + 200$

**17.** Use a 30-60-90 triangle to find $x = 4\sqrt{3}$.

area = semicircle − triangle

$= \dfrac{1}{2}\pi(4)^2 - \dfrac{1}{2}(4)(4\sqrt{3}) = 8\pi - 8\sqrt{3}$

**18.** $r = 10/2 = 5$

area = circle − 4 right triangles

$= \pi(5)^2 - 4 \cdot \dfrac{1}{2}(5)(5) = 25\pi - 50$

**19.** 2. Corresponding ∠s on parallel lines are ≅.

3. Reflexive Property

4. AA

**20.** 2. Def. of trapezoid

3. Alternate interior ∠s on parallel lines are ≅.

4. Vertical angles are congruent.

5. AA

6. Corresponding sides of similar triangles are proportional.

## LESSON 110

1. $A = bh = 8(5.5) = 44$

2. $A = \frac{1}{2}bh = \frac{1}{2}(8 + 12)(11) = 110$

3. Use a 3-4-5 triangle to find $a = 3$.
   Opposite sides of a rectangle are congruent, so $b = 5$.
   $A = \frac{1}{2}h(b_1 + b_2) = \frac{1}{2}(4)(3 + 5 + 5) = 26$

4. Diagonals bisect each other, so $a = 6$.
   Use a multiple of a 3-4-5 triangle to find $b = 8$.
   $A = \frac{1}{2}d_1 d_2 = \frac{1}{2}(2b)(2a) = \frac{1}{2}(16)(12) = 96$

5. $A = \frac{1}{2}sa \cdot n = \frac{1}{2}(5.8)(4)(5) = 58$

6. Use a 30-60-90 triangle to find $x = 3$ and $a = 3\sqrt{3}$.
   $A = \frac{1}{2}sa \cdot n = \frac{1}{2}(6)(3\sqrt{3})(6) = 54\sqrt{3}$

7. perimeter ratio = 1/2
   area ratio = 1/4
   $\frac{1}{4} = \frac{20}{x}$
   $x = 80 \text{ cm}^2$

8. area ratio = 4/9
   side ratio = 2/3
   $\frac{2}{3} = \frac{10}{x}$
   $2x = 3(10)$
   $x = 15 \text{ ft}$

9. $C = 2\pi r = 2\pi(3) = 6\pi$
   $A = \pi r^2 = \pi(3)^2 = 9\pi$

10. $C = \pi d = 10\pi$
    $A = \pi r^2 = \pi(5)^2 = 25\pi$

11. $\frac{150}{360} = \frac{x}{2\pi}$
    $360x = 150(2\pi)$
    $x = (5/6)\pi$ radians

12. $\frac{x}{360} = \frac{\pi/3}{2\pi}$
    $2\pi x = 360(\pi/3)$
    $x = 60°$

13. $s = \frac{150}{360} \cdot 2\pi(6) = 5\pi$
    $A = \frac{150}{360} \cdot \pi(6)^2 = 15\pi$

14. $s = \frac{240}{360} \cdot 2\pi(9) = 12\pi$
    $A = \frac{240}{360} \cdot \pi(9)^2 = 54\pi$

15. $s = \frac{\pi}{3}(6) = 2\pi$
    $A = \frac{1}{2} \cdot \frac{\pi}{3}(6)^2 = 6\pi$

16. $s = \frac{11\pi}{6}(12) = 22\pi$
    $A = \frac{1}{2} \cdot \frac{11\pi}{6}(12)^2 = 132\pi$

17. sector area $= \frac{90}{360} \cdot \pi(2)^2 = \pi$
    triangle area $= \frac{1}{2}(2)(2) = 2$
    segment area $= \pi - 2$

18. sector area $= \frac{120}{360} \cdot \pi(6)^2 = 12\pi$
    triangle area $= \frac{1}{2}(6\sqrt{3})(3) = 9\sqrt{3}$
    segment area $= 12\pi - 9\sqrt{3}$

19. area = semicircle + rectangle
    $= \frac{1}{2}\pi(6)^2 + 10(12) = 18\pi + 120$

20. Use a 45-45-90 triangle to find $r = 4$.
    area = semicircle − triangle
    $= \frac{1}{2}\pi(4)^2 - \frac{1}{2}(8)(4) = 8\pi - 16$

21. length = circumference of a circle with diameter 100 + two sides of a square with side length 100
    $= 100\pi + 2(100) \approx 100(22/7) + 2(100) \approx 514$
    The length of the track is about 514 meters.

22. time = distance / speed
    $= (514)(4)/2 = 1028$ seconds $\approx 17$ minutes
    It will take about 17 minutes.

23. $a = (129 - 63)/2 = 33$

24. $a = 360 - 230 = 130$
    $b = (230 - a)/2 = (230 - 130)/2 = 50$

## LESSON 111

1. not a polyhedron

2. polyhedron (6 faces, 10 edges, 6 vertices)

3. not a polyhedron

4. polyhedron (6 faces, 12 edges, 8 vertices)

5. 5 faces, 8 edges, 5 vertices; 5 + 5 = 8 + 2

6. 6 faces, 12 edges, 8 vertices; 6 + 8 = 12 + 2

7. 4 faces, 6 edges, 4 vertices; 4 + 4 = 6 + 2

8. 5 faces, 9 edges, 6 vertices; 5 + 6 = 9 + 2

9. $20 + V = 30 + 2$
   $V = 12$ vertices

10. $F + 6 = 12 + 2$
    $F = 8$ faces

11. Problem 7

12. Problem 6

13. Problem 5

14. Problem 4

15. Problem 3

16. Problem 8

17. Problem 1

18. Problem 6

19. It has a curved surface.

20. See Problem 7.

21. $F = 6, E = 12, V = 8$
    $6 + 8 = 12 + 2$

22. $12 + V = 30 + 2$
    $V = 20$ vertices

**23.** $F + 15 = 20 + 2$
$F = 7$ faces

**24.** $F + 8 = 6 + 2$
$F = 0$
It is not possible.

**25.** tetrahedron:   4 faces, 6 edges, 4 vertices
$4 + 4 = 6 + 2$

cube:   6 faces, 12 edges, 8 vertices
$6 + 8 = 12 + 2$

octahedron:   8 faces, 12 edges, 6 vertices
$8 + 6 = 12 + 2$

dodecahedron:   12 faces, 30 edges, 20 vertices
$12 + 20 = 30 + 2$

icosahedron:   20 faces, 30 edges, 12 vertices
$20 + 12 = 30 + 2$

**26.** $m\angle AOC = 2(m\angle BOC)$
$3x + 15 = 2(2x)$
$x = 15$

**27.** $x + 2x + 3x = 180$
$x = 30$
The angles are 30°, 60°, and 90°.

## LESSON 112

*Note that all areas are in square units.*

**1.** Use the Pythagorean Theorem to find $x = 17$.
perimeter = $8 + 15 + 17 = 40$

area $= \frac{1}{2}bh = \frac{1}{2}(8)(15) = 60$

**2.** An altitude divides an equilateral triangle into two congruent 30-60-90 triangles.
Use a 30-60-90 triangle to find $h = 3\sqrt{3}$.
perimeter = $6 + 6 + 6 = 18$

area $= \frac{1}{2}bh = \frac{1}{2}(6)(3\sqrt{3}) = 9\sqrt{3}$

**3.** Use a multiple of a 3-4-5 triangle to find $h = 8$.
Opposite sides of a rectangle are congruent, so $x = 8$.
perimeter = top + right side + bottom + left side
$= (6 + 8) + 8 + 8 + 10 = 40$

area $= \frac{1}{2}h(b_1 + b_2) = \frac{1}{2}(8)(6 + 8 + 8) = 88$

**4.** $a = 3, b = 4, c = 5, h = 5$
area = 2 right triangles + 1 large rectangle

$= 2 \cdot \frac{1}{2}ab + (a + b + c)(h)$

$= 2 \cdot \frac{1}{2}(3)(4) + (3 + 4 + 5)(5) = 12 + 60 = 72$

**5.** $r = 4, h = 6, x$ = circumference of base = $8\pi$
area = 2 circles + 1 large rectangle
$= 2\pi r^2 + xh$
$= 2\pi(4)^2 + (8\pi)(6) = 32\pi + 48\pi = 80\pi$

**6.** $LA = Ph = (14 + 7 + 14 + 7)(8) = 336$
$SA = 2B + LA = 2(14)(7) + 336 = 532$

**7.** Use the Pythagorean Theorem to find $x = 17$.
$LA = Ph = (8 + 15 + 17)(9) = 360$
$SA = 2B + LA = 2 \cdot \frac{1}{2}(8)(15) + 360 = 480$

**8.** $SA = 2\pi r^2 + 2\pi rh$
$= 2\pi(9)^2 + 2\pi(9)(8) = 162\pi + 144\pi = 306\pi$

**9.** $SA = 2\pi r^2 + 2\pi rh$
$= 2\pi(7)^2 + 2\pi(7)(12) = 98\pi + 168\pi = 266\pi$

**10.** $LA = Ph = (16 + 5 + 16 + 5)(7) = 294$
$SA = 2B + LA = 2(16)(5) + 294 = 454$

**11.** $SA = 2\pi r^2 + 2\pi rh$
$= 2\pi(3)^2 + 2\pi(3)(7) = 18\pi + 42\pi = 60\pi$

**12.** $SA = 2\pi r^2 + 2\pi rh$
$= 2\pi(10)^2 + 2\pi(10)(6) = 200\pi + 120\pi = 320\pi$

**13.** The bases are right triangles.
Use a 5-12-13 triangle to find $x = 13$.
$LA = Ph = (5 + 12 + 13)(10) = 300$

$SA = 2B + LA = 2 \cdot \frac{1}{2}(5)(12) + 300 = 360$

**14.** The bases are equilateral triangles.
Use a 30-60-90 triangle to find $h = 3\sqrt{3}$.
$LA = Ph = (6 + 6 + 6)(5) = 90$

$SA = 2B + LA = 2 \cdot \frac{1}{2}(6)(3\sqrt{3}) + 90 = 18\sqrt{3} + 90$

**15.** The bases are trapezoids.
You found in Problem 3 that $h = 8$.
$LA = Ph = (14 + 8 + 8 + 10)(5) = 200$

$SA = 2B + LA = 2 \cdot \frac{1}{2}(8)(14 + 8) + 200 = 376$

**16.** The bases are squares. The base side length is 9 cm and the base perimeter is 4(9) = 36 cm.
$LA = Ph = 36(4) = 144$ cm$^2$

**17.** $SA = 2\pi r^2 + 2\pi rh$
$80\pi = 2\pi(5)^2 + 2\pi(5)h$
$10h = 30$
$h = 3$ inches

**18.** An inscribed angle measures half its intercepted arc. See Theorem 95.1.

## LESSON 113 ·····································

**1.** $\dfrac{\text{sector area}}{\text{circle area}} = \dfrac{\text{arc length}}{\text{circumference}}$

$\dfrac{x}{81\pi} = \dfrac{6\pi}{18\pi} = \dfrac{1}{3} \quad \rightarrow \quad 3x = 81\pi \quad \rightarrow \quad x = 27\pi$

**2.** $\dfrac{\text{arc length}}{\text{circumference}} = \dfrac{\text{sector area}}{\text{circle area}}$

$\dfrac{x}{20\pi} = \dfrac{25\pi}{100\pi} = \dfrac{1}{4} \quad \rightarrow \quad 4x = 20\pi \quad \rightarrow \quad x = 5\pi$

**3.** $s = 4, l = 5$
area = square + 4 triangles

$= 4(4) + 4 \cdot \dfrac{1}{2}(4)(5) = 16 + 40 = 56$

**4.** $r = 3, l = 9, s = $ circumference of base $= 6\pi$
area = circle + sector
$= \pi(3)^2 + 27\pi = 9\pi + 27\pi = 36\pi$

The sector has radius $l = 9$ and arc length $s = 6\pi$. You found in Problem 1 that the area of this sector is $27\pi$.

**5.** $LA = n$ triangles with base $s$ and height $l$

$= n \cdot \dfrac{1}{2} sl = \dfrac{1}{2} nsl = \dfrac{1}{2} Pl$

**6.** $LA = \dfrac{1}{2} Pl = \dfrac{1}{2}(32)(10) = 160$

$SA = B + LA = 8(8) + 160 = 224$

**7.** $B = \dfrac{1}{2} sa \cdot n = \dfrac{1}{2}(5)(3.4)(5) = 42.5$

$LA = \dfrac{1}{2} Pl = \dfrac{1}{2}(25)(8) = 100$

$SA = B + LA = 42.5 + 100 = 142.5$

**8.** $s = $ circumference of base $= 2\pi r$
$LA = $ area of a sector with radius $l$ and arc length $s$

$\dfrac{\text{sector area } LA}{\text{circle area}} = \dfrac{\text{arc length } s}{\text{circumference}}$

$\dfrac{LA}{\pi l^2} = \dfrac{2\pi r}{2\pi l} \quad \rightarrow \quad LA = \dfrac{2\pi r}{2\pi l} \cdot \pi l^2 = \pi rl$

**9.** Use a multiple of a 3-4-5 triangle to find $l = 10$.
$SA = \pi r^2 + \pi rl$
$= \pi(6)^2 + \pi(6)(10) = 36\pi + 60\pi = 96\pi$

**10.** Use a 5-12-13 triangle to find $r = 5$.
$SA = \pi r^2 + \pi rl$
$= \pi(5)^2 + \pi(5)(13) = 25\pi + 65\pi = 90\pi$

**11.** $LA = \dfrac{1}{2} Pl = \dfrac{1}{2}(24)(7) = 84$

$SA = B + LA = 6(6) + 84 = 120$

**12.** $LA = \dfrac{1}{2} Pl = \dfrac{1}{2}(80)(15) = 600$

$SA = B + LA = 20(20) + 600 = 1{,}000$

**13.** $SA = \pi r^2 + \pi rl$
$= \pi(9)^2 + \pi(9)(15) = 81\pi + 135\pi = 216\pi$

**14.** The base is an equilateral triangle with side length 8. Use a 30-60-90 triangle to find $h = 4\sqrt{3}$.

$B = \dfrac{1}{2} bh = \dfrac{1}{2}(8)(4\sqrt{3}) = 16\sqrt{3}$

$LA = \dfrac{1}{2} Pl = \dfrac{1}{2}(24)(9) = 108$

$SA = B + LA = 16\sqrt{3} + 108$

**15.** Use a 45-45-90 triangle to find $l = 6\sqrt{2}$.

$LA = \dfrac{1}{2} Pl = \dfrac{1}{2}(48)(6\sqrt{2}) = 144\sqrt{2}$

$SA = B + LA = 12(12) + 144\sqrt{2} = 144 + 144\sqrt{2}$

**16.** Use the Pythagorean Theorem to find $l = 3\sqrt{2}$.
$SA = \pi r^2 + \pi rl$
$= \pi(\sqrt{2})^2 + \pi(\sqrt{2})(3\sqrt{2}) = 2\pi + 6\pi = 8\pi$

**17.** $(x, y) \rightarrow (x + 5, y - 2) = (-1, 4)$
$x + 5 = -1, y - 2 = 4$
$x = -6, y = 6$
So, the preimage is $(-6, 6)$.

## LESSON 114 ·····································

*Note that all areas are in square units and all volumes are in cubic units.*

**1.** An equilateral triangle has 60° angles, so $\theta = 60°$. Use a 30-60-90 triangle to find $h = 3\sqrt{3}$.

$A = \dfrac{1}{2} bh = \dfrac{1}{2}(6)(3\sqrt{3}) = 9\sqrt{3}$

**2.** $A = \dfrac{1}{2} sa \cdot n = \dfrac{1}{2}(7.3)(5)(5) = 91.25$

**3.** central angle of a hexagon $= 360/6 = 60°$
$\theta = $ (central angle)$/2 = 60/2 = 30°$
Use a 30-60-90 triangle to find $a = 2\sqrt{3}$.

$A = \dfrac{1}{2} sa \cdot n = \dfrac{1}{2}(4)(2\sqrt{3})(6) = 24\sqrt{3}$

**4.** $LA = Ph = (12 + 10 + 12 + 10)(9) = 396$
$SA = 2B + LA = 2(12)(10) + 396 = 636$

**5.** $LA = \dfrac{1}{2} Pl = \dfrac{1}{2}(24)(7) = 84$

$SA = B + LA = 6(6) + 84 = 120$

**6.** $SA = \pi r^2 + \pi rl$
$= \pi(9)^2 + \pi(9)(15) = 81\pi + 135\pi = 216\pi$

7. $B = bh = 14(7) = 98$

   $V = Bh = 98(8) = 784$

8. $B = \frac{1}{2}bh = \frac{1}{2}(8)(15) = 60$

   $V = Bh = 60(6) = 360$

9. $B = bh = 5(4) = 20$

   $V = Bh = 20(7) = 140$

10. The bases are equiangular triangles, and all equiangular triangles are equilateral. The area of an equilateral triangle with side length 6 is found in Problem 1.

    $B = \frac{1}{2}bh = \frac{1}{2}(6)(3\sqrt{3}) = 9\sqrt{3}$

    $V = Bh = (9\sqrt{3})(8) = 72\sqrt{3}$

11. $V = \pi r^2 h = \pi(8)^2(6) = 384\pi$

12. $V = \pi r^2 h = \pi(9)^2(15) = 1{,}215\pi$

13. $B = bh = 13(10) = 130$
    $V = Bh = 130(10) = 1{,}300$

14. The bases are equilateral triangles with side length 10.

    $B = \frac{1}{2}bh = \frac{1}{2}(10)(5\sqrt{3}) = 25\sqrt{3}$

    $V = Bh = (25\sqrt{3})(8) = 200\sqrt{3}$

15. The bases are regular hexagons. The area of a regular hexagon with side length 4 is found in Problem 3.

    $B = \frac{1}{2}sa \cdot n = \frac{1}{2}(4)(2\sqrt{3})(6) = 24\sqrt{3}$

    $V = Bh = (24\sqrt{3})(5) = 120\sqrt{3}$

16. $B = bh = 10(9) = 90$
    $V = Bh = 90(12) = 1{,}080$

17. $B = \frac{1}{2}bh = \frac{1}{2}(4)(5) = 10$

    $V = Bh = (10)(7) = 70$

18. $V = \pi r^2 h = \pi(7)^2(12) = 588\pi$

19. Let $s$ = side length of the cube.
    $V = Bh = s^3 = 27; s = 3$
    $SA = 6$ square faces $= 6s^2 = 6(3)^2 = 54$
    So, the surface area is 54 ft$^2$.

20. Let $h$ = height of the prism.
    $V = Bh = 36h = 180; h = 5$
    So, the height is 5 cm.

21. Let $r$ = base radius and $h$ = cylinder height.
    $C = 2\pi r = 10\pi; r = 5$
    $V = \pi r^2 h = \pi(5)^2 h = 100\pi; h = 4$
    So, the height is 4 ft.

22 ~ 23. *Answers may vary. Samples are given.*

22. a reflection over the $x$-axis and then a translation of 2 units left

23. a dilation about the origin by scale factor 1/2 and then a translation of 3 units left and 4 units up

## LESSON 115

1. The bases are equilateral triangles.
   Use a 30-60-90 triangle to find $h = 3\sqrt{3}$.
   $LA = Ph = (6 + 6 + 6)(5) = 90$

   $SA = 2B + LA = 2 \cdot \frac{1}{2}(6)(3\sqrt{3}) + 90 = 18\sqrt{3} + 90$

2. $SA = 2\pi r^2 + 2\pi rh$
   $= 2\pi(9)^2 + 2\pi(9)(8) = 162\pi + 144\pi = 306\pi$

3. $SA = \pi r^2 + \pi rl$
   $= \pi(6)^2 + \pi(6)(10) = 36\pi + 60\pi = 96\pi$

4. The bases are isosceles triangles.
   Use a multiple of a 3-4-5 triangle to find $h = 8$.

   $B = \frac{1}{2}bh = \frac{1}{2}(12)(8) = 48$

   $V = Bh = (48)(7) = 336$

5. $B = bh = 10(9) = 90$
   $V = Bh = 90(12) = 1{,}080$

6. $V = \pi r^2 h = \pi(7)^2(10) = 490\pi$

7. $B = \frac{1}{2}bh = \frac{1}{2}(4)(7) = 14$

   $V = \frac{1}{3}Bh = \frac{1}{3}(14)(6) = 28$

8. $(2\sqrt{13})^2 = 4^2 + h^2$, so $h = 6$.
   $B = bh = 8(8) = 64$

   $V = \frac{1}{3}Bh = \frac{1}{3}(64)(6) = 128$

9. $V = \frac{1}{3}\pi r^2 h = \frac{1}{3}\pi(5)^2(9) = 75\pi$

10. Use a multiple of a 3-4-5 triangle to find $h = 12$.

    $V = \frac{1}{3}\pi r^2 h = \frac{1}{3}\pi(9)^2(12) = 324\pi$

11. $B = bh = 5(5) = 25$

    $V = \frac{1}{3}Bh = \frac{1}{3}(25)(6) = 50$

12. $B = \frac{1}{2}bh = \frac{1}{2}(9)(4) = 18$

    $V = \frac{1}{3}Bh = \frac{1}{3}(18)(6) = 36$

**13.** $V = \frac{1}{3}\pi r^2 h = \frac{1}{3}\pi(9)^2(12) = 324\pi$

**14.** Use a multiple of a 3-4-5 triangle to find $h = 8$.

$B = bh = 12(12) = 144$

$V = \frac{1}{3}Bh = \frac{1}{3}(144)(8) = 384$

**15.** Use a 30-60-90 triangle to find $h = 6\sqrt{3}$.

$B = \frac{1}{2}bh = \frac{1}{2}(6)(10) = 30$

$V = \frac{1}{3}Bh = \frac{1}{3}(30)(6\sqrt{3}) = 60\sqrt{3}$

**16.** Use a 30-60-90 triangle to find $h = 7\sqrt{3}$.

$V = \frac{1}{3}\pi r^2 h = \frac{1}{3}\pi(6)^2(7\sqrt{3}) = 84\pi\sqrt{3}$

**17.** 60 m³; The volume of the prism is three times the volume of the pyramid.

**18.** $V = \frac{1}{3}Bh = \frac{1}{3}(36)h = 120$

$36h = 3(120)$; $h = 10$

So, the height is 10 cm.

**19.** $V = \frac{1}{3}\pi r^2 h = \frac{1}{3}\pi r^2(3) = 25\pi$

$r^2 = 25$; $r = 5$

So, the radius is 5 in.

**20.** Use the surface area to find the slant height.
$SA = \pi r^2 + \pi rl = \pi(7)^2 + \pi(7)l = 224\pi$
$49 + 7l = 224$; $l = 25$

Use the Pythagorean Theorem or the 7-24-25 Pythagorean triple to find $h = 24$.

$V = \frac{1}{3}\pi r^2 h = \frac{1}{3}\pi(7)^2(24) = 392\pi$

So, the volume is $392\pi$ cm³.

**21.** 21, 25; Each term is 4 more than the previous term.

**22.** The number 5 has only two factors.

**23.** Addition Property

**24.** $\angle 1$ and $\angle 2$ must be supplementary. If two angles are congruent and supplementary, then they are right angles. So, $m\angle 1 = m\angle 2 = 90°$.

## LESSON 116

**1.** $SA = 2\pi r^2 + 2\pi rh = 2\pi(15)^2 + 2\pi(15)(10) = 750\pi$

$V = \pi r^2 h = \pi(15)^2(10) = 2250\pi$

**2.** Use a multiple of a 3-4-5 triangle to find $h = 8$.

$LA = \frac{1}{2}Pl = \frac{1}{2}(48)(10) = 240$

$SA = B + LA = 12(12) + 240 = 384$

$V = \frac{1}{3}Bh = \frac{1}{3}(12)(12)(8) = 384$

**3.** Use a 30-60-90 triangle to find $l = 6$.

$SA = \pi r^2 + \pi rl = \pi(3)^2 + \pi(3)(6) = 27\pi$

$V = \frac{1}{3}\pi r^2 h = \frac{1}{3}\pi(3)^2(3\sqrt{3}) = 9\pi\sqrt{3}$

**4.** not a polyhedron; A sphere has no vertices, no edges, and no flat faces.

**5.** true

**6.** The cylinder has radius $r$ and height $2r$.
$SA$ = lateral area of the cylinder
= (base circumference)(height)
= $(2\pi r)(2r) = 4\pi r^2$

**7.** $SA = 4\pi r^2 = 4\pi(2)^2 = 16\pi$

**8.** $C = 2\pi r = 10\pi$; $r = 5$

$SA = 4\pi r^2 = 4\pi(5)^2 = 100\pi$

**9.** $V = \frac{4}{3}\pi r^3 = \frac{4}{3}\pi(6)^3 = 288\pi$

**10.** $C = 2\pi r = 6\pi$; $r = 3$

$V = \frac{4}{3}\pi r^3 = \frac{4}{3}\pi(2)^3 = 36\pi$

**11.** $SA = 4\pi r^2 = 4\pi(4)^2 = 64\pi$

$V = \frac{4}{3}\pi r^3 = \frac{4}{3}\pi(4)^3 = (256/3)\pi$

**12.** $SA = 4\pi r^2 = 4\pi(15)^2 = 900\pi$

$V = \frac{4}{3}\pi r^3 = \frac{4}{3}\pi(15)^3 = 4{,}500\pi$

**13.** $C = 2\pi r = 2\pi$; $r = 1$

$SA = 4\pi r^2 = 4\pi(1)^2 = 4\pi$

$V = \frac{4}{3}\pi r^3 = \frac{4}{3}\pi(1)^3 = (4/3)\pi$

**14.** $SA = \pi r^2 + \frac{1}{2} \cdot 4\pi r^2 = \pi(2)^2 + \frac{1}{2} \cdot 4\pi(2)^2 = 12\pi$

$V = \frac{1}{2} \cdot \frac{4}{3}\pi r^3 = \frac{1}{2} \cdot \frac{4}{3}\pi(2)^3 = (16/3)\pi$

**15.** $SA = \pi r^2 + \frac{1}{2} \cdot 4\pi r^2 = \pi(9)^2 + \frac{1}{2} \cdot 4\pi(9)^2 = 243\pi$

$V = \frac{1}{2} \cdot \frac{4}{3} \pi r^3 = \frac{1}{2} \cdot \frac{4}{3} \pi(9)^3 = 486\pi$

**16.** $C = 2\pi r = 12\pi; \; r = 6$

$SA = \pi r^2 + \frac{1}{2} \cdot 4\pi r^2 = \pi(6)^2 + \frac{1}{2} \cdot 4\pi(6)^2 = 108\pi$

$V = \frac{1}{2} \cdot \frac{4}{3} \pi r^3 = \frac{1}{2} \cdot \frac{4}{3} \pi(6)^3 = 144\pi$

**17.** $SA = 4\pi r^2 = 64\pi$

$r^2 = 16; \; r = 4$

$C = 2\pi r = 2\pi(4) = 8\pi$

So, the circumference is $8\pi$ cm.

**18.** $V = \frac{4}{3}\pi r^3 = 36\pi$

$r^3 = 27; \; r = 3$

$SA = 4\pi r^2 = 4\pi(3)^2 = 36\pi$

So, the surface area is $36\pi$ in$^2$.

**19.** $SA = \pi r^2 + \frac{1}{2} \cdot 4\pi r^2 = 3\pi r^2 = 12\pi$

$r^2 = 4; \; r = 2$

$V = \frac{1}{2} \cdot \frac{4}{3} \pi r^3 = \frac{4}{3}\pi(2)^3 = (16/3)\pi$

So, the volume is $(16/3)\pi$ m$^3$.

**20.** sphere $V$ = cylinder $V$ − cone $V$

$V = \pi r^2 h - \frac{1}{3}\pi r^2 h$

$= \pi r^2(2r) - \frac{1}{3}\pi r^2(2r) = 2\pi r^3 - \frac{2}{3}\pi r^3 = \frac{4}{3}\pi r^3$

**21.** $\sin 45° = \frac{1}{\sqrt{2}} = \frac{\sqrt{2}}{2} \qquad \cos 45° = \frac{\sqrt{2}}{2} \qquad \tan 45° = 1$

## LESSON 117

**1.** perimeter ratio = 2:3 or 2/3
area ratio = 4:9 or 4/9

**2.** perimeter ratio = 1/2
area ratio = 1/4

$\frac{1}{4} = \frac{10}{x}$

$x = 4(10) = 40$
The area is 40 cm$^2$.

**3.** area ratio = 9/4
side ratio = 3/2

$\frac{3}{2} = \frac{15}{x}$

$3x = 2(15)$
$x = 10$
The hypotenuse is 10 in.

**4.** no; 18/12 = 12/8 ≠ 10/6

**5.**
a. ratio of radii = 4/10 = 2/5
b. ratio of heights = 6/15 = 2/5
c. ratio of base circumferences = 8π/20π = 2/5
d. ratio of lateral areas = 48π/300π = 4/25
e. ratio of surface areas = 80π/500π = 4/25
f. ratio of volumes = 96π/1500π = 8/125

**6.** volume ratio = 1/8

**7.** area ratio = 4/9

**8.** side ratio = 3/2

**9.** side ratio = 5/6
volume ratio = 125/216

**10.** side ratio = 4/8 = 1/2
volume ratio = 1/8

$\frac{1}{8} = \frac{x}{32}$

$8x = 32$
$x = 4$
The volume is 4 in$^3$.

**11.** area ratio = 1/9
volume ratio = 1/27

$\frac{1}{27} = \frac{x}{243}$

$27x = 243$
$x = 9$
The volume is 9 cm$^3$.

**12.** yes; 20/12 = 15/9 = 25/15

**13.** no; 6/8 = 9/12 ≠ 10/16

**14.** yes; 20/15 = 24/18

**15.** no; 6/9 ≠ 15/25

**16.** radius ratio = height ratio = 6/10 = 3/5

**17.** area ratio = 48/27 = 16/9
height ratio = 4/3

**18.** side ratio = 2/4 = 1/2
volume ratio = 1/8

**19.** area ratio = 54/24 = 9/4
perimeter ratio = 3/2

$\frac{3}{2} = \frac{x}{8}$

$2x = 3(8)$
$x = 12$
The perimeter is 12 in.

**20.** volume ratio = 1/27
area ratio = 1/9

$\frac{1}{9} = \frac{9}{x}$

$x = 81$
The base area is 81 ft$^2$.

**21.** $\angle B \cong \angle E$; The included angles must be congruent.

**22.** Use the Altitude Rule [68.1].
$8^2 = x(4x)$
$x^2 = 16$
$x = 4$

The segments are 4 cm and 16 cm.

## LESSON 118

**1.** $LA = Ph = (14 + 7 + 14 + 7)(8) = 336$

$SA = 2B + LA = 2(14)(7) + 336 = 532$

$V = Bh = 14(7)(8) = 784$

2. Use the Pythagorean Theorem to find $x = 17$.

$B = \frac{1}{2}bh = \frac{1}{2}(8)(15) = 60$

$LA = Ph = (8 + 15 + 17)(6) = 240$

$SA = 2B + LA = 2(60) + 240 = 360$

$V = Bh = 60(6) = 360$

3. $SA = 2\pi r^2 + 2\pi rh = 2\pi(4)^2 + 2\pi(4)(6) = 80\pi$

$V = \pi r^2 h = \pi(4)^2(6) = 96\pi$

4. Use a 3-4-5 triangle to find $h = 4$.

$LA = \frac{1}{2}Pl = \frac{1}{2}(24)(5) = 60$

$SA = B + LA = 6(6) + 60 = 96$

$V = \frac{1}{3}Bh = \frac{1}{3}(6)(6)(4) = 48$

5. Use a 5-12-13 triangle to find $r = 5$.

$SA = \pi r^2 + \pi rl = \pi(5)^2 + \pi(5)(13) = 90\pi$

$V = \frac{1}{3}\pi r^2 h = \frac{1}{3}\pi(5)^2(12) = 100\pi$

6. $SA = 4\pi r^2 = 4\pi(3)^2 = 36\pi$

$V = \frac{4}{3}\pi r^3 = \frac{4}{3}\pi(3)^3 = 36\pi$

7. $SA = $ hemisphere $LA + $ cylinder $LA + $ cylinder $B$

$= \frac{1}{2} \cdot 4\pi r^2 + 2\pi rh + \pi r^2$

$= \frac{1}{2} \cdot 4\pi(6)^2 + 2\pi(6)(6) + \pi(6)^2$

$= 72\pi + 72\pi + 36\pi = 180\pi$

$V = $ hemisphere $V + $ cylinder $V$

$= \frac{1}{2} \cdot \frac{4}{3}\pi r^3 + \pi r^2 h$

$= \frac{1}{2} \cdot \frac{4}{3}\pi(6)^3 + \pi(6)^2(6)$

$= 144\pi + 216\pi = 360\pi$

8. $SA = $ cone $LA + $ cylinder $LA + $ cylinder $B$

$= \pi rl + 2\pi rh + \pi r^2$

$= \pi(8)(10) + 2\pi(8)(7) + \pi(8)^2$

$= 80\pi + 112\pi + 64\pi = 256\pi$

Use a multiple of a 3-4-5 triangle to find cone $h = 6$.

$V = $ cone $V + $ cylinder $V$

$= \frac{1}{3}\pi r^2 h + \pi r^2 h$

$= \frac{1}{3}\pi(8)^2(6) + \pi(8)^2(7)$

$= 128\pi + 448\pi = 576\pi$

9. $SA = $ pyramid $LA + $ prism $LA + $ prism $B$

$= \frac{1}{2}Pl + Ph + B$

$= \frac{1}{2}(40)(13) + 40(3) + 10(10)$

$= 260 + 120 + 100 = 480$

Use a 5-12-13 triangle to find pyramid $h = 12$.

$V = $ pyramid $V + $ prism $V$

$= \frac{1}{3}Bh + Bh$

$= \frac{1}{3}(10)(10)(12) + (10)(10)(3)$

$= 400 + 300 = 700$

10. a. hemisphere $LA = \frac{1}{2} \cdot 4\pi r^2 = \frac{1}{2} \cdot 4\pi(10)^2 = 200\pi$

   b. cylinder $LA = 2\pi rh = 2\pi(10)(15) = 300\pi$

   c. cylinder $B = \pi r^2 = \pi(10)^2 = 100\pi$

   d. $SA = $ hemisphere $LA + $ cylinder $LA + $ cylinder $B$

      $= 200\pi + 300\pi + 100\pi = 600\pi$

11. a. $B = $ larger circle $-$ smaller circle

      $= \pi(5)^2 - \pi(3)^2 = 16\pi$

   b. larger cylinder $LA = 2\pi rh = 2\pi(5)(6) = 60\pi$

   c. smaller cylinder $LA = 2\pi rh = 2\pi(3)(6) = 36\pi$

   d. $SA = 2B + $ larger cylinder $LA + $ smaller cylinder $LA$

      $= 2(16\pi) + 60\pi + 36\pi = 128\pi$

12. a. prism $V = Bh = 8(10)(4) = 320$

   b. half-cylinder $V = \frac{1}{2} \cdot \pi r^2 h = \frac{1}{2} \cdot \pi(4)^2(10) = 80\pi$

   c. $V = $ prism $V + $ half-cylinder $V = 320 + 80\pi$

13. $V = $ rectangular prism $V + $ triangular prism $V$

   $= 20(18)(12) + \frac{1}{2}(12)(16)(18) = 4320 + 1728 = 6048$

14. $V = $ sphere $V + $ cylinder $V$

   $= \frac{4}{3}\pi(3)^3 + \pi(3)^2(4) = 36\pi + 36\pi = 72\pi$

15. Use a multiple of a 3-4-5 triangle to find cone $h = 8$.

   $V = $ cone $V + $ cylinder $V$

   $= \frac{1}{3}\pi r^2 h + \pi r^2 h$

   $= \frac{1}{3}\pi(6)^2(8) + \pi(9)^2(8)$

   $= 96\pi + 648\pi = 744\pi$

**16.** A, B, E

C is false because the diagonals of a rectangle are congruent but not necessarily perpendicular. D is false because the diagonals of a kite are perpendicular but not congruent.

## LESSON 119

**1.** $SA = 4\pi r^2 = 4\pi(6)^2 = 144\pi$

$V = \dfrac{4}{3}\pi r^3 = \dfrac{4}{3}\pi(6)^3 = 288\pi$

**2.** Use a 3-4-5 triangle to find $l = 5$.

$SA = \pi r^2 + \pi rl = \pi(3)^2 + \pi(3)(5) = 24\pi$

$V = \dfrac{1}{3}\pi r^2 h = \dfrac{1}{3}\pi(3)^2(4) = 12\pi$

**3.** Use a multiple of a 3-4-5 triangle to find $l = 15$.

$SA =$ cone $LA +$ cylinder $LA +$ cylinder $B$

$\quad = \pi rl + 2\pi rh + \pi r^2$

$\quad = \pi(12)(15) + 2\pi(12)(7) + \pi(12)^2$

$\quad = 180\pi + 168\pi + 144\pi = 492\pi$

$V =$ cone $V +$ cylinder $V$

$\quad = \dfrac{1}{3}\pi r^2 h + \pi r^2 h$

$\quad = \dfrac{1}{3}\pi(12)^2(9) + \pi(12)^2(7)$

$\quad = 432\pi + 1008\pi = 1440\pi$

**4.** The cross section is a circle.

**5.** The cross section is a rectangle.

**6.** The solid is a cone with radius 4 and height 7.

**7.** The solid is a sphere with radius 5.

**8.**  The solid is a hemisphere with radius 2.

$SA =$ base circle $A +$ hemisphere $LA$

$\quad = \pi r^2 + \dfrac{1}{2} \cdot 4\pi r^2 = \pi(2)^2 + \dfrac{1}{2} \cdot 4\pi(2)^2 = 12\pi$

$V = \dfrac{1}{2} \cdot \dfrac{4}{3}\pi r^3 = \dfrac{1}{2} \cdot \dfrac{4}{3}\pi(2)^3 = (16/3)\pi$

**9.** 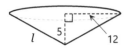 The solid is an upside-down cone with radius 12 and height 5.

Use a 5-12-13 triangle to find $l = 13$.

$SA = \pi r^2 + \pi rl = \pi(12)^2 + \pi(12)(13) = 300\pi$

$V = \dfrac{1}{3}\pi r^2 h = \dfrac{1}{3}\pi(12)^2(5) = 240\pi$

**10.**  The solid is a cylinder with a hemisphere on top. The hemisphere has radius 6. The cylinder has radius 6 and height 6.

$SA =$ hemisphere $LA +$ cylinder $LA +$ cylinder $B$

$\quad = \dfrac{1}{2} \cdot 4\pi r^2 + 2\pi rh + \pi r^2$

$\quad = \dfrac{1}{2} \cdot 4\pi(6)^2 + 2\pi(6)(6) + \pi(6)^2$

$\quad = 72\pi + 72\pi + 36\pi = 180\pi$

$V =$ hemisphere $V +$ cylinder $V$

$\quad = \dfrac{1}{2} \cdot \dfrac{4}{3}\pi r^3 + \pi r^2 h$

$\quad = \dfrac{1}{2} \cdot \dfrac{4}{3}\pi(6)^3 + \pi(6)^2(6) = 144\pi + 216\pi = 360\pi$

**11.** circle

**12.** rectangle

**13.** triangle

**14.** triangle

**15.** rectangle

**16.** parallelogram

**17.**  The solid is a cylinder with radius 10 and height 5.

$SA = 2\pi r^2 + 2\pi rh = 2\pi(10)^2 + 2\pi(10)(5) = 300\pi$

$V = \pi r^2 h = \pi(10)^2(5) = 500\pi$

**18.**  The solid is a sphere with radius 9.

$SA = 4\pi r^2 = 4\pi(9)^2 = 324\pi$

$V = \dfrac{4}{3}\pi r^3 = \dfrac{4}{3}\pi(9)^3 = 972\pi$

**19.** The solid is a cone with a hemisphere on top. The hemisphere has radius 6. The cone has radius 6 and height 8.

Use a multiple of a 3-4-5 triangle to find $l = 10$.

$SA =$ hemisphere $LA +$ cone $LA$

$\quad = \dfrac{1}{2} \cdot 4\pi r^2 + \pi rl = \dfrac{1}{2} \cdot 4\pi(6)^2 + \pi(6)(10) = 132\pi$

$V =$ hemisphere $V +$ cone $V$

$\quad = \dfrac{1}{2} \cdot \dfrac{4}{3}\pi r^3 + \dfrac{1}{3}\pi r^2 h$

$\quad = \dfrac{1}{2} \cdot \dfrac{4}{3}\pi(6)^3 + \dfrac{1}{3}\pi(6)^2(8) = 144\pi + 96\pi = 240\pi$

**20.** Two pairs of corresponding angles are congruent, so the triangles are similar by AA.

**21.** $\dfrac{x}{10} = \dfrac{21}{15}$ $\rightarrow$ $15x = 10(21)$ $\rightarrow$ $x = 14$

**22.** The side ratio is 21/15 = 7/5, so the area ratio is 49/25.

## LESSON 120

*Note that answers may vary slightly due to rounding.*

1. The box is a rectangular prism.
   $LA = Ph = (12 + 8 + 12 + 8)(6) = 240$
   $SA = 2B + LA = 2(12)(8) + 240 = 432$
   So, he will need 432 in² of paper.

2. The water tank is a cylinder.
   $V = \pi r^2 h = \pi(3)^2(5) = 45\pi \approx 45(22/7) \approx 141$
   time = volume / rate $\approx 141/3 \approx 47$
   So, it will take about 47 minutes.

3. The marble is a sphere.
   $V = \frac{4}{3}\pi r^3 = \frac{4}{3}\pi(3)^3 = 36\pi \approx 36(22/7) \approx 113.1$
   density = mass/volume $\approx 290/113.1 \approx 2.6$
   So, the density is about 2.6 g/cm³.

4. $19 = 570/x$; $x = 30$
   So, the volume is 30 cm³.

5. The water tank is a rectangular prism.
   $V = Bh = 5(3)(2) = 30$
   $997 = x/30$; $x = 29910$
   So, the tank can hold 29,910 kilograms of water.

6. population density = people/land area
   $= 704,800/80 = 8,810$
   So, the population density is 8,810 people/mile².

7. $4,680 = x/2$; $x = 9,360$
   So, the population is 9,360.

8. The fence is the lateral surface of a cylinder with radius 120 feet and height 3 feet.
   $LA = 2\pi rh = 2\pi(120)(3) = 720\pi \approx 720(22/7) \approx 2263$
   So, about 2,263 ft² of fence material is used.

9. The aquarium is a rectangular prism with one base.
   $LA = Ph = (4 + 3 + 4 + 3)(2) = 28$
   $SA = B + LA = 4(3) + 28 = 40$
   So, he will need 40 ft² of glass.

10. The height of the cone is 4(1.5) = 6.
    $V = \frac{1}{3}\pi r^2 h = \frac{1}{3}\pi(2)^2(6) = 8\pi \approx (8)(22/7) \approx 25$
    So, the volume is about 25 in³.

11. $V = \frac{4}{3}\pi r^3 = \frac{4}{3}\pi(9)^3 = 972\pi \approx 972(22/7) \approx 3055$
    time = volume / rate $\approx 3055/13 \approx 235$
    So, it will take about 235 minutes.

12. $V = \pi r^2 h = \pi(2)^2(2) = 8\pi \approx 8(22/7) \approx 25$
    density = mass/volume $\approx 227/25 \approx 9$
    So, the density is about 9 pounds per cubic foot.

13. $8 = 440/x$; $x = 55$
    So, the volume is 55 cm³.

14. $V = Bh = 3(3)(3) = 27$
    $9 = x/27$; $x = 243$
    So, the mass is 243 g.

15. $V = \frac{4}{3}\pi r^3 = \frac{4}{3}\pi(6)^3 = 288\pi \approx 288(22/7) \approx 905$
    $62 = x/905$; $x = 56110$
    So, the tank can hold about 56,110 pounds of water.

16. $10,065 = x/6.28$; $x = 63208.2$
    So, the population is about 63,208 people.

17. land area $= \pi r^2 = \pi(2)^2 = 4\pi \approx 4(22/7) \approx 13$
    population density = people/land area
    $\approx 124,800/13 \approx 9600$
    So, the population density is about 9,600 people/mile².

18. $\sin 40° = a/15$     $\cos 40° = b/15$
    $a = 15 \sin 40°$     $b = 15 \cos 40°$
    $a \approx 9.6$        $b \approx 11.5$

19. $\cos 37° = x/16$
    $x = 16 \cos 37° \approx 12.8$
    So, it is about 12.8 ft away from the wall.
    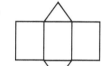

## LESSON 121

1. triangular prism

2. (diagram)

3. $F = 5$, $E = 9$, $V = 6$
   $5 + 6 = 9 + 2$

4. The bases are right triangles.
   Use a 5-12-13 triangle to find $x = 13$.
   $B = \frac{1}{2}bh = \frac{1}{2}(5)(12) = 30$
   $LA = Ph = (5 + 12 + 13)(10) = 300$
   $SA = 2B + LA = 2(30) + 300 = 360$
   $V = Bh = 30(10) = 300$

5. $SA = 2\pi r^2 + 2\pi rh = 2\pi(5)^2 + 2\pi(5)(4) = 90\pi$
   $V = \pi r^2 h = \pi(5)^2(4) = 100\pi$

6. Use a multiple of a 3-4-5 triangle to find $h = 8$.
   $LA = \frac{1}{2}Pl = \frac{1}{2}(48)(10) = 240$
   $SA = B + LA = 12(12) + 240 = 384$
   $V = \frac{1}{3}Bh = \frac{1}{3}(12)(12)(8) = 384$

**7.** Use a 30-60-90 triangle to find $h = 3\sqrt{3}$.

$SA = \pi r^2 + \pi rl = \pi(3)^2 + \pi(3)(6) = 27\pi$

$V = \frac{1}{3}\pi r^2 h = \frac{1}{3}\pi(3)^2(3\sqrt{3}) = 9\pi\sqrt{3}$

**8.** $SA = 4\pi r^2 = 4\pi(3)^2 = 36\pi$

$V = \frac{4}{3}\pi r^3 = \frac{4}{3}\pi(3)^3 = 36\pi$

**9.** $SA = \pi r^2 + \frac{1}{2} \cdot 4\pi r^2 = \pi(2)^2 + \frac{1}{2} \cdot 4\pi(2)^2 = 12\pi$

$V = \frac{1}{2} \cdot \frac{4}{3}\pi r^3 = \frac{1}{2} \cdot \frac{4}{3}\pi(2)^3 = (16/3)\pi$

**10.** $SA$ = hemisphere $LA$ + cylinder $LA$ + cylinder $B$

$= \frac{1}{2} \cdot 4\pi r^2 + 2\pi rh + \pi r^2$

$= \frac{1}{2} \cdot 4\pi(6)^2 + 2\pi(6)(8) + \pi(6)^2$

$= 72\pi + 96\pi + 36\pi = 204\pi$

$V$ = cylinder $V$ – hemisphere $V$

$= \pi r^2 h - \frac{1}{2} \cdot \frac{4}{3}\pi r^3$

$= \pi(6)^2(8) - \frac{1}{2} \cdot \frac{4}{3}\pi(6)^3$

$= 288\pi - 144\pi = 144\pi$

**11.** $SA$ = pyramid $LA$ + prism $LA$ + prism $B$

$= \frac{1}{2}Pl + Ph + B$

$= \frac{1}{2}(24)(5) + 24(3) + 6(6)$

$= 60 + 72 + 36 = 168$

Use a 3-4-5 triangle to find pyramid $h = 4$.

$V$ = pyramid $V$ + prism $V$

$= \frac{1}{3}Bh + Bh$

$= \frac{1}{3}(6)(6)(4) + (6)(6)(3)$

$= 48 + 108 = 156$

**12** $V = \pi r^2 h = \pi(7)^2(12) = 588\pi$

**13.** $B = \frac{1}{2}bh = \frac{1}{2}(4)(7) = 14$

$V = \frac{1}{3}Bh = \frac{1}{3}(14)(6) = 28$

**14.** no; $18/12 = 12/8 \neq 10/6$

**15.** area ratio = 32/50 = 16/25 = $4^2/5^2$

volume ratio = $4^3/5^3$ = 64/125

$\frac{64}{125} = \frac{128}{x}$  $\rightarrow$  $64x = 125(128)$  $\rightarrow$  $x = 250$

The volume of the larger prism is 250 cm$^3$.

**16.** The cross section is a circle.

**17.** The solid is a cylinder with radius 10 and height 5.

**18.** $SA = 2\pi r^2 + 2\pi rh = 2\pi(10)^2 + 2\pi(10)(5) = 300\pi$

$V = \pi r^2 h = \pi(10)^2(5) = 500\pi$

**19.** Cans are shaped like right cylinders. You need to find the lateral area of a cylinder with radius 3 and height 5.

$LA = 2\pi rh = 2\pi(3)(5) = 30\pi \approx 30(22/7) \approx 94$

So, 94 in$^2$ of paper was used.

**20.** $V = Bh = 3(3)(3) = 27$

density = mass/volume = 7.4/27 = 0.3

So, the density is 0.3 g/cm$^3$.

**21.** land area = $\pi r^2 = \pi(9)^2 = 9\pi \approx 9(22/7) \approx 28$

population density = people/land area

$\approx 20,900/28 \approx 746$

So, the population density is about 746 people/mile$^2$.

**22.** one line

**23.** If a point is on the bisector of an angle, then it is equidistant from the sides of the angle.

If a point is equidistant from the sides of an angle, then it is on the bisector of the angle.

**24.** area $= \frac{1}{2}d_1 d_2 = \frac{1}{2}(8)(10) = 40$ in$^2$

**25.** arc length $= \frac{\theta}{360} \cdot 2\pi r = \frac{150}{360} \cdot 2\pi(6) = 5\pi$ cm

## LESSON 122

**1.** $-3 + x = 3(2)$

$x = 9$

**2.** $1 + y = -5(2)$

$y = -11$

**3.** $x^2 = 7^2 + 14^2$

$x^2 = 245$

$x = 7\sqrt{5}$

**4.** $d = \sqrt{(0-3)^2 + (-8-1)^2} = \sqrt{90} = 3\sqrt{10}$

**5.** $d = \sqrt{(4-(-2))^2 + (-9-(-1))^2} = \sqrt{100} = 10$

**6.** radius = distance between (3, 0) and (4, –2)

$= \sqrt{(4-3)^2 + (-2-0)^2} = \sqrt{5}$

**7.** $M = \left(\frac{6+0}{2}, \frac{1-7}{2}\right) = \left(\frac{6}{2}, \frac{-6}{2}\right) = (3, -3)$

**8.** $M = \left(\frac{-2+4}{2}, \frac{-1+9}{2}\right) = \left(\frac{2}{2}, \frac{8}{2}\right) = (1, 4)$

**9.** $(9 + x)/2 = 5$    and    $(-3 + y)/2 = 2$

$9 + x = 5(2)$           $-3 + y = 2(2)$

$x = 1$                   $y = 7$

So, the other endpoint is (1, 7).

**10.** $(2 + x)/2 = -1$        $(8 + y)/2 = 4$

$2 + x = -1(2)$         $8 + y = 4(2)$

$x = -4$               $y = 0$

So, the other endpoint is (−4, 0).

**11.** center = midpoint between (5, −1) and (−3, 5)

$$= \left(\frac{5 - 3}{2}, \frac{-1 + 5}{2}\right) = \left(\frac{2}{2}, \frac{4}{2}\right) = (1, 2)$$

radius = distance between (1, 2) and (5, −1)

$$= \sqrt{(5 - 1)^2 + (-1 - 2)^2} = \sqrt{25} = 5$$

**12.** $P(-3, 2)$ and $Q(3, -2)$

$$PQ = \sqrt{(3 - (-3))^2 + (-2 - 2)^2} = 2\sqrt{13}$$

$$M = \left(\frac{-3 + 3}{2}, \frac{2 - 2}{2}\right) = (0, 0)$$

**13.** $P(2, 2)$ and $Q(-1, -4)$

$$PQ = \sqrt{(-1 - 2)^2 + (-4 - 2)^2} = \sqrt{45} = 3\sqrt{5}$$

$$M = \left(\frac{2 - 1}{2}, \frac{2 - 4}{2}\right) = \left(\frac{1}{2}, -1\right)$$

**14.** $P(0, 3)$ and $Q(-4, 0)$

$$PQ = \sqrt{(-4 - 0)^2 + (0 - 3)^2} = \sqrt{25} = 5$$

$$M = \left(\frac{0 - 4}{2}, \frac{3 + 0}{2}\right) = \left(-2, \frac{3}{2}\right)$$

**15.** radius = distance between (−4, 6) and (1, −6)

$$= \sqrt{(1 - (-4))^2 + (-6 - 6)^2} = \sqrt{169} = 13$$

**16.** center = midpoint between (9, −5) and (11, 15)

$$= \left(\frac{9 + 11}{2}, \frac{-5 + 15}{2}\right) = (10, 5)$$

**17.** $(-1 + x)/2 = 5$    and    $(4 + y)/2 = 9$

$-1 + x = 5(2)$         $4 + y = 9(2)$

$x = 11$             $y = 14$

So, the other endpoint is (11, 14).

**18.** $(7 + x)/2 = 1$    and    $(3 + y)/2 = -1$

$7 + x = 1(2)$          $3 + y = -1(2)$

$x = -5$            $y = -5$

So, the other endpoint is (−5, −5).

**19.** distance from Jacob's house to the grocery

$$= \sqrt{(-3 - 2)^2 + (2 - 7)^2} = \sqrt{50}$$

distance from Ella's house to the grocery

$$= \sqrt{(-3 - 5)^2 + (2 - (-1))^2} = \sqrt{73}$$

So, Jacob lives closer to the grocery.

**20.** distance from Morgan's house to the library

$$= \sqrt{(4 - 0)^2 + (7 - 4)^2} = \sqrt{25} = 5 \text{ km}$$

time = distance/speed = 5/10 = 0.5 hour

So, it took half an hour (or 30 minutes).

**21.** slope $m = (6 - 0)/(0 - 2) = -3$

$y$-intercept $b = 6$

So, the slope intercept equation is $y = -3x + 6$.

## LESSON 123

**1.** 3:2                    **2.** 3:1

**3.** $XY = \sqrt{(-6 - 2)^2 + (6 - 0)^2} = \sqrt{100} = 10$

$$M = \left(\frac{2 - 6}{2}, \frac{0 + 6}{2}\right) = (-2, 3)$$

**4.** $XY = \sqrt{(1 - (-3))^2 + (-6 - 2)^2} = \sqrt{80} = 4\sqrt{5}$

$$M = \left(\frac{-3 + 1}{2}, \frac{2 - 6}{2}\right) = (-1, -2)$$

**5.** $AB = 8 - 2 = 6$

$AP = 2/3$ of $AB = (2/3)(6) = 4$

$P = A + AP = 2 + 4 = 6$

So, $P$ is at 6.

**6.** $AB = 11 - (-10) = 21$

$AP = 5/7$ of $AB = (5/7)(21) = 15$

$P = A + AP = -10 + 15 = 5$

So, $P$ is at 5.

**7.** $x$-length of $\overline{AB} = 8 - (-7) = 15$

$x$ of $P = x$ of $A + (2/3)(x\text{-length}) = -7 + (2/3)(15) = 3$

$y$-length of $\overline{AB} = 20 - 2 = 18$

$y$ of $P = y$ of $A + (2/3)(y\text{-length}) = 2 + (2/3)(18) = 14$

So, $P$ is at (3, 14).

**8.** You need to move left and up to find $P$.

$x$-length of $\overline{AB} = 2 - (-3) = 5$

$x$ of $P = x$ of $A - (3/5)(x\text{-length}) = 2 - (3/5)(5) = -1$

$y$-length of $\overline{AB} = 9 - (-1) = 10$

$y$ of $P = y$ of $A + (3/5)(y\text{-length}) = -1 + (3/5)(10) = 5$

So, $P$ is at (−1, 5).

**9.** 4:2 or 2:1

**10.** $XP = (4/6)18 = 12$

**11.** $AB = 17 - 2 = 15$

$P = A + 1/3$ of $AB = 2 + (1/3)(15) = 7$

So, $P$ is at 7.

**12.** $AB = 4 - (-10) = 14$

$P = A + 3/7$ of $AB = -10 + (3/7)(14) = -4$

So, $P$ is at −4.

13. $x$-length of $\overline{AB} = 6 - 1 = 5$

   $x$ of $P = x$ of $A + (1/5)(x\text{-length}) = 1 + (1/5)(5) = 2$

   $y$-length of $\overline{AB} = 7 - (-3) = 10$

   $y$ of $P = y$ of $A + (1/5)(y\text{-length}) = -3 + (1/5)(10) = -1$

   So, $P$ is at $(2, -1)$.

14. You need to move left and up to find $P$.

   $x$-length of $\overline{AB} = 5 - (-4) = 9$

   $x$ of $P = x$ of $A - (2/3)(x\text{-length}) = 5 - (2/3)(9) = -1$

   $y$-length of $\overline{AB} = 9 - 0 = 9$

   $y$ of $P = y$ of $A + (2/3)(y\text{-length}) = 0 + (2/3)(9) = 6$

   So, $P$ is at $(-1, 6)$.

15. You need to move right and down to find $P$.

   $x$-length of $\overline{AB} = 10 - 0 = 10$

   $x$ of $P = x$ of $A + (3/5)(x\text{-length}) = 0 + (3/5)(10) = 6$

   $y$-length of $\overline{AB} = 6 - 1 = 5$

   $y$ of $P = y$ of $A - (3/5)(y\text{-length}) = 6 - (3/5)(5) = 3$

   So, $P$ is at $(6, 3)$.

16. You need to move left and down to find $P$.

   $x$-length of $\overline{AB} = 10 - (-8) = 18$

   $x$ of $P = x$ of $A - (4/9)(x\text{-length}) = 10 - (4/9)(18) = 2$

   $y$-length of $\overline{AB} = 24 - (-12) = 36$

   $y$ of $P = y$ of $A - (4/9)(y\text{-length}) = 24 - (4/9)(36) = 8$

   So, $P$ is at $(2, 8)$.

17. $\angle ACB \cong \angle E$ as right angles. $\angle ACB$ and $\angle E$ are corresponding angles on $\overline{BC}$ and $\overline{DE}$ cut by $\overline{AE}$. Two lines cut by a transversal are parallel if corresponding angles are congruent. Therefore, $\overline{BC}$ is parallel to $\overline{DE}$.

18. $AB : BD = AC : CE$

## LESSON 124

1. $y = 4$

2. $-2y = -x + 6$ $\qquad$ slope $m = 1/2$
   $y = (1/2)x - 3$ $\qquad$ $y$-intercept $= -3$

3. slope $m = (-5 - 3)/(3 - (-1)) = -2$
   point-slope form: $y - 3 = -2(x - (-1))$
   slope-intercept form: $y = -2x + 1$

4. parallel; Both lines are vertical.

5. perpendicular; $(1)(-1) = -1$

6. parallel; Both lines have slope 4.

7. neither; The lines have slopes 3/2 and 2/3.

8. original $m = 3$ $\qquad$ 9. original $m = -4$
   parallel $m = 3$ $\qquad\qquad$ parallel $m = -4$
   $y - (-2) = 3(x - 1)$ $\qquad$ $y - 0 = -4(x - (-3))$
   $y = 3x - 5$ $\qquad\qquad$ $y = -4x - 12$

10. original $m = -1$ $\qquad$ 11. original $m = 2/3$
   perpendicular $m = 1$ $\qquad$ perpendicular $m = -3/2$
   $y - 2 = (x - 7)$ $\qquad\qquad$ $y - 1 = (-3/2)(x - (-2))$
   $y = x - 5$ $\qquad\qquad$ $y = (-3/2)x - 2$

12. perpendicular; $x = 5$ is vertical and $y = 2$ is horizontal.

13. parallel; Both lines have slope 5.

14. neither; The lines have slopes 2 and –2.

15. perpendicular; $(-4/3)(3/4) = -1$

16. slope $m = -3$ $\qquad\qquad$ 17. $x = 6$
   $y - 5 = -3(x - (-1))$
   $y = -3x + 2$

18. original $m = -1$ $\qquad$ 19. original $m = 1/5$
   parallel $m = -1$ $\qquad\qquad$ parallel $m = 1/5$
   $y$-intercept $= 7$ $\qquad\qquad$ $y - (-1) = (1/5)(x - 5)$
   $y = -x + 7$ $\qquad\qquad$ $y = (1/5)x - 2$

20. original $m = -1$ $\qquad$ 21. original $m = -3$
   perpendicular $m = 1$ $\qquad$ perpendicular $m = 1/3$
   $y - 7 = x - 2$ $\qquad\qquad$ $y - 5 = (1/3)(x - 9)$
   $y = x + 5$ $\qquad\qquad$ $y = (1/3)x + 2$

22. interior angle sum $= 180(n - 2) = 180(4 - 2) = 360°$

23. interior angle sum $= 180(n - 2) = 180(10 - 2) = 1440°$
   one interior angle $= 1440/10 = 144°$

## LESSON 125

1. Plug eq2 into eq1: $\quad x - (-2x + 1) = 2$
   Solve for $x$: $\qquad\qquad x = 1$
   Use eq2 to find $y$: $\quad y = -2(1) + 1 = -1$
   Write the solution: $\quad x = 1, y = -1$

2. The lines intersect at $(1, -1)$.

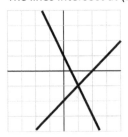

3. $d = \sqrt{(-1 - 2)^2 + (4 - 3)^2} = \sqrt{10}$

4. original slope $= -1$
   perpendicular slope $= 1$
   point-slope form: $y - 2 = x - 7$
   slope-intercept form: $y = x - 5$

5. Plug eq1 into eq2: $\quad 3x + 2(x - 2) = 4$
   Solve for $x$: $\qquad\qquad x = 8/5$
   Use eq1 to find $y$: $\quad y = (8/5) - 2 = -2/5$
   Write the solution: $\quad x = 8/5, y = -2/5$

6.  a.  original slope = 1/2

    perpendicular slope = –2

    point-slope form: $y - 5 = -2(x - (-2))$

    slope-intercept form: $y = -2x + 1$

    b.  Solve the system of $x - 2y = 3$ and $y = -2x + 1$.

    $x - 2(-2x + 1) = 3$

    $x = 1$

    $y = -2(1) + 1 = -1$

    The lines intersect at (1, –1).

    c.  distance between (–2, 5) and (1, –1)

    $= \sqrt{(1 - (-2))^2 + (-1 - 5)^2} = 3\sqrt{5}$

7.  $d = 4 - (-3) = 7$

8.  a.  (0, 3)

    b.  original slope = –2

    perpendicular slope = 1/2

    point-slope form: $y - 3 = (1/2)(x - 0)$

    slope-intercept form: $y = (1/2)x + 3$

    c.  Solve the system of $2x + y = 8$ and $y = (1/2)x + 3$.

    $2x + (1/2)x + 3 = 8$

    $4x + x + 6 = 16$ (Multiply both sides by 2.)

    $x = 2$

    $y = (1/2)(2) + 3 = 4$

    The lines intersect at (2, 4).

    d.  distance between (0, 3) and (2, 4)

    $= \sqrt{(2 - 0)^2 + (4 - 3)^2} = \sqrt{5}$

9.  Plug eq1 into eq2.

    $-x = 3x + 4$

    $x = -1$

    $y = -(-1) = 1$

    Solution: (–1, 1)

10. eq1 × 2 + eq2

    $7x = 5$

    $x = 5/7$

    $2(5/7) - y = 1$

    $y = 3/7$

    Solution: (5/7, 3/7)

11. $d = 6 - 1 = 5$

12. a.  Find the line perpendicular to $y = x$ passing through (2, –2).

    original slope = 1

    perpendicular slope = –1

    point-slope form: $y - (-2) = (-1)(x - 2)$

    slope-intercept form: $y = -x$

    b.  Find the Intersection between $y = x$ and $y = -x$.

    $x = -x$; $x = 0$; $y = 0$

    The lines intersect at (0, 0).

    c.  Find the distance between (2, –2) and (0, 0).

    $d = \sqrt{(0 - 2)^2 + (0 - (-2))^2} = 2\sqrt{2}$

13. a.  Find the line perpendicular to $x - 3y = 7$ passing through (0, 1).

    original slope = 1/3

    perpendicular slope = –3

    point-slope form: $y - 1 = (-3)(x - 0)$

    slope-intercept form: $y = -3x + 1$

    b.  Find the Intersection between $x - 3y = 7$ and $y = -3x + 1$.

    $x - 3(-3x + 1) = 7$

    $x = 1$

    $y = -3(1) + 1 = -2$

    The lines intersect at (1, –2).

    c.  Find the distance between (0, 1) and (1, –2).

    $d = \sqrt{(1 - 0)^2 + (-2 - 1)^2} = \sqrt{10}$

14. a.  Find the line perpendicular to $4x + y = -1$ passing through (4, 0).

    original slope = –4

    perpendicular slope = 1/4

    point-slope form: $y - 0 = (1/4)(x - 4)$

    slope-intercept form: $y = (1/4)x - 1$

    b.  Find the Intersection between $4x + y = -1$ and $y = (1/4)x - 1$.

    $4x + (1/4)x - 1 = -1$

    $16x + x - 4 = -4$ (Multiply both sides by 4.)

    $x = 0$

    $y = (1/4)(0) - 1 = -1$

    The lines intersect at (0, – 1).

    c.  Find the distance between (4, 0) and (0, – 1).

    $d = \sqrt{(0 - 4)^2 + (-1 - 0)^2} = \sqrt{17}$

15. a.  The $y$-intercept of $y = -x + 2$ is (0, 2).

    b.  Find the line perpendicular to $x + y = 6$ passing through (0, 2).

    original slope = –1

    perpendicular slope = 1

    point-slope form: $y - 2 = x - 0$

    slope-intercept form: $y = x + 2$

    c.  Find the intersection between $x + y = 6$ and $y = x + 2$.

    $x + (x + 2) = 6$

    $x = 2$

    $y = 2 + 2 = 4$

    The lines intersect at (2, 4).

    d.  Find the distance between (0, 2) and (2, 4).

    $d = \sqrt{(2 - 0)^2 + (4 - 2)^2} = 2\sqrt{2}$

**16.** a. The $y$-intercept of $y = 2x - 1$ is $(0, -1)$.

b. Find the line perpendicular to $2x - y = 6$ passing through $(0, -1)$.

original slope = 2

perpendicular slope = $-1/2$

point-slope form: $y - (-1) = (-1/2)(x - 0)$

slope-intercept form: $y = (-1/2)x - 1$

c. Find the intersection between $2x - y = 6$ and $y = (-1/2)x - 1$.

$2x - ((-1/2)x - 1) = 6$

$2x + (1/2)x + 1 = 6$

$4x + x + 2 = 12$ (Multiply both sides by 2.)

$x = 2$

$y = (-1/2)(2) - 1 = -2$

The lines intersect at $(2, -2)$.

d. Find the distance between $(0, -1)$ and $(2, -2)$.

$d = \sqrt{(2 - 0)^2 + (-2 - (-1))^2} = \sqrt{5}$

**17.** $(4, 1)$      **18.** $(-4, 1)$

**19.** $(12, -3)$

## LESSON 126

**1.** slope $= \dfrac{5 - (-1)}{0 - 2} = -3$

distance $= \sqrt{(0 - 2)^2 + (5 - (-1))^2} = 2\sqrt{10}$

midpoint $= \left(\dfrac{2 + 0}{2}, \dfrac{-1 + 5}{2}\right) = (1, 2)$

**2.** slope $= \dfrac{9 - 2}{-2 - (-1)} = -7$

distance $= \sqrt{(-2 - (-1))^2 + (9 - 2)^2} = 5\sqrt{2}$

midpoint $= \left(\dfrac{-1 - 2}{2}, \dfrac{2 + 9}{2}\right) = \left(-\dfrac{3}{2}, \dfrac{11}{2}\right)$

**3.** slope of $\overline{AB} = \dfrac{3 - 0}{0 - (-3)} = 1$

slope of $\overline{CD} = \dfrac{-1 - 5}{2 - (-4)} = -1$

The product of the slopes is $-1$, so the segments are perpendicular.

**4.** slope of $\overline{AB} = \dfrac{7 - 1}{5 - 2} = 2$

slope of $\overline{CD} = \dfrac{3 - (-3)}{1 - (-2)} = 2$

The slopes are equal, so the segments are parallel.

**5.** $D(3, 0)$, $E(-3, 2)$, $F(-3, -2)$

$DE = \sqrt{(-3 - 3)^2 + (2 - 0)^2} = 2\sqrt{10}$

$EF = |-2 - 2| = 4$

$DF = \sqrt{(-3 - 3)^2 + (-2 - 0)^2} = 2\sqrt{10}$

So, the perimeter is $4 + 4\sqrt{10}$.

**6.** Draw $\overline{HF}$ to divide $EFGH$.

area of $\triangle EHF = (7)(2)/2 = 7$

area of $\triangle GHF = (7)(4)/2 = 14$

area of $EFGH = 7 + 14 = 21$

**7.** 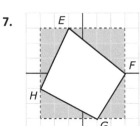 Draw a box around $EFGH$.

area of box = 6(6) = 36

area of 4 shaded $\triangle$s

    = 6 + 3 + 4 + 4 = 17

area of $EFGH$

    = 36 - 17 = 19

**8.**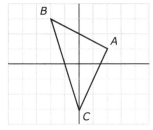

a. $AB = \sqrt{(-2 - 2)^2 + (3 - 1)^2} = 2\sqrt{5}$

$BC = \sqrt{(0 - (-2))^2 + (-3 - 3)^2} = 2\sqrt{10}$

$AC = \sqrt{(0 - 2)^2 + (-3 - 1)^2} = 2\sqrt{5}$

b. slope of $\overline{AB} = \dfrac{3 - 1}{-2 - 2} = -\dfrac{1}{2}$

slope of $\overline{BC} = \dfrac{-3 - 3}{0 - (-2)} = -3$

slope of $\overline{AC} = \dfrac{-3 - 1}{0 - 2} = 2$

c. $AB = AC$, so the triangle is isosceles.

d. The product of the slopes of $\overline{AB}$ and $\overline{AC}$ is $-1$, meaning that $\overline{AB}$ and $\overline{AC}$ are perpendicular. So, the triangle is a right triangle.

You could use the Pythagorean Theorem [74.1] to find that $BC^2 = AB^2 + AC^2$ and thus the triangle is a right triangle.

**9.**

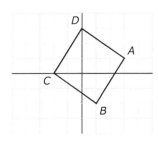

a. $AB = \sqrt{(1-3)^2 + (-2-1)^2} = \sqrt{13}$

   $BC = \sqrt{(-2-1)^2 + (0-(-2))^2} = \sqrt{13}$

   $CD = \sqrt{(0-(-2))^2 + (3-0)^2} = \sqrt{13}$

   $AD = \sqrt{(0-3)^2 + (3-1)^2} = \sqrt{13}$

b. slope of $\overline{AB} = \dfrac{-2-1}{1-3} = \dfrac{3}{2}$

   slope of $\overline{BC} = \dfrac{0-(-2)}{-2-1} = -\dfrac{2}{3}$

   slope of $\overline{CD} = \dfrac{3-0}{0-(-2)} = \dfrac{3}{2}$

   slope of $\overline{AD} = \dfrac{3-1}{0-3} = -\dfrac{2}{3}$

c. The slopes of opposite sides are equal, meaning that opposite sides are parallel. So, $ABCD$ is a parallelogram.

   You can also say that $ABCD$ is a parallelogram because opposite sides are congruent.

d. All sides are congruent. So, $ABCD$ is a rhombus.

e. The product of the slopes of adjacent sides is −1, meaning that adjacent sides are perpendicular and $ABCD$ is a rectangle. Because $ABCD$ is a rhombus and a rectangle, it is a square.

**10.**

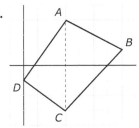

area of $\triangle ABC$
= (6)(4)/2 = 12

area of $\triangle ADC$
= (6)(3)/2 = 9

area of $ABCD$
= 12 + 9 = 21 units$^2$

**11.**

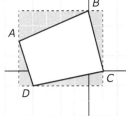

Draw a box around $ABCD$.

area of box = 6(5) = 30

area of 4 shaded $\triangle$s
= 5 + 2 + 2.5 + 1.5 = 11

area of $ABCD$
= 30 − 11 = 19

**12.** $AB = \sqrt{(4-1)^2 + (-1-6)^2} = \sqrt{58}$

$BC = \sqrt{(-2-4)^2 + (3-(-1))^2} = 2\sqrt{13}$

$AC = \sqrt{(-2-1)^2 + (3-6)^2} = 3\sqrt{2}$

All sides are different lengths, so it is a scalene triangle.

**13.** $AB = \sqrt{(-2-3)^2 + (0-5)^2} = 5\sqrt{2}$

$BC = \sqrt{(5-(-2))^2 + (-1-0)^2} = 5\sqrt{2}$

$AC = \sqrt{(5-3)^2 + (-1-5)^2} = 2\sqrt{10}$

Two sides are congruent, so it is an isosceles triangle.

**14.** slope of $\overline{AB} = \dfrac{1-4}{0-1} = 3$

slope of $\overline{BC} = \dfrac{-1-1}{6-0} = -\dfrac{1}{3}$

slope of $\overline{AC} = \dfrac{-1-4}{6-1} = -1$

$\overline{AB}$ and $\overline{BC}$ are perpendicular, so it is a right triangle.

**15.** slope of $\overline{AB} = \dfrac{6-0}{0-3} = -2$

slope of $\overline{BC} = \dfrac{3-6}{-3-0} = 1$

slope of $\overline{AC} = \dfrac{3-0}{-3-3} = -\dfrac{1}{2}$

No two sides are perpendicular, so it is not a right triangle.

**16.**

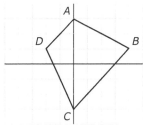

You can tell from the graph that it is not a parallelogram. It looks like an isosceles trapezoid. Check if $\overline{AD} \parallel \overline{BC}$ and $\overline{AB} \cong \overline{CD}$.

slope of $\overline{AD} = \dfrac{1-3}{-2-0} = 1$

slope of $\overline{BC} = \dfrac{-3-1}{0-4} = 1$

$AB = \sqrt{(4-0)^2 + (1-3)^2} = 2\sqrt{5}$

$CD = \sqrt{(-2-0)^2 + (1-(-3))^2} = 2\sqrt{5}$

One pair of sides is parallel and the non-parallel sides are congruent, so it is an isosceles trapezoid.

**17.**

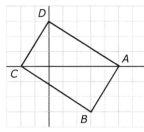

You can tell from the graph that it is not a rhombus. It looks like a parallelogram or a rectangle. Check the slopes of the sides.

slope of $\overline{AB}$ = $\dfrac{-3-0}{3-5}$ = $\dfrac{3}{2}$

slope of $\overline{BC}$ = $\dfrac{0-(-3)}{-2-3}$ = $-\dfrac{3}{5}$

slope of $\overline{CD}$ = $\dfrac{3-0}{0-(-2)}$ = $\dfrac{3}{2}$

slope of $\overline{AD}$ = $\dfrac{3-0}{0-5}$ = $-\dfrac{3}{5}$

Opposite sides are parallel, but adjacent sides are not perpendicular. So, it is a parallelogram but not a rectangle.

**18.** Each term is 10 times the previous term. The next two terms are 70,000 and 700,000.

**19.** If segments have the same length, then they are congruent.

**20.** Division Property; Divide both sides by 4.

## LESSON 127

**1.** (2, 6)

**2.** (−2, −6)

**3.** $\pi r^2 = 4\pi$
$r = 2$

**4.** $2\pi r = 10\pi$
$r = 5$

**5.** $x^2 + (y-4)^2 = 9$

**6.** $(x+2)^2 + (y-1)^2 = 16$

**7.** center: (0, 0)
radius = 2

**8.** center: (2, −1)
radius = 3

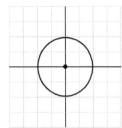

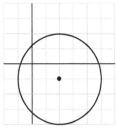

**9.** radius = distance between (5, 0) and (7, 2)
$= \sqrt{(7-5)^2 + (2-0)^2}$ = $\sqrt{8}$
So, the equation is $(x-5)^2 + y^2 = 8$.

**10.** $\pi r^2 = 25\pi$, so the radius is 5.
So, the equation is $(x-4)^2 + (y+1)^2 = 25$.

**11.** center = midpoint between (−1, 0) and (5, −6)
$= \left(\dfrac{-1+5}{2}, \dfrac{0-6}{2}\right)$ = (2, − 3)
radius = distance between (2, –3) and (–1, 0)
$= \sqrt{(-1-2)^2 + (0-(-3))^2}$ = $\sqrt{18}$
So, the equation is $(x-2)^2 + (y+3)^2 = 18$.

**12.** The preimage has center (1, 2) and radius 7.
The image has center (–1, 2) and radius 7.
So, the equation is $(x+1)^2 + (y-2)^2 = 16$.

**13.** center: (0, 2)
radius = 8

**14.** center: (−5, 0)
radius 10

**15.** center: (4, 8)
radius = 5

**16.** center: (−7, 9)
radius = 6

**17.** radius = distance between (1, 2) and (5, 0)
$= \sqrt{(5-1)^2 + (0-2)^2}$ = $\sqrt{20}$
So, the equation is $(x-1)^2 + (y-2)^2 = 20$.

**18.** $2\pi r = 6\pi$, so the radius is 3.
So, the equation is $(x+3)^2 + (y-4)^2 = 9$.

**19.** center = midpoint between (1, 1) and (9, 7)
$= \left(\dfrac{1+9}{2}, \dfrac{1+7}{2}\right)$ = (5, 4)
radius = distance between (5, 4) and (1, 1)
$= \sqrt{(1-5)^2 + (1-4)^2}$ = $\sqrt{25}$
So, the equation is $(x-5)^2 + (y-4)^2 = 25$.

**20.** center = midpoint between (−3, 5) and (1, −1)
$= \left(\dfrac{-3+1}{2}, \dfrac{5-1}{2}\right)$ = (−1, 2)
radius = distance between (−1, 2) and (1, −1)
$= \sqrt{(1-(-1))^2 + (-1-2)^2}$ = $\sqrt{13}$
So, the equation is $(x+1)^2 + (y-2)^2 = 13$.

**21.** The preimage has center (0, 0) and radius 2.
The image has center (4, 0) and radius 2.
So, the equation is $(x-4)^2 + y^2 = 4$.

**22.** The preimage has center (−7, 2) and radius $\sqrt{10}$.
The image has center (−7, −5) and radius $\sqrt{10}$.
So, the equation is $(x+7)^2 + (y+5)^2 = 10$.

**23.** Tangent and radius are perpendicular, so $m\angle A = 90°$.
$m\angle B = 180 - m\angle A - m\angle C = 180 - 90 - 55 = 35°$

**24.** Use the Pythagorean Theorem [74.1].
$(x+4)^2 = x^2 + 8^2$
$x^2 + 8x + 16 = x^2 + 64$
$8x = 48$
$x = 6$

1. $(x + 7)^2 + (y - 9)^2 - 36 = 0$
   $(x^2 + 14x + 49) + (y^2 - 18y + 81) - 36 = 0$
   $x^2 + y^2 + 14x - 18y + 94 = 0$

2. $x^2 + y^2 + 6x - 2y = -6$
   $x^2 + 6x + y^2 - 2y = -6$
   $(x^2 + 6x + 9) + (y^2 - 2y + 1) = -6 + 9 + 1$
   $(x + 3)^2 + (y - 1)^2 = 4$

3. standard equation: $x^2 + (y - 1)^2 = 9$
   general equation: $x^2 + y^2 - 2y - 8 = 0$

4. standard equation: $(x + 4)^2 + (y - 5)^2 = 36$
   general equation: $x^2 + y^2 + 8x - 10y + 5 = 0$

5. $x^2 + y^2 - 4y + 3 = 0$
   $x^2 + y^2 - 4y = -3$
   $x^2 + y^2 - 4y + 4 = -3 + 4$
   $x^2 + (y - 2)^2 = 1$
   The circle has center (0, 2) and radius 1.

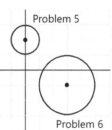
Problem 5
Problem 6

6. $x^2 + y^2 - 6x + 2y = -6$
   $x^2 - 6x + y^2 + 2y = -6$
   $x^2 - 6x + 9 + y^2 + 2y + 1 = -6 + 9 + 1$
   $(x - 3)^2 + (y + 1)^2 = 4$
   The circle has center (3, −1) and radius 2.

7. a. The slope of $\overline{CP}$ is 1/2.
   b. The tangent line is perpendicular to $\overline{CP}$, so the slope of the tangent line is −2.
   c. The tangent line has slope −2 and passes through $P(4, 2)$, so the point-slope form is $y - 2 = -2(x - 4)$.

8. a. $y = x + 2$
   b. $(x + 2)^2 + (x + 2)^2 = 8$
      $2(x + 2)^2 = 8$
      $(x + 2)^2 = 4$
      $x + 2 = 2, x + 2 = -2$
      $x = 0, x = -4$
   c. If $x = 0$, then $y = 0 + 2 = 2$.
      If $x = -4$, then $y = -4 + 2 = -2$.
      So, they intersect at (0, 2) and (−4, −2).

9. $x^2 + 2x + y^2 = 3$
   $x^2 + 2x + 1 + y^2 = 3 + 1$
   $(x + 1)^2 + y^2 = 4$
   The circle has center (−1, 0) and radius 2.

10. $x^2 + y^2 + 6y = 7$
    $x^2 + y^2 + 6y + 9 = 7 + 9$
    $x^2 + (y + 3)^2 = 16$
    The circle has center (0, −3) and radius 4.

11. $x^2 - 6x + y^2 - 4y = 0$
    $x^2 - 6x + 9 + y^2 - 4y + 4 = 9 + 4$
    $(x - 3)^2 + (y - 2)^2 = 13$
    The circle has center (3, 2) and radius $\sqrt{13}$.

12. $x^2 + 8x + y^2 - 10y = -5$
    $x^2 + 8x + 16 + y^2 - 10y + 25 = -5 + 16 + 25$
    $(x + 4)^2 + (y - 5)^2 = 36$
    The circle has center (−4, 5) and radius 6.

13. The standard equation is $(x - 1)^2 + y^2 = 16$.
    The general equation is $x^2 + y^2 - 2x - 15 = 0$.

14. radius = distance between (3, 2) and (5, 0)
    $= \sqrt{(5 - 3)^2 + (0 - 2)^2} = \sqrt{8}$
    The standard equation is $(x - 3)^2 + (y - 2)^2 = 8$.
    The general equation is $x^2 + y^2 - 6x - 4y + 5 = 0$.

15. $2\pi r = 10\pi$, so the radius is 5.
    The standard equation is $(x - 7)^2 + (y + 5)^2 = 25$.
    The general equation is $x^2 + y^2 - 14x + 10y + 49 = 0$.

16. center = midpoint between (0, 6) and (8, 6) = (4, 6)
    radius = distance between (4, 6) and (0, 6) = 4 − 0 = 4
    The standard equation is $(x - 4)^2 + (y - 6)^2 = 16$.
    The general equation is $x^2 + y^2 - 8x - 12y + 36 = 0$.

17. center = midpoint between (−1, 4) and (5, 2) = (2, 3)
    radius = distance between (2, 3) and (5, 2)
    $= \sqrt{(5 - 2)^2 + (2 - 3)^2} = \sqrt{10}$
    The standard equation is $(x - 2)^2 + (y - 3)^2 = 10$.
    The general equation is $x^2 + y^2 - 4x - 6y + 3 = 0$.

18. The preimage has center (4, −1) and radius $\sqrt{6}$.
    The image has center (−4, −1) and radius $\sqrt{6}$.
    The standard equation is $(x + 4)^2 + (y + 1)^2 = 6$.
    The general equation is $x^2 + y^2 + 8x + 2y + 11 = 0$.

19. The slope of $\overline{CP}$ is −1/3, meaning that the tangent line has slope 3 and passes through (3, 0). So, the point-slope form of the tangent line is $y = 3(x - 3)$.

**20.** $(x-1)^2 + (-x+4-2)^2 = 13$

$2x^2 - 6x - 8 = 0$

$x^2 - 3x - 4 = 0$

$(x-4)(x+1) = 0$

$x = 4, x = -1$

If $x = 4$, then $y = -4 + 4 = 0$.

If $x = -1$, then $y = -(-1) + 4 = 5$.

So, they intersect at $(4, 0)$ and $(-1, 5)$.

**21.** An angle inscribed in a semicircle is a right angle. So, $m\angle ABC = 90°$.

**22.** Because $\overline{OB} \cong \overline{OC}$ as radii, $\triangle OBC$ is equilateral. So, $m\angle C = 60°$ and $m\angle A = 30°$.

## LESSON 129

**1.** parallelogram

**2.** rhombus

**3.** rectangle

**4.** square

**5.** square

**6.** slope $= \dfrac{9-2}{-2-(-1)} = -7$

distance $= \sqrt{(-2-(-1))^2 + (9-2)^2} = 5\sqrt{2}$

midpoint $= \left(\dfrac{-1-2}{2}, \dfrac{2+9}{2}\right) = \left(-\dfrac{3}{2}, \dfrac{11}{2}\right)$

**7.** slope $= \dfrac{5-(-1)}{0-2} = -3$

distance $= \sqrt{(0-2)^2 + (5-(-1))^2} = 2\sqrt{10}$

midpoint $= \left(\dfrac{2+0}{2}, \dfrac{-1+5}{2}\right) = (1, 2)$

**8.** slope of $\overline{AB} = \dfrac{7-1}{5-2} = 2$

slope of $\overline{CD} = \dfrac{3-(-3)}{1-(-2)} = 2$

The slopes are equal, so the segments are parallel.

**9.** slope of $\overline{AB} = \dfrac{3-0}{0-(-3)} = 1$

slope of $\overline{CD} = \dfrac{-1-5}{2-(-4)} = -1$

The product of the slopes is $-1$, so the segments are perpendicular.

**10.** The circle has center $(4, 8)$ and radius 5.

**11.** $x^2 + 8x + y^2 - 10y = -5$

$x^2 + 8x + 16 + y^2 - 10y + 25 = -5 + 16 + 25$

$(x+4)^2 + (y-5)^2 = 36$

The circle has center $(-4, 5)$ and radius 6.

**12.** $D(2, 2)$, $E(-3, 1)$, $F(1, -3)$

$DE = \sqrt{(-3-2)^2 + (1-2)^2} = \sqrt{26}$

$EF = \sqrt{(1-(-3))^2 + (-3-1)^2} = \sqrt{32}$

$DF = \sqrt{(1-2)^2 + (-3-2)^2} = \sqrt{26}$

$DE = DF$, so the triangle is isosceles.

**13.** $P(1, 2)$, $Q(3, 0)$, $R(-1, -2)$, $S(-3, 0)$

a. $PQ = \sqrt{(3-1)^2 + (0-2)^2} = \sqrt{8}$

$QR = \sqrt{(-1-3)^2 + (-2-0)^2} = \sqrt{20}$

$RS = \sqrt{(-3-(-1))^2 + (0-(-2))^2} = \sqrt{8}$

$PS = \sqrt{(-3-1)^2 + (0-2)^2} = \sqrt{20}$

$PQ = RS$ and $QR = PS$, so it is a parallelogram.

b. slope of $\overline{PQ} = \dfrac{0-2}{3-1} = -1$

slope of $\overline{RS} = \dfrac{0-(-2)}{-3-(-1)} = -1$

$\overline{PQ} \parallel \overline{RS}$ and $PQ = RS$, so it is a parallelogram.

c. midpoint of $\overline{PR} = \left(\dfrac{1-1}{2}, \dfrac{2-2}{2}\right) = (0, 0)$

midpoint of $\overline{QS} = \left(\dfrac{3-3}{2}, \dfrac{0-0}{2}\right) = (0, 0)$

$\overline{PR}$ and $\overline{QS}$ bisect each other because they have the same midpoint. So, it is a parallelogram.

**14.** $CP$ = radius = distance between $(-3, 5)$ and $(-1, 3)$

$= \sqrt{(-1-(-3))^2 + (3-5)^2} = \sqrt{8}$

$CQ$ = distance between $(-3, 5)$ and $(-5, 6)$

$= \sqrt{(-5-(-3))^2 + (6-5)^2} = \sqrt{5}$

$CQ$ is less than the radius, so $Q$ is inside the circle.

**15.** The circle has center $C(1, 2)$ and radius 3.

$CR$ = distance between $(1, 2)$ and $(3, -1)$

$= \sqrt{(3-1)^2 + (-1-2)^2} = \sqrt{13}$

$CR$ is greater than the radius ($\sqrt{13} > \sqrt{9}$), so $R$ is outside the circle.

**16.** $A(0, 4)$, $B(3, 2)$, $C(0, 0)$, $D(-3, 2)$

$AB = \sqrt{(3-0)^2 + (2-4)^2} = \sqrt{13}$

$BC = \sqrt{(0-3)^2 + (0-2)^2} = \sqrt{13}$

$CD = \sqrt{(-3-0)^2 + (2-0)^2} = \sqrt{13}$

$AD = \sqrt{(-3-0)^2 + (2-4)^2} = \sqrt{13}$

All sides are congruent, so it is a rhombus.

**17.** $\overline{AC}$ and $\overline{BD}$ bisect each other because they have the same midpoint $(0, 2)$. $\overline{AC}$ and $\overline{BD}$ are perpendicular because $\overline{AC}$ is vertical and $\overline{BD}$ is horizontal. So, it is a rhombus.

**18.** $E(-2, 2)$, $F(2, 0)$, $G(1, -2)$, $H(-3, 0)$

slope of $\overline{EF} = \dfrac{0 - 2}{2 - (-2)} = -\dfrac{1}{2}$

slope of $\overline{FG} = \dfrac{-2 - 0}{1 - 2} = 2$

slope of $\overline{GH} = \dfrac{0 - (-2)}{-3 - 1} = -\dfrac{1}{2}$

slope of $\overline{EH} = \dfrac{0 - 2}{-3 - (-2)} = 2$

The product of the slopes of adjacent sides is $-1$. Adjacent sides are perpendicular, so it is a rectangle.

**19.** midpoint of $\overline{EG} = \left(\dfrac{-2 + 1}{2}, \dfrac{2 - 2}{2}\right) = \left(-\dfrac{1}{2}, 0\right)$

midpoint of $\overline{FH} = \left(\dfrac{2 - 3}{2}, \dfrac{0 - 0}{2}\right) = \left(-\dfrac{1}{2}, 0\right)$

$EG = \sqrt{(1 - (-2))^2 + (-2 - 2)^2} = 5$

$FH = |-3 - 2| = 5$

Diagonals bisect each other and are congruent, so it is a rectangle.

**20.** $CP$ = radius = distance between $(0, 4)$ and $(2, 5)$

$= \sqrt{(2 - 0)^2 + (5 - 4)^2} = \sqrt{5}$

$CQ$ = distance between $(0, 4)$ and $(-2, 2)$

$= \sqrt{(-2 - 0)^2 + (2 - 4)^2} = \sqrt{8}$

$CQ$ is greater than the radius, $Q$ is outside the circle.

**21.** The circle has center $C(1, 2)$ and radius 4.

$CR$ = distance between $(1, 2)$ and $(0, 5)$

$= \sqrt{(0 - 1)^2 + (5 - 2)^2} = \sqrt{10}$

$CR$ is less than the radius ($\sqrt{10} < \sqrt{16}$), so $R$ is inside the circle.

**22.** In a parallelogram, opposite angles are congruent, and consecutive angles are supplementary. So, the other three angles are 120°, 60°, and 120°.

**23.** A translation of 2 units left and 2 units up followed by a dilation about $(0, -3)$ by scale factor 2 will map circle $C$ onto circle $D$. Therefore, the two circles are similar.

## LESSON 130

**1.** By the slope formula,

slope of $\overline{AB} = -2/3$    slope of $\overline{BC} = 2/3$

slope of $\overline{CD} = -2/3$    slope of $\overline{AD} = 2/3$

Opposite sides are parallel, so it is a parallelogram.

You could use "rise over run" instead of the slope formula. For example, $\overline{AB}$ has a rise of 2 and a run of $-3$, which gives a slope of $-2/3$.

**2.** By the distance formula, the length of each side is $\sqrt{13}$. All sides are congruent, so it is a rhombus.

You could use the Pythagorean Theorem instead of the distance formula. For example, you can find $AB$ by finding the length of the hypotenuse of a right triangle with legs 3 and 2. Use whichever is easier for you.

**3.** The length of $\overline{AC}$ is 4. The length of $\overline{BD}$ is 6. The diagonals are not congruent, so it is not a rectangle.

**4.** midpoint of $\overline{OA} = \left(\dfrac{0 + b}{2}, \dfrac{0 + h}{2}\right) = \left(\dfrac{b}{2}, \dfrac{h}{2}\right)$

length of $\overline{OA} = \sqrt{(b - 0)^2 + (h - 0)^2} = \sqrt{b^2 + h^2}$

**5.** a. $C(0, h)$

b. $OB$ = distance between $(0, 0)$ and $(b, h)$

$= \sqrt{(b - 0)^2 + (h - 0)^2} = \sqrt{b^2 + h^2}$

$AC$ = distance between $(b, 0)$ and $(0, h)$

$= \sqrt{(0 - b)^2 + (h - 0)^2} = \sqrt{b^2 + h^2}$

The two segments have the same length.

c. The diagonals of a rectangle are congruent.

**6.** a. $A(-a, 0)$, $B(-b, h)$

b. $AC$ = distance between $(-a, 0)$ and $(b, h)$

$= \sqrt{(b - (-a))^2 + (h - 0)^2} = \sqrt{(a + b)^2 + h^2}$

$BD$ = distance between $(-b, h)$ and $(a, 0)$

$= \sqrt{(a - (-b))^2 + (0 - h)^2} = \sqrt{(a + b)^2 + h^2}$

The two segments have the same length.

c. The diagonals of an isosceles trapezoid are congruent.

**7.** a. $M = \left(\dfrac{0 + 2b}{2}, \dfrac{0 + 2c}{2}\right) = (b, c)$

$N = \left(\dfrac{2b + 2a}{2}, \dfrac{2c + 0}{2}\right) = (a + b, c)$

b. $\overline{MN}$ is horizontal because $M$ and $N$ have the same $y$-coordinate. $\overline{OB}$ is horizontal for the same reason. The two segments are both horizontal and thus parallel. Horizontal lines have a slope of 0.

c. $OB = 2a$ and $MN = |(a + b) - b| = a$. This means that $OB$ is twice $MN$, or $MN$ is half of $OB$.

d. A midsegment is parallel to the third side and half the length of the third side.

**8.** midpoint of $\overline{OB} = \left(\dfrac{0 + a + b}{2}, \dfrac{0 + c}{2}\right) = \left(\dfrac{a + b}{2}, \dfrac{c}{2}\right)$

midpoint of $\overline{AC} = \left(\dfrac{a + b}{2}, \dfrac{0 + c}{2}\right) = \left(\dfrac{a + b}{2}, \dfrac{c}{2}\right)$

The two segments have the same midpoint, so they bisect each other.

**9.** $OA = |\,a - 0\,| = a$

$OC = \sqrt{(b - 0)^2 + (c - 0)^2} = \sqrt{b^2 + c^2}$

$BC = |(a + b) - b| = a$

$AB = \sqrt{(a + b - a)^2 + (c - 0)^2} = \sqrt{b^2 + c^2}$

$\overline{OA} \cong \overline{BC}$ and $\overline{OC} \cong \overline{AB}$ because each pair has the same length. $\overline{AC} \cong \overline{CA}$ by the Reflexive Property. Therefore, $\triangle COA \cong \triangle ABC$ by SSS.

**10.** $E(-a, 0), F(0, b), G(a, 0), H(0, -b)$

**11.** $P = \left(\dfrac{-a + 0}{2}, \dfrac{0 + b}{2}\right) = \left(-\dfrac{a}{2}, \dfrac{b}{2}\right)$

$Q = \left(\dfrac{0 + a}{2}, \dfrac{b + 0}{2}\right) = \left(\dfrac{a}{2}, \dfrac{b}{2}\right)$

$R = \left(\dfrac{a + 0}{2}, \dfrac{0 - b}{2}\right) = \left(\dfrac{a}{2}, -\dfrac{b}{2}\right)$

$S = \left(\dfrac{-a + 0}{2}, \dfrac{0 - b}{2}\right) = \left(-\dfrac{a}{2}, -\dfrac{b}{2}\right)$

**12.** $\overline{PQ}$ is horizontal because $P$ and $Q$ have the same $y$-coordinate. For the same reason, $\overline{RS}$ is horizontal.

$\overline{PS}$ is vertical because $P$ and $S$ have the same $x$-coordinate. For the same reason, $\overline{QR}$ is vertical.

Horizontal and vertical lines are perpendicular to each other. This means that adjacent sides of $PQRS$ are perpendicular to each other. So, $PQRS$ is a rectangle.

**13.** $E(2b, 2h)$

**14.** $P(b, h), Q(3b, h), R(2b, 0)$

**15.** $\overline{OD}$ is horizontal because it is on the $x$-axis. $\overline{ER}$ is vertical because $E$ and $R$ have the same $x$-coordinate. So, $\overline{OD}$ and $\overline{ER}$ are perpendicular to each other.

**16** $OQ = \sqrt{(3b - 0)^2 + (h - 0)^2} = \sqrt{9b^2 + h^2}$

$DP = \sqrt{(b - 4b)^2 + (h - 0)^2} = \sqrt{9b^2 + h^2}$

The two segments have the same length.

**17.**

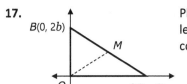

Place a right triangle with legs $2a$ and $2b$ on a coordinate plane.

Let $M$ be the midpoint of $\overline{AB}$. By the midpoint formula,

$M = \left(\dfrac{2a + 0}{2}, \dfrac{0 + 2b}{2}\right) = (a, b)$

By the distance formula,

$MO = \sqrt{(0 - a)^2 + (0 - b)^2} = \sqrt{a^2 + b^2}$

$MA = \sqrt{(2a - a)^2 + (0 - b)^2} = \sqrt{a^2 + b^2}$

$MB = \sqrt{(0 - a)^2 + (2b - b)^2} = \sqrt{a^2 + b^2}$

$MO = MA = MB$, so $M$ is equidistant from each vertex.

**18.** $\angle A \cong \angle C$ or $\angle B \cong \angle D$

**19.** $\overline{BE} \cong \overline{DE}$

## LESSON 131

**1.** length = distance between two endpoints
$= \sqrt{(5 - (-1))^2 + (-2 - 4)^2} = 6\sqrt{2}$

**2.** radius = distance between $(0, -2)$ and $(1, 3)$
$= \sqrt{(1 - 0)^2 + (3 - (-2))^2} = \sqrt{26}$

**3.** midpoint $= \left(\dfrac{-3 + 1}{2}, \dfrac{9 + 5}{2}\right) = (-1, 7)$

**4.** center = midpoint between two endpoints
$= \left(\dfrac{4 + 8}{2}, \dfrac{-2 + 6}{2}\right) = (6, 2)$

**5.** $AB = 15 - 3 = 12$
$P = A + 1/3 \text{ of } AB = 3 + (1/3)(12) = 7$
So, $P$ is at 7.

**6.** You need to move left and up to find $P$.
$x$-length of $\overline{AB} = 9 - (-3) = 12$
$x$ of $P = x$ of $A - (2/3)(x\text{-length}) = 9 - (2/3)(12) = 1$
$y$-length of $\overline{AB} = 5 - (-1) = 6$
$y$ of $P = y$ of $A + (2/3)(y\text{-length}) = -1 + (2/3)(6) = 3$
So, $P$ is at $(1, 3)$.

**7.** original slope = 2
parallel slope = 2
point-slope form: $y - 1 = 2(x - 4)$
slope-intercept form: $y = 2x - 7$

**8.** original slope = 1/3
perpendicular slope = $-3$
point-slope form: $y - (-3) = -3(x - 1)$
slope-intercept form: $y = -3x$

**9.** distance = $|7 - (-3)| = 10$

**10. a.** Find the line perpendicular to $x - 2y = 3$ passing through $(-2, 5)$.

original slope = 1/2

perpendicular slope = $-2$

point-slope form: $y - 5 = -2(x - (-2))$

slope-intercept form: $y = -2x + 1$

**b.** Find the Intersection between $x - 2y = 3$ and $y = -2x + 1$.

$x - 2(-2x + 1) = 3$

$x = 1$

$y = -2(1) + 1 = -1$

The lines intersect at $(1, -1)$.

**c.** Find the distance between $(-2, 5)$ and $(1, -1)$.

$d = \sqrt{(1 - (-2))^2 + (-1 - 5)^2} = 3\sqrt{5}$

**11.** $A(1, 2), B(1, -2), C(-3, -1)$

$AB = |-2 - 2| = 4$

$BC = \sqrt{(-3 - 1)^2 + (-1 - (-2))^2} = \sqrt{17}$

$AC = \sqrt{(-3 - 1)^2 + (-1 - 2)^2} = 5$

So, the perimeter is $9 + \sqrt{17}$ units.

**12.**

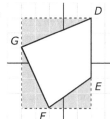

Draw a box around $DEFG$.

area of box = 5(6) = 30

area of 3 shaded △s

= 3 + 4 + 5 = 12

area of $DEFG$

= 30 − 12 = 18

**13.** $AB = \sqrt{(-2 - 2)^2 + (3 - 1)^2} = 2\sqrt{5}$

$BC = \sqrt{(0 - (-2))^2 + (-3 - 3)^2} = 2\sqrt{10}$

$AC = \sqrt{(0 - 2)^2 + (-3 - 1)^2} = 2\sqrt{5}$

$AB = AC$, so the triangle is isosceles.

**14.**

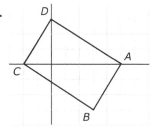

You can tell from the graph that it is not a rhombus. It looks like a parallelogram or a rectangle. Check the slopes of the sides.

slope of $\overline{AB}$ = 3/2      slope of $\overline{BC}$ = −3/5

slope of $\overline{CD}$ = 3/2      slope of $\overline{AD}$ = −3/5

Opposite sides are parallel, but adjacent sides are not perpendicular. So, it is a parallelogram but not a rectangle.

**15.** $x^2 + y^2 = 9$

**16.** $\pi r^2 = 9\pi$ gives $r = 3$.

So, the equation is $(x - 7)^2 + (y + 2)^2 = 9$.

**17.** $r$ = distance between $(0, 5)$ and $(1, 3)$

$= \sqrt{(1 - 0)^2 + (3 - 5)^2} = \sqrt{5}$

So, the equation is $x^2 + (y - 5)^2 = 5$.

**18.** $x^2 + 8x + y^2 - 10y = -5$

$x^2 + 8x + 16 + y^2 - 10y + 25 = -5 + 16 + 25$

$(x + 4)^2 + (y - 5)^2 = 36$

**19.** Find the slope and length of each side.

slope of $\overline{AB}$ = −1          length of $\overline{AB}$ = $2\sqrt{2}$

slope of $\overline{BC}$ = 3           length of $\overline{BC}$ = $\sqrt{10}$

slope of $\overline{CD}$ = −1          length of $\overline{CD}$ = $4\sqrt{2}$

slope of $\overline{AD}$ = 1/3         length of $\overline{AD}$ = $\sqrt{10}$

One pair of opposite sides is parallel but not congruent, and the other pair is congruent but not parallel. So, it is an isosceles trapezoid.

**20. a.** $A(b, 0), B(b, h), C(0, h)$

**b.** Find the length of each diagonal.

$OB = \sqrt{(b - 0)^2 + (h - 0)^2} = \sqrt{b^2 + h^2}$

$AC = \sqrt{(0 - b)^2 + (h - 0)^2} = \sqrt{b^2 + h^2}$

The two segments have the same length, so the diagonals of a rectangle are congruent.

**21.** Transitive Property

**22.** Assume that a triangle can have two right angles.

**23.** Let $x$ = base angle and $2x$ = vertex angle.

$x + x + 2x = 180; x = 45$

The triangle has angles 45°, 45°, and 90°.

**24.** A midsegment is half the length of the third side.

$5x - 8 = 2(11); x = 6$

## LESSON 132 ·············································

**1.** slope $m = (6 - 4)/(3 - 2) = 2$

point-slope form: $y - 4 = 2(x - 2)$

slope-intercept form: $y = 2x$

**2.** Add the two equations to get $3x = 6$ and $x = 2$.

Use the first equation to get $2 - y = 3$ and $y = -1$.

So, the lines intersect at $(2, -1)$.

**3.** By factoring:                    By completing the square:

$x^2 + 2x - 3 = 0$               $x^2 + 2x + 1 = 3 + 1$

$(x - 1)(x + 3) = 0$             $(x + 1)^2 = 4$

$x = 1, x = -3$                  $x + 1 = 2, x + 1 = -2$

                                $x = 1, x = -3$

**4.**
A    B    C

**5.** Use the Angle Addition Postulate [7.7].

$m\angle XOY + m\angle YOZ = m\angle XOZ$

$2m\angle YOZ + m\angle YOZ = 150°$

$m\angle YOZ = 50°$

**6.** complementary angles

$2x + x = 90$

$x = 30$

**7.** alternate interior angles

$5x + 6 = 116$

$x = 22$

**8.** $\triangle$ angle sum = 180

$x + 100 + 46 = 180$

$x = 34$

**9.** quad. angle sum = 360

$5x + 4x + 5x + 4x = 360$

$x = 20$

**10.** interior angle sum = $180(n - 2) = 180(5 - 2) = 540°$

one interior angle = 540/5 = 108°

exterior angle sum of any polygon = 360°

one exterior angle = 360/5 = 72°

**11.** interior angle sum = one interior angle × $n$

$180(n - 2) = 135n$; $n = 8$

The polygon has 8 sides.

**12.** (−3, −4)      **13.** (−4, 2)

**14.** a rotation of 180° about the origin; A composition of reflections over two intersecting lines is a rotation.

**15.** 11111

**16.** *Answers may vary. Sample(s):*

two equilateral triangles with different side lengths

**17.** If two segments are congruent, then they have the same length.

If two segments have the same length, then they are congruent.

**18.** If a figure is a rhombus, then it is a quadrilateral.

**19.** Substitution Property

**20.** Transitive Property

**21.** Addition Property; Add 7 to both sides.

**22.** Assume that $\angle 1$ and $\angle 2$ are both right angles.

**23.** $\triangle PEF \cong \triangle PGH$ by SAS.

**24.** There is not enough information.

**25.** 2. Alternate interior $\angle$s on parallel lines are $\cong$.

   3. ASA

   4. CPCTC

**26.** $\triangle DEF$ is equilateral and thus equiangular, so $a = 60$.

$\triangle DFG$ is isosceles with $m\angle DFG = 120°$, so $b = 30$.

**27.** $\triangle RSV$ is isosceles, so $a = m\angle V = 40$.

$\triangle RTU$ is isosceles with vertex angle 46°, so $b = 67$.

$c$ is an exterior angle of $\triangle RTU$, so $c = 46 + b = 113$.

## LESSON 133

**1.** perpendicular bisector, circumcenter

**2.** angle bisector, incenter

**3.** median, centroid

**4.** altitude, orthocenter

**5.** $\angle 1$ is larger than $\angle 2$ because 34 > 33.

**6.** $\angle 1$ is smaller than $\angle 2$ because 16 < 18.

**7.** Opposite angles are congruent, so $x = 62$.

Consecutive angles are supplementary, so $y = z = 180 - 62 = 118$.

**8.** The midsegment is half the sum of the bases, so $x = (7 + 9)/2 = 8$.

Base angles are congruent, so $y = 80$.

Non-base angles are supplementary, so $z = 180 - y = 100$.

**9.** Diagonals bisect opposite angles, so $m\angle 1 = 60°$.

Diagonals are perpendicular, so $m\angle 2 = 90°$.

Alternate interior angles are congruent, so $m\angle 3 = 60°$.

Diagonals bisect opposite angles, so $m\angle 4 = m\angle 3 = 60°$.

A triangle has 180°, so $m\angle 5 = 180 - 90 - m\angle 3 = 30°$.

There are many ways to find these angle measures that are all correct. For example, you could say $m\angle 1 = m\angle 2 = m\angle 3 = 60°$ because the four right triangles are congruent.

**10.** Non-vertex angles are congruent, so $m\angle 1 = 113°$.

Vertex angles are bisected by a diagonal, so $m\angle 2 = 27°$.

A triangle has 180°, so $m\angle 3 = 180 - 113 - m\angle 2 = 40°$.

A triangle has 180°, so $m\angle 4 = 180 - 27 - m\angle 1 = 40°$.

**11.** Statements (Reasons)

1. $\overline{AB} \cong \overline{CD}, \overline{BC} \cong \overline{DA}$ (Given)

2. $\overline{AC} \cong \overline{CA}$ (Reflexive Property)

3. $\triangle ABC \cong \triangle CDA$ (SSS)

4. $\angle BAC \cong \angle DCA, \angle BCA \cong \angle DAC$ (CPCTC)

5. $\overline{BA} \parallel \overline{CD}, \overline{BC} \parallel \overline{AD}$ (If alternate interior angles are congruent, then lines are parallel.)

6. $ABCD$ is a parallelogram. (Def. of parallelogram)

**12.** Corresponding angles must be congruent, so both triangles have angles 51°, 39°, and $a°$.

A triangle has 180°, so $a = 180 - 51 - 39 = 90$.

**13.** Corresponding sides must be proportional.

$\dfrac{16}{16 + 8} = \dfrac{10}{a}$   →   $16a = 10(16 + 8)$   →   $a = 15$

$\dfrac{16}{16 + 8} = \dfrac{b}{b + 7}$   →   $16(b + 7) = b(16 + 8)$   →   $b = 14$

**14.** Use the Altitude Rule [68.1].

$x^2 = 14(8)$; $x = 4\sqrt{7}$

**15.** Use the Triangle Side Splitter Theorem [69.1].

$\dfrac{20}{12} = \dfrac{15}{x}$ → $20x = 12(15)$ → $x = 9$

**16.** Use the Triangle Angle Bisector Theorem [70.1].

$\dfrac{4}{x} = \dfrac{15}{18}$ → $15x = 4(18)$ → $x = 24/5$

**17.** Use the Three Parallel Lines Theorem [69.2].

$\dfrac{12}{x} = \dfrac{16}{10}$ → $16x = 12(10)$ → $x = 15/2$

**18.** $AB = \sqrt{7^2 + 10^2} = \sqrt{149} \approx 12.2$

$m\angle A = \tan^{-1}(10/7) \approx 55°$

$m\angle B \approx 90 - 55 = 35°$

**19.** $AC = 14 \tan 24° \approx 6.2$

$AB = 14 / \cos 24° \approx 15.3$

$m\angle A = 90 - 24 = 66°$

**20.** area $= \dfrac{1}{2}(15)(19) \sin 40° \approx 91.6$

**21.** included angle $= 180 - 103 = 77°$

area $= (6)(10) \sin 77° \approx 58.5$

**22 ~ 24.** *Diagrams are not drawn to scale.*

**22.** $\dfrac{8}{8 + 16} = \dfrac{5.2}{x}$

$8x = (5.2)(8 + 16)$

$x = 15.6$

The street lamp is 15.6 feet tall.

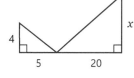

**23.** $\dfrac{4}{x} = \dfrac{5}{20}$

$5x = 4(20)$

$x = 16$

The tree is 16 feet tall.

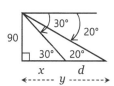

**24.** $x = 90 / \tan 30° \approx 155.9$

$y = 90 / \tan 20° \approx 247.3$

$d = y - x \approx 91.4$

The distance between the two boats is about 91.4 ft.

## LESSON 134

**1.** $(6 + 6)^2 = 6^2 + a^2$

$a = \sqrt{108} = 6\sqrt{3}$

**2.** $a = 6$

$b = 180 - 116 = 64$

**3.** $a + a + 166 = 360$

$a = 97$

**4.** $a = 90$

$b = 180 - 102 = 78$

$c = b/2 = 39$

**5.** $a = 154/2 = 77$

$b = 2(36) = 72$

**6.** $a = 2(124) = 248$

$b = 360 - a = 112$

**7.** $a = 180 - 93 = 87$

$b = (a + 129)/2 = 108$

**8.** $a = 360 - 117 = 243$

$b = (a - 117)/2 = 63$

**9.** $8a = 6(10)$

$a = 15/2$

**10.** $6(6 + 12) = 8(8 + a)$

$a = 11/2$

**11.** 3. All radii of a circle are congruent.

4. Reflexive Property

5. SSS

**12 ~ 27.** *All areas are in square units.*

**12.** area $= bh = 12(11) = 132$

**13.** Use the 3-4-5 Pythagorean triple to find $a = 3$.

Opposite sides of a rectangle are congruent, so $b = 5$.

area $= \dfrac{1}{2}h(b_1 + b_2) = \dfrac{1}{2}(4)(3 + 5 + 5) = 26$

**14.** area $= \dfrac{1}{2}sa \cdot n = \dfrac{1}{2}(7.4)(6)(5) = 111$

**15.** Use a 30-60-90 triangle to find $a = 4\sqrt{3}$.

area $= \dfrac{1}{2}sa \cdot n = \dfrac{1}{2}(8)(4\sqrt{3})(6) = 96\sqrt{3}$

**16.** The area ratio is 4:25 or 4/25.

**17.** The area ratio is 54/6 = 9/1, so the side ratio is 3/1. Set up and solve the proportion 3/1 = 15/x to get x = 5.

So, the hypotenuse of the similar triangle is 5 in.

**18.** circumference $= 2\pi r = 2\pi(5) = 10\pi$ in

**19.** arc length $= \dfrac{\theta}{360} \cdot 2\pi r = \dfrac{80}{360} \cdot 2\pi(9) = 4\pi$ cm

**20.** $14\pi = \dfrac{\theta}{360} \cdot 2\pi(18)$

$\theta = 14(360) \cdot \dfrac{1}{2(18)} = 140°$

**21.** radius $= 20/2 = 10$ in

area $= \pi r^2 = \pi(10)^2 = 100\pi$ in$^2$

**22.** area $= \dfrac{\theta}{360} \cdot \pi r^2 = \dfrac{110}{360} \cdot \pi(6)^2 = 11\pi$ cm$^2$

**23.** $150\pi = \dfrac{240}{360} \cdot \pi r^2$

$r^2 = 150 \cdot \dfrac{360}{240} = 225$

$r = 15$

**24.** $\dfrac{120}{360} = \dfrac{x}{2\pi}$

$360x = 120(2\pi)$

$x = (2/3)\pi$ radians

**25.** $\dfrac{x}{360} = \dfrac{\pi/6}{2\pi}$

$2\pi x = 360(\pi/6)$

$x = 30°$

**26.** Use the Pythagorean Theorem to find $x = 6$.

area = large rectangle – triangle

$$= 12(6) - \frac{1}{2}(3)(6) = 72 - 9 = 63$$

**27.** Radius is half diameter, so $r = 4$.

Use a 30-60-90 triangle to find $h = 4\sqrt{3}$.

area = semicircle + triangle

$$= \frac{1}{2}\pi r^2 + \frac{1}{2}bh = \frac{1}{2}\pi(4)^2 + \frac{1}{2}(8)(4\sqrt{3})$$

$$= 8\pi + 16\sqrt{3}$$

## LESSON 135

**1.** triangular pyramid

**2.** $F = 4, E = 6, V = 4$

$4 + 4 = 6 + 2$

**3 ~ 14.** *All areas are in square units.*

*All volumes are in cubic units.*

**3.** $LA = Ph = (16 + 5 + 16 + 5)(7) = 294$

$SA = 2B + LA = 2(16)(5) + 294 = 454$

$V = Bh = 16(5)(7) = 560$

**4.** $SA = 2\pi r^2 + 2\pi rh = 2\pi(10)^2 + 2\pi(10)(6) = 320\pi$

$V = \pi r^2 h = \pi(10)^2(6) = 600\pi$

**5.** The dashed triangle has hypotenuse 17 and base 8. Use the Pythagorean Theorem to find $h = 15$.

$$LA = \frac{1}{2}Pl = \frac{1}{2}(4)(16)(17) = 544$$

$$SA = B + LA = 16(16) + 544 = 800$$

$$V = \frac{1}{3}Bh = \frac{1}{3}(16)(16)(15) = 1{,}280$$

**6.** Use the 5-12-13 Pythagorean triple to find $l = 13$.

$$SA = \pi r^2 + \pi rl = \pi(5)^2 + \pi(5)(13) = 90\pi$$

$$V = \frac{1}{3}\pi r^2 h = \frac{1}{3}\pi(5)^2(12) = 100\pi$$

**7.** $SA = 4\pi r^2 = 4\pi(6)^2 = 144\pi$

$$V = \frac{4}{3}\pi r^3 = \frac{4}{3}\pi(6)^3 = 288\pi$$

**8.** $SA$ = hemisphere $LA$ + cylinder $LA$ + hemisphere $LA$

= sphere $SA$ + cylinder $LA$

= $4\pi r^2 + 2\pi rh = 4\pi(3)^2 + 2\pi(3)(4) = 60\pi$

$V$ = hemisphere $V$ + cylinder $V$ + hemisphere $V$

= sphere $V$ + cylinder $V$

$$= \frac{4}{3}\pi r^3 + \pi r^2 h = \frac{4}{3}\pi(3)^3 + \pi(3)^2(4) = 72\pi$$

**9.** The volume ratio is 15/405 = 1/27, so the side ratio is 1/3 and the area ratio is 1/9. Set up and solve the proportion $1/9 = 9/x$ to get $x = 81$.

So, the base area of the larger pyramid is 81 ft².

**10.** The cross section is a square.

**11.** The solid of revolution is a cone.

**12.** balloon $V = \frac{4}{3}\pi r^3 = \frac{4}{3}\pi(6)^3 = 288\pi$

$\approx 288(22/7) \approx 905.1$ in³

time = volume / rate $\approx 905.1/5 \approx 181$

So, it will take about 181 minutes.

**13.** aquarium $V = Bh = 10(5)(5) = 250$

density = mass/volume

$62 = x/250$; $x = 15500$

So, the aquarium can hold 15,500 pounds of water.

**14.** population density = people/land area

$250 = x/82$; $x = 20500$

So, there are 20,500 people in the town.

**15.** length = distance between two endpoints

$$= \sqrt{(1 - 3)^2 + (-4 - 2)^2} = 2\sqrt{10}$$

**16.** midpoint $= \left(\dfrac{2 + 6}{2}, \dfrac{-9 + 7}{2}\right) = (4, -1)$

**17.** $AB = 17 - 2 = 15$

$P = A + 1/3$ of $AB = 2 + (1/3)(15) = 7$

So, $P$ is at 7.

**18.** You need to move left and up to find $P$.

$x$-length of $\overline{AB} = 6 - 1 = 5$

$x$ of $P = x$ of $A - (3/5)(x\text{-length}) = 6 - (3/5)(5) = 3$

$y$-length of $\overline{AB} = 10 - (-5) = 15$

$y$ of $P = y$ of $A + (3/5)(y\text{-length}) = -5 + (3/5)(15) = 4$

So, $P$ is at (3, 4).

**19.** original slope = 3

parallel slope = 3

point-slope form: $y - 1 = 3(x - 2)$

slope-intercept form: $y = 3x - 5$

**20.** original slope = 1/2

perpendicular slope = –2

point-slope form: $y - (-1) = (-2)(x - 1)$

slope-intercept form: $y = -2x + 1$

**21.** a. Find the line perpendicular to $y = x + 4$ passing through (0, –2).

original slope = 1

perpendicular slope = –1

$y$-intercept = –2

slope-intercept form: $y = -x - 2$

**21. b.** Find the Intersection between $y = x + 4$ and $y = -x - 2$.

$x + 4 = -x - 2$

$x = -3$

$y = -3 + 4 = 1$

The lines intersect at $(-3, 1)$.

**c.** Find the distance between $(0, -2)$ and $(-3, 1)$.

$d = \sqrt{(-3 - 0)^2 + (1 - (-2))^2} = 3\sqrt{2}$

**22.** $A(2, 1), B(-2, 3), C(0, -3)$

$AB = \sqrt{(-2 - 2)^2 + (3 - 1)^2} = 2\sqrt{5}$

$BC = \sqrt{(0 - (-2))^2 + (-3 - 3)^2} = 2\sqrt{10}$

$AC = \sqrt{(0 - 2)^2 + (-3 - 1)^2} = 2\sqrt{5}$

$AB = AC$, so the triangle is isosceles.

**23.** $A(5, 0), B(3, -3), C(-2, 0), D(0, 3)$

You can tell from the graph that it is not a rhombus. It looks like a parallelogram or a rectangle. Check the slopes of the sides. By the slope formula,

slope of $\overline{AB} = \dfrac{-3 - 0}{3 - 5} = \dfrac{3}{2}$

slope of $\overline{BC} = \dfrac{0 - (-3)}{-2 - 3} = -\dfrac{3}{5}$

slope of $\overline{CD} = \dfrac{3 - 0}{0 - (-2)} = \dfrac{3}{2}$

slope of $\overline{AD} = \dfrac{3 - 0}{0 - 5} = -\dfrac{3}{5}$

Opposite sides are parallel, but adjacent sides are not perpendicular. So, it is a parallelogram but not a rectangle.

**24.** radius = distance between $(1, 2)$ and $(5, 0)$

$= \sqrt{(5 - 1)^2 + (0 - 2)^2} = \sqrt{20}$

So, the equation is $(x - 1)^2 + (y - 2)^2 = 20$.

**25.** $x^2 + 6x + y^2 - 4y = 12$

$x^2 + 6x + 9 + y^2 - 4y + 4 = 12 + 9 + 4$

$(x + 3)^2 + (y - 2)^2 = 25$

The circle has center $(-3, 2)$ and radius 5.

**26.** $M = \left(\dfrac{0 + 2b}{2}, \dfrac{0 + 2c}{2}\right) = (b, c)$

$N = \left(\dfrac{2b + 2a}{2}, \dfrac{2c + 0}{2}\right) = (a + b, c)$

**27.** $\overline{MN}$ and $\overline{OB}$ are both horizontal segments and thus parallel. The length of $\overline{OB}$ is $2a$, and the length of $\overline{MN}$ is $|(a + b) - b| = a$.

So, $\overline{MN}$ is parallel to $\overline{OB}$ and half the length of $\overline{OB}$.

## LESSON 136 ·······················································

**1.** See Lessons 36 through 38.

**2 ~ 7.** Use your ruler and protractor to check the accuracy of your construction.

**8.**

**9.**

**10.**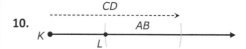

**11.** **12.**

**13 ~ 14.** Use your ruler and protractor to check the accuracy of your construction.

**15.** ASA

**16.** Use the Segment Addition Postulate [7.6].

$XY + YZ = XZ$

$XY + 3XY = 24$

$XY = 6$

**17.** Corresponding angles are congruent, so $m\angle R = m\angle W$.

$m\angle Q = 180 - m\angle P - m\angle R = 180 - 30 - 45 = 105°$.

**18.** 90°; An angle inscribed in a semicircle is a right angle.

**19.** $x^2 + (y - 4)^2 = 9$

## LESSON 137 ·······················································

**1.** $m\angle CBE = m\angle CBD + m\angle DBE$

$5x = 3x - 5 + 3x - 5; x = 10$

$m\angle CBE = 5(10) = 50°$

**2.** $AC = AB + BC$

$11 = 2x + 3x + 1; x = 2$

$BC = 3(2) + 1 = 7$

**3 ~ 4.** Use your ruler and protractor to check the accuracy of your construction.

**5.** $3x = 5x - 8; x = 4$     **6.** $7 - x = 14; x = -7$

**7.** $5x = 4x + 5; x = 5$

**8 ~ 10.** Use your ruler and protractor to check the accuracy of your construction.

**11.**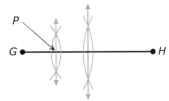

**12.**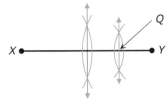

**13 ~ 14.** Use your ruler and protractor to check the accuracy of your construction.

**15.** Construct the perpendicular bisector of each side of the triangle. If your construction is correct, the perpendicular bisectors should meet in one point. That point is the circumcenter of your triangle.

**16.** If your construction is correct, the circumcenter should be equidistant from all three vertices of your triangle.

**17.** If your construction is correct, the circumcenter should be the midpoint of the hypotenuse of your triangle.

**18.** altitude, median, perpendicular bisector, angle bisector

**19.** $\triangle SFT \cong \triangle SFU$ by SAS, ASA, or AAS.
$\overline{ST} \cong \overline{SU}$ by CPCTC, so $\triangle STU$ is isosceles.

**20.** Base angles of an isosceles triangle are congruent, so $m\angle T = m\angle U = 50°$.

**21.** false; $SF = x \cos \theta$

## LESSON 138

**1.** yes; Alternate interior angles are congruent.

**2.** yes; Corresponding angles are congruent.

**3.** no

**4 ~ 15.** Use your ruler and protractor to check the accuracy of your construction.

**14.**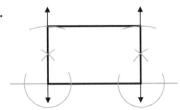

**16.** $\sin 60° = \dfrac{\sqrt{3}}{2}$    $\cos 60° = \dfrac{1}{2}$    $\tan 60° = \sqrt{3}$

## LESSON 139

**1.** interior angle sum = $180(n - 2) = 180(4 - 2) = 360°$

**2.** A parallelogram has congruent opposite angles and supplementary consecutive angles. So, the other three angles are 140°, 40°, and 140°.

**3.** Let $ABCD$ be a parallelogram with $m\angle A = 90°$. Opposite angles are congruent, so $m\angle C = 90°$. Consecutive angles are supplementary, $m\angle B = m\angle D = 180 - 90 = 90°$. All four angles are right angles, so $ABCD$ is a rectangle.

**4.** A rhombus is a parallelogram. A parallelogram with one right angle is a rectangle. A quadrilateral that is a rhombus and a rectangle is a square.

**5.** A rectangle is a parallelogram. Opposite sides of a parallelogram are congruent, so a parallelogram with congruent adjacent sides is a rhombus. A quadrilateral that is a rectangle and a rhombus is a square.

**6.** A parallelogram with congruent diagonals is a rectangle. A parallelogram with perpendicular diagonals is a rhombus. A quadrilateral that is a rectangle and a rhombus is a square.

**7 ~ 11.** Use your ruler and protractor to check the accuracy of your construction.

**12 ~ 15.** *Constructions may vary. Samples are given.*

**12.** Construct a 30°, then bisect it.

**13.** Construct two 60° consecutively.

**14.** Construct 90° and 45° consecutively.

**15.** Construct 60°, 60°, 60°, and 30° consecutively.

**16 ~ 17.** Use your ruler and protractor to check the accuracy of your construction.

**18.** $\angle B$ is an inscribed angle, so $m\widehat{AC} = 2(76) = 152°$.

**19.** A circle has 360°, so $m\widehat{BC} = 360 - m\widehat{AB} - m\widehat{AC} = 108°$.

**20.** no; $\overline{AB} \not\cong \overline{AC}$ because $\widehat{AB} \not\cong \widehat{AB}$.

## LESSON 140

1. $\overline{CP}$ and $\overline{CQ}$ are radii, $\angle PCQ$ is a central angle, and $\overline{CT}$ is an apothem.

2. $\triangle CPT$ is a 30-60-90 triangle, so $PT = 5$ and $CT = 5\sqrt{3}$.

$$A = \frac{1}{2}sa \cdot n = \frac{1}{2}(10)(5\sqrt{3})(6) = 150\sqrt{3}$$

**3 ~ 14.** Use your ruler and protractor to check the accuracy of your construction.

15. base of right $\triangle = 20/2 = 10$

$r^2 = 5^2 + 10^2$

$r^2 = 125$

$r = 5\sqrt{5}$

The radius is $5\sqrt{5}$ cm.

16. Use a 30-60-90 triangle to find that the height of the triangle is $3\sqrt{3}$.

$$A = \frac{1}{2}bh = \frac{1}{2}(6)(3\sqrt{3}) = 9\sqrt{3}$$

The area is $9\sqrt{3}$ cm².

17. true

## LESSON 141

1. perpendicular bisector
2. angle bisector
3. median
4. altitude
5. altitude
6. median
7. perpendicular bisector
8. angle bisector
9. altitude
10. altitude, median, perpendicular bisector, angle bisector

**11 ~ 17.** Use your ruler and protractor to check the accuracy of your construction.

18. If your construction is correct, the circumcenter should be the midpoint of the hypotenuse of your triangle.

19. If your construction is correct, the circumcenter should be outside of your triangle.

20. If your construction is correct, the orthocenter should be the vertex of the right angle of your triangle.

21. If your construction is correct, the orthocenter should be outside of your triangle.

**22 ~ 24.** Use your ruler and protractor to check the accuracy of your construction.

25. $P$ is the centroid and divides $\overline{AM}$ in the ratio 2:1.
$AP = (2/3)AM = (2/3)6 = 4$

26. incenter, centroid; Angle bisectors and medians are always inside a triangle.

27. Angles in a triangle add up to 180°.
$m\angle Z = 180 - 55 - 65 = 60°$

The larger angle has the longer opposite side.
$YZ < XY < XZ$ because $m\angle X < m\angle Z < m\angle Y$.

## LESSON 142

1. Tangent and radius are perpendicular.
$90 + 63 + x = 180$; $x = 27$

2. Angles in a quadrilateral add up to 360°.
$90 + 90 + 132 + x = 360$; $x = 48$

You could use Theorem 98.1 to find the measure of an angle formed by two tangent segments.
$x = ((360 - 132) - 132)/2 = 48$

3. Tangent segments to a circle from a point are ≅.
$5x - 9 = 11$; $x = 4$

**4 ~ 9.** Use your ruler and protractor to check the accuracy of your construction.

10. Tangent segments to a circle from a point outside the circle are congruent. See Theorem 91.2.

11. $\overline{OA} \cong \overline{OB} \cong \overline{OC}$ as radii. $\overline{OA} \perp \overline{DE}$, $\overline{OB} \perp \overline{EF}$, $\overline{OC} \perp \overline{DF}$ because $\overline{DE}$, $\overline{EF}$, and $\overline{DF}$ are tangents. This means that $O$ is equidistant from each side of $\triangle DEF$ and thus $O$ is the incenter of the triangle.

The incenter of a triangle is where the angle bisectors intersect, so your angle bisectors should meet at $O$.

12. Tangent and radius are perpendicular, so $m\angle G = m\angle H = 90°$. Angles in a quadrilateral add up to 360°, so $m\angle P + m\angle G + m\angle H + m\angle I = 135 + 90 + 90 + m\angle I = 360°$. This gives $m\angle I = 45°$.

13. $\overline{QJ} \cong \overline{RK}$ as radii of congruent circles. $\overline{QJ} \perp \overline{QR}$ and $\overline{RK} \perp \overline{QR}$ by construction. $\overline{QJ} \parallel \overline{RK}$ because they are perpendicular to the same line. One pair of sides is congruent and parallel, so $QRKJ$ is a parallelogram. Opposite angles of a parallelogram are congruent, so $\angle QJK$ and $\angle RKJ$ are also right angles.

14. $a = 156/2 = 78$
$b = 360 - 156 = 204$

15. $a = (35 + 65)/2 = 50$
$b = 180 - 50 = 130$

16. $a = (153 - 37)/2 = 58$

## LESSON 143

**1 ~ 15.** Use your ruler and protractor to check the accuracy of your construction.

**16.** If your construction is correct, the circumcenter should be the midpoint of the hypotenuse of your triangle. The hypotenuse should be 5 inches, and the distance from each vertex to your circumcenter should be 2.5 inches.

**17.** If your construction is correct, the median to the base should be 5 inches. The distance from the centroid to the midpoint of the base along the median should be $(1/3)(5) = 1.666… ≈ 1.67$ inches.

**18 ~ 19.** Use your ruler and protractor to check the accuracy of your construction.

**20.** $6x + 92 + 80 + 86 = 360$
$x = 17$

**21.** $90 + 2x + 102 + 78 = 540$
$x = 135$

**22.** $9x = 6(12)$
$x = 8$

**23.** $x(x + 6) = 4(4 + 5)$
$x^2 + 6x − 36 = 0$
$x = −3 + 3\sqrt{5}$

**24.** 2. Tangent and radius are perpendicular.
4. An angle inscribed in a semicircle is a right angle.
6. Reflexive Property
7. AA

## LESSON 144

**1.** $P = 2/6 = 1/3$
2 favorable: 3, 6

**2.** $P = 3/6 = 1/2$
3 favorable: 2, 3, 5

**3.** $P = 4/18 = 2/9$

**4.** $P = 5/20 = 1/4$
The team lost 5 games.

**5.** 8 possible outcomes: HHH, HHT, HTH, HTT, THH, THT, TTH, TTT
$P(\text{no heads}) = P(\text{all tails}) = P(\text{TTT}) = 1/8$
$P(\text{at least one heads}) = 1 − P(\text{no heads}) = 7/8$

**6.** $P = 2/8 = 1/4$

**7.** $P = 6/20 = 3/10$

**8.** $P = (8 − 2)/8 = 3/4$

**9.** $P = (20 − 4)/20 = 4/5$

**10.** $P = (2 + 4)/8 = 3/4$

**11.** $P = (4 + 10)/20 = 7/10$

**12.** $P = 10/100 = 10\%$
10 favorable:
10, 20, 30, …, 90, 100

**13.** $P = 5/100 = 5\%$
5 favorable:
11, 31, 41, 61, 71

**14.** $P = 13/100 = 13\%$
13 favorable:
1, 4, 9, 16, 25, 36, 49, 64, 81, 100 / 1, 8, 27, 64 / 1 is both.

**15.** $P = 0/100 = 0\%$
0 favorable:
The square of a number is never negative.

**16.** 36 possible outcomes: 11, 12, 13, …, 66
$P(\text{sum} = 12) = P(\text{rolling a 6 twice}) = 1/36$
$P(\text{sum} < 12) = 1 − P(\text{sum} = 12) = 35/36$

**17.** 50 possible outcomes: 1, 2, …, 50
$P(\text{multiple of 9}) = P(9, 18, 27, 36, \text{ or } 45) = 5/50 = 1/10$
$P(\text{not multiple of 9}) = 1 − P(\text{multiple of 9}) = 9/10$

**18.** Use the Euler's formula ($F + V = E + 2$).
$12 + V = 30 + 2; V = 20$
The polyhedron has 20 vertices.

**19.** Use the volume formula for a cylinder, $V = \pi r^2 h$.
$\pi(2)^2 h = 20\pi; h = 5$
The height is 5 cm.

## LESSON 145

**1.** $P = 3/6 = 1/2$
3 favorable: 2, 3, 5

**2.** $P = 10/25 = 2/5$

**3.** $2 × 2 × 2 × 2 × 2 = 32$

**4.** $6 × 3 = 18$
10s place: 1 to 6
1s place: 1, 3, 5

**5.** $2 × 6 = 12$
10s place: 5, 6
1s place: 1 to 6

**6.** $3 × 3 = 9$
10s place: 1, 2, 3
1s place: 2, 4, 6

**7.** $6 × 5 = 30$
10s place: 1 to 6
1s place: 6 − 1 ways

**8.** $3 × 5 = 15$
1s place: 2, 4, 6
10s place: 6 − 1 ways

**9.** $3 × 5 × 4 = 60$
100s place: 4, 5, 6
10s place: 6 − 1 ways
1s place: 6 − 2 ways

**10.** $2 × 2 × 6 = 24$

**11.** $4 × 3 × 6 = 72$

**12.** $6 × 7 × 12 = 504$

**13.** $4 × 4 × 4 = 64$

**14.** $9 × 8 = 72$
10s place: 1 to 9
1s place: 9 − 1 ways

**15.** $1 × 4 × 4 = 16$
1s place: 2
10s place: 2, 3, 5, 7
100s place: 2, 3, 5, 7

**16.** $1 × 3 × 2 = 6$
1s place: 2
10s place: 4 − 1 ways
100s place: 4 − 2 ways

**17.** $9 × 9 × 9 × 9 = 6,561$
1st digit: 1 to 9
2nd digit: 1 to 9
3rd digit: 1 to 9
4th digit: 1 to 9

**18.** $5 × 25 × 24 × 23 = 69,000$
1st letter: 5 vowels
2nd letter: 26 − 1 ways
3rd letter: 26 − 2 ways
4th letter: 26 − 3 ways

**19.** area ratio = 54/6 = 9/1
side ratio = 3/1
$3/1 = 15/x$
$x = 5$
The hypotenuse is 5 in.

**20.** A great circle has the same radius as its sphere.
So, the circumference is $2\pi r = 2\pi(5) = 10\pi$ cm.

**21.** population density = people/land area
$250 = x/82; x = 20500$
So, there are 20,500 people in the town.

## LESSON 146

1. $P = 8/(3 + 5 + 8) = 1/2$

2. $P = 12/22 = 6/11$

3. $5 \times 5 = 25$
   10s place: 1 to 5
   1s place: 1 to 5

4. $5 \times 2 = 10$
   10s place: 1 to 5
   1s place: 2, 4

5. $P(2) \times P(4)$
   $= \dfrac{1}{5} \times \dfrac{1}{5} = \dfrac{1}{25}$

6. $P(\text{odd}) \times P(\text{even})$
   $= \dfrac{3}{5} \times \dfrac{2}{5} = \dfrac{6}{25}$

7. $P(\text{odd}) \times P(\text{odd})$
   $= \dfrac{3}{5} \times \dfrac{3}{5} = \dfrac{9}{25}$

8. $P(\text{1st} > 4) \times P(\text{2nd} > 4)$
   $= \dfrac{1}{5} \times \dfrac{1}{5} = \dfrac{1}{25}$

9. $P(\text{red}) \times P(\text{pink})$
   $= \dfrac{2}{6} \times \dfrac{4}{6} = \dfrac{2}{9}$

10. $P(\text{pink}) \times P(\text{red})$
    $= \dfrac{4}{6} \times \dfrac{2}{6} = \dfrac{2}{9}$

11. $P(\text{red}) \times P(\text{red})$
    $= \dfrac{2}{6} \times \dfrac{2}{6} = \dfrac{1}{9}$

12. $P(\text{pink}) \times P(\text{pink})$
    $= \dfrac{4}{6} \times \dfrac{4}{6} = \dfrac{4}{9}$

13. $P(\text{odd}) \times P(\text{odd})$
    $= \dfrac{3}{6} \times \dfrac{3}{6} = \dfrac{1}{4}$

14. $P(\text{prime}) \times P(\text{prime})$
    $= \dfrac{3}{6} \times \dfrac{3}{6} = \dfrac{1}{4}$

15. $P(\text{tails}) \times P(\text{negative})$
    $= \dfrac{1}{2} \times \dfrac{0}{6} = 0$

16. $P(\text{black}) \times P(\text{white})$
    $= \dfrac{2}{8} \times \dfrac{6}{8} = \dfrac{3}{16}$

17. $P(\text{odd}) \times P(\text{Mon or Tue})$
    $= \dfrac{3}{6} \times \dfrac{2}{7} = \dfrac{1}{7}$

18. $P(\text{vowel}) \times P(\text{vowel})$
    $= \dfrac{2}{5} \times \dfrac{2}{5} = \dfrac{4}{25}$

19. $P(\text{correct}) \times P(\text{correct}) \times P(\text{correct}) \times P(\text{correct})$
    $= \dfrac{1}{2} \times \dfrac{1}{2} \times \dfrac{1}{2} \times \dfrac{1}{2} = \dfrac{1}{16}$

20. $P(2) \times P(3)$
    $= \dfrac{1}{9} \times \dfrac{1}{9} = \dfrac{1}{81}$

21. $P(8) \times P(8)$
    $= \dfrac{1}{9} \times \dfrac{1}{9} = \dfrac{1}{81}$

22. $P(\text{1st digit} < 4) \times$
    $P(\text{2nd digit any})$
    $= \dfrac{3}{9} \times \dfrac{9}{9} = \dfrac{1}{3}$

23. $P(\text{1st digit any}) \times$
    $P(\text{2nd digit} = 5)$
    $= \dfrac{9}{9} \times \dfrac{1}{9} = \dfrac{1}{9}$

24. Use the Three Parallel Lines Theorem [69.2].
    $420/555 = 448/x$; $x = 592$
    The distance is 592 feet.

## LESSON 147

1. $5 \times 4 = 20$
   10s place: 1 to 5
   1s place: 5 − 1 ways

2. $2 \times 4 = 8$
   1s place: 2, 4
   10s place: 5 − 1 ways

3. $P(\text{heads}) \times P(5)$
   $= \dfrac{1}{2} \times \dfrac{1}{6} = \dfrac{1}{12}$

4. $P(\text{red}) \times P(\text{pink})$
   $= \dfrac{2}{8} \times \dfrac{6}{8} = \dfrac{3}{16}$

5. $P(2) \times P(4 \mid 2)$
   $= \dfrac{1}{5} \times \dfrac{1}{4} = \dfrac{1}{20}$

6. $P(\text{odd}) \times P(\text{even} \mid \text{odd})$
   $= \dfrac{3}{5} \times \dfrac{2}{4} = \dfrac{3}{10}$

7. $P(\text{odd}) \times P(\text{odd} \mid \text{odd})$
   $= \dfrac{3}{5} \times \dfrac{2}{4} = \dfrac{3}{10}$

8. $P(5) \times P(5 \mid 5)$
   $= \dfrac{1}{5} \times \dfrac{0}{4} = 0$

9. $P(\text{red}) \times P(\text{pink} \mid \text{red})$
   $= \dfrac{2}{6} \times \dfrac{4}{5} = \dfrac{4}{15}$

10. $P(\text{pink}) \times P(\text{red} \mid \text{pink})$
    $= \dfrac{4}{6} \times \dfrac{2}{5} = \dfrac{4}{15}$

11. $P(\text{red}) \times P(\text{red} \mid \text{red})$
    $= \dfrac{2}{6} \times \dfrac{1}{5} = \dfrac{1}{15}$

12. $P(\text{pink}) \times P(\text{pink} \mid \text{pink})$
    $= \dfrac{4}{6} \times \dfrac{3}{5} = \dfrac{2}{5}$

13. $P = 6/36 = 1/6$
    6 favorable: 11, 22, ..., 66

14. $P = 3/36 = 1/12$
    3 favorable: 46, 55, 64

15. $P(\text{red}) \times P(\text{red} \mid \text{red})$
    $= \dfrac{3}{6} \times \dfrac{2}{5} = \dfrac{1}{5}$

16. $P(\text{even}) \times P(\text{even} \mid \text{even})$
    $= \dfrac{4}{9} \times \dfrac{3}{8} = \dfrac{1}{6}$

17. $P(\text{vowel}) \times P(\text{vowel} \mid \text{vowel})$
    $= \dfrac{2}{5} \times \dfrac{1}{4} = \dfrac{1}{10}$

18. $P(\text{green}) \times P(\text{green} \mid \text{green}) \times P(\text{green} \mid \text{two greens})$
    $= \dfrac{4}{10} \times \dfrac{3}{9} \times \dfrac{2}{8} = \dfrac{1}{30}$

19. $P = 3/36 = 1/12$
    3 favorable:
    11, 12, 21

20. $P = 15/36 = 5/12$
    15 favorable:
    12, 13, 14, 15, 16 /
    23, 24, 25, 26 /
    34, 35, 36 / 45, 46 / 56

21. $P(2) \times P(3 \mid 2)$
    $= \dfrac{1}{9} \times \dfrac{1}{8} = \dfrac{1}{72}$

22. $P(8) \times P(8 \mid 8)$
    $= \dfrac{1}{9} \times \dfrac{0}{8} = 0$

23. $P(\text{1st digit} < 4) \times$
    $P(\text{2nd digit any} \mid \text{1st} < 4)$
    $= \dfrac{3}{9} \times \dfrac{8}{8} = \dfrac{1}{3}$

24. $P(\text{2nd digit} = 5) \times$
    $P(\text{1st digit any} \mid \text{2nd} = 5)$
    $= \dfrac{1}{9} \times \dfrac{8}{8} = \dfrac{1}{9}$

25. The triangle is obtuse because $8^2 > 3^2 + 6^2$.

26. arc length $= \dfrac{\theta}{360} \cdot 2\pi r = \dfrac{60}{360} \cdot 2\pi(6) = 2\pi$

## LESSON 148

1. $P(\text{odd}) \times P(\text{odd})$

$$= \frac{3}{6} \times \frac{3}{6} = \frac{1}{4}$$

2. $P = 2/36 = 1/18$

   2 favorable: 12, 21

3. $P = 1 - P(\text{same numbers})$

   $= 1 - P(11, 22, ..., 66)$

   $= 1 - 6/36 = 5/6$

4. $P = 21/36 = 7/12$

   21 favorable:

   11 / 21, 22 / 31 ~ 33 /
   41 ~ 44 / 51 ~ 55 /
   61 ~ 66

5. $P(\text{heart}) + P(\text{face}) - P(\text{heart and face})$

$$= \frac{13}{52} + \frac{12}{52} - \frac{3}{52} = \frac{11}{26}$$

6. $P(\text{red}) + P(\text{number}) - P(\text{red and number})$

$$= \frac{26}{52} + \frac{36}{52} - \frac{18}{52} = \frac{11}{13}$$

7. $P(\text{face}) + P(\text{king}) - P(\text{face and king})$

$$= \frac{12}{52} + \frac{4}{52} - \frac{4}{52} = \frac{3}{13}$$

8. $P(\text{spade}) + P(\text{number} < 5) - P(\text{spade and number} < 5)$

$$= \frac{13}{52} + \frac{12}{52} - \frac{3}{52} = \frac{11}{26}$$

9. $P(\text{red}) + P(\text{spade})$

$$= \frac{26}{52} + \frac{13}{52} = \frac{3}{4}$$

10. $P(\text{heart}) + P(\text{diamond})$

$$= \frac{13}{52} + \frac{13}{52} = \frac{1}{2}$$

11. $P(\text{ace}) + P(\text{face})$

$$= \frac{4}{52} + \frac{12}{52} = \frac{4}{13}$$

12. $P(\text{face}) + P(\text{number} < 5)$

$$= \frac{12}{52} + \frac{12}{52} = \frac{6}{13}$$

13. $P(\text{odd}) + P(\text{prime}) - P(\text{odd and prime})$

$$= \frac{3}{6} + \frac{3}{6} - \frac{2}{6} = \frac{2}{3}$$

14. $P(\text{odd}) + P(2\text{'s multiple}) - P(\text{odd and 2's multiple})$

$$= \frac{3}{6} + \frac{3}{6} - \frac{0}{6} = 1$$

15. $P(\text{even}) + P(\text{number} < 4) - P(\text{even and number} < 4)$

$$= \frac{3}{6} + \frac{3}{6} - \frac{1}{6} = \frac{5}{6}$$

16. $P(\text{king}) + P(\text{queen}) - P(\text{king and queen})$

$$= \frac{4}{52} + \frac{4}{52} - \frac{0}{52} = \frac{2}{13}$$

17. $P(\text{ace}) + P(\text{club}) - P(\text{ace and club})$

$$= \frac{4}{52} + \frac{13}{52} - \frac{1}{52} = \frac{4}{13}$$

18. $P(\text{red}) + P(\text{face}) - P(\text{red and face})$

$$= \frac{26}{52} + \frac{12}{52} - \frac{6}{52} = \frac{8}{13}$$

19. $P = 36/81 = 4/9$

   $9 \times 9 = 81$ possible

   $4 \times 9 = 36$ favorable:

   10s place: 1, 2, 3, 4

   1s place: 1 to 9

20. $P = 45/81 = 5/9$

   $9 \times 9 = 81$ possible

   $9 \times 5 = 45$ favorable:

   10s place: 1 to 9

   1s place: 1, 3, 5, 7, 9

21. $P(\text{1st digit} < 5) \times P(\text{2nd digit odd})$

$$= \frac{4}{9} \times \frac{5}{9} = \frac{20}{81}$$

22. Use the probabilities from Problems 19 through 21.

   $P(\text{less than 50}) + P(\text{odd}) - P(\text{less than 50 and odd})$

$$= \frac{4}{9} + \frac{5}{9} - \frac{20}{81} = \frac{61}{81}$$

23. The side lengths are 3, $3\sqrt{3}$, and 6.

24. The solid is a cone with radius $3\sqrt{3}$ and height 3.

25. volume $= \frac{1}{3}\pi r^2 h = \frac{1}{3}\pi(3\sqrt{3})^2(3) = 27\pi$

## LESSON 149

1. $P(\text{heads}) \times P(\text{odd})$

$$= \frac{1}{2} \times \frac{3}{6} = \frac{1}{4}$$

2. $P(\text{red}) \times P(\text{red})$

$$= \frac{4}{10} \times \frac{4}{10} = \frac{4}{25}$$

3. $P(\text{odd}) \times P(\text{odd} | \text{odd})$

$$= \frac{2}{4} \times \frac{1}{3} = \frac{1}{6}$$

4. $P(\text{red}) \times P(\text{red} | \text{red})$

$$= \frac{4}{10} \times \frac{3}{9} = \frac{2}{15}$$

5. $P(\text{club}) + P(\text{number}) - P(\text{club and number})$

$$= \frac{13}{52} + \frac{36}{52} - \frac{9}{52} = \frac{10}{13}$$

6. $P(\text{club}) + P(\text{red}) - P(\text{club and red})$

$$= \frac{13}{52} + \frac{26}{52} - \frac{0}{52} = \frac{3}{4}$$

7. $P(\text{sum} = 12) = P(\text{rolling a 6 twice}) = 1/36$

   $P(\text{sum} \neq 12) = 1 - P(\text{sum} = 12) = 1 - 1/36 = 35/36$

8. $P(\text{sum} \leq 3) = P(11, 12, \text{ or } 21) = 3/36 = 1/12$

   $P(\text{sum} > 3) = 1 - P(\text{sum} \leq 3) = 1 - 1/12 = 11/12$

9. $P(\text{same numbers}) = P(11, 22, 33, 44, 55, \text{ or } 66) = 1/6$

   $P(\text{different numbers}) = 1 - P(\text{same numbers}) = 5/6$

10. $P(\text{even}) + P(\text{prime}) - P(\text{even and prime})$

$$= \frac{3}{6} + \frac{3}{6} - \frac{1}{6} = \frac{5}{6}$$

11. $P(\text{odd}) + P(2\text{'s multiple}) - P(\text{odd and 2's multiple})$

$$= \frac{3}{6} + \frac{3}{6} - \frac{0}{6} = 1$$

12. $P(\text{red}) \times P(\text{pink} | \text{red})$

$$= \frac{2}{5} \times \frac{3}{4} = \frac{3}{10}$$

13. $P(\text{red}) \times P(\text{pink})$

$$= \frac{2}{5} \times \frac{3}{5} = \frac{6}{25}$$

**14.** $P(\text{number}) = 36/52 = 9/13$

$P(\text{not number}) = 1 - P(\text{number}) = 1 - 9/13 = 4/13$

**15.** $P(\text{red}) + P(\text{ace}) - P(\text{red and ace})$

$= \dfrac{26}{52} + \dfrac{4}{52} - \dfrac{2}{52} = \dfrac{7}{13}$

**16.** $P(\text{face}) + P(\text{heart}) - P(\text{face and heart})$

$= \dfrac{12}{52} + \dfrac{13}{52} - \dfrac{3}{52} = \dfrac{11}{26}$

**17.** $P(\text{heart or king})$

$= P(\text{heart}) + P(\text{king}) - P(\text{heart and king})$

$= \dfrac{13}{52} + \dfrac{4}{52} - \dfrac{1}{52} = \dfrac{4}{13}$

$P(\text{neither heart nor king}) = 1 - P(\text{heart or king}) = 9/13$

**18.** $P(\text{king}) \times P(\text{king}\,|\,\text{king})$

$= \dfrac{4}{52} \times \dfrac{3}{51} = \dfrac{1}{221}$

**19.** $P(\text{heart}) \times P(\text{heart}\,|\,\text{heart})$

$= \dfrac{13}{52} \times \dfrac{12}{51} = \dfrac{1}{17}$

**20.** $P(\text{2 hearts}) + P(\text{2 diamonds}) + P(\text{2 clubs}) + P(\text{2 spades})$

$= \left(\dfrac{13}{52} \times \dfrac{12}{51}\right) + \left(\dfrac{13}{52} \times \dfrac{12}{51}\right) + \left(\dfrac{13}{52} \times \dfrac{12}{51}\right) + \left(\dfrac{13}{52} \times \dfrac{12}{51}\right)$

$= \dfrac{1}{17} + \dfrac{1}{17} + \dfrac{1}{17} + \dfrac{1}{17} = \dfrac{4}{17}$

**21.** The complement of "at least one card is not a diamond" is "both cards are diamonds."

$1 - P(\text{2 diamonds}) = 1 - 1/17 = 16/17$

**22.** $P(\text{odd}) \times P(\text{odd}) \times P(\text{odd}) \times P(\text{odd}) \times P(\text{odd})$

$= \dfrac{3}{6} \times \dfrac{3}{6} \times \dfrac{3}{6} \times \dfrac{3}{6} \times \dfrac{3}{6} = \dfrac{1}{32}$

**23.** $P(x \text{ is odd and } y \text{ is odd}) = P(x \text{ is odd}) \times P(y \text{ is odd})$

$= \dfrac{5}{9} \times \dfrac{5}{9} = \dfrac{25}{81}$

**24.** There are 9 x 10 = 90 possible outcomes because the zero cannot be in the tens place. There are 9 x 2 = 18 favorable outcomes because numbers ending in 0 or 5 are divisible by 5.

So, the probability is 18/90 = 1/5.

**25.** $\dfrac{2}{5} = \dfrac{y}{x + 2x + y}$ gives $y = 2x$.

$P(\text{red}) = \dfrac{x}{x + 2x + y} = \dfrac{x}{x + 2x + 2x} = \dfrac{x}{5x} = \dfrac{1}{5}$

**26.** 45°

**27.** $\dfrac{60}{360} = \dfrac{x}{2\pi}$ gives $x = 3/\pi$ radians.

---

**1.** 6 + 3 + 7 + 4 = 20 students

**2.** 6 + 3 = 9 students

**3.** 6 + 3 + 7 = 16 students

**4.**
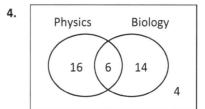

**5.** $P(\text{Physics but not Biology}) = 16/40 = 2/5$

**6.** $P(\text{Physics or Biology}) = (16 + 6 + 14)/40 = 9/10$

**7.** $P(\text{not Biology}) = 1 - P(\text{Biology}) = 1 - 20/40 = 1/2$

**8.** $P(\text{neither}) = 4/40 = 1/10$

**9.**
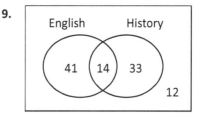

**10.** 41 students

**11.** $P(\text{English only or History only}) = (41 + 33)/100 = 37/50$

**12.** $P(\text{neither}) = 12/100 = 3/25$

**13.**
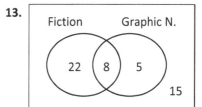

**14.** 5 students

**15.** $P(\text{not fiction books}) = 1 - P(\text{fiction books})$

$= 1 - 30/50 = 2/5$

**16.** $P(\text{not graphic novels}) = 1 - P(\text{graphic novels})$

$= 1 - 13/50 = 37/50$

**17.** $x$ = number of members who have taken both

aerobics only + both + rock c. only + neither = 30

$(15 - x) + x + (17 - x) + 5 = 30; x = 7$

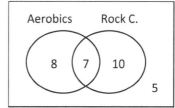

EP Math Geometry Workbook Answers

**18.** 7 students

**19.** $P$(rock climbing) = 17/30

**20.** $P$(rock climbing only) = 10/30 = 1/3

**21.** $x$ = number of members who play basketball only
$2x$ = number of members who play tennis only
tennis only + both + basketball only + neither = 40
$2x + 7 + x + 6 = 40$; $x = 9$

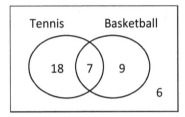

**22.** 18 students

**23.** $P$(not tennis) = 1 − $P$(tennis) = 1 − (18 + 7)/40 = 3/8

**24.** $P$(tennis or basketball) = (18 + 7 + 9)/40 = 17/20

**25.** The sum of two sides of a triangle must be greater than the third side. Let $x$ be the third side.

| | | |
|---|---|---|
| $x + 5 > 9$ | $x + 9 > 5$ | $5 + 9 > x$ |
| $x > 4$ | $x > -4$ | $x < 14$ |

Combine the inequalities to get $4 < x < 14$. So, the third side must be longer than 4 and shorter than 14.

**26.** area $= \dfrac{\theta}{360} \cdot \pi r^2 = \dfrac{30}{360} \cdot \pi(12)^2 = 12\pi$ cm$^2$

## LESSON 151

**1.** 80 female students     **2.** 128 students

**3.** 120 + 128 − 80 = 168 students

**4.**

| | Tablet | No tablet | Total |
|---|---|---|---|
| Desktop | 10 | 5 | 15 |
| No desktop | 8 | 2 | 10 |
| Total | 18 | 7 | 25 |

**5.** $P$(desktop) = 15/25 = 3/5

**6.** $P$(desktop but no tablet) = 5/25 = 1/5

**7.** $P$(both) = 10/25 = 2/5

**8.** $P$(desktop or tablet)
= $P$(desktop) + $P$(tablet) − $P$(both)
= 15/25 + 18/25 − 10/25 = 23/25

**9.**

| | Online | In-store | Total |
|---|---|---|---|
| Teens | 18 | 9 | 27 |
| Adults | 12 | 21 | 33 |
| Total | 30 | 30 | 60 |

**10.** 60 people

**11.** 30 people

**12.** $P$(teen) = 27/60 = 9/20

**13.** $P$(teen and online) = 18/60 = 3/10

**14.** $P$(teen or online)
= $P$(teen) + $P$(online) − $P$(teen and online)
= 27/60 + 30/60 − 18/60 = 13/20

**15.**

| | Steak | Pasta | Total |
|---|---|---|---|
| Soup | 40 | 32 | 72 |
| Salad | 68 | 60 | 128 |
| Total | 108 | 92 | 200 |

**16.** 60 customers

**17.** 92 + 72 − 32 = 132 customers

**18.** $P$(pasta) = 92/200 = 23/50

**19.** $P$(soup) = 72/200 = 9/25

**20.** $P$(steak and salad) = 68/200 = 17/50

**21.** $P$(steak or salad)
= $P$(steak) + $P$(salad) − $P$(steak and salad)
= 108/200 + 128/200 − 68/200 = 21/25

**22.** 2 lines of symmetry

**23.** order of rotational symmetry = 6

**24.** The side ratio is 1/2, so the volume ratio is 1/8.

## LESSON 152

**1.**

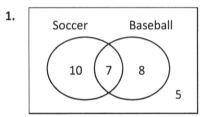

**2.** 10 students

**3.** $P$(neither) = 5/30 = 1/6

**4.**

| | Cat(s) | No cat | Total |
|---|---|---|---|
| Dog(s) | 8 | 17 | 25 |
| No dog | 12 | 13 | 25 |
| Total | 20 | 30 | 50 |

**5.** 13 students

**6.** $P$(cat or dog)
= $P$(cat) + $P$(dog) − $P$(both)
= 20/50 + 25/50 − 8/50 = 37/50

**7.** $P(\text{soccer}|\text{baseball}) = \text{both}/\text{baseball} = 7/15$

**8.** $P(\text{baseball}|\text{soccer}) = \text{both}/\text{soccer} = 7/17$

**9.** $P(C|D) = P(C) = 3/4$, so $C$ and $D$ are independent.

**10.**

History     Chemistry

41   14   33

12

**11.** $P(\text{History}) = 55/100 = 11/20$

**12.** $P(\text{History}|\text{Chemistry}) = \text{both}/\text{Chemistry} = 14/47$

**13.** Use your answers in Problems 11 and 12.

The two events are not independent because $P(\text{History}|\text{Chemistry}) \neq P(\text{History})$.

**14.**

|  | Swim | Not swim | Total |
|---|---|---|---|
| Teens | 15 | 45 | 60 |
| Adults | 25 | 75 | 100 |
| Total | 40 | 120 | 160 |

**15.** $P(\text{swim}) = 40/160 = 1/4$

**16.** $P(\text{swim}|\text{teen}) = (\text{teen and swim})/\text{teen} = 15/60 = 1/4$

**17.** Use your answers in Problems 15 and 16.

The two events are independent because $P(\text{swim}|\text{teen}) = P(\text{swim})$.

**18.**

|  | Juice | Soda | Total |
|---|---|---|---|
| Juniors | 12 | 13 | 25 |
| Seniors | 9 | 16 | 25 |
| Total | 21 | 29 | 50 |

**19.** $P(\text{juice}) = 21/50$

$P(\text{juice}|\text{junior}) = (\text{juice and junior})/\text{junior} = 12/25$

The two events are not independent because $P(\text{juice}|\text{junior}) \neq P(\text{juice})$.

You could compare $P(\text{junior})$ and $P(\text{junior}|\text{juice})$.
$P(\text{junior}) = 25/50 = 1/2$
$P(\text{junior}|\text{juice}) = (\text{junior and juice})/\text{juice} = 12/21 = 4/7$

**20.** In an isosceles trapezoid, each pair of base angles is congruent, and non-base angles are supplementary. So, the other three angles are 50°, 130°, and 130°.

**21.** Use the volume formula for a cone, $V = (1/3)\pi r^2 h$.
$(1/3)\pi(6)^2 h = 48\pi$; $h = 4$
The height is 4 cm.

**LESSON 153** ·······························

**1.** Use a 45-45-90 triangle to find $x = 4$.

$A = \frac{1}{2}bh = \frac{1}{2}(4)(4) = 8$

**2.** $A = \pi r^2 = \pi(9)^2 = 81\pi$

**3.** $A = \frac{\theta}{360} \cdot \pi r^2 = \frac{140}{360} \cdot \pi(6)^2 = 14\pi \text{ cm}^2$

**4.** $P(Y \text{ on } \overline{AB}) = \frac{AB}{AD} = \frac{9}{9+5+7} = \frac{3}{7}$

**5.** $P(Y \text{ not on } \overline{BC}) = \frac{AB + CD}{AD} = \frac{9+7}{9+5+7} = \frac{16}{21}$

You could use the complement rule.
$P(Y \text{ not on } \overline{BC}) = 1 - P(Y \text{ on } \overline{BC}) = 1 - 5/21 = 16/21$

**6.** entire area = semicircle with radius 14 = $98\pi$
favorable area = semicircle with radius 4 = $8\pi$

$P(X \text{ inside shaded region}) = \frac{8\pi}{98\pi} = \frac{4}{49}$

**7.** favorable area
= semicircle with radius 14 – semicircle with radius 8
= $98\pi - 32\pi = 66\pi$

$P(X \text{ outside shaded region}) = \frac{66\pi}{98\pi} = \frac{33}{49}$

**8.** If you show up anytime between $A$ and $B$, you will wait for 15 minutes or more.

$P(15 \text{ minutes or more}) = \frac{AB}{AC} = \frac{5}{20} = \frac{1}{4}$

**9.** The shaded region is closer to the center than to the edge.
entire area = 10(10) = 100
favorable area = 5(5) = 25

$P(\text{closer to the center than to the edge}) = \frac{25}{100} = \frac{1}{4}$

**10.** $P(X \text{ on } \overline{CD}) = \frac{CD}{AD} = \frac{5}{8+7+5} = \frac{5}{20} = \frac{1}{4}$

**11.** $P(X \text{ not on } \overline{BD}) = \frac{AB}{AD} = \frac{8}{8+7+5} = \frac{8}{20} = \frac{2}{5}$

**12.** entire area = $\pi r^2 = \pi(3)^2 = 9\pi$

favorable area = $\frac{\theta}{360} \cdot \pi r^2 = \frac{120}{360} \cdot \pi(3)^2 = 3\pi$

$P(\text{shaded region}) = \frac{3\pi}{9\pi} = \frac{1}{3}$

13. entire area = circle with radius 6 = $\pi r^2 = \pi(6)^2 = 36\pi$

favorable area = 4 isosceles right triangles with legs 6

$$= 4 \cdot \frac{1}{2} bh = 4 \cdot \frac{1}{2}(6)(6) = 72$$

$$P(\text{shaded region}) = \frac{72}{36\pi} = \frac{2}{\pi}$$

14. entire area = rectangle = $bh = 12(8) = 96$

favorable area = circle + semicircle

$$= \pi r^2 + \frac{1}{2}\pi r^2 = \frac{3}{2}\pi r^2 = \frac{3}{2}\pi(4)^2 = 24\pi$$

$$P(\text{shaded region}) = \frac{24\pi}{96} = \frac{\pi}{4}$$

15. $P(\text{green}) = \dfrac{60}{60 + 10 + 50} = \dfrac{60}{120} = \dfrac{1}{2}$

16. entire area = circle with radius 20 = $\pi(20)^2 = 400\pi$

bullseye = circle with radius 2 = $\pi(2)^2 = 4\pi$

favorable area = circle − bullseye = $400\pi − 4\pi = 396\pi$

$$P(\text{missing bullseye}) = \frac{396\pi}{400\pi} = \frac{99}{100}$$

17. entire area = circle with radius 12 = $\pi(12)^2 = 144\pi$

favorable area = red sector + yellow sector

$$= \frac{80}{360} \cdot \pi(12)^2 + \frac{160}{360} \cdot \pi(12)^2$$

$$= 32\pi + 64\pi = 96\pi$$

$$P(\text{red or yellow}) = \frac{96\pi}{144\pi} = \frac{2}{3}$$

18. $P(5, 7) \rightarrow P'(7, 5) \rightarrow P''(3, 5)$

The final image is (3, 5).

## LESSON 154

1. $P = 1/8$

8 possible: $2 \times 2 \times 2$

1 favorable: HHH

2. $P = 2/36 = 1/18$

36 possible: $6 \times 6$

2 favorable: 12, 21

3.

| $Y$ | 1 | 2 | 3 | 4 |
|---|---|---|---|---|
| $P(Y)$ | $\frac{1}{1000}$ | $\frac{9}{1000}$ | $\frac{9}{100}$ | $\frac{9}{10}$ |

$P(\text{1 digit}) = P(0 \sim 9) = 10/10000 = 1/1000$

$P(\text{2 digits}) = P(10 \sim 99) = 90/10000 = 9/1000$

$P(\text{3 digits}) = P(100 \sim 999) = 900/10000 = 9/100$

$P(\text{4 digits}) = P(1000 \sim 9999) = 9000/10000 = 9/10$

4. $P(Y \geq 3) = P(Y = 3) + P(Y = 4)$

$\qquad = 9/100 + 9/10 = 99/100$

5. $E(Y) = 1(0.1) + 3(0.35) + 5(0.25) + 7(0.3) = 4.5$

6. $E(Z) = (-20)(1/8) + (-10)(1/4) + 0(1/8) +$

$\qquad 10(3/8) + 20(1/8) = 5/4$

7.

| $X$ | 0 | 1 | 2 |
|---|---|---|---|
| $P(Y)$ | $\frac{9}{16}$ | $\frac{3}{8}$ | $\frac{1}{16}$ |

$P(0) = P(\text{1st wrong and 2nd wrong})$

$\qquad = P(\text{1st wrong}) \times P(\text{2nd wrong})$

$\qquad = 3/4 \times 3/4 = 9/16$

$P(1) = P(\text{1st correct and 2nd wrong}) +$

$\qquad P(\text{1st wrong and 2nd correct})$

$\qquad = 1/4 \times 3/4 + 3/4 \times 1/4 = 3/8$

$P(2) = P(\text{1st correct and 2nd correct})$

$\qquad = P(\text{1st correct}) \times P(\text{2nd correct})$

$\qquad = 1/4 \times 1/4 = 1/16$

8. $P(X \geq 1) = P(X = 1) + P(X = 2)$

$\qquad = 3/8 + 1/16 = 7/16$

9. $E(X) = 0(9/16) + 1(3/8) + 2(1/16) = 1/2$

10.

| $X$ | 2 | 3 | 4 | 5 | 6 | 7 |
|---|---|---|---|---|---|---|
| $P(Y)$ | $\frac{1}{36}$ | $\frac{1}{18}$ | $\frac{1}{12}$ | $\frac{1}{9}$ | $\frac{5}{36}$ | $\frac{1}{6}$ |

| $X$ | 8 | 9 | 10 | 11 | 12 |
|---|---|---|---|---|---|
| $P(Y)$ | $\frac{5}{36}$ | $\frac{1}{9}$ | $\frac{1}{12}$ | $\frac{1}{18}$ | $\frac{1}{36}$ |

11. $P(X \leq 4) = P(X = 2) + P(X = 3) + P(X = 4)$

$\qquad = 1/36 + 1/18 + 1/12 = 1/6$

12. $P(X \text{ is odd})$

$= P(X = 3) + P(X = 5) + P(X = 7) + P(X = 9) + P(X = 11)$

$= 1/18 + 1/9 + 1/6 + 1/9 + 1/18 = 1/2$

13. $E(X) = 2(1/36) + 3(1/18) + 4(1/12) + 5(1/9) +$

$\qquad 6(5/36) + 7(1/6) + 8(5/36) + 9(1/9) +$

$\qquad 10(1/12) + 11(1/18) + 12(1/36)$

$\qquad = 7$

14.

| $X$ | 4 | 9 | 12 | 16 |
|---|---|---|---|---|
| $P(Y)$ | $\frac{1}{8}$ | $\frac{1}{6}$ | $\frac{1}{3}$ | $\frac{3}{8}$ |

probability of landing on a sector with angle $\theta$

$$= \frac{\text{sector area}}{\text{circle area}} = \frac{(\theta/360)\pi r^2}{\pi r^2} = \frac{\theta}{360}$$

$P(4) = P(\text{sector with angle } 45°) = 45/360 = 1/8$

$P(9) = P(\text{sector with angle } 60°) = 60/360 = 1/6$

$P(12) = P(\text{sector with angle } 120°) = 120/360 = 1/3$

$P(16) = P(\text{sector with angle } 135°) = 135/360 = 3/8$

**15.** $P(X \geq 10) = P(X = 12) + P(X = 16)$
$= 1/3 + 3/8 = 17/24$

**16.** $E(X) = 4(1/8) + 9(1/6) + 12(1/3) + 16(3/8) = 12$
You can expect to earn about $12 \times 200 = 2400$ points.

**17.**

| $X$ | −20 | 20 | 12 |
|---|---|---|---|
| $P(Y)$ | $\dfrac{3}{8}$ | $\dfrac{1}{2}$ | $\dfrac{1}{8}$ |

**18.** $E(X) = (-20)(3/8) + 20(1/2) + 12(1/8) = 4$

The game is favorable to the player because the expected value is positive. There is no right or wrong answer for whether to play the game as long as you can give reasoning for your answer.

**19.** $\angle P \cong \angle R$ and $\angle Q \cong \angle S$ as alternate interior angles.
So, $\triangle PQT \sim \triangle RST$ by AA.

**20.** $\angle PTQ \cong \angle RTS$ as vertical angles.
$\overline{PT} \cong \overline{RT}$ and $\overline{QT} \cong \overline{ST}$ by the definition of bisect.
So, $\triangle PQT \cong \triangle RST$ by SAS.

**21.** $\overline{PQ} \cong \overline{RS}$ by the given statement.
$\angle PTQ \cong \angle RTS$ as vertical angles.
$\angle P \cong \angle R$ and $\angle Q \cong \angle S$ as alternate interior angles.
So, $\triangle PQT \cong \triangle RST$ by ASA or AAS.

## LESSON 155

1. $3 \times 3 \times 3 = 9$ passwords

2. $3 \times 2 \times 1 = 6$ passwords

3. ABC, ACB, BAC, BCA, CAB, CBA

4. permutation

5. combination

6. permutation

7. $5 \times 4 \times 3 \times 2 \times 1 = 120$ ways

8. $7 \times 6 \times 5 \times 4 = 840$ ways

9. $(6 \times 5 \times 4 \times 3)/(4 \times 3 \times 2 \times 1) = 15$ teams

10. $(10 \times 9 \times 8)/(3 \times 2 \times 1) = 120$ committees

11. permutation, $6 \times 5 \times 4 \times 3 \times 2 \times 1 = 720$ ways

12. permutation, $6 \times 5 \times 4 = 120$ ways

13. combination, $(8 \times 7 \times 6 \times 5)/(4 \times 3 \times 2 \times 1) = 70$ ways

14. combination, $(52 \times 51 \times 50)/(3 \times 2 \times 1) = 22{,}100$ ways

15. permutation, $11 \times 10 \times 9 = 990$ ways

16. permutation, $20 \times 19 \times 18 \times 17 = 116{,}280$ ways

17. combination, $(25 \times 24 \times 23)/(3 \times 2 \times 1) = 2{,}300$ ways

18. combination, $(10 \times 9)/(2 \times 1) = 45$ matches

**19.** Let $B = (x, y)$. By the midpoint formula,
$(3 + x)/2 = -2; x = -7$
$(2 + y)/2 = 4; y = 6$
So, $B$ is at $(-7, 6)$.

**20.**

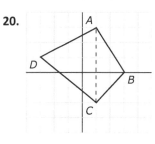

Draw $\overline{AC}$ to divide $ABCD$.
area of $\triangle ABC$
$= bh/2 = (5)(2)/2 = 5$
area of $\triangle ADC$
$= bh/2 = (5)(4)/2 = 10$
area of $ABCD$
$= 5 + 10 = 15$

## LESSON 156

1. combination, $(5 \times 4 \times 3)/(3 \times 2 \times 1) = 10$ teams

2. permutation, $6 \times 5 \times 4 \times 3 \times 2 \times 1 = 720$ ways

3. permutation, $5 \times 4 \times 3 = 60$ ways

4. combination, $(7 \times 6)/(2 \times 1) = 21$ ways

5. $\dfrac{8 \times 7 \times 6 \times 5!}{5!} = 8 \times 7 \times 6 = 336$

6. $\dfrac{7 \times 6 \times 5 \times 4!}{3!\,4!} = \dfrac{7 \times 6 \times 5}{3!} = \dfrac{7 \times 6 \times 5}{3 \times 2 \times 1} = 7 \times 5 = 35$

7. $P(5, 5) = \dfrac{5!}{(5-5)!} = \dfrac{5!}{0!} = \dfrac{5!}{1} = 5 \times 4 \times 3 \times 2 \times 1 = 120$

8. $P(8, 3) = \dfrac{8!}{(8-3)!} = \dfrac{8!}{5!} = 8 \times 7 \times 6 = 336$

9. $C(8, 2) = \dfrac{8!}{(8-2)!\,2!} = \dfrac{8!}{6!\,2!} = \dfrac{8 \times 7}{2 \times 1} = 28$

10. $C(10, 4) = \dfrac{10!}{(10-4)!\,4!} = \dfrac{10!}{6!\,4!} = \dfrac{10 \times 9 \times 8 \times 7}{4 \times 3 \times 2 \times 1} = 210$

11. $\dfrac{6 \times 5 \times 4!}{4!} = 6 \times 5 = 30$

12. $\dfrac{8 \times 7 \times 6 \times 5!}{5!\,3!} = \dfrac{8 \times 7 \times 6}{3!} = \dfrac{8 \times 7 \times 6}{3 \times 2 \times 1} = 8 \times 7 = 56$

13. $\dfrac{9!}{(9-4)!} = \dfrac{9!}{5!} = 9 \times 8 \times 7 \times 6 = 3{,}024$

14. $\dfrac{10!}{(10-7)!\,7!} = \dfrac{10!}{3!\,7!} = \dfrac{10 \times 9 \times 8}{3 \times 2 \times 1} = 120$

15. $P(8, 8) = \dfrac{8!}{(8-8)!} = \dfrac{8!}{0!} = \dfrac{8!}{1} = 40{,}320$

16. $C(15, 5) = \dfrac{15!}{(15-5)!\,5!} = \dfrac{15!}{10!\,5!} = 3{,}003$

17. $P(30, 3) = \dfrac{30!}{(30-3)!} = \dfrac{30!}{27!} = 24{,}360$

**18.** $C(40, 2) = \dfrac{40!}{(40-2)!\,2!} = \dfrac{40!}{38!\,2!} = 780$

**19.** $P(9, 4) = \dfrac{9!}{(9-4)!} = \dfrac{9!}{5!} = 3{,}024$

**20.** $P(15, 4) = \dfrac{15!}{(15-4)!} = \dfrac{15!}{11!} = 32{,}760$

**21.** $C(10, 3) = \dfrac{10!}{(10-3)!\,3!} = \dfrac{10!}{7!\,3!} = 120$

**22.** 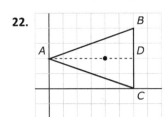   A centroid divides a median in the ratio 2:1.

The point (4, 2) divides median $\overline{AD}$ in the ratio 2:1, so the centroid is at (4, 2).

**23.** Convert to the standard form.

$x^2 + 2x + y^2 = 3$

$x^2 + 2x + 1 + y^2 = 3 + 1$

$(x + 1)^2 + y^2 = 4$

The circle has center (−1, 0) and radius 2.

# LESSON 157

**1.** $P(\text{odd}) \times P(\text{odd}\,|\,\text{odd})$

$= \dfrac{3}{5} \times \dfrac{2}{4} = \dfrac{3}{10}$

**2.** $P(\text{pink}) \times P(\text{pink}\,|\,\text{pink})$

$= \dfrac{4}{6} \times \dfrac{3}{5} = \dfrac{2}{5}$

**3.** $P(5, 5) = \dfrac{5!}{(5-5)!} = \dfrac{5!}{0!} = \dfrac{5!}{1} = 5! = 120$

**4.** $C(8, 2) = \dfrac{8!}{(8-2)!\,2!} = \dfrac{8!}{6!\,2!} = \dfrac{8 \times 7}{2 \times 1} = 28$

**5.** possible outcomes = $P(6, 6)$

favorable outcomes = permutations of 5 remaining people after seating Emma in the first seat = $P(5, 5)$

probability = $\dfrac{P(5, 5)}{P(6, 6)} = \dfrac{5!}{6!} = \dfrac{1}{6}$

**6.** possible outcomes = $P(6, 6)$

favorable outcomes = permutations of 4 remaining people after seating Emma first and Brian last = $P(4, 4)$

probability = $\dfrac{P(4, 4)}{P(6, 6)} = \dfrac{4!}{6!} = \dfrac{1}{6 \times 5} = \dfrac{1}{30}$

**7.** possible outcomes = $P(6, 6)$

favorable outcomes = Emma first and Brian last + Brian first and Emma last = $P(4, 4) + P(4, 4) = P(4, 4) \times 2$

probability = $\dfrac{P(4, 4) \times 2}{P(6, 6)} = \dfrac{4! \times 2}{6!} = \dfrac{2}{6 \times 5} = \dfrac{1}{15}$

**8.** possible outcomes = $C(7, 2)$

favorable outcomes = combinations of drawing 2 balls from 3 white balls = $C(3, 2)$

probability = $\dfrac{C(3, 2)}{C(7, 2)} = \dfrac{3}{21} = \dfrac{1}{7}$

**9.** possible outcomes = $C(7, 2)$

favorable outcomes = combinations of drawing 2 balls from 4 black balls = $C(4, 2)$

probability = $\dfrac{C(4, 2)}{C(7, 2)} = \dfrac{6}{21} = \dfrac{2}{7}$

**10.** possible outcomes = $C(7, 2)$

favorable outcomes = 3 ways to draw a white ball × 4 ways to draw a black ball = 3 × 4

probability = $\dfrac{3 \times 4}{C(7, 2)} = \dfrac{12}{21} = \dfrac{4}{7}$

**11.** possible outcomes = $P(8, 8)$

favorable outcomes = permutations of 7 remaining people after seating Emma in the first seat = $P(7, 7)$

probability = $\dfrac{P(7, 7)}{P(8, 8)} = \dfrac{7!}{8!} = \dfrac{1}{8}$

**12.** possible outcomes = $P(8, 8)$

favorable outcomes = permutations of 6 remaining people after seating Emma first and Brian last = $P(6, 6)$

probability = $\dfrac{P(6, 6)}{P(8, 8)} = \dfrac{6!}{8!} = \dfrac{1}{8 \times 7} = \dfrac{1}{56}$

**13.** possible outcomes = $P(8, 8)$

favorable outcomes = Emma first and Brian last + Brian first and Emma last = $P(6, 6) + P(6, 6) = P(6, 6) \times 2$

probability = $\dfrac{P(6, 6) \times 2}{P(8, 8)} = \dfrac{6! \times 2}{8!} = \dfrac{2}{8 \times 7} = \dfrac{1}{28}$

**14.** possible outcomes = $P(5, 5)$

favorable outcomes = 1

probability = $\dfrac{1}{P(5, 5)} = \dfrac{1}{5!} = \dfrac{1}{120}$

**15.** possible outcomes = $P(5, 5)$

favorable outcomes = permutations of 4 remaining letters after placing W first = $P(4, 4)$

probability = $\dfrac{P(4, 4)}{P(5, 5)} = \dfrac{4!}{5!} = \dfrac{1}{5}$

**16.** possible outcomes = $P(5, 5)$

favorable outcomes = permutations of 4 remaining letters after placing A or E first = $P(4, 4) \times 2$

probability = $\dfrac{P(4, 4) \times 2}{P(5, 5)} = \dfrac{4! \times 2}{5!} = \dfrac{2}{5}$

**17.** possible outcomes = $C(12, 3)$

favorable outcomes = combinations of drawing 3 balls from 5 pink balls = $C(5, 3)$

probability = $\dfrac{C(5, 3)}{C(12, 3)} = \dfrac{10}{220} = \dfrac{1}{22}$

**18.** possible outcomes = $C(12, 3)$

favorable outcomes = combinations of drawing 3 balls from 3 red and 5 pink balls = $C(8, 3)$

probability = $\dfrac{C(8, 3)}{C(12, 3)} = \dfrac{56}{220} = \dfrac{14}{55}$

**19.** possible outcomes = $C(12, 3)$

favorable outcomes = 3 ways to draw a red ball × 5 ways to draw a pink ball × 4 ways to draw a yellow ball = $3 \times 5 \times 4$

probability = $\dfrac{3 \times 5 \times 4}{C(12, 3)} = \dfrac{60}{220} = \dfrac{3}{11}$

**20.** possible outcomes = $P(9, 3)$

favorable outcomes = permutations of choosing 3 boys out of 5 = $P(5, 3)$

probability = $\dfrac{P(5, 3)}{P(9, 3)} = \dfrac{60}{504} = \dfrac{5}{42}$

**21.** possible outcomes = $P(9, 3)$

favorable outcomes = ways of choosing 1 girl out of 4 × permutations of choosing 2 boys out of 5 = $4 \times P(5, 2)$

probability = $\dfrac{4 \times P(5, 2)}{P(9, 3)} = \dfrac{4 \times 20}{504} = \dfrac{10}{63}$

**22.** possible outcomes = $P(9, 3)$

favorable outcomes = all outcomes − permutations of choosing 3 girls out of 4 = $P(9, 3) - P(4, 3)$

probability = $\dfrac{P(9, 3) - P(4, 3)}{P(9, 3)} = \dfrac{504 - 24}{504} = \dfrac{20}{21}$

You could use the complement rule.

$P$(at least one position is filled by a boy)

= $1 - P$(all three positions are filled by girls)

= $1 - \dfrac{P(4, 3)}{P(9, 3)} = 1 - \dfrac{24}{504} = \dfrac{20}{21}$

**23.** Use the circumference formula, $C = 2\pi r$.

$2\pi r = 4\pi$, so the radius is 2.

**24.** Parallel lines have the same slope.

$(a - 4)/(2 - 1) = 2$ gives $a = 6$.

**25.** $x^2 + (y - 2)^2 = 4$

---

## LESSON 158

**1.** $P = 1/4$

**2.** $P = 6/20 = 3/10$

**3.** $4 \times 4 \times 4 = 64$

100s place: 1, 3, 5, 6
10s place: 1, 3, 5, 6
1s place: 1, 3, 5, 6

**4.** $4 \times 3 \times 2 = 24$

100s place: 1, 3, 5, 6
10s place: 4 − 1 ways
1s place: 4 − 2 ways

**5.** $1 \times 3 \times 2 = 6$

1s place: 6
10s place: 4 − 1 ways
100s place: 4 − 2 ways

**6.** $P$(odd) × $P$(odd)

= $\dfrac{3}{5} \times \dfrac{3}{5} = \dfrac{9}{25}$

**7.** $P$(odd) × $P$(odd|odd)

= $\dfrac{3}{5} \times \dfrac{2}{4} = \dfrac{3}{10}$

**8.** $P$(clear) × $P$(clear)

= $\dfrac{6}{10} \times \dfrac{6}{10} = \dfrac{9}{25}$

**9.** $P$(clear) × $P$(clear|clear)

= $\dfrac{6}{10} \times \dfrac{5}{9} = \dfrac{1}{3}$

**10.** $P$(red) + $P$(heart) − $P$(red and heart)

= $\dfrac{26}{52} + \dfrac{13}{52} - \dfrac{13}{52} = \dfrac{1}{2}$

**11.** $P$(king) + $P$(queen) − $P$(king and queen)

= $\dfrac{4}{52} + \dfrac{4}{52} - \dfrac{0}{52} = \dfrac{2}{13}$

**12.**

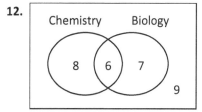

**13.** $P$(Chemistry only or Biology only) = (8 + 7)/30 = 1/2

**14.** $P$(Biology|Chemistry) = both/Chemistry = 6/14 = 3/7

**15.**

|        | Drive | Cannot | Total |
|--------|-------|--------|-------|
| Swim   | 45    | 30     | 75    |
| Cannot | 15    | 10     | 25    |
| Total  | 60    | 40     | 100   |

**16.** $P$(drive|swim) = both/swim = 45/75 = 3/5

**17.** $P$(drive) = 60/100 = 3/5

The two events are independent because $P$(drive|swim) = $P$(drive).

**18.**

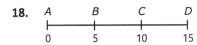

Suppose a bus arrives at A. Then the next bus will arrive at D. If you show up anytime between B and D, you will wait for 10 minutes or less.

$$P(10 \text{ minutes or less}) = \frac{BD}{AD} = \frac{10}{15} = \frac{2}{3}$$

**19.** If you show up anytime between A and C, you will wait for 5 minutes or more.

$$P(5 \text{ minutes or more}) = \frac{AC}{AD} = \frac{10}{15} = \frac{2}{3}$$

**20.**

| X | 2 | 3 | 6 | 10 |
|---|---|---|---|----|
| $P(Y)$ | $\frac{1}{8}$ | $\frac{1}{6}$ | $\frac{5}{24}$ | $\frac{1}{2}$ |

probability of landing on a sector with angle $\theta$

$$= \frac{\text{sector area}}{\text{circle area}} = \frac{(\theta/360)\pi r^2}{\pi r^2} = \frac{\theta}{360}$$

angle of the sector with 6 points = $180 - 60 - 45 = 75°$

$P(2) = P(\text{sector with angle } 45°) = 45/360 = 1/8$

$P(5) = P(\text{sector with angle } 60°) = 60/360 = 1/6$

$P(6) = P(\text{sector with angle } 75°) = 75/360 = 5/24$

$P(10) = P(\text{sector with angle } 180°) = 180/360 = 1/2$

$E(X) = 2(1/8) + 3(1/6) + 6(5/24) + 10(1/2) = 7$

**21.** You can expect to earn about $7 \times 1000 = 7000$ points.

**22.** $P(5, 5) = \dfrac{5!}{(5-5)!} = \dfrac{5!}{0!} = \dfrac{5!}{1} = 5 \times 4 \times 3 \times 2 \times 1 = 120$

**23.** possible outcomes = $P(5, 5)$

favorable outcomes = permutations of 4 remaining letters after placing H first = $P(4, 4)$

probability = $\dfrac{P(4, 4)}{P(5, 5)} = \dfrac{4!}{5!} = \dfrac{1}{5}$

**24.** possible outcomes = $P(5, 5)$

favorable outcomes = permutations of 4 remaining letters after placing O or E first = $P(4, 4) \times 2$

probability = $\dfrac{P(4, 4) \times 2}{P(5, 5)} = \dfrac{4! \times 2}{5!} = \dfrac{2}{5}$

**25.** $C(52, 2) = \dfrac{52!}{(52-2)! \, 2!} = \dfrac{52!}{50! \, 2!} = \dfrac{52 \times 51}{2 \times 1} = 1326$

**26.** possible outcomes = $C(52, 2)$

favorable outcomes = combinations of drawing 2 cards from 13 clubs = $C(13, 2)$

probability = $\dfrac{C(13, 2)}{C(52, 2)} = \dfrac{78}{1326} = \dfrac{1}{17}$

**27.** possible outcomes = $C(52, 2)$

favorable outcomes = 26 ways to draw a red card × 26 ways to draw a black card = $26 \times 26$

probability = $\dfrac{26 \times 26}{C(52, 3)} = \dfrac{26 \times 26}{1326} = \dfrac{26}{51}$

**28.** Supplementary angles add up to 180°. So, if they are congruent, then each must measure 90°.

**29.** Use the Altitude Rule [68.1].

$x^2 = 5(10)$

$x = 5\sqrt{2}$

## LESSON 159

**1.**
A) false; A line has no endpoints.

B) false; $\overleftrightarrow{AB}$ and $\overleftrightarrow{BA}$ are the same lines.

C) true; $\overrightarrow{AB}$ has endpoint $A$, but $\overrightarrow{BA}$ has endpoint $B$.

D) true; All points on a line are coplanar.

E) true

F) false; The intersection of two planes is a line.

G) false; Vertical angles are never adjacent.

H) true

I) false; Only acute angles have complements.

J) false; A straight angle does not have a supplement.

K) false; Angles in a triangle must add up to 180°.

L) true

M) true

N) false; A circle is made of a curve.

O) true; A square is equilateral and equiangular.

P) false; A rectangle has four right angles.

**2.** Use the Segment Addition Postulate [7.6].

$AB + BC = AC$

$x + (x + 5) = 3x + 1; \; x = 4$

$AC = 3(4) + 1 = 13$

**3.** A midpoint divides a segment into two ≅ segments.

$PQ = 2PM$

$12 = 2(x - 4); \; x = 10$

**4.** An angle bisector divides an angle into two ≅ angles.

$m\angle ABP = m\angle CBP$

$3x + 7 = 5x - 1; \; x = 4$

$m\angle ABP = 3(4) + 7 = 19°$

$m\angle ABC = 2(m\angle ABP) = 2(19) = 38°$

**5.** linear pairs: $\angle 3$ and $\angle 4$, $\angle 4$ and $\angle 5$

vertical angles: $\angle 3$ and $\angle 5$

6.  $m\angle 1 = 90°$
    $m\angle 2 = 90 - m\angle 3 = 58°$ (complementary angles)
    $m\angle 4 = 180 - m\angle 3 = 148°$ (supplementary angles)
    $m\angle 5 = m\angle 3 = 32°$ (vertical angles)

7.  $6x + 3x = 90; x = 10$

8.  4 pairs

9.  yes; $\angle 1$ and $\angle 2$ are alternate exterior angles. If alternate exterior angles are congruent, then lines are parallel.

10. $m\angle 1 = 58°$ (alternate interior angles)
    $m\angle 2 = 180 - 90 - 58 = 32°$ ($\triangle$ angle sum = 180)
    $m\angle 3 = m\angle 2 = 32°$ (alternate interior angles)
    $m\angle 4 = 180 - m\angle 2 = 148°$ (supplementary angles)

11. $m\angle 1 = 180 - 105 = 75°$ (supplementary angles)
    $m\angle 2 = 105°$ (alternate interior angles)
    $m\angle 3 = 105°$ (corresponding angles)
    $m\angle 4 = 105°$ (alternate interior angles)
    $m\angle 5 = 105°$ (corresponding angles)
    $m\angle 6 = 180 - m\angle 5 = 75°$ (consecutive interior angles)
    $m\angle 7 = m\angle 6 = 75°$ (vertical angles)

12. obtuse; 130° is an obtuse angle.

13. no; The angles do not add up to 180°.

14. Angles in a triangle add up to 180°.
    $x + x + 120 = 180; x = 30$

15. An exterior $\angle$ is the sum of its two remote interior $\angle$s.
    $75 + (2x + 4) = 109; x = 15$

16. rhombus, square

17. rectangle, square

18. The figure is not a polygon because it is not closed.

19. interior angle sum = $180(n - 2) = 180(7 - 2) = 900°$

20. interior angle sum of a pentagon = $180(5 - 2) = 540°$
    $92 + 145 + 3x + 102 + 111 = 540; x = 30$

21. exterior angle sum of any polygon = 360°
    $80 + 80 + 5x + (5x + 10) = 360; x = 19$

22. Let $x$ be each angle of the quadrilateral. Angles in a quadrilateral add up to 360°, so $4x = 360$ and $x = 90$. This means that each angle must be a right angle. A quadrilateral with four right angles is a rectangle.

23. A regular polygon with $n$ sides has $n$ angles.
    one interior angle = interior angle sum/# of angles
    $\qquad = 180(n - 2)/n$

24. exterior angle sum of any polygon = 360°
    one exterior angle = exterior angle sum/ # of angles
    $\qquad = 360/n$

## LESSON 160

1.  B, C, D
    A parallelogram has no reflectional symmetry. A trapezoid has no reflectional symmetry and no rotational symmetry. A kite has no rotational symmetry.

2.  3 lines of symmetry

3.  $180/3 = 60°$

4.  $\overline{X'Y'}$

5.  $(-2, -4)$

6.  $(x, y) \rightarrow (x + 2, y - 1)$

7.  $\overline{YY'}$ and $\overline{ZZ'}$

8.  $(3, 6)$

9.  $y$-axis or $x = 0$

10. $\angle YCY'$ and $\angle ZCZ'$

11. $(6, 3)$

12. 270°

13. $X'Y' = 5XY = 5(2) = 10$

14. $(6, -12)$

15. 4

16. Let $k$ = scale factor $\quad \dashrightarrow$ Use $k$ to find $x$.
    $kAB = A'B' \qquad\qquad x = B'C' = kBC$
    $8k = 12 \qquad\qquad\qquad = (3/2)12 = 18$
    $k = 3/2$

    A dilation produces similar figures, so you could set up and solve the proportion $AB/A'B' = BC/B'C'$ to find $x$.

17. A, B, C

18. A, B, C, D

19. A, D

20. The translation maps $P(3, -6)$ to $P'(0, -6)$.
    The reflection maps $P'(0, -6)$ to $P''(0, -6)$.
    So, the final image is $(0, -6)$.

21. The dilation maps $P(3, -6)$ to $P'(1, -2)$.
    The rotation maps $P'(1, -2)$ to $P''(-1, 2)$.
    The final image is $(-1, 2)$.

22. *Answers may vary. Sample(s):*
    a reflection over the $y$-axis followed by a translation of 1 unit left and 5 units down

23. *Answers may vary. Sample(s):*
    a dilation about the origin by scale factor 5/2 followed by a translation of 1 unit down

24. a translation by the rule $(x, y) \rightarrow (x, y - 2)$; A composition of translations is a translation.

25. a rotation of 180° about the origin; A composition of reflections over two intersecting lines is a rotation.

26. A, B, E

## LESSON 161

1. 55555

2. ⇨

3. *Counterexamples may vary. Samples are given.*
   A) false; $1 + 3 = 4$
   B) true
   C) true
   D) false; $1 - (-1) = 2$
   E) true; $x + (x + 1) + (x + 2) = 3x + 3 = 3(x + 1)$
   F) false; $|0| = 0$. Zero is neither negative nor positive.

4. If an angle measures 180°, then it is a straight angle.
   If an angle is a straight angle, then it measures 180°.

5. Two angles are adjacent if and only if they have a common vertex and a common side but do not overlap.
   If two angles are adjacent, then they have a common vertex and a common side but do not overlap.
   If two angles have a common vertex and a common side but do not overlap, then they are adjacent.

6. If $M$ bisects $\overline{PQ}$, then $PM = MQ$.

7. A) Division Property
   B) Subtraction Property
   C) Symmetric Property
   D) Transitive Property

8. 2. Distributive Property
   4. Subtraction Property

9. 3. All right angles are congruent.
   4. Definition of congruent angles

10. C, A, D, E, B

11. *Answers may vary. Sample(s):*
    A reflection over the $x$-axis followed by a translation of 4 units right will map $\triangle ABC$ to $\triangle DEF$. Therefore, the two triangles are congruent.

12. 2. Definition of complementary angles
    3. $m\angle 1 + m\angle 3 = m\angle 2 + m\angle 3$
    4. Subtraction Property
    5. Definition of congruent angles

13. 2. If alternate exterior angles are congruent, then lines are parallel.
    4. If alternate interior angles are congruent, then lines are parallel.
    5. Transitive Property

14. parallel, perpendicular

15. Statements (Reasons)
    1. $\overline{AC} \parallel l$ (Given)
    2. $\angle 4 \cong \angle 1$, $\angle 5 \cong \angle 3$ (If lines are parallel, then alternate interior angles are congruent.)
    3. $m\angle 4 = m\angle 1$, $m\angle 5 = m\angle 3$ (Definition of congruent angles)
    4. $m\angle 4 + m\angle 2 + m\angle 5 = 180°$ (Angle Addition Postulate)
    5. $m\angle 1 + m\angle 2 + m\angle 3 = 180°$ (Substitution Property)

16. A polygon with $n$ sides can be divided into $n - 2$ triangles by the diagonals drawn from one vertex. Because the interior angle sum of each triangle is 180°, the interior angle sum of the polygon is $180(n - 2)°$.

## LESSON 162

1. A, D

2. Corresponding angles are congruent.
   $m\angle N = m\angle U = 33°$
   Angles in a triangle add up to 180°.
   $90 + 33 + (8x + 1) = 180$; $x = 7$

3. $\triangle MNL \cong \triangle TUS$, $\triangle MLN \cong \triangle TSU$

4. 2. Reflexive Property
   3. SSS

5. $\overline{AB} \cong \overline{AC}$

6. 2. Def. of bisect
   5. All right $\angle$s are $\cong$.
   7. SAS

7. $\overline{PE} \cong \overline{PG}$

8. 2. alternate interior $\angle$s
   3. Reflexive Property
   4. ASA
   5. CPCTC

9. $\angle BAD \cong \angle CAD$

10. $\angle E \cong \angle G$

11. $\overline{PQ} \cong \overline{RS}$ or $\overline{QR} \cong \overline{SP}$

12. 3. Reflexive Property
    4. AAS
    5. CPCTC

13. Base $\angle$s of an isosceles $\triangle$ are congruent, so $a = 43$.
    A triangle has 180°, so $b = 180 - 2(43) = 94$.

14. An equiangular triangle is equilateral, so $a = b = 15$.

15. interior angle sum = $180(5 - 2) = 540°$
    one interior angle = $540/5 = 108°$
    $\triangle EAD$ is an isosceles $\triangle$ with vertex angle 108°.
    $108 + 2a = 180$; $a = 36$
    $b = m\angle D - a = 108 - 36 = 72$

16. 3. Base angles of an isosceles triangle are congruent.
    5. SAS
    6. CPCTC
    7. Definition of isosceles triangle

## LESSON 163

1. A midsegment is half the length of the third side.
   $PQ = AC/2 = 16/8 = 8$

2. A midsegment is parallel to the third side, so $\overline{PQ} \parallel \overline{AC}$.
   Corresponding $\angle$s on $\parallel$ lines are $\cong$, so $\angle A \cong \angle BPQ$.
   $m\angle A = m\angle BPQ = 180 - m\angle APQ = 180 - 118 = 62°$

3. A midsegment is half the length of the third side.
   perimeter of $\triangle PQR = PQ + QR + PR$
   $= AB/2 + BC/2 + AC/2$
   $= 7 + 8 + 9 = 24$

4. Any point on the perpendicular bisector of a segment is equidistant from the endpoints of the segment.
   $x + 7 = 4x + 1; x = 2$

5. An angle bisector divides an angle into two congruent angles. Angles in a triangle add up to 180°.
   $90 + 2(29) + (5x - 3) = 180; x = 7$

6. A median divides the side to which it is drawn into two congruent segments.
   $7 - x = 2x - 5; x = 4$

7. An altitude forms right angles with the side to which it is drawn. Angles in a triangle add up to 180°.
   $90 + 53 + (8x - 3) = 180; x = 5$

8. A) 4, B) 3, C) 1, D) 2

9. A) incenter, B) circumcenter

10. A centroid divides a median in the ratio 2:1.
    $KT = (2/3)KN = (2/3)(15) = 10$
    $TN = (1/3)KN = (1/3)(15) = 5$

11. $\overline{XP}, \overline{YP}, \overline{ZQ}$

12. $\overline{AD}$ and $\overline{BE}$ are medians. The centroid is $K$.

13. $\overline{AB}, \overline{BF},$ and $\overline{CB}$ are altitudes. The orthocenter is $B$.

14. C; $5 + 5 > 10$ is false. The sum of two sides of a triangle must be greater than the third side.

15. The longer side has the larger opposite angle.
    $m\angle P < m\angle Q < m\angle R$ because $QR < PR < PQ$.

16. Angles in a triangle add up to 180°.
    $m\angle D = 180 - 98 - 39 = 43°$

    The larger angle has the longer opposite side.
    $DE < EF < DF$ because $m\angle F < m\angle D < m\angle E$.

17. The sum of two sides of a triangle must be greater than the third side. Let $x$ be the third side.

    | $x + 10 > 15$ | $x + 15 > 10$ | $10 + 15 > x$ |
    |---|---|---|
    | $x > 5$ | $x > -5$ | $x < 25$ |

    Combine the inequalities to get $5 < x < 25$. So, the third side must be longer than 5 and shorter than 25.

18. $25 - 5x > 15$ because $45° > 36°$ (Hinge Theorem [53.1]).
    $25 - 5x > 0$ because side lengths must be positive.
    Solve each inequality to get $x < 2$ and $x < 5$.
    Combine the two inequalities to get $x < 2$.

19. 2. Definition of median
    3. Definition of midpoint
    4. Reflexive Property
    5. SSS
    6. CPCTC
    7. Definition of bisect (or angle bisector)

20. Statements (Reasons)
    1. $m\angle C = 90°$ (Given)
    2. $m\angle A + m\angle B + m\angle C = 180°$ (Angles in a triangle add up to 180°. See the Triangle Sum Theorem [32.1].)
    3. $m\angle A + m\angle B = 180 - m\angle C$ (Subtraction Property)
    4. $m\angle A + m\angle B = 180 - 90$ (Substitution Property)
    5. $m\angle A + m\angle B = 90$ (Simplify)
    6. $m\angle A < 90, m\angle B < 90$ (Definition of less than)
    7. $m\angle A < m\angle C, m\angle B < m\angle C$ (Substitution Property)
    8. $BC < AB, AC < AB$ (The larger angle has the longer opposite side. See Theorem 52.2.)

## LESSON 164

1. A) Opposite sides are parallel.
   B) Opposite angles are congruent.
   C) Opposite sides are congruent.
   F) Diagonals bisect each other.
   H) One pair of sides is parallel and congruent.

2. Opposite angles are congruent, so $x = 62$.
   Consecutive angles are supplementary, so $y = z = 118$.

3. Opposite sides must be congruent.
   $x + 2y = 26$ and $x + y = 18$

   Subtract eq2 from eq1 to get $y = 8$.
   Plug $y$ into eq2 to get $x = 10$.
   So, $x = 10$ and $y = 8$.

4. Diagonals must bisect each other.
   $x - 4y = 7$ and $2x + y = 5$
   $x = 4y + 7$ and $2x + y = 5$
   $2(4y + 7) + y = 5$
   $y = -1$
   $x = 4(-1) + 7 = 3$
   So, $x = 3$ and $y = -1$.

5. In a parallelogram, opposite angles are congruent, and consecutive angles are supplementary.
   Let $x$ and $3x$ be the two angles.
   $x + 3x = 180; x = 45$
   So, the angles are 45°, 135°, 45°, and 135°.

**6.** Base ∠s of an isosceles △ are congruent, so $m\angle 1 = 31°$.
A triangle has 180°, so $m\angle 2 = 180 - 31 - m\angle 1 = 118°$.
Diagonals bisect opposite angles, so $m\angle 3 = m\angle 1 = 31°$.
Opposite angles are congruent, so $m\angle 4 = m\angle 2 = 118°$.

There are many ways to find these angle measures that are all correct. For example, you could say $m\angle 1 = m\angle 3$ and $m\angle 2 = m\angle 4$ because A diagonal divides a rhombus into two congruent isosceles triangles.

**7.** Diagonals are perpendicular, so $m\angle 1 = 90°$.
A triangle has 180°, so $m\angle 2 = 180 - 57 - m\angle 1 = 33°$.
Diagonals bisect opposite angles, so $m\angle 3 = 57°$.
Alt. interior ∠s are congruent, so $m\angle 4 = m\angle 2 = 33°$.
Alt. interior ∠s are congruent, so $m\angle 5 = 57°$.

**8.** Diagonals are congruent and bisect each other.
$PR = QS = 2QX$
$5x - 11 = 2(x + 5); x = 7$
$PR = QS = 5(7) - 11 = 24$

**9.** The midsegment is half the sum of the bases.
$30 = (x + 36)/2; x = 24$

**10.** Base angles are congruent, so $x = 80$.
Non-base angles are supplementary, so $y = 100$.
Base angles are congruent, so $z = y = 100$.

**11.** C; Diagonals are not necessarily perpendicular.

**12.** Non-vertex angles are congruent, so $m\angle 1 = m\angle 2$.
Angles in a quadrilateral add up to 360°.
$m\angle 1 + m\angle 2 + 57 + 85 = 360$
$m\angle 1 + m\angle 1 + 57 + 85 = 360$
$m\angle 1 = m\angle 2 = 109°$

**13.** Diagonals are perpendicular, so $m\angle 1 = 90°$.
A triangle has 180°, so $m\angle 2 = 180 - 50 - m\angle 1 = 40°$.
Vertex angles are bisected by a diagonal, so $m\angle 3 = 50°$.

**14.** parallelogram, rhombus, rectangle, square

**15.** D; A quadrilateral with congruent opposite sides is a parallelogram. A parallelogram with perpendicular diagonals is a rhombus.

**16.** 2. Angles in a quadrilateral add up to 360°.
3. Distributive Property
4. Division Property
5. Definition of supplementary angles
6. If consecutive interior angles are supplementary, then lines are parallel.
7. Definition of parallelogram

**17.** Both pairs of opposite sides are parallel.
Both pairs of opposite sides are congruent.
One pair of opposite sides is parallel and congruent.

**1.** B, C

**2.** D; The included angles must be congruent.

**3.** $m\angle E = 180 - 120 = 60°$
$m\angle D = 180 - 44 - m\angle E = 76°$
∠DHE ≅ ∠FHG because vertical angles are congruent.
∠D ≅ ∠F because their measures are equal.
So, △DHE ~ △FHG by AA.

**4.** ∠B ≅ ∠B by the Reflexive Property.
$BC/BD = 18/(18 + 12) = 3/5$
$BF/BE = 21/(21 + 14) = 3/5$
So, △BCF ~ △BDE by SAS.

**5.** $AB/DE = 12/15 = 4/5$
$BC/EF = 15/20 = 3/4$
$AC/DF = 20/25 = 4/5$
So, the triangles are not similar.

**6.** Corresponding angles must be congruent, so both triangles have angles 90°, 33°, and $a°$.
A triangle has 180°, so $a = 180 - 90 - 33 = 57$.

**7.** Corresponding sides must be proportional.
$\dfrac{15}{10} = \dfrac{18}{a}$ → $15a = 10(18)$ → $a = 12$
$\dfrac{15}{10} = \dfrac{12}{b}$ → $15b = 10(12)$ → $b = 8$

**8.** Corresponding sides must be proportional.
$\dfrac{16}{16 + 8} = \dfrac{a}{a + 7}$ → $16(a + 7) = 24a$ → $a = 14$
$\dfrac{16}{16 + 8} = \dfrac{10}{b}$ → $16b = 24(10)$ → $b = 15$

**9.** … rotation of 90° … a scale factor of 2 …

**10.** △ABC ~ △ACD ~ △CBD

**11.** Use the Leg Rule [68.2].    Use the Altitude Rule [68.1].
$x^2 = 5(5 + 10)$          $y^2 = 5(10)$
$x = 5\sqrt{3}$             $y = 5\sqrt{2}$

**12.** Use the Altitude Rule [68.1].
$10^2 = x(4x)$
$x^2 = 25$
$x = 5$
The shorter segment is 5 cm.

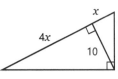

**13.** Use the Triangle Side Splitter Theorem [69.1].
$\dfrac{24}{8} = \dfrac{x}{7}$ → $8x = 24(7)$ → $x = 21$

**14.** Use the Three Parallel Lines Theorem [69.2].

$$\frac{5}{x} = \frac{6}{4} \qquad \rightarrow \qquad 6x = 5(4) \qquad \rightarrow \qquad x = 10/3$$

**15.** Use the Triangle Angle Bisector Theorem [70.1].

$$\frac{x}{20 - x} = \frac{18}{12} \qquad \rightarrow \qquad 12x = 18(20 - x) \qquad \rightarrow \qquad x = 12$$

**16.** 2. Vertical angles are congruent.

3. AA

4. Corresponding sides of similar triangles are proportional (CSSTP).

**17.** $\dfrac{20}{135} = \dfrac{24}{x} \qquad \rightarrow \qquad 20x = 135(24) \qquad \rightarrow \qquad x = 162$

The shadow is 162 m long.

**18.** $\dfrac{4}{x} = \dfrac{5}{20}$

$5x = 4(20)$

$x = 16$

The tree is 16 feet tall.

**19.** There are two pairs of similar triangles, so set up two proportions. Let $EF = x$ and $BF = y$. Then $DF = 48 - y$.

$\triangle BEF \sim \triangle BCD$ 　　　　 $\triangle DEF \sim \triangle DAB$

$$\frac{EF}{CD} = \frac{BF}{BD} \qquad\qquad \frac{EF}{AB} = \frac{DF}{DB}$$

$$\frac{x}{24} = \frac{y}{48} \qquad\qquad \frac{x}{12} = \frac{48 - y}{48}$$

$48x = 24y$　　　　　　　$48x = 12(48 - y)$

$y = 2x$ 　　　　　　　　 $4x = 48 - y$

　　　　　　　　　　　　 $4x = 48 - 2x$

　　　　　　　　　　　　　　 $x = 8$

So, the intersection is 8 m above the ground.

## LESSON 166

**1.** $14^2 = 6^2 + x^2$

$x^2 = 160$

$x = 4\sqrt{10}$

**2.** A

**3.** no; $(2\sqrt{15})^2 \neq 7^2 + 3^2$

**4.** obtuse; $12^2 > 6^2 + 10^2$

**5.** A 45-45-90 triangle has sides in the ratio $1:1:\sqrt{2}$. So, $a = 5$ and $b = 5\sqrt{2}$.

**6.** A 30-60-90 triangle has sides in the ratio $1 : \sqrt{3} : 2$. So, $a = 4\sqrt{3}$ and $b = 2(4) = 8$.

**7.** $\sin\theta = \dfrac{3}{5} \qquad \cos\theta = \dfrac{4}{5} \qquad \tan\theta = \dfrac{3}{4}$

**8.** $\sin\theta = \dfrac{2\sqrt{2}}{3} \qquad \cos\theta = \dfrac{1}{3} \qquad \tan\theta = 2\sqrt{2}$

**9.**

|  | 30° | 45° | 60° |
|---|---|---|---|
| sin | $\dfrac{1}{2}$ | $\dfrac{1}{\sqrt{2}} = \dfrac{\sqrt{2}}{2}$ | $\dfrac{\sqrt{3}}{2}$ |
| cos | $\dfrac{\sqrt{3}}{2}$ | $\dfrac{1}{\sqrt{2}} = \dfrac{\sqrt{2}}{2}$ | $\dfrac{1}{2}$ |
| tan | $\dfrac{1}{\sqrt{3}} = \dfrac{\sqrt{3}}{3}$ | 1 | $\sqrt{3}$ |

**10.** $\sin 53° = 0.79863... \approx 0.7986$

$\cos 53° = 0.60181... \approx 0.6018$

$\tan 53° = 1.32704... \approx 1.327$

**11.** The sine of an acute angle is equal to the cosine of its complement. The cosine of an acute angle is equal to the sine of its complement.

$\sin 25° = \cos(90° - 25°) = \cos 65°$

$\cos 25° = \sin(90° - 25°) = \sin 65°$

**12.** $x°$ and $y°$ are complementary. The sine of an acute angle is equal to the cosine of its complement.

$\sin\angle y° = \cos x° = 5/13$

**13.** The tangent of an acute angle is the reciprocal of the tangent of its complement.

$\tan y° = 3$

**14.** $\sin 68° = \dfrac{15}{a}$ 　and　 $\tan 68° = \dfrac{15}{b}$

$a \sin 68° = 15$ 　　　　 $b \tan 68° = 15$

$a = \dfrac{15}{\sin 68°}$ 　　　　 $b = \dfrac{15}{\tan 68°}$

$a \approx 16.2$ 　　　　　　 $b \approx 6.1$

**15.** A, D, E

**16.** $\tan\theta = \dfrac{27}{12}$

$\theta = \tan^{-1}(27/12)$

$\theta \approx 66°$

**17.** $AB = \sqrt{5^2 + 10^2} = \sqrt{125} \approx 11.2$

$m\angle A = \tan^{-1}(10/5) \approx 63.4°$

$m\angle B \approx 180 - 90 - 63.4 = 26.6°$

**18.** $m\angle A = 180 - 90 - 75 = 15°$

$AC = 20 \sin 75° \approx 19.3$

$BC = 20 \cos 75° \approx 5.2$

**19.** included angle $= 180 - 41 - 72 = 67°$

area $= \dfrac{1}{2}ab\sin\theta = \dfrac{1}{2}(16)(11)\sin 67° \approx 81$

**20 ~ 22.** *Diagrams are not drawn to scale.*

**20.** $x = 5 \sin 65° \approx 4.5$

The top of the ladder
reaches about 4.5 m high.

**21.** $\theta = 20°$

$x = 56 / \tan 20° \approx 153.9$

The boat is about 153.9 ft
away from the lighthouse.

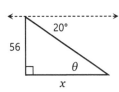

**22.** $h = 50000 - 10000$

$\quad = 40000$ feet

$x = 10$ miles x 5280 feet

$\quad = 52800$ feet

$\theta = \tan^{-1}(h/x) \approx 37°$

The angle of depression is about 37 degrees.

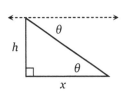

## LESSON 167

**1.** Tangent and radius are perpendicular.

$(r + 8)^2 = r^2 + 12^2$

$r = 5$

**2.** Tangent segments to a circle from a point are $\cong$.

$AE = AH = 8$

$BE = 15 - AE = 7$

$BF = BE = 7$

$CF = CG = 10$

$DG = DH = 5$

perimeter
$= AB + BC + CD + AD$
$= 15 + 17 + 15 + 13$
$= 60$

**3.** 180°; A diameter divides a circle into two semicircles. A semicircle measures 180°.

**4.** A radius perpendicular to a chord bisects the chord and its arc. A semicircle measures 180°.

$x = 6$

$y = 180 - 64 = 116$

**5.** A radius perpendicular to a chord bisects the chord.
base of right $\triangle = 14/2 = 7$

$r^2 = 4^2 + 7^2$

$r = \sqrt{65}$

**6.** Chords equidistant from the center are congruent.

$x = 9$

Congruent chords have congruent arcs. A circle measures 360°.

$y + y + 166 = 360; y = 97$

**7.** A circle measures 360°.

$a = 360 - 90 - 134 = 136$

An inscribed angle measures half its intercepted arc.

$b = a/2 = 136/2 = 68$

**8.** An angle inscribed in a semicircle is a right angle.

$m\angle B = 90°$

Base angles of an isosceles triangle are congruent.

$m\angle A = m\angle C = 45°$

A diameter is twice a radius.

$AC = 2(5\sqrt{2}) = 10\sqrt{2}$

A 45-45-90 triangle has sides in the ratio 1:1:$\sqrt{2}$.

$AB = BC = 10$

**9.** An inscribed angle measures half its intercepted arc.

$m\angle 1 = (100 + 118)/2 = 109°$

Opposite angles of an inscribed quadrilateral are supplementary.

$m\angle 2 = 180 - 90 = 90°$

$m\angle 3 = 180 - m\angle 1 = 180 - 109 = 71°$

**10.** A chord-tangent angle measures half its intercepted arc.

$m\angle 1 = 154/2 = 77°$

$m\angle 2 = 180 - m\angle 1 = 180 - 77 = 103°$

**11.** A chord-chord angle measures half the sum of the intercepted arcs.

$m\angle 1 = (54 + 70)/2 = 62°$

$m\angle 2 = 180 - m\angle 1 = 180 - 62 = 118°$

**12.** A secant-secant angle measures half the difference of the intercepted arcs.

$m\angle 1 = (129 - 63)/2 = 33°$

**13.** A tangent-tangent angle measures half the difference of the intercepted arcs.

$m\angle 1 = ((360 - 117) - 117)/2 = 63°$

**14.** The product of the segments of one chord equals the product of the segments of the other chord.

$9x = 6(12); x = 8$

**15.** The product of the secant segment and its external part is equal to the square of the tangent segment.

$x(x + 8) = 9^2$

$x^2 + 8x - 81 = 0$

$x = -4 + \sqrt{97}$

**16.** $\overline{OA} \cong \overline{OB} \cong \overline{OC} \cong \overline{OD}$ as radii of the same circle.

$\angle AOB \cong \angle COD$ as vertical angles.

So, $\triangle AOB \cong \triangle COD$ by SAS.

**17.** B, D

**18.** $m\widehat{BC} = 180 - m\widehat{CD} = 180 - 60 = 120°$

$m\widehat{AE} = 180 - m\widehat{AB} - m\widehat{DE} = 180 - 46 - 46 = 88°$

$m\angle 1 = 90°$ (inscribed in a semicircle)

$m\angle 2 = (m\widehat{AB} + m\widehat{DE})/2 = 46°$ (chord-chord angle)

$m\angle 3 = 90°$ (inscribed in a semicircle)

$m\angle 4 = m\widehat{CD}/2 = 30°$ (inscribed angle)

$m\angle 5 = m\widehat{BC}/2 = 60°$ (inscribed angle)

$m\angle 6 = m\widehat{CD}/2 = 30°$ (chord-tangent angle)

$m\angle 7 = (m\widehat{BAD} - m\widehat{CD})/2 = 60°$ (secant-tangent angle)

There are many ways to find these angle measures that are all correct. For example, you could use the Triangle Exterior Angle Theorem [32.2] to find $m\angle 7 = m\angle 3 - m\angle 6 = 90 - 30 = 60°$.

## LESSON 168

*Note that all areas are in square units.*

**1.** area = $bh = 12(11) = 132$

**2.** area $= \frac{1}{2}h(b_1 + b_2) = \frac{1}{2}(10)(10 + 6 + 12) = 140$

**3.** Diagonals of a kite are perpendicular.

Use the Pythagorean theorem or Pythagorean triples (3-4-5 and 5-12-13) to find $b = 9$ and $c = 5$.

area $= \frac{1}{2}d_1 d_2 = \frac{1}{2}(12 + 12)(9 + 5) = 168$

**4.** An altitude divides an equilateral triangle into two congruent 30-60-90 triangles.

Use a 30-60-90 triangle to find $h = 5\sqrt{3}$.

area $= \frac{1}{2}bh = \frac{1}{2}(10)(5\sqrt{3}) = 25\sqrt{3}$

**5.** The triangle can be divided into two congruent 30-60-90 triangles.

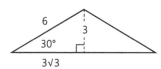

Use a 30-60-90 triangle to find $h = 3$ and $b = 6\sqrt{3}$.

area $= \frac{1}{2}bh = \frac{1}{2}(6\sqrt{3})(3) = 9\sqrt{3}$

**6.** area $= \frac{1}{2}sa \cdot n = \frac{1}{2}(5)(6)(8) = 120$

**7.** A regular hexagon is made up of 6 equilateral triangles. The apothem is the height of each equilateral triangle.

Use a 30-60-90 triangle to find $a = 2\sqrt{3}$.

area $= \frac{1}{2}sa \cdot n = \frac{1}{2}(4)(2\sqrt{3})(6) = 24\sqrt{3}$

**8.** Use a 30-60-90 triangle to find $s = 8$ and $a = 4\sqrt{3}$.

area $= \frac{1}{2}sa \cdot n = \frac{1}{2}(8)(4\sqrt{3})(6) = 96\sqrt{3}$

**9.** side ratio = perimeter ratio = 90/54 = 5/3

$\frac{5}{3} = \frac{x}{15}$ → $3x = 5(15)$ → $x = 25$

$\frac{5}{3} = \frac{20}{y}$ → $5y = 3(20)$ → $y = 12$

**10.** area ratio = 216/96 = 9/4, side ratio = 3/2

$\frac{3}{2} = \frac{18}{x}$ → $3x = 2(18)$ → $x = 12$ cm

**11.** circumference = $2\pi r = \pi d = 20\pi$

area = $\pi r^2 = \pi(10)^2 = 100\pi$

**12.** arc length $= \frac{\theta}{360} \cdot 2\pi r = \frac{225}{360} \cdot 2\pi(8) = 10\pi$

area $= \frac{\theta}{360} \cdot \pi r^2 = \frac{225}{360} \cdot \pi(8)^2 = 40\pi$

**13.** arc length $= \frac{\theta}{2\pi} \cdot 2\pi r = \theta r = \frac{5\pi}{9}(18) = 10\pi$

area $= \frac{\theta}{2\pi} \cdot \pi r^2 = \frac{1}{2}\theta r^2 = \frac{1}{2} \cdot \frac{5\pi}{9}(18)^2 = 90\pi$

**14.** 360°, $2\pi$, circumference, circle area

**15.** $\frac{45}{360} = \frac{x}{2\pi}$

$360x = 45(2\pi)$

$x = \pi/4$ radians

**16.** $\frac{x}{360} = \frac{2\pi/5}{2\pi}$

$2\pi x = 360(2\pi/5)$

$x = 72°$

**17.** $\dfrac{\text{arc length}}{\text{circumference}} = \dfrac{\text{sector area}}{\text{circle area}}$

$\frac{x}{12\pi} = \frac{15\pi}{36\pi} = \frac{5}{12}$ → $12x = 5(12)\pi$ → $x = 5\pi$

**18.** The area of the triangle is found in Problem 5.

sector area $= \frac{\theta}{360} \cdot \pi r^2 = \frac{120}{360} \cdot \pi(6)^2 = 12\pi$

triangle area $= \frac{1}{2}bh = \frac{1}{2}(6\sqrt{3})(3) = 9\sqrt{3}$

segment area = sector − triangle = $12\pi - 9\sqrt{3}$

**19.** radius = 10/2 = 5

area = circle − 4 right triangles with legs 5

$= \pi(5)^2 - 4 \cdot \frac{1}{2}(5)(5) = 25\pi - 50$

**20.** An intercepted arc measures twice its inscribed angle.

$m\overset{\frown}{BC} = 2m\angle A = 80°$

An arc measure equals the measure of its central angle.

$m\angle BPC = m\overset{\frown}{BC} = 80°$

Sector $BPC$ has radius 9 and angle 80°.

area $= \dfrac{\theta}{360} \cdot \pi r^2 = \dfrac{80}{360} \cdot \pi(9)^2 = 18\pi$

**21.** A circle has 360°. There are 12 hours on a clock, so each number position is 360/12 = 30° around the clock. At 2:00, the minute hand is on the 12 and the hour hand is on the 2. So, the angle between them is 2(30) = 60°.

## LESSON 169 ·······························································

*Note that all areas are in square units and all volumes are in cubic units.*

**1.**

**2.** Use the Euler's formula.
$F + V = E + 2$
$20 + V = 30 + 2$
$V = 12$
It has 12 vertices.

**3.** $LA = Ph = (18 + 6 + 18 + 6)(7) = 336$
$SA = 2B + LA = 2(18)(6) + 336 = 552$
$V = Bh = 18(6)(7) = 756$

**4.** $SA = 2\pi r^2 + 2\pi rh = 2\pi(3)^2 + 2\pi(3)(7) = 60\pi$
$V = \pi r^2 h = \pi(3)^2(7) = 63\pi$

**5.** The dashed triangle has hypotenuse 10 and base 6. Use the 6-8-10 Pythagorean triple to find $h = 8$.

$LA = \dfrac{1}{2}Pl = \dfrac{1}{2}4(12)(10) = 240$

$SA = B + LA = 12(12) + 240 = 384$

$V = \dfrac{1}{3}Bh = \dfrac{1}{3}(12)(12)(8) = 384$

**6.** Use the 3-4-5 Pythagorean triple to find $l = 5$.
$SA = \pi r^2 + \pi rl = \pi(3)^2 + \pi(3)(5) = 24\pi$

$V = \dfrac{1}{3}\pi r^2 h = \dfrac{1}{3}\pi(3)^2(4) = 12\pi$

**7.** $SA = 4\pi r^2 = 4\pi(2)^2 = 16\pi$

$V = \dfrac{4}{3}\pi r^3 = \dfrac{4}{3}\pi(2)^3 = (32/3)\pi$

**8.** $SA =$ cone $LA +$ cylinder $LA +$ cylinder $B$
$= \pi rl + 2\pi rh + \pi r^2$
$= \pi(12)(15) + 2\pi(12)(7) + \pi(12)^2 = 492\pi$

$V =$ cone $V +$ cylinder $V$

$= \dfrac{1}{3}\pi r^2 h + \pi r^2 h = \dfrac{1}{3}\pi(12)^2(9) + \pi(12)^2(7) = 1440\pi$

**9.** $V = \pi r^2 h = \pi(7)^2(12) = 588\pi$

**10.** The cons are not similar because corresponding linear dimensions are not proportional (25/15 ≠ 9/6).

**11.** volume ratio = 40/135 = 8/27
side ratio = 2/3, area ratio = 4/9

$\dfrac{4}{9} = \dfrac{12}{x}$ → $4x = 9(12)$ → $x = 27$ ft²

**12.** rectangle

**13.** C

**14.**

The solid is a cylinder with a hemisphere on top. The hemisphere has radius 6. The cylinder has radius 6 and height 6.

**15.** $SA =$ hemisphere $LA +$ cylinder $LA +$ cylinder $B$

$= \dfrac{1}{2} \cdot 4\pi r^2 + 2\pi rh + \pi r^2$

$= \dfrac{1}{2} \cdot 4\pi(6)^2 + 2\pi(6)(6) + \pi(6)^2 = 180\pi$

$V =$ hemisphere $V +$ cylinder $V$

$= \dfrac{1}{2} \cdot \dfrac{4}{3}\pi r^3 + \pi r^2 h$

$= \dfrac{1}{2} \cdot \dfrac{4}{3}\pi(6)^3 + \pi(6)^2(6) = 360\pi$

**16.** The amount of air in the balloon is the volume of a sphere with radius 15 inches.

balloon $V = \dfrac{4}{3}\pi r^3 = \dfrac{4}{3}\pi(15)^3 = 4500\pi$

$\approx 4500(22/7) \approx 14143$ in³
time = volume / rate $\approx 14143/30 \approx 471$
So, it will take about 471 minutes.

**17.** aquarium $V = Bh = 12(6)(6) = 432$ ft³
density = mass/volume
$62 = x/432; x = 26784$
So, the aquarium can hold 26,784 pounds of water.

**18.** cube $V = Bh = 2(2)(2) = 8$ cm³
cube density = mass/volume = 6/8 = 0.75 g/cm³
The cube is less dense than water, so it will float.

**19.** population density = people/land area
$320 = x/92; x = 29440$
So, there are 29,440 people in the town.

**20.** sphere $SA =$ sphere $V$

$4\pi r^2 = \dfrac{4}{3}\pi r^3$

$3(4)\pi r^2 = 4\pi r^3$

$r = 3$

**21.** All cross sections are rectangles. The largest possible cross section is a rectangle with width = diameter = 10 and height = 6. So, its area is 10(6) = 60 cm².

**22.**

The solid is a truncated cone, a cone whose top is cut off. The entire cone has radius 6 and height 6. The cut-off cone has radius 3 and height 3.

$V$ = entire cone $V$ − cut-off cone $V$

$$= \frac{1}{3}\pi(6)^2(6) - \frac{1}{3}\pi(3)^2(3) = 63\pi$$

**23.** rate = 12 − 3 = 9 ft²/min

volume = 10(10)(10) = 1000 ft²

time = volume / rate = 1000/9 ≈ 111

So, it will take about 111 minutes.

## LESSON 170

**1.** $P(5, 2)$ and $Q(-1, -2)$

$PQ = \sqrt{(-1-5)^2 + (-2-2)^2} = 2\sqrt{13}$

**2.** center = midpoint between (8, 0) and (−2, 4)

$$= \left(\frac{8-2}{2}, \frac{0+4}{2}\right) = (3, 2)$$

**3.** $AB$ = 13 − 3 = 10

$P = A + 2/5$ of $AB$ = 3 + (2/5)(10) = 7

So, $P$ is at 7.

**4.** You need to move right and down to find $P$.

$x$-length of $\overline{AB}$ = 15 − 3 = 12

$x$ of $P$ = $x$ of $A$ + (1/4)($x$-length) = 3 + (1/4)(12) = 6

$y$-length of $\overline{AB}$ = 1 − (−3) = 4

$y$ of $P$ = $y$ of $A$ − (1/4)($y$-length) = 1 − (1/4)(4) = 0

So, $P$ is at (6, 0).

**5.**
A) vertical
B) vertical
C) horizontal
D) slope = 2
E) slope = 1/2
F) slope = 2
G) slope = −2

Parallel lines: A and B, D and F

Perpendicular lines: A and C, B and C, E and G

**6.** original slope = 3

parallel slope = 3

point-slope form: $y - 2 = 3(x - 0)$

slope-intercept form: $y = 3x + 2$

**7.** Find a line perpendicular to $\overline{AB}$ and passing through the midpoint of $\overline{AB}$.

slope of $\overline{AB}$ = −1

midpoint of $\overline{AB}$ = (−1, 0)

perpendicular slope = 1

point-slope form: $y - 0 = (1)(x - (-1))$

slope-intercept form: $y = x + 1$

**8.** Subtract eq2 from eq1 to get $3y = 3$ and $y = 1$.

Plug $y$ into eq1 to get $x - 1 = 5$ and $x = 6$.

So, the lines intersect at (6, 1).

**9.** a. Find the line perpendicular to $x + 3y = 6$ passing through (2, −2).

original slope = −1/3

perpendicular slope = 3

point-slope form: $y - (-2) = 3(x - 2)$

slope-intercept form: $y = 3x - 8$

b. Find the Intersection between $x + 3y = 6$ and $y = 3x - 8$.

$x + 3(3x - 8) = 6$; $x = 3$

$y = 3(3) - 8 = 1$

The lines intersect at (3, 1).

c. Find the distance between (2, −2) and (3, 1).

$d = \sqrt{(3-2)^2 + (1-(-2))^2} = \sqrt{10}$

**10.** Draw $\overline{AC}$ to divide $ABCD$.

area of $ABCD$ = area of $\triangle ABC$ + area of $\triangle ADC$

$$= (4)(2)/2 + (4)(4)/2 = 12$$

**11.**

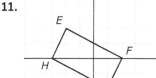

You can tell from the graph that it is not a rhombus. It looks like a parallelogram or a rectangle. Check the slopes of the sides.

slope of $\overline{EF} = \dfrac{0-2}{2-(-2)} = -\dfrac{1}{2}$

slope of $\overline{FG} = \dfrac{-2-0}{1-2} = 2$

slope of $\overline{GH} = \dfrac{0-(-2)}{-3-1} = -\dfrac{1}{2}$

slope of $\overline{EH} = \dfrac{0-2}{-3-(-2)} = 2$

The product of the slopes of adjacent sides is −1. Adjacent sides are perpendicular, so it is a rectangle.

**12.** center: (3, 2), radius = 3

So, the equation is $(x - 3)^2 + (y - 2)^2 = 9$.

**13.** $\pi r^2 = 25\pi; r = 5$

So, the equation is $(x - 2)^2 + (y + 6)^2 = 25$.

**14.** $r$ = distance between (5, 1) and (3, 7)

$= \sqrt{(3-5)^2 + (7-1)^2} = \sqrt{40}$

So, the equation is $(x - 5)^2 + (y - 1)^2 = 40$.

**15.** $x^2 + 4x + y^2 = 5$

$x^2 + 4x + 4 + y^2 = 5 + 4$

$(x + 2)^2 + y^2 = 9$

So, the circle has center (−2, 0) and radius 3.

**16.** The preimage has center (0, −5) and radius 2.

The image has center (0, 5) and radius 2.

So, the equation is $x^2 + (y - 5)^2 = 4$.

**17.** A, D, E, F

**18.** $CP$ = radius = distance between (1, 3) and (2, 0)

$= \sqrt{(2-1)^2 + (0-3)^2} = \sqrt{10}$

$CQ$ = distance between (1, 3) and (−1, 5)

$= \sqrt{(-1-1)^2 + (5-3)^2} = \sqrt{8}$

$CQ$ is less than the radius, $Q$ is inside the circle.

**19.** $P(x, x), Q(x, -x), R(-x, -x), S(-x, x)$

**20.** $PR = \sqrt{(-x - x)^2 + (-x - x)^2} = \sqrt{8}x$

$SQ = \sqrt{(x - (-x))^2 + (-x - x)^2} = \sqrt{8}x$

$PR = SQ$, so the diagonals of a square are congruent.

**21.**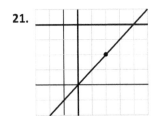

The circumcenter of a right triangle is the midpoint of the hypotenuse, so the circumcenter is at (3, 2).

**22.**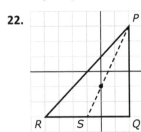

A centroid divides a median in the ratio 2:1.

Th point (0, −1) divides median $\overline{PS}$ in the ratio 2:1, so the centroid is at (0, −1).

**23.**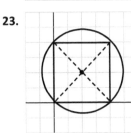

The circumcircle has center (2, 2) and radius $2\sqrt{2}$, so the standard equation is $(x - 2)^2 + (y - 2)^2 = 8$.

## LESSON 171

**1 ~ 12.** Use your ruler and protractor to check the accuracy of your construction.

**7.** *Sample steps:*

Construct equilateral $\triangle ABC$.

Construct a line through $A$ parallel to $\overline{BC}$.

Construct a line through $C$ parallel to $\overline{AB}$.

Label the intersection of the two lines as $D$.

$ABCD$ is a parallelogram with one angle 60°.

**8.** *Sample steps:*

Construct equilateral $\triangle ABC$.

Construct a line through $A$ perpendicular to $\overline{BC}$.

This line is an altitude of $\triangle ABC$.

**13.** A

**14.** corresponding angles

**15.** D; A, B, and C construct 60°, 30°, and 90° respectively.

**16.** D    **17.** B    **18.** B    **19.** A    **20.** B

## LESSON 172

**1.** $P$(multiple of 3) = $P$(3, 6, or 9) = 3/10

**2.** $P$(hit) = 15/25 = 3/5

**3.** The complement of "at least one heads" is "no heads."

8 possible outcomes: HHH, HHT, HTH, HTT,

THH, THT, TTH, TTT

$P$(no heads) = $P$(all tails) = $P$(TTT) = 1/8

$P$(at least one heads) = $1 - P$(no heads) = $1 - 1/8 = 7/8$

**4.** $P$(correct) × $P$(correct) × $P$(correct) × $P$(correct)

$= \dfrac{1}{2} \times \dfrac{1}{2} \times \dfrac{1}{2} \times \dfrac{1}{2} = \dfrac{1}{16}$

**5.** $P$(clear) × $P$(clear)

$= \dfrac{6}{10} \times \dfrac{6}{10} = \dfrac{9}{25}$

**6.** 6 x 6 = 36 possible outcomes

6 favorable outcomes: 11, 22, 33, ..., 66

$P$(same numbers) = 6/36 = 1/6

**7.** $P$(clear) × $P$(clear|clear)

$= \dfrac{6}{10} \times \dfrac{5}{9} = \dfrac{1}{3}$

**8.** $P$(club) × $P$(club|club)

$= \dfrac{13}{52} \times \dfrac{12}{51} = \dfrac{1}{17}$

**9.** $P$(heart) + $P$(face) − $P$(heart and face)

$= \dfrac{13}{52} + \dfrac{12}{52} - \dfrac{3}{52} = \dfrac{11}{26}$

10. swimming only = 22 − 7 = 15

    rock climbing only = 19 − 7 = 12

    swimming only or rock climbing only = 15 + 12 = 27

    $P$(swimming only or rock climbing only) = 27/40

11. $P$(vanilla|mint) = (vanilla and mint)/mint

    $= 10/(10 + 15) = 2/5$

12. $P$(coffee) = 26/40 = 13/20

13. $P$(tea|male) = (tea and male)/male = 6/18 = 1/3

14. $P$(red) = red/(green + yellow + red)

    $= 80/(50 + 10 + 80) = 4/7$

15. entire area = circle with radius 9 = $\pi(9)^2 = 81\pi$

    favorable area

    = circle with radius 6 − circle with radius 3

    $= 36\pi − 9\pi = 27\pi$

    $P$(shaded region) $= \dfrac{\text{favorable area}}{\text{entire area}} = \dfrac{27\pi}{81\pi} = \dfrac{1}{3}$

16. 4 possible outcomes: HH, HT, TH, TT

    possible values of $X$: 0, 1, 2

    $P(0) = P$(no heads) = $P$(TT) = 1/4

    $P(1) = P$(one heads) = $P$(HT or TH) = 1/2

    $P(2) = P$(two heads) = $P$(HH) = 1/4

    $E(X) = 0 \times P(0) + 1 \times P(1) + 2 \times P(2)$

    $= 0(1/4) + 1(1/2) + 2(1/4) = 1$

    So, the expected value is 1.

17. Find the number of permutations of 5.

    $P(5, 5) = \dfrac{5!}{(5-5)!} = \dfrac{5!}{0!} = \dfrac{5!}{1} = 5 \times 4 \times 3 \times 2 \times 1 = 120$

18. Find the number of permutations of 4 out of 6.

    $P(6, 4) = \dfrac{6!}{(6-4)!} = \dfrac{6!}{2!} = 6 \times 5 \times 4 \times 3 = 360$

19. Find the number of combinations of 3 out of 12.

    $C(12, 3) = \dfrac{12!}{(12-3)!\,3!} = \dfrac{12!}{9!\,3!} = \dfrac{12 \times 11 \times 10}{3 \times 2 \times 1} = 220$

20. Two points determine a line. Because order does not matter, the number of lines is the number of combinations of 2 out of 10.

    $C(10, 2) = \dfrac{10!}{(10-2)!\,2!} = \dfrac{10!}{8!\,2!} = \dfrac{10 \times 9}{2 \times 1} = 45$

21. possible outcomes = $P(5, 5)$

    favorable outcomes = permutations of 4 remaining letters after placing 5 first = $P(4, 4)$

    probability $= \dfrac{P(4, 4)}{P(5, 5)} = \dfrac{4!}{5!} = \dfrac{1}{5}$

22. possible outcomes = $C(10, 2)$

    favorable outcomes = combinations of choosing 2 teens out of 4 = $C(4, 2)$

    probability $= \dfrac{C(4, 2)}{C(10, 2)} = \dfrac{6}{45} = \dfrac{2}{15}$

23. Emma and Brian must sit next to each other, so group them together and treat them as one person.

    possible outcomes = $P(8, 8)$

    favorable outcomes = permutations of 7 people with Emma-Brian + permutations of 7 people with Brian-Emma = $P(7, 7) + P(7, 7) = P(7, 7) \times 2$

    probability $= \dfrac{P(7, 7) \times 2}{P(8, 8)} = \dfrac{7! \times 2}{8!} = \dfrac{1}{4}$

24. The vowels should be placed second and fourth.

    possible outcomes = $P(5, 5)$

    favorable outcomes = permutations of 3 consonants with A second and E fourth + permutations of 3 consonants with E second and A fourth = $P(3, 3) \times 2$

    probability $= \dfrac{P(3, 3) \times 2}{P(5, 5)} = \dfrac{3! \times 2}{5!} = \dfrac{1}{10}$

    You could use the counting principle.

    possible outcomes = $5 \times 4 \times 3 \times 2 \times 1 = 120$

    favorable outcomes = $3 \times 2 \times 2 \times 1 \times 1 = 12$

       1st place: 3 consonants

       2nd place: 2 vowels

       3rd place: 3 − 1 = 2 consonants

       4th place: 2 − 1 = 1 vowel

       5th place: 3 − 2 = 1 consonant

    probability = 12/120 = 1/10

## LESSON 173

1. Use the Angle Addition Postulate [7.7].

    $m\angle AOB + m\angle BOC + m\angle COD = 180°$

    $m\angle AOB + 112° + m\angle AOB = 180°$

    $2m\angle AOB = 68°$

    $m\angle AOB = 34°$

2. $\angle 1 \cong \angle 2$ as vertical angles.

    $\angle 3 \cong \angle 4$ as vertical angles.

    $\angle 1 \cong \angle 3$ as corresponding angles.

    $\angle 2 \cong \angle 4$ as corresponding angles.

    $\angle 1 \cong \angle 4$ as alternate exterior angles.

    $\angle 2 \cong \angle 3$ as alternate interior angles.

3. An exterior $\angle$ is the sum of its two remote interior $\angle$s.

    $3x + 10 = 68 + 74$; $x = 44$

4. interior angle sum = $180(n - 2) = 180(12 - 2) = 1800°$

    exterior angle sum of any polygon = $360°$

**5.** The reflection maps $P(-2, 3)$ to $P'(-2, -3)$.
The translation maps $P'(-2, -3)$ to $P''(1, -3)$.
So, the final image is $(1, -3)$.

**6.** a translation of 4 units right; A composition of reflections over two parallel lines is a translation. Use a simple point like $(0, 0)$ to find the rule.

**7.** *Answers may vary. Sample(s):*

a dilation about the origin by scale factor 2/3, a reflection over the $y$-axis, and then a translation of 2 units right and 1 unit up

**8.** Each term is 4 more than the previous term. The next term is $17 + 4 = 21$.

**9.** Addition Property; Add 3 to both sides.

**10.** Assume that a quadrilateral can have 4 obtuse angles.

**11.** 3. Definition of bisect (or angle bisector)
    4. Reflexive Property
    5. AAS
    6. CPCTC

**12.** SSS, SAS, HL

**13.** A midsegment is parallel to the third side and half the length of the third side.

$x$ and 74 are corresponding angles, so $x = 74$.
$y$ is twice the length of the midsegment, so $y = 14$.

**14.** A) 4, B) 3, C) 1, D) 2

**15.** $P$ is the centroid and divides $\overline{AD}$ in the ratio 2:1.
$PD = AP/2 = 10/2 = 5$
$AD = AP + PD = 10 + 5 = 15$

**16.** Angles in a triangle add up to 180°.
$m\angle Z = 180 - 48 - 82 = 50°$

The larger angle has the longer opposite side.
$YZ < XY < XZ$ because $m\angle X < m\angle Z < m\angle Y$.

**17.** square; A quadrilateral with bisecting diagonals is a parallelogram. A parallelogram with congruent diagonals is a rectangle. A parallelogram with perpendicular diagonals is a rhombus. A quadrilateral that is a rhombus and a rectangle is a square.

**18.** Corresponding sides must be proportional.

$\dfrac{12}{18} = \dfrac{a}{a + 15}$ $\rightarrow$ $12(a + 15) = 18a$ $\rightarrow$ $a = 30$

$\dfrac{12}{18} = \dfrac{24}{24 + b}$ $\rightarrow$ $12(24 + b) = 18(24)$ $\rightarrow$ $b = 12$

**19.** Use the Altitude Rule [68.1].
$4^2 = 8x; x = 2$

Use the Leg Rule [68.2].
$y^2 = x(x + 8); y = 2\sqrt{5}$

**20.** $\triangle ADE \sim \triangle ABC$ by AA.

$\dfrac{AD}{AB} = \dfrac{DE}{BC}$ $\rightarrow$ $\dfrac{24}{36} = \dfrac{DE}{15}$ $\rightarrow$ $\begin{array}{c} 36DE = 24(15) \\ DE = 10 \end{array}$

He is 10 m high from the ground.

**21.** $\sin 30° = \dfrac{1}{2}$     $\cos 30° = \dfrac{\sqrt{3}}{2}$     $\tan 30° = \dfrac{1}{\sqrt{3}} = \dfrac{\sqrt{3}}{3}$

**22.** Find $XY$:    $XY^2 = YZ^2 + XZ^2$
       $XZ = \sqrt{12^2 - 4^2} = \sqrt{128} \approx 11.3$
Find $m\angle Y$:   $\cos Y = 4/12$
          $m\angle Y = \cos^{-1}(4/12) \approx 70.5°$
Find $m\angle X$:   $m\angle X \approx 180 - 90 - 70.5 = 19.5°$

**23.** $\sin\theta = 30/80$
$\theta = \sin^{-1}(30/80) \approx 22°$
The angle of depression is about 22°.

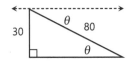

## LESSON 174

**1.** Tangent segments to a circle from a point are $\cong$.
$AD = AF = 10$     $\rightarrow$ perimeter
$BE = BD = 15$         $= AB + BC + AC$
$CE = CF = 9$           $= 25 + 24 + 19 = 68$

**2.** Congruent chords are equidistant from the center.
$x = 6/2 = 3$

A radius perpendicular to a chord bisects the chord.
base of right $\triangle = 8/2 = 4$

Use the Pythagorean Theorem or the 3-4-5 Pythagorean triple to find $y = 5$.

**3.** An inscribed angle measures half its intercepted arc.
$m\angle 1 = 118/2 = 59°$

A chord-chord angle measures half the sum of the intercepted arcs.
$m\angle 2 = (86 + 118)/2 = 102°$

**4.** An angle inscribed in a semicircle is a right angle.
$m\angle 1 = 90°$

An inscribed angle measures half its intercepted arc.
$m\angle 2 = 60/2 = 30°$

Angles in a triangle add up to 180°.
$m\angle 3 = 180 - m\angle 1 - m\angle 2 = 60°$

**5.** The product of the secant segment and its external part is equal to the square of the tangent segment.
$x^2 = 15(15 + 10 + 7); x = 4\sqrt{30}$

The product of the segments of one chord equals the product of the segments of the other chord.
$14y = 7(10); y = 5$

**6.**  An equilateral triangle can be divided into two congruent 30-60-90 triangles. Use a 30-60-90 triangle to find that the height is $2\sqrt{3}$.

$$\text{area} = \frac{1}{2}bh = \frac{1}{2}(4)(2\sqrt{3}) = 4\sqrt{3}$$

**7.**  A regular hexagon is made up of 6 equilateral triangles. The apothem is the height of each equilateral triangle. Use a 30-60-90 triangle to find that the apothem is $3\sqrt{3}$.

$$\text{area} = \frac{1}{2}sa \cdot n = \frac{1}{2}(6)(3\sqrt{3})(6) = 54\sqrt{3}$$

**8.** $\text{arc length} = \dfrac{\theta}{360} \cdot 2\pi r = \dfrac{150}{360} \cdot 2\pi(12) = 10\pi$

$\text{area} = \dfrac{\theta}{360} \cdot \pi r^2 = \dfrac{150}{360} \cdot \pi(12)^2 = 60\pi$

**9.** 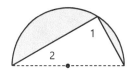 An angle inscribed in a semicircle is a right angle, so $m\angle 1 = 90°$. An inscribed angle measures half its intercepted arc, so $m\angle 2 =$ 60/2 = 30°. So, the triangle is a 30-60-90 triangle with hypotenuse 20 and legs 10 and $10\sqrt{3}$.

$\text{area} = \text{semicircle} - \text{triangle}$

$$= \frac{1}{2}\pi(10)^2 - \frac{1}{2}(10)(10\sqrt{3}) = 50\pi - 50\sqrt{3}$$

**10.** $SA = 2\pi r^2 + 2\pi rh = 2\pi(5)^2 + 2\pi(5)(6) = 110\pi$

$V = \pi r^2 h = \pi(5)^2(6) = 150\pi$

**11.**  The solid is a cone with a hemisphere on top. The hemisphere has radius 6. The cone has radius 6 and height 8.

**12.** Use the Pythagorean Theorem or a multiple of the 3-4-5 Pythagorean triple to find that the slant height of the cone is 10.

$SA = \text{hemisphere } LA + \text{cone } LA$

$$= \frac{1}{2} \cdot 4\pi r^2 + \pi rl = \frac{1}{2} \cdot 4\pi(6)^2 + \pi(6)(10) = 132\pi$$

$V = \text{hemisphere } V + \text{cone } V$

$$= \frac{1}{2} \cdot \frac{4}{3}\pi r^3 + \frac{1}{3}\pi r^2 h$$

$$= \frac{1}{2} \cdot \frac{4}{3}\pi(6)^3 + \frac{1}{3}\pi(6)^2(8) = 144\pi + 96\pi = 240\pi$$

**13.** area ratio = 48/27 = 16/9 = $4^2/3^2$
height ratio = side ratio = 4/3
volume ratio = $4^3/3^3$ = 64/27

**14.** tank $V = \dfrac{4}{3}\pi r^3 = \dfrac{4}{3}\pi(12)^3 = 2304\pi$

$\approx 2304(22/7) \approx 7241$

time = volume / rate $\approx 7241/50 \approx 145$

So, it will take about 145 minutes.

**15.** cylinder $V = \pi r^2 h = \pi(2)^2(2) = 8\pi$

$\approx 8(22/7) \approx 25.1$

density = mass/volume $\approx 227/25.1 \approx 9$

So, the density is about 9 pounds per cubic foot.

**16.** population density = people/land area
= 504,000/60 = 8400

So, the population density is 8,400 people/mile$^2$.

**17.** center = midpoint between (–5, 2) and (3, –2)

$$= \left(\frac{-5+3}{2}, \frac{2-2}{2}\right) = (-1, 0)$$

radius = distance between (–1, 0) and (3, –2)

$$= \sqrt{(3-(-1))^2 + (-2-0)^2} = \sqrt{20}$$

So, the equation is $(x+1)^2 + y^2 = 20$.

**18.** You need to move right and up to find $P$.
$x$-length of $\overline{AB}$ = 8 – (–7) = 15
$x$ of $P$ = $x$ of $A$ + (3/5)($x$-length) = –7 + (3/5)15 = 2

$y$-length of $\overline{AB}$ = 4 – (–1) = 5
$y$ of $P$ = $y$ of $A$ + (3/5)($y$-length) = –1 + (3/5)5 = 2

So, $P$ is at (2, 2).

**19.** Find a line perpendicular to $\overline{AB}$ and passing through the midpoint of $\overline{AB}$.

slope of $\overline{AB}$ = 1/3
midpoint of $\overline{AB}$ = (2, 2)
perpendicular slope = –3
point-slope form: $y - 2 = -3(x - 2)$
slope-intercept form: $y = -3x + 8$

**20.** You can tell from the graph that it is not a rhombus. It looks like a parallelogram or a rectangle. Check the slopes of the sides. By the slope formula,

slope of $\overline{AB}$ = 3/2          slope of $\overline{BC}$ = –3/5
slope of $\overline{CD}$ = 3/2          slope of $\overline{AD}$ = –3/5

Opposite sides are parallel, but adjacent sides are not perpendicular. So, it is a parallelogram but not a rectangle.

**21 ~ 22.** Use your ruler and protractor to check the accuracy of your construction.

**23.** Use the complement rule.
$P$(sum is 5) = $P$(14, 23, 32, or 41) = 4/36 = 1/9
$P$(sum is not 5) = 1 – $P$(sum is 5) = 1 – 1/9 = 8/9

**24.** Let $x$ = number of students who speak both.

Spanish only + French only + both + neither = 30

$(17 - x) + (14 - x) + x + 4 = 30$; $x = 5$

$P$(both) = 5/30 = 1/6

**25.** entire area = rectangle = 10(10) = 100

favorable area = circle = $\pi(5)^2 = 25\pi$

$P(\text{shaded region}) = \dfrac{\text{favorable area}}{\text{entire area}} = \dfrac{25\pi}{100} = \dfrac{\pi}{4}$

**26.** Order does not matter, so find the number of combinations of 3 out of 8.

$C(8, 3) = \dfrac{8!}{(8-3)!\,3!} = \dfrac{8!}{5!\,3!} = \dfrac{8 \times 7 \times 6}{3 \times 2 \times 1} = 56$

**27.**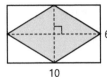

The area of the rhombus is half the area of the rectangle, so the probability is 1/2.

# LESSON 179

**1.** A (vertical angles)

D (corresponding angles on parallel lines)

**2.** A, B, C, E

D is false because a straight angle does not have a supplement. F is false because a square is a rhombus but not all rhombuses are squares.

**3.** $m\angle ACB = 180 - 132 = 48°$ (supplementary angles)

$m\angle ABC = m\angle ACB = 48°$ (base angles of isosceles $\triangle$)

$m\angle 1 = m\angle ABC = 48°$ (alternate interior angles)

**4.** A, B, C, D

**5.** If the tangent is 1, then the legs must be congruent. A right triangle with congruent legs is a 45-45-90 triangle.

$\cos y° = \cos 45° = \dfrac{1}{\sqrt{2}} = \dfrac{1}{\sqrt{2}} \cdot \dfrac{\sqrt{2}}{\sqrt{2}} = \dfrac{\sqrt{2}}{2}$

**6.** 2. Vertical angles are congruent.

3. AAS

**7.** 4 possible outcomes: HH, HT, TH, TT

3 favorable outcomes: HH, HT, TH

$P$(at least one heads) = 3/4

You could use the complement rule.

$P$(at least one heads) = 1 - $P$(no heads)

$\qquad\qquad\qquad\qquad$ = 1 - $P$(TT) = 1 - 1/4 = 3/4

**8.** C, B, A, D

**9.** Use a 30-60-90 triangle to find that the height is $6\sqrt{3}$.

area $= \dfrac{1}{2} h(b_1 + b_2) = \dfrac{1}{2}(6\sqrt{3})(11 + 6 + 11) = 84\sqrt{3}$

**10.** Tangent segments to a circle from a point are $\cong$.

perimeter = (8 + 9) + (9 + 12) + (8 + 12) = 58

**11.** Let $b$ be the base of the right triangle. Then the Pythagorean Theorem gives $b = 3\sqrt{3}$.

A radius perpendicular to a chord bisects the chord, so the length of the chord is $2b = 6\sqrt{3}$.

**12.** A, B, C, D

**13.** A midsegment is parallel to the third side.

$\angle 1$ and 76° are congruent as corresponding angles. $\angle 1$ and $\angle 2$ are congruent as alternate interior angles.

So, $m\angle 1 = m\angle 2 = 76°$.

**14.** Find a line perpendicular to $\overline{AB}$ and passing through the midpoint of $\overline{AB}$.

slope of $\overline{AB}$ = 1/4

midpoint of $\overline{AB}$ = (1, 2)

perpendicular slope = −4

point-slope form: $y - 2 = -4(x - 1)$

slope-intercept form: $y = -4x + 6$

**15.** A

**16.** $\angle ACD$ (angle formed by a tangent and a diameter)

$\angle ABC$ (angle inscribed in a semicircle)

$\angle CBD$ (angle supplementary to a right angle)

**17.** You need to move right and down to find $P$.

$x$-length of $\overline{AB}$ = 5 − 1 = 4

$x$ of $P = x$ of $A + (1/4)(x\text{-length}) = 1 + (1/4)4 = 2$

$y$-length of $\overline{AB}$ = 9 − 1 = 8

$y$ of $P = y$ of $A - (1/4)(y\text{-length}) = 9 - (1/4)8 = 7$

So, $P$ is at (2, 7).

**18.** An intercepted arc measures twice its inscribed angle.

$m\overset{\frown}{AC} = 2m\angle B = 90°$

An arc measure equals the measure of its central angle.

$m\angle APC = m\overset{\frown}{AC} = 90°$

Sector $APC$ has radius 4 and angle 90°.

area $= \dfrac{\theta}{360} \cdot \pi r^2 = \dfrac{90}{360} \cdot \pi(4)^2 = 4\pi$

**19.** D; A composition of reflections over two intersecting lines is a rotation.

**20.** A, C

B is false because a circumcenter is equidistant from the vertices of its triangle. D is false because an incenter is where the angle bisectors of a triangle meet.

**21.** $ACDE$ is a rectangle, so $AE = CD = 5$ and $ED = AC = 16$.

$$\tan 18° = \frac{BC}{AC} = \frac{BC}{16}$$

$BC = 16 \tan 18° \approx 5.2$

$BD = BC + CD \approx 5.2 + 5 = 10.2$

So, the tree is about 10.2 ft tall.

**22.** Let $x$ = number of students who take both.

Biology only + Chemistry only + both + neither = 40

$(25 - x) + (20 - x) + x + 7 = 40$; $x = 12$

$P$(Chemistry only) = $(20 - 12)/40 = 1/5 = 20\%$

**23.** Tangent and radius are perpendicular. Angles in a quadrilateral add up to 360°.

$90 + 90 + x + y = 360$; $x + y = 180$

So, the value of $x + y$ is always 180.

**24.** center: $(-3, 1)$, radius = 2

So, the equation is $(x + 3)^2 + (y - 1)^2 = 4$.

**25.** Use the Altitude Rule [68.1].

$9^2 = x(3x)$; $x = \sqrt{27} = 3\sqrt{3}$

So, the shorter segment is $3\sqrt{3}$ cm.

**26.** $\triangle EGH$ is a right triangle. The Pythagorean Theorem or the 5-12-13 Pythagorean triple gives $EG = 13$.

Because the diagonals of a rectangle are congruent, $FH = EG = 13$.

**27.** The product of the secant segment and its external part is equal to the square of the tangent segment.

$x^2 = 5(5 + 8)$; $x = \sqrt{65}$

**28.** B

A can use HL. C can use ASA. D can use SSS.

**29.** Any three points on a circle cannot be collinear. Three non-collinear points determine a triangle. Because order does not matter, the number of triangles is the number of combinations of 3 out of 8.

$$C(8, 3) = \frac{8!}{(8 - 3)! \, 3!} = \frac{8!}{5! \, 3!} = \frac{8 \times 7 \times 6}{3 \times 2 \times 1} = 56$$

**30.** Use the Pythagorean Theorem or the distance formula to find the length of each side.

$A(0, 2)$, $B(4, -1)$, $C(-3, -2)$

$AB = \sqrt{(4 - 0)^2 + (-1 - 2)^2} = 5$

$BC = \sqrt{(-3 - 4)^2 + (-2 - (-1))^2} = 5\sqrt{2}$

$AC = \sqrt{(-3 - 0)^2 + (-2 - 2)^2} = 5$

So, the perimeter is $10 + 5\sqrt{2}$ units.

**31.**

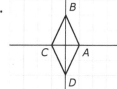

All sides are congruent, so it is a rhombus. The answer is B.

**32.** Use the Triangle Side Splitter Theorem [69.1].

$$\frac{20}{4x} = \frac{5x}{9} \quad \rightarrow \quad 4x(5x) = 20(9) \quad \rightarrow \quad x = 3$$

**33.** aquarium $V = Bh = 4(3)(2) = 24$

density = mass/volume

$62 = x/24$; $x = 1488$

So, the aquarium can hold 1,488 pounds of water.

**34.** balloon $V = \frac{4}{3}\pi r^3 = \frac{4}{3}\pi(6)^3 = 288\pi$

$\approx 288(22/7) \approx 905$ in$^3$

time = volume / rate $\approx 905/20 = 45$

So, it will take about 45 minutes.

**35.** entire area = circle with radius 6 = $\pi(6)^2 = 36\pi$

favorable area = a rhombus with diagonals 12 and 12

$$= \frac{1}{2}(12)(12) = 72$$

$$P(\text{shaded region}) = \frac{\text{favorable area}}{\text{entire area}} = \frac{72}{36\pi} = \frac{2}{\pi}$$

## LESSON 180

**1.** A (alternate interior angles)

B (corresponding angles)

**2.** C

**3.** B

**4.** A, B, D

*Counterexamples may vary. Sample(s):*

A) The statement is false when $a = 1$, $b = 2$, $c = 0$.

B) A 45-45-90 triangle and a 60-60-60 triangle are not similar because their angles are not congruent.

D) Side lengths 1, 1, and 5 cannot form a triangle.

**5.** $m\angle AEB = 180 - 90 - 52 = 38°$ ($\triangle$ angle sum = 180)

$m\angle ADC = m\angle AEB = 38°$ (corresponding angles)

$m\angle 1 = 180 - m\angle ADC = 142°$ (supplementary angles)

**6.**

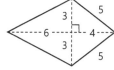

The diagonals of a kite are perpendicular. Use the Pythagorean Theorem or the 3-4-5 Pythagorean triple to find that the length of the vertical diagonal is $3 + 3 = 6$.

area $= \frac{1}{2}d_1 d_2 = \frac{1}{2}(4 + 6)(3 + 3) = 30$ units$^2$

**7.** 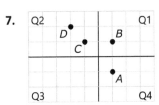 Use any point in Q4. The reflection maps $A$ to $B$, the rotation maps $B$ to $C$, and the dilation maps $C$ to $D$.

So, the resulting image is in Quadrant 2.

**8.** D; An orthocenter is the point where the altitudes of a triangle intersect.

**9.** 3. If lines are parallel, then alternate interior angles are congruent.

   4. Reflexive Property

   5. ASA

**10.** Use the Three Parallel Lines Theorem [69.2].

$$\frac{8}{6x} = \frac{5x}{15} \quad \rightarrow \quad (6x)(5x) = 8(15) \quad \rightarrow \quad x = 2$$

**11.** C

**12.** B, D, F

**13.** A radius perpendicular to a chord bisects the chord, so the base of the right triangle is 20/2 = 10.

Let $r$ be the radius of the circle. The right triangle has base 10, height 5, and hypotenuse $r$. By the Pythagorean Theorem,

$$r^2 = 5^2 + 10^2$$

$$r = \sqrt{125} = 5\sqrt{5}$$

So, the radius of the circle is $5\sqrt{5}$ inches.

**14.** D

**15.** An intercepted arc measures twice its inscribed angle.

$$m\widehat{AC} = 2m\angle B = 50°$$

An arc measure equals the measure of its central angle.

$$m\angle APC = m\widehat{AC} = 50°$$

Sector $APC$ has radius 18 and angle 50°.

$$\text{area} = \frac{\theta}{360} \cdot \pi r^2 = \frac{50}{360} \cdot \pi (18)^2 = 45\pi$$

**16.** $x°$ and $y°$ are complementary. The cosine of an acute angle is equal to the sine of its complement.

$$\cos y° = \sin x° = 5/13$$

**17.** The circle has center (1, 4) and radius $\sqrt{5}$. By the distance formula,

distance between (1, 4) and (−1, 2)

$$= \sqrt{(-1-1)^2 + (2-4)^2} = \sqrt{8}$$

The distance is greater than the radius ($\sqrt{8} > \sqrt{5}$), so the point is outside the circle.

**18.** Parallel lines have the same slope.

original slope = 4

parallel slope = 4

point-slope form: $y - 1 = 4(x + 1)$

slope-intercept form: $y = 4x + 5$

**19.** Use the Secant-Secant Product Theorem [99.2].

$$8(8 + x) = 7(7 + x + 3)$$

$$64 + 8x = 7x + 70$$

$$x = 6$$

**20.** The diagonals of a parallelogram bisect each other.

$4x = 8$  ┌→  $10 - x = 5y - 2$

$x = 2$  └--┘  $10 - 2 = 5y$ - 2

$y = 2$

**21.** $P$ is the centroid and divides $\overline{BD}$ in the ratio 2:1.

$PD = BP / 2 = 8/2 = 4$

$BD = BP + PD = 8 + 4 = 12$

**22.** 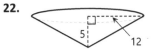 The solid is an upside-down cone with radius 12 and height 5.

$$\text{volume} = \frac{1}{3}\pi r^2 h = \frac{1}{3}\pi(12)^2(5) = 240\pi$$

**23.** Use the Pythagorean inequality theorems.

A is a right triangle because $5^2 = 3^2 + 4^2$.

B is an acute triangle because $6^2 < 4^2 + 5^2$.

C is a right triangle because $13^2 = 5^2 + 12^2$.

D is an obtuse triangle because $15^2 > 8^2 + 2^2$.

So, the answer is B.

**24.** C, E, F

**25.** You need to move right and up to find $P$.

$x$-length of $\overline{AB}$ = 8 − (−2) = 10

$x$ of $P = x$ of $A + (3/5)(x$-length$) = -2 + (3/5)10 = 4$

$y$-length of $\overline{AB}$ = 5 − 0 = 5

$y$ of $P = y$ of $A + (3/5)(y$-length$) = 0 + (3/5)5 = 3$

So, $P$ is at (4, 3).

**26.** The preimage has center (2, −7) and radius 5.

The image has center (2, 7) and radius 5.

So, the equation is $(x - 2)^2 + (y - 7)^2 = 25$.

**27.** Use the complement rule.

$P$(sum is 3) = $P$(12 or 21) = 2/36 = 1/18

$P$(sum is not 3) = 1 − $P$(sum is 3) = 1 − 1/18 = 17/18

**28.** 10 × 9 × 8 = 720 ways

**29.** By the slope formula,

slope of $\overline{AB}$ = –2          slope of $\overline{BC}$ = 1/2

slope of $\overline{CD}$ = –2          slope of $\overline{AD}$ = 1/2

By the Pythagorean Theorem or the distance formula,

length of $\overline{AB}$ = $2\sqrt{5}$       length of $\overline{AB}$ = $2\sqrt{5}$

length of $\overline{CD}$ = $2\sqrt{5}$       length of $\overline{CD}$ = $2\sqrt{5}$

Adjacent sides are perpendicular (the product of the slopes of adjacent sides is –1), so it is a rectangle. All sides are congruent, so it is a rhombus. A quadrilateral that is a rectangle and a rhombus is a square.

The answer is A.

**30.** tank surface area = $4\pi r^2 = 4\pi(15)^2 = 900\pi$

$\approx 900(22/7) \approx 2829$ ft$^2$

number of cans $\approx 2829/180 \approx 16$

So, about 16 cans will be needed.

**31.** population density = people/land area

$979 = x/11787$

$x = 11{,}539{,}473 \approx 11{,}539{,}000$

So, the population is about 11,539,000 people.

**32.** Let $x$ be the number of students who play neither.

soccer only + baseball only + both + neither = 50

$(30 - 14) + (22 - 14) + 14 + x = 50$

$x = 12$

So, $P$(neither) = 12/50 = 6/25.

**33 ~ 34.** *Diagrams are not drawn to scale.*

**33.** $\dfrac{15}{15 + 10} = \dfrac{6}{x}$

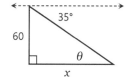

$15x = 6(15 + 10)$

$x = 10$

The street lamp is 10 feet tall.

**34.** $\theta = 35°$

$\tan 35° = 60/x$

$x = 60 / \tan 35° \approx 85.7$

The boat is about 85.7 ft away from the lighthouse.

**35.** entire area = circle with radius 12 = $\pi(12)^2 = 144\pi$

favorable area

= circle with radius 6 – circle with radius 3

= $36\pi - 9\pi = 27\pi$

$P$(shaded region) = $\dfrac{\text{favorable area}}{\text{entire area}} = \dfrac{27\pi}{144\pi} = \dfrac{3}{16}$

Made in United States
Troutdale, OR
12/02/2024

25657779R00077